Days of the Lord
THE LITURGICAL YEAR

Days of the Lord

THE LITURGICAL YEAR

Volume 4.

Ordinary Time, Year A

THE LITURGICAL PRESS
Collegeville, Minnesota

The English translation of Volume 4 of this series is by Madeleine Beaumont. The original French text of *Days of the Lord (Jours du Seigneur*, Brepols: Publications de Saint-André, 1988) was written by the authors of the *Missel dominical de l'assemblée* and *Missel de l'assemblée pour la semaine* under the direction of Robert Gantoy and Romain Swaeles, Benedictines of Saint-André de Clerlande.

ACKNOWLEDGMENTS
Excerpts from the English translation of *Lectionary for Mass* © 1969, International Committee on English in the Liturgy, Inc. (ICEL); excerpts from the English translation of *The Roman Missal* © 1973, ICEL; excerpts from the English translation of *Documents on the Liturgy, 1963–1979: Conciliar, Papal, and Curial Texts* © 1982, ICEL. All rights reserved.

Scripture selections are taken from the New American Bible *Lectionary for Mass*, © 1970 by the Confraternity of Christian Doctrine, Washington, D.C., and are used by license of said copyright owner. All rights reserved. No part of the New American Bible *Lectionary for Mass* may be reproduced in any form without written permission from the copyright owner.

Scripture quotations are from the *New American Bible with Revised New Testament*, © 1986 Confraternity of Christian Doctrine. The text of the Old Testament in *The New American Bible with Revised New Testament* was published in *The New American Bible*, © 1970 Confraternity of Christian Doctrine. Other quotations, as indicated, are from *The Jerusalem Bible*, © 1966 by Darton, Longman & Todd, Ltd. and Doubleday & Company, Inc.

Cover design by Monica Bokinskie.

Library of Congress Cataloging-in-Publication Data

(Revised for vol. 4)

Days of the Lord.

   Translation of: Jours du Seigneur.
   Includes bibliographical references.
   Contents: v. 1. Season of Advent. Season of Christmas/Epiphany —   — v. 4. Ordinary time, Year A —   — v. 6. Ordinary time, Year C.
   1. Church year. 2. Catholic Church—Liturgy.
BX1970.J67313 1990   263'.9   90-22253
ISBN 0-8146-1899-5 (v. 1)
ISBN 0-8146-1902-9 (v. 4)
ISBN 0-8146-1904-5 (v. 6)

Contents

Ordinary Time

Since the liturgical reform, the longest part of the year is called "Ordinary Time." Because of its novelty, this expression was sometimes misunderstood, especially in the beginning. The numerous explanations that have been given, plus the very use of this term, have dispelled the ambiguities. It is now common knowledge that this time is called "ordinary" in order to distinguish it from other periods of the liturgical year, which are qualified by the context of the specific mystery being celebrated: the coming of salvation and its preparation today as yesterday (Advent); the birth of the Lord and his manifestation, his Epiphany, to all nations; the ascent toward Easter and the preparation of catechumens for baptism (Lent); Christ's Pasch and ours.

During Ordinary Time—thirty-three or thirty-four weeks, depending on the years—what is celebrated is "Christ's mystery, not under any particular aspect, but rather in all its scope," as it unfolds in the sequence of days from Pentecost "until the expectation of the blessed hope and of the advent of the Lord."[1]

Ordinary Time a Monotonous Time?

Although we are accustomed to it, the use of the term "ordinary" to designate this time causes perplexity. The person insufficiently familiar with this term could think that we are speaking of a period of the liturgical year devoid of interest—in a word, of a "dull" time in comparison with the other times, frequently called "special" times. In any event, even when we recognize that the adjective "ordinary" does not have this slightly pejorative meaning, many persons perceive this long period of the year, especially from the feast of the Body and Blood of Christ to that of Christ the King, as rather monotonous.

Whatever its other aspects, too often forgotten, Advent benefits from the strong attraction of the feast of Christmas, the radiance of which extends to the celebration of the two Sundays following, the Holy Family and Epiphany.[2] Easily enough, Lent can be considered an ascent toward Holy Week and the paschal celebrations, the "apex of the liturgical year."[3] In fact, tension slackens during the Easter season, a season meant to be thought of as "one single feastday, or better, one great Sunday" of

1

Easter.[4] But it must be admitted that it is difficult to live in that way. Seven Sundays, each with one excerpt from the Acts of the Apostles, a paschal catechesis from the apostolic epistles, and an account of one appearance of the risen Christ, seems long to many persons, in spite of the feasts of Ascension and Pentecost. But what shall we say of the last six months of the liturgical year? One is more or less tempted to yield to a slumber hardly interrupted by the few feasts, the number of which depends on the years.[5]

This sort of miring that the liturgical year undergoes during this period is furthermore accentuated by the fact that in Europe and North America, summer vacations upset the customary rhythm of the Christian communities' life. Even if they continue to participate in Sunday celebrations, those who go away for vacation are no longer completely within the dynamic time-frame of Ordinary Time.[6] For those who stay at home, especially in cities, it is very often the time of poorly attended liturgical assemblies and lackluster celebrations. Only with the start of the school year is the connection with Ordinary Time reestablished after a gap of two to three months.[7]

Such are some of the difficulties of Ordinary Time. Rather than discourage us, they should spur us on to a better consciousness of the importance, value, and meaning of this long period of the liturgical year.

Being Attentive to the Rhythm and Calls of Daily Life

Ordinary Time is the time of the Church, of the daily life of every Christian community, and of each one of us. It is the time not of a brief effort during which one hurries or even runs in order to progress on the way, but the time when one goes at a measured pace in order to cover a long distance.

As a rule, it is not the time for great conversions, for decisive choices made at one time or another in one's life. But it is the time for a painstaking, though at times wavering, faithfulness; the time for an obscure faith that sustains daily life; the time for a self-effacing hope that holds us steadfast and keeps us from stopping at the first difficulty; the time for charity writ small.

To be sure, this is not the time when we can overcome large obstacles in one leap. But this is the time when progress is made in spite of the rocks or holes along the way. This is the time for unceasingly announcing and preaching the gospel, not with raised voices, but in season and out of season. This is the time that allows for the slow germinations of

God's Word, the cultivating and pruning of the vine, the regular treatments that prevent and cure diseases, the fertilizing repeated whenever rain or storm have compromised the preceding application. This is the time for lamps to be replenished with oil; for the daily bread, sometimes stale but nonetheless nourishing; for the simple glass of water that quenches thirst. This is the time when one draws new and old from the treasury of the Church and of God's Word. This is the time of regular prayer, of assiduous attention to the apostles' teaching, and to the breaking of the bread dispensed by the Church, Sunday in and Sunday out.

Ordinary Time is the opportunity for us to take our time without wasting it.

Being Open to All Possibilities

Everything is possible at any time for God, and for us, with his grace always proffered. But Ordinary Time is very specially marked by this openness to all possibilities. Would not this openness be its special character, first of all, by reason of its length? In the course of six months, many things can happen in the world, in the Church, in our community, and in ourselves. Thus, what happens during Ordinary Time is welcomed and lived in faith, hope, and love. Indeed, it does not focus the attention on a particular aspect of the mystery of salvation, but on its unfolding in the succession of days.

The point of departure for the liturgies is one of the three Synoptic Gospels, each of which was written for a specific community. The Gospel can therefore be reread, here and now, within an unceasing and dialectical confrontation between God's revelation, the person of Christ, the message, and, on the other hand, each community, the Church, today's world—all with their riches and flaws, their resolve and failures, their questions and difficulties, their mission, their opening to the Spirit.

Ordinary Time is also given to each community and to each of us to recapture, strengthen, redress, and rebuild our own Christian and ecclesial personalities. Without our becoming self-absorbed (quite the contrary), this is the favorable time to check up on and, if need be, to renew our commitment to the Church, one in its diversity. This is the time for witnessing humbly and discreetly, but effectively, within the reality of daily life. This is the time for proclaiming God's Word, announced day in and day out, or carried afar by brothers and sisters who come to tell of the wonders wrought by the Spirit. This is the time for sowing and burying the grain that will germinate in due time.

This is the favorable time for welcoming our vacationing brothers and sisters in simplicity, joy, and love. Summer months offer a good opportunity for this. The assemblies open up. They recognize that we are brothers and sisters celebrating the same Lord and living by the same Spirit, albeit in different situations and according to different customs, including liturgical ones.

The long sequence of Sunday celebrations in Ordinary Time has many surprises in store. This one Gospel excerpt, forgotten or heard as if for the first time; this light striking unexpectedly after so many gray days; this forward leap taken almost unawares; this wide vista opening, at the turn in the path, upon the mystery of the total Christ, of his bride the Church, and of the world that must be transfigured.

Ordinary Time allows us to welcome simply, without rigidity or formality, the unforeseen riches of God, of others, of ourselves in the community, in the assembly, in life.

This is the time of all possibilities.

Through the Prism of the Gospels
Among the directions given by Vatican II is the following: "The treasures of the Bible are to be opened up more lavishly, so that richer fare may be provided for the faithful at the table of God's Word. In this way a more representative portion of the holy Scriptures will be read to the people over a set cycle of years."[8] It is in accordance with these guidelines of the Council that the new Lectionaries[9] have been composed, the number of biblical Sunday readings has been increased from two to three [including one from the Old Testament, which up to then was read only during the week],[10] and the three-year Sunday cycle has been established. Each of these years is characterized by the reading, termed "semi-continuous,"[11] of one of the three Synoptic Gospels: Matthew (Year A), Mark (Year B), and Luke (Year C).

During Year A, on the Third Sunday, the Gospel of Matthew is begun with the inauguration of Jesus' ministry in Capernaum (Matt 4:12-23), and the reading is continued up to the discourse on the Last Judgment (Matt 25:31-45).

During Year B, the Gospel of Mark is taken almost from its beginning, after Jesus' temptation in the desert (Mark 1:14-20), and the reading continues up to the words Jesus pronounces before his passion (Mark 13:24-30).[12]

Finally, during Year C, the Gospel of Luke is read from the beginning (Luke 1:1-4); then from the beginning of the preaching in Galilee and at Nazareth (Luke 4:14-21), up to the discourse on Jerusalem's ruin and on the persecutions (Luke 21:5-19).

Never, before the liturgical reform, had it been thus legislated to make a "continuous reading" of each of the three Synoptic Gospels.[13] But beyond this abundance of evangelical texts, the important fact is that the mystery of salvation is presented to us through the prism of the Gospels.

"The Gospel of Jesus Christ according to Matthew . . . Mark . . . Luke." We perhaps pay insufficient attention to this formula. It says a great deal, however, and it says something fundamental. The Gospel of John ends with this statement: "There are also many other things that Jesus did, but if these were to be described individually, I do not think the whole world would contain the books that would be written" (John 21:25). The very existence of Gospels "according to" Matthew, Mark, Luke—to speak only of these[14]—shows concretely, better than all explanations, that one single testimony, one single reading, is unable to express or give a full account of the entire gospel, i.e., the good news proclaimed. Each Gospel proclaims not only Jesus' words and actions but his person and his mystery, the kingdom and its advent, God whom Jesus has revealed.

Matthew, Mark, and Luke speak of all that, of the same Jesus, of the same kingdom he came to announce and establish, of the same Father whom he revealed. Far from contradicting one another, their three testimonies are in harmony, but not in the way of duplication. Their agreement is all the stronger, as it is not explicit but implicit.[15] Indeed, the three testimonies are not reducible to a single one. This originality is not limited to nuances of detail, since each has personally looked at, listened to, endeavored to understand Jesus, and received the data of tradition. Besides, each was acting as an original author. And this is as it should be, inasmuch as the gospel calls for the personal commitment of those who receive and announce it, on the one hand, and on the other, it is not a dead letter, but the living Word for the life of humankind and of the communities of every race, people, and nation for all time. The one gospel of Jesus Christ must be received and lived within the diversity of the readings. No one—be it an individual, a community, a tradition— can pretend to the exclusive privilege of understanding, announcing, and living it in its totality. Matthew, Mark, and Luke attest to the necessity of this pluralism, but also of its limits, or rather its demands.

At the same time, they show that the Gospel is neither a mere material reading, nor a stereotyped retelling of the event that is Jesus Christ. Each of the evangelists has retained, adapted—we would say made relevant— what he received from the tradition, with regard to the possibilities, the needs, the questions, etc., of a concrete community. Furthermore, the same is true of the other apostolic witnesses. For instance, Paul, wherever he was going, does not indefinitely repeat everywhere the same discourse. His letters to the Churches are inspired by each Church's situation. Thus, would he have spoken of what the Lord did on the eve of the day he was to die if the assemblies at Corinth had not been the occasion of intolerable disorders? We too, therefore, must again and again read the Gospels anew, under the Spirit's guidance, for the Spirit is given today as yesterday to each one, to our communities, to the Church, to the prophets, to the doctors, to the little ones.

Furthermore, the yearly reading of one of the Synoptics keeps us from the temptation to reduce the three, or the four Gospels into one. We succumb unawares to this temptation when, reading a page from one evangelist, we bring in what another evangelist says in his own narrative of the same event, in his own parallel presentation of Jesus' words. This comparison is useful, to be sure, but only inasmuch as it helps to better understand what the evangelist we are reading says or wants to say, and inasmuch as it illuminates his originality. In this book we shall sometimes resort to such a comparison. But as a rule, we shall focus on the one evangelist under study.

In this manner, one really listens to the Gospel "according to" Matthew, Mark, Luke. Otherwise, we blot out the riches of each in order to keep only what they hold in common or to artificially reconstitute a text that belongs to none of them. Would it occur to anyone to superimpose tracings of paintings of Christ by three great artists in order to obtain a fourth one based on the features common to the three? This would be worse than a bad composite portrait.

The gospel—with the meaning outlined above—was therefore, from the beginning, preached and transmitted in the framework of a living tradition that is also a source of revelation and not just its channel. It is not merely a transmission, materially and objectively faithful, of an inert treasure, of an immobile deposit passed in its entirety—nothing subtracted, nothing added—from hand to hand, from generation to generation. It implied, on the contrary, the *now* of each generation, each Christian community in the unity of its diversity. In its committed and responsible faithfulness. In this living tradition we insert ourselves in turn, welcoming the heritage of the past to make it fruitful today, with an eye to tomorrow's fruits. Tradition is not traditionalism.

The Table of the Word Too Abundant?

The reading of the Gospel is accompanied by two other readings. During Advent, Christmas and Epiphany, Lent, and Easter, these have been chosen in accordance with the Gospel or the liturgical context of these diverse periods of the liturgical year.[16] The same is not quite true for the Sundays of Ordinary Time. Whereas the text of the Old Testament has been selected to match the Gospel at most other times, for the Sundays of Ordinary Time the second reading is an excerpt from an apostolic letter given in the course of "semi-continuous" reading.[17]

Certain persons think—and say—that this is too much, blaming less the number of texts than the fact that they might distract the attention in the absence of logical or educational unity. These people would be content with the Gospel alone, perhaps highlighted by another text. Indeed, for pastoral reasons, it is permitted to omit one of the two readings before the Gospel. But even when the readings before the Gospel are retained, these people often remain unconvinced of their importance. The homily forgets about them; it bears principally on the Gospel.[18]

In this book, we resolutely confront these difficulties, not to show that they are not insurmountable, but simply to help Christians derive the maximum profit from the spiritual food of the table of the Word, set by the Church. Therefore, we begin by reading each text in the order in which the Sunday liturgy or Ordinary Time presents it. This method has two advantages. First and foremost, it obliges us to take the time to really read one text after the other. We thus avoid the temptation to go directly to the Gospel, eventually clarified by some feature from the other two readings rapidly glanced at. To succumb to the temptation very quickly leads, as we have said, to reading only the Gospel with serious consideration[19] and to a willingness, soon reached, to do away with the other two texts.[20]

Second, we think we shall effectively help the readers to really hear these other two readings. It will become clear to them that after lingering over each text, they are able to grasp the real coherence, the articulations, the original and complementary contributions of the texts, thus avoiding arbitrary choices that prove more or less narrow, unjustified, and awkward. The three biblical texts of the Sunday liturgy form a "montage," the judicious and harmonious construction of which will be appreciated.

A Series of Sequences

During Ordinary Time, the Liturgy of the Word constitutes the immediate and, so to speak, only context of the Sunday celebration. It gives its stamp to each Sunday of Ordinary Time. Its main part is the Gospel taken, in the course of each year, from Matthew, Mark, or Luke.[21]

Ancient authors did not present their writings as we do, dividing them into chapters and paragraphs with titles and subtitles, and including a table of contents.[22] Of course, they did not write their books without a plan, without a precise idea of the way in which they intended to set down what Luke calls "an orderly sequence" (Luke 1:4). Much to the contrary, certain authors seem to have employed a number of purposeful, elaborate, and often remarkable literary devices. But they did not disclose the principles and the rules guiding them. We must discover them through what we gather from other sources concerning the modes of composition of their time. We must attentively read their writings, which sometimes lead us to detect the type of literary model that might have inspired them.[23]

In a certain way, the selection of evangelical texts found in the Lectionary for Ordinary Time allows us, on the basis of exegetical data, to make groupings, here called "sequences." The term adequately suggests the viewpoint chosen and why it was chosen. First of all, to look at each text in isolation does not take into account the fact that the Lectionary offers a "continuous reading" of one Gospel, which is beyond doubt the particular grace of Ordinary Time. At the same time, we would do violence to a text by reading it by itself, especially whenever its connection with the preceding or following passage is clear. In a word, we would mark time instead of letting ourselves follow the road marked out by the evangelist. Besides, there is a great risk in looking only for a "moral lesson" in each Gospel page.

To speak of "sequences" is to allude to a certain unity, but one that is not simply a logical development within a larger one. Rather what is meant is a small, coherent ensemble that also is part of a larger whole, the Gospel as its author composed it. From one sequence to the other, we progress not only in the "continuous reading" but especially in the work as its author conceived it and meant for us to understand it. This is similar to a film montage that allows us to discern levels and sequences and to progressively grasp the meaning of the whole. Thus we are kept in suspense, eager for what follows, attentive.

We certainly would not pretend that our manner of dividing into sequences excludes all others. But such division was not done arbitrarily. It is based upon the work of those who have studied the composition of the Gospels of Matthew, Mark, and Luke.[24] This is not the place to go into detail by citing the reasons of internal criticism that would justify our choice. It will suffice to rapidly underscore, as we go along, the coherence of each sequence and the manner in which it is joined to the preceding one.

Right away, we perceive the immediate usefulness of this grouping into small units. The drawbacks and the risks of such partitioning are counteracted by the restraints of the continuity and dynamism of a "continuous reading." We are within the context of the liturgy and of Ordinary Time, which do not proceed along the lines of any intellectual type of logic or in piecemeal fashion. A celebration is an ensemble of small parts, Ordinary Time being a long portion of the liturgical year.

Liturgical Proclamation of the Word

In the liturgy, God's word is directed to the heart, or rather to the intelligence of the heart, more than to the reason. It is proclaimed not to enrich the mind with new knowledge but to orient the assembly toward the mystery and to guide it into the celebration under the Spirit's guidance. This is a viewpoint and an attitude wholly different from those adopted for individual or group Bible reading.

In the liturgy, God's Word, proclaimed by a member of the assembly, is meant to be heard together. Each one does not read it separately in a book.[25] The homily is not an explanation of the text read but is, instead, a proclamation of the reality of salvation today, made by the person entrusted with this ministry in the assembly. In brief, the homily is a word on the Word.[26]

Sitting at a desk or in a Bible class, each one has the text under study, often even in several translations, which can prove very useful. Unless one of the members has thoroughly studied the text under consideration, it is good to have, if not a professional exegete, at least a person particularly knowledgeable in Holy Scripture. In any case, the members are able to consult commentaries and exegetical studies. They page through their Bibles to find parallel texts and passages that throw light on the page under scrutiny. In a word, they have recourse to all the available means to come to a better understanding of Scripture.[27]

Even if it leads to personal prayer or prayer in the group—which is usually the case—this approach does not coincide with the nature or purpose of the liturgy's approach to Scripture. Liturgy does not tarry on biblical texts; it proclaims them. This proclamation is only a stage of the liturgy, not its goal, and therefore requires a personal response from each and all. This response manifests itself in immediate prayer and, after the celebration, in our daily lives lived in the midst of the world. But if the proclamation takes only a brief time, it is because it wants to lead us forthwith into the celebration of the mystery, relevant to the present, of which the word unveils one aspect, one facet. Direct exegesis must encumber neither the liturgy nor this book.

The Biblical Readings in Ordinary Time

During Ordinary Time, the biblical texts that are proclaimed not only constitute the immediate context of each Sunday celebration. They also orient and nurture the spirituality proper to this period of the liturgical year. It is fitting to linger over the Lectionary of the long succession of "green Sundays."[28] Then we shall celebrate and live each one of the Days of the Lord in its newness. But it is not a question of drifting toward pious generalities, of wandering outside the itinerary set by the liturgy and marked out by a choice of biblical texts offered by the Church. The "continuous reading" of a Gospel is an opportunity or grace too important not to deserve all the resources of the intelligence of the heart.

In order to help the reader, it was necessary to begin by applying ourselves to the serious study of the texts, with the exegetes' irreplaceable aid. But we do not present an exegetical approach to the Scripture. Having taken in what the exegetes say, we devoted ourselves to listening to the Word anew in the attitude of Christians who allow the Word to be heard.[29] It is for everyone to hear it, to keep it "with a generous and good heart" in order to bear fruit through perseverance—a hundred- or sixty- or thirtyfold—according to what the Spirit grants. Jesus has taught this himself in the parable related by the three Synoptics (Matt 13:1-23; Mark 4:1-20; Luke 8:4-15).

The Prayer of the Psalms—Response to God's Word

The liturgy is under the sign and guidance of God's initiative throughout. It is God who summons the assembly and makes of this coming together the symbolic movement through which a Christian community, gathered as a Church, covers a new stage of the journey toward the Lord who came, is coming, and will come. We assemble first of all to listen to God's Word. It is through Christ, with him, and in him, that in the Spirit we give thanks to God. It is God who, in Christ's peace, sends us to announce the good news and bring our witness to the whole world. Finally, it is God who puts on our unschooled lips words of prayer because "we do not know how to pray as we ought." But "the Spirit itself intercedes with inexpressible groanings" (Rom 8:26).

In the assembly, this prayer is expressed under diverse forms: prayers pronounced in the name of all by the presider, general intercessions, individual intentions, silence. In one way or another, more or less explicitly, we find in this prayer the dialogue between the "we" of the Church and the "I" of God—Father, Son, and Spirit; the Church's desire to enter into communion with God by thanksgiving; its inability to reach this by itself, urging it on a journey of conversion so that God may celebrate God's own glory in us; the Church's acknowledgment of dependence upon that God to whom it renders thanks; its plea that God may perfect what was inaugurated in Christ and may gather it into the fully realized kingdom. All this is sought not through words that explain or exhort, but through an action, an approach that unveils what we are by grace, that is, a Church, a people living in thanksgiving.[30]

Now the liturgical celebration explicitly urges us to consciously undertake this course by giving us simple and easily grasped means. Indeed, after the first reading, the Lectionary proposes a few well chosen verses from a psalm, interspersed with a refrain sung by the assembly. Here we are invited to respond to God's Word by appropriating an inspired prayer. Why is it so often replaced by another song that in spite of its qualities does not possess the guarantee of divine authority? Little attention is needed to understand how this psalm is an answer to the Word just proclaimed and how this page from the Old Testament is suitable to the Christian assembly's prayer.

From Sunday to Sunday, we recognize, unsurprisingly at times, always with wonder, how fitting are these psalms, which belong to the tradition of Israel and the Church, to the diverse attitudes of prayer. To discover them so close to us is a cause for endless admiration. Without ever being abstract or disembodied, these responsorial psalms keep us from abandoning ourselves to our own subjectivity by giving it direction. To the singer or hearer, the unadorned manner in which these psalms are sung succeeds in creating a much needed climate. Indeed, this chanting that sets off the text allows it to be easily appropriated by each of us in spiritual freedom. Far from hindering recollection and meditation, it opens doors to them. In the Liturgy of the Word, the responsorial psalm provides a blessed and fruitful time, a breathing space, while each of us benefits from communal participation.[31]

Among all the texts of the formulary, the responsorial psalm is the only one given here in full. This exceptional treatment does more than highlight an important element of the liturgy that is somewhat neglected; it provides the reader an opportunity for a moment of prayer.

The More Familiar Translations

In this book the biblical texts are quoted according to the official translation of the Lectionary as it is found in any missal of the faithful. Being repeatedly heard, they become familiar; such is the value of reminiscence.

We also thought it useful to indicate on what Sunday the reader hears these texts. Thus, this book can be easily and fruitfully read, with the sole help of the missal one is used to.[32]

Finally, we make reference primarily to the Lectionary of the current year, especially for the evangelical texts. Therefore, we cite most often Matthew, Mark, or Luke in Year A, Year B, and Year C, respectively.

The Detailed Account of Sundays

Ordinary Time is divided into two periods: from the Monday following the Baptism of the Lord to the Tuesday preceding Ash Wednesday and from the Monday after Pentecost to the morning of the Saturday preceding the First Sunday of Advent.[33]

In the first period, owing to the mobility of Easter and, accordingly, of Ash Wednesday, the number of Sundays in Ordinary Time varies from year to year.[34]

The same is true of the second period. But the numbering of these Sundays starts from the last one, always the Thirty-fourth, and goes backward to the Sunday following the feast of the Body and Blood of Christ. Therefore, all thirty-four formularies of Ordinary Time are rarely used for lack of available Sundays in the first or second period and because of the occurrence of feasts having their proper formularies.[35] It is easy for the reader to consult yearly liturgical calendars or those found in any missal.[36]

The Cycle of Readings

We have seen that there is a three-year cycle (A, B, and C) for the readings of Sundays in Ordinary Time, and that each liturgical year is characterized by the "continuous reading" of Matthew, Mark, or Luke. The first reading, taken from the Old Testament, is chosen in relation to the Gospel. Furthermore, the Sunday Lectionary proposes the "semi-continuous reading" of the apostolic letters.[37]

On the other hand, for the weekday Lectionary of Ordinary Time—two readings a day—there is a one-year cycle for the Gospel readings, but a two-year one for the first readings: even years (1), odd years (2).

It would be tedious and useless to set up the whole list of these texts and to record their distribution among the days. It suffices to know that the weekday Lectionary takes in almost all the biblical books in the course of the year. The same texts come back every year during Advent, the time from Christmas to Epiphany, Lent and Paschal Time; but they come back every other year in Ordinary Time. Certain books rarely appear, even once: 2 Chronicles, Esther, the Song of Songs, Lamentations, and also Nahum, Habakkuk, the Letter to Philemon, the Second and Third Letters of John. But these latter six are very short. The only books not used for the weekdays in Ordinary Time, on either the even or odd years, are 1 Chronicles, Judith, and Obadiah.[38]

Ordinary Time is decidedly not a nondescript period of the liturgical year; it is not trite or commonplace, in the rather pejorative sense of these words in current usage.[39] It deserves to be lived with intensity, not only at the time of the common celebration, but in the "ordinariness" of daily life. Whether it be in each believer, in communities, in the Church, in the world, many things are at work at each level. It is important for us to become imbued with the spirituality of Ordinary Time, which is not monotonous, which is open to all possibilities.

May the volumes devoted to this longest period of the liturgical year help us as the Days of the Lord succeed one another.

Ordinary Time A

The Sundays of the first year of the liturgical cycle—Year A—are set apart for the reading of the Gospel of Matthew, which is used no less than thirty-two times. This Gospel consists of twenty-eight chapters divided into 1,064 verses; 593, or a little more than half, are read in the Sunday liturgies. The better part of these are found in the Sunday Lectionary for Ordinary Time. We begin with Jesus' Galilean ministry (Matt 4) and end with his words on the Last Judgment (Matt 25:31-46).[1] It is easy to make an integral reading of these twenty-three chapters by perusing during the week the verses that are between the texts of two consecutive Sundays. This would be a good way to better understand and savor the Gospel reading of each Sunday in Ordinary Time.[2]

The texts of the first reading, chosen in relation to the Gospel and generally very short, are taken from fifteen books of the Old Testament: Exodus (twice), Leviticus (once), Deuteronomy (once), 1 Kings (twice), 2 Kings (once), Proverbs (once), Wisdom (twice), Sirach (twice), Isaiah (twelve times), Jeremiah (twice), Ezekiel (three times), Hosea (once), Zephaniah (once), Zechariah (once), and Malachi (once).

The second readings, however, are taken solely from four of Paul's letters: 1 Corinthians (eight times—Second to Seventh Sunday and Christ the King), Romans (sixteen times—Ninth to Twenty-fourth Sunday), Philippians (four times—Twenty-fifth to Twenty-eighth Sunday), and 1 Thessalonians (five times—Twenty-ninth to Thirty-third Sunday). The Letter to the Romans is most often read,[3] and all the excerpts are from the central part of the letter (3:21–14:9), which remains most pertinent today.[4]

Such are the scriptural signposts for Ordinary Time in Year A.[5]

Practical Plan of the Gospel of Matthew

The evangelists did not compose their books as we do, following a plan shown in a "Table of Contents" and dividing their texts into chapters and paragraphs that indicate the progression of their thinking.[1] They wrote according to their personal criteria, e.g., to their own literary purposes. An attentive reading reveals this. However, the exact determination of their principles of composition, based as it is on internal textual criticism, remains open to question. This is why the exegetes come up with Gospel plans that do not exactly coincide. They are unanimous only in discerning certain wholes, certain units. For instance, in Matthew, there is agreement concerning "the origins of Jesus Christ" and "the infancy narrative" (Matt 1:1–2:23), and the "Sermon on the Mount" (Matt 5:1–7:29).[2] Likewise, it is clear that this evangelist alternates "narrative sections" and "discourses."[3] The various plans are based on the recognition of these divisions and on some other considerations.[4] Taken by itself, each of these plans is appealing because of its satisfying clarity and because of its coherence as explained by the author. But when compared among themselves, these plans prove to be arbitrary in part. The same can be said of the plan that we are proposing here. Its only purpose is to offer to readers of this book some reliable landmarks.[5]

1. Infancy narrative and preparation for Jesus' ministry	Matt 1:1–4:16
Jesus' genealogy and infancy Son of Abraham, Son of David, Son of God	Matt 1–2
Preaching of John the Baptist, baptism and temptation of Jesus	Matt 3:1–4:16
2. The preaching of the kingdom in word and act	Matt 4:17–11:30
Preface: "Jesus began to preach and say 'Repent, for the kingdom of heaven is at hand,' " and he calls his first disciples.	Matt 4:17-25

A. Sermon on the Mount	Matt 5–7
B. Narratives of miracles	Matt 8–9
C. Discourse to the Twelve	Matt 10 (1-42)[6]
Conclusion: The question of Jesus'	Matt 11 (1-30)
identity is posed: Is he the one who is to come?	

3. Belief and unbelief in response to the teaching and behavior of Jesus   Matt 12:1–16:12

A. Five controversies	Matt 12 (1-50)
B. Discourse in parables	Matt 13 (1-58)
C. Teaching given to the disciples after John the Baptist's death	Matt 14 (1-36)
D. New controversies	Matt 15:1–16:12

4. The Christian community   Matt 16:13–20:34

A. Foundation of the Church and journeys of faith	Matt 16:13–17:27
B. Ethical rules for the community[7]	Matt 18 (1-35)
C. Instructions on Christian life	Matt 19–20

5. The last days in Jerusalem   Matt 21–25

A. The great crisis: controversies and parables	Matt 21–22
B. Discourse addressed to Scribes and Pharisees	Matt 23 (1-39)
C. Discourse on the end of time[8]	Matt 24–25

6. Passion and resurrection of the Lord   Matt 26–28

A. Suffering and death of the just one	Matt 26–27
B. Resurrection and the mission of the disciples	Matt 28 (1-30)

We should add to this practical plan a general introduction to the reading of Matthew. But such introductions are readily available to the reader.[9] In any case, repeated exposure to Matthew, Sunday after Sunday, will be the best way of knowing him better and of perceiving the originality and emphases in his way of announcing the good news of Jesus Christ, the Lord.

The Texts of the Lectionary

Sunday	1st Reading	Psalm	2nd Reading	Gospel
2nd	Isa 49:3,5-6	40	1 Cor 1:1-3	John 1:29-34
3rd	8:23b-9:3	27	1:10-13, 17	Matt 4:12-23
4th	Zeph 2:3, 3:12-13	146	1:26-31	5:1-12a
5th	Isa 58:7-10	112	2:1-5	5:13-16
6th	Sir 15:15-20	119	2:6-10	5:17-37
7th	Lev 19:1-2, 17-18	103	3:16-23	5:38-48
8th	Isa 49:14-15	62	4:1-5	6:24-34
9th	Deut 11:18, 26-28	31	Rom 3:21-25a, 28	7:21-27
10th	Hos 6:3-6	50	4:18-25	9:9-13
11th	Exod 19:2-6a	100	5:6-11	9:36–10:8
12th	Jer 20:10-13	69	5:12-15	10:26-33
13th	2 Kgs 4:8-11, 14-16a	89	6:3b-4, 8-11	10:37-42
14th	Zech 9:9-10	145	8:9, 11-13	11:25-30
15th	Isa 55:10-11	65	8:18-23	13:1-23
16th	Wis 12:13, 16-19	86	8:26-27	13:24-43
17th	1 Kgs 3:5, 7-12	119	8:28-30	13:44-52
18th	Isa 55:1-3	145	8:35, 37-39	14:13-21
19th	1 Kgs 19:9a, 11-13a	85	9:1-5	14:22-32
20th	Isa 56:1, 6-7	67	11:13-15, 29-32	15:21-28
21st	22:15, 19-23	138	11:33-36	16:13-20
22nd	Jer 20:7-9	63	12:1-2	16:21-27
23rd	Ezek 33:7-9	95	13:8-10	18:15-20
24th	Sir 27:30–28:7	103	14:7-9	18:21-35
25th	Isa 55:6-9	145	Phil 1:20c-24, 27a	20:1-16a
26th	Ezek 18:25-28	25	2:1-11	21:28-32
27th	Isa 5:1-7	80	4:6-9	21:33-43
28th	25:6-10a	23	4:12-14, 19-20	22:1-14
29th	45:1, 4-6a	96	1 Thess 1:1-5b	22:15-21
30th	Exod 22:20-26	18	1:5c-10	22:34-40
31st	Mal 1:14b–2:2b, 8-10	131	2:7b-9, 13	23:1-12
32nd	Wis 6:12-16	63	4:13-18	25:1-13
33rd	Prov 31:10-13, 19-20, 30-31	128	5:1-6	25:14-30
34th (Christ the King)	Ezek 34:11-12, 15-17	23	1 Cor 15:20-26, 28	25:31-46

The Division of Sundays into "Sequences" Ordinary Time, Year A

This division is determined by the Gospel readings that form the framework of the Liturgy of the Word on each Sunday. It does not pretend to exclude any other division, but it has its foundation in the "plan" of the Gospel of Matthew and the selection of texts given in the Lectionary.

2nd and 3rd Sundays

Isa 49:3, 5-6	1 Cor 1:1-3	John 1:29-34
8:23b-9:3	1:10-13, 17	Matt 4:12-23

4th and 5th Sundays

Zeph 2:3, 3:12-13	1 Cor 1:26-31	Matt 5:1-12a
Isa 58:7-10	2:1-5	5:13-16

6th, 7th, 8th, and 9th Sundays

Sir 15:15-20	1 Cor 2:6-10	Matt 5:17-37
Lev 19:1-2, 17-18	3:16-23	5:38-48
Isa 49:14-15	4:1-5	6:24-34
Deut 11:18, 26-28	Rom 3:21-25a, 28	7:21-27

10th and 11th Sundays

Hos 6:3-6	Rom 4:18-25	Matt 9:9-13
Exod 19:2-6a	5:6-11	9:36–10:8

12th, 13th, and 14th Sundays

Jer 20:10-13	Rom 5:12-15	Matt 10:26-33
2 Kgs 4:8-11, 14-16a	6:3b-4, 8-11	10:37-42
Zech 9:9-10	8:9, 11-13	11:25-30

15th, 16th, and 17th Sundays

Isa 55:10-11	Rom 8:18-23	Matt 13:1-23
Wis 12:13, 16-19	8:26-27	13:24-43
1 Kgs 3:5, 7-12	8:28-30	13:44-52

18th, 19th, and 20th Sundays

Isa 55:1-3	Rom 8:35, 37-39	Matt 14:13-21
1 Kgs 19:9a, 11-13a	9:1-5	14:22-33
Isa 56:1, 6-7	11:13-15, 29-32	15:21-28

21st and 22nd Sundays

Isa 22:15, 19-23	Rom 11:33-36	Matt 16:13-20
Jer 20:7-9	12:1-2	16:21-27

23rd, 24th, and 25th Sundays

Ezek 33:7-9	Rom 13:8-10	Matt 18:15-20
Sir 27:30-28:7	14:7-9	18:21-35
Isa 55:6-9	Phil 1:20c-24, 27a	20:1-16a

26th, 27th, and 28th Sundays

Ezek 18:25-28	Phil 2:1-11	Matt 21:28-32
Isa 5:1-7	4:6-9	21:33-43
25:6-10a	4:12-14, 19-20	22:1-14

29th, 30th, and 31st Sundays

Isa 45:1, 4-6a	1 Thess 1:1-5b	Matt 22:15-21

| Exod 22:20-26 | 1:5c-10 | 22:34-40 |
| Mal 1:14b-2:2b, 8-10 | 2:7b-9, 13 | 23:1-12 |

32nd and 33rd Sundays

| Wis 6:12-16 | 1 Thess 4:13-18 | Matt 25:1-13 |
| Prov 31:10-13, 19-20, 30-31 | 5:1-6 | 25:14-30 |

34th Sunday: Christ the King

| Ezek 34:11-12, 15-17 | 1 Cor 15:20-26, 28 | Matt 25:31-46 |

In this volume, when we refer to a Sunday without further qualification, we are speaking of a Sunday in Ordinary Time, Year A. When we refer to a Sunday in another part of the liturgical year, we also are speaking of Year A.

The Second and Third Sundays in Ordinary Time

Every year, on the Second Sunday in Ordinary Time, the third reading is taken from the Gospel of John rather than from that of Matthew. Matthew's Gospel, however, is going to be used in a "semi-continuous" reading on the following Sundays. The purpose of this choice is to place Ordinary Time in continuity with the manifestation of the Lord, celebrated at Epiphany and at the Baptism of the Lord.[1]

During Year A, on the Second Sunday in Ordinary Time, the passage from John speaks of the witness given to Jesus by John the Baptist. The "semi-continuous" reading of the Gospel of Matthew begins with Jesus' ministry in Nazareth "when he heard that John had been arrested." Therefore, the Second and Third Sundays constitute the first "sequence."[2] This is made clear since, on the following Sunday, the Sermon on the Mount forms a characteristic unit of the Gospel of Matthew.

Second Sunday

Recognizing the Lord's Presence

God's Servant, Light of the Nations
The Liturgy of the Word begins, on this Sunday, with the proclamation of one of the oracle-poems of the Book of Isaiah, called "Servant-of-the-Lord" oracles (Isa 49:3, 5-6).[1]

In the Book of Isaiah, the second poem contains six verses, of which the Lectionary keeps only three: those that pertain to the religious and universal mission of the mysterious Servant.[2] This kind of selection is normal in the liturgy and quite legitimate.[3] It is not a question of arbitrarily omitting verses, claiming that they are too hard, distasteful, or giving some similar reason. The objective of the liturgy is not primarily to have us read the Bible, but rather to celebrate the mystery illumined by God's Word. The Bible is offered as a food, the "table of the Word." Its proclamation and its function are ritual ones.[4] Finally, when it is a question of correlating two passages of the Scripture, the choice of texts or excerpts from texts is made to form a coherent montage. This happens on Sundays in Ordinary Time, for the choice of the first reading (Old Testament) depends on what Gospel is to be read.[5] Such is the case on this Sunday.

The mysterious Servant of whom the Book of Isaiah speaks has been chosen by God who formed him "from the womb." His mission is to reunite God's people, "to raise up the tribes of Jacob and restore the survivors of Israel." Moreover, God is going to make of him "a light to the nations," that God's salvation "may reach to the ends of the earth."

Whatever the historic identity and mission of this emissary,[6] the person remains mysterious and the mission so extraordinary that, in all times, believers have read and reread this oracle into the present moment of their own history.

From apostolic times, Christians have recognized the features of Christ in those of this mysterious Servant of God (see Matt 3:17 and Luke 2:32). The Fourth Gospel sees in Jesus' destiny the realization of the prophesies concerning the Servant. Jesus died "so that the whole nation may not perish," and "to gather into one the dispersed children of God" (John 11:50-53). This is why "when he came into the world, he said, 'Sacrifice

22

and offering you did not desire, but a body you prepared for me; holocausts and sin offerings you took no delight in. Then I said, "As is written of me in the scroll, behold I come to do your will, O God" ' " (Heb 10:5-7).

Having heard this text from the Book of Isaiah, we could do nothing better than repeat, following Jesus and in the name of the whole Body of Christ, Psalm 40. While we sing the verses punctuated by the refrain, the overtones of this prophetic text unfold, as we more and more intently fix our eyes on Christ.

> *Here am I, LORD;*
> *I come to do your will.*
>
> I have waited, waited for the LORD,
>   and he stooped toward me and heard my cry.
> And he put a new song into my mouth,
>   a hymn to our God.
>
> Sacrifice or oblation you wished not,
>   but ears open to obedience you gave me.
> Holocausts or sin-offerings you sought not;
>   then said I, "Behold I come."
>
> "In the written scroll it is prescribed for me,
>   to do your will, O my God, is my delight,
> And your law is within my heart!"
>
> I announced your justice in the vast assembly;
>   I did not restrain my lips, as you, O LORD, know.
> (Ps 40)

Grace and Peace Be with You All

From the Second to the Eighth Sundays in Ordinary Time during Year A, we read excerpts from the First Letter of Paul to the Corinthians,[7] beginning with the first words: the address and the opening salutation (1 Cor 1:1-3).

St. Paul's manner of beginning his letters is never trite: "Paul, called to be an apostle of Christ Jesus by the will of God." The solemnity of the formula reveals the writer's authority and the official character of his epistle. This is not without importance in view of the topics about to be discussed. Besides, by speaking with such solemnity, the Apostle shields himself against those who would be tempted to call upon a lesser authority than his.[8]

"To the church of God that is in Corinth." This formula recalls the solemn assemblies of the chosen people gathered in the desert, then in the

Jerusalem temple after Ezra's and Nehemiah's reform.[9] The assembly of Corinthian Christians is heir to this lineage, but it also anticipates the immense gathering of the elect at the end of time. There is only one single assembly, one single group called by divine summons, a fraction of which is gathered in Corinth. But it already contains in reality the mystery of the Church that the following passage reveals.

"Sanctified in Christ Jesus," the members of the Church in Corinth are "called to be holy." The originator of the call is God. Christ's role is to lead to sanctity those called to faith by God and bound to be holy because of the grace they have received.

But Paul widens significantly the audience to whom he addresses his letter, to "all those everywhere who call upon the name of our Lord Jesus Christ, their Lord and ours." The newness of the gospel is this: from now on the holy people is made of all those who have faith in the one and only Lord Jesus Christ, in whom they find their fundamental unity.

By the same token, the Apostle suggests that the counsels and guidelines he addresses to the community in Corinth are meant for the whole Church, in all times and places, including the actual communities that to this day read the Apostle's letter during the Liturgy of the Word. From that time, all believers, past, present, and future, receive the classical salutation that concludes the reading on this Sunday. St. Paul wishes them "peace,"—the typically Jewish greeting—and "grace"—a more distinctly Greek formula, bespeaking the newness brought by Christ—in other words, salvation, the supreme gift offered to all in Jesus Christ.

The strong voice of the Apostle, who worked to the limit of his strength to root the Church, reaches us. And it reaches us whether we read his letters or hear the teaching and exhortations of those who today in the Church exercise the ministry of the word. "Receive from us the right teaching of faith as transmitted by our fathers in order to be strengthened, you in whom the purity of perfect faith resides, you most holy assembly of the Church, you who rely upon God's help and in whom God rests."[10]

John's Testimony for Our Faith

By a particularly fortunate inspiration, the editors of the Sunday Lectionary invite us to hear again, before we begin reading the Gospel of Matthew, the testimony of John the Baptist concerning Jesus (John: 1:29-34).

"I did not know him, but . . ." These words recur twice in the Precursor's mouth. However, Jesus was his cousin, barely six months younger than he (Luke 1:36). After the Annunciation, Mary, Jesus' mother, had visited a pregnant Elizabeth and had remained with her until John's birth (Luke 1:56). It would be very surprising if Elizabeth had been indifferent to the happy outcome of Mary's pregnancy, if she had not been informed of Jesus' birth, if the two women had never met again, if the two children had never become acquainted. And yet John states, "I did not know him." There are different ways of knowing. There are indeed many persons whom we know and of whom we say that, in fact, we do not know them. We might sense that they are out of the ordinary until, one day, because of an incident, a word, whatever—it does not matter—we suddenly discover their true and deep identities. "No indeed, I did not know him." All the more, those who approached Jesus must have known this commonplace experience: John, the disciples, but also Mary. The Gospels have preserved the memory of John's interrogations and hesitations concerning Jesus. Steeped in prophetic oracles, he was carrying in his mind an image of the Messiah that did not exactly square with that given by Jesus in his behavior (Matt 3:7-10; 11:2-3). And then there was the common saying that no one would know from where the Messiah was coming (John 7:27); that after his birth, which was to take place in Bethlehem (Matt 2:5-6), he would abide in an unknown place—heaven?—until his dazzling manifestation (Matt: 24:26). But John saw the Spirit descend from the heavens and rest upon Jesus. Whatever the questions that linger in his mind, he cannot forget this divine intervention that led him to discover him whom he did not know beforehand.[11] Here is the reason why he says and proclaims, "Now I have seen and testified." John was sent by God to testify to the light come into the world.[12] By so speaking, he fulfills his mission. But at the same time, he witnesses to the manner in which one normally becomes a believer.

The sudden and evident discovery of the Lord, for instance, that by Saul on the way to Damascus (Acts 9:1-19), remains the exception. Ordinarily, Jesus' true face reveals itself little by little, at the end of a slow, even laborious journey, under the light of the Spirit that illuminates by degrees. To tell the truth, we never succeed in fully knowing here on earth the one whom, however, we have already "seen." We will have to wait for the time of the face-to-face (1 Cor 13:12). This applies to the whole Church and, the more so, to each believer.

This progressive knowledge of Jesus is the fruit of the unceasingly renewed reading of the Gospels—this year, that of Matthew—as it is done, above all, in the framework of the liturgy,[13] within a group, or in one's "inner room" (Matt 6:6), by the light of the Spirit and in a prayerful climate. This reading must be coupled with a conscious, full, and complete participation in the sacraments of the faith, which celebrate and unveil the mystery. Let us not forget, besides, that we become Christians in proportion to how much we live according to Christ.

He Is Coming After Me; He Ranks Ahead of Me

The evangelist John artfully suggests much with few words, or even one word, to which he suddenly gives a meaning that opens us to the mystery. The Baptist *sees* Jesus *coming* towards him. The verbs have their most current meaning: John catches sight of Jesus advancing in his direction. Everyone around the Baptist could do the same. Then John repeats what he already has said (John 1:27), "The one who is coming after me ranks ahead of me." The verb "to come" has here special overtones: Jesus is "the one who comes," "the one who is to come" (Matt 11:3). He "ranks ahead" because "he existed before me." No doubt, we are now speaking about the Messiah. "It is he." In this context, this way of speaking recalls that used to designate God himself—"He-is."[14] And we acclaim the Lord by singing to "him who is and who was and who is to come" (Rev: 1:4, 8).

At this moment, the witness takes his proper place in relation to the one he points to; he has no other mission than to prepare his manifestation.

The Lamb of God

The coming of him whom John the Baptist points to—"It is he"—had already been announced by the great messianic prophecies: "A shoot shall sprout from the stump of Jesse" (Isa 11:1, Second Sunday of Advent) and the "Servant-of-the-Lord oracles." The Messiah's manifestation was to be accompanied by an extraordinary outpouring of the Spirit,[15] who would rest on him.[16] However, the features of the hoped-for Messiah were too vague to allow a clear identification. He was the unknown Messiah and was to remain so for those who did not recognize or accept his coming (John 1:11).

All through his Gospel, Matthew presents Jesus as the one who fulfills the Scriptures.[17] Likewise, the evangelist is very interested in the messianic titles given to Jesus and in those his disciples used for him.[18] The title "Lamb of God" appears only in the Fourth Gospel and, as a proper name, twenty-nine times in Revelation. We are familiar with this title, difficult to understand in itself, but rich in meanings. Recalling its nomadic past, the people around the Baptist might have thought of the ram walking before the flock, overcoming the obstacles in the way of the ewes. And, in fact, John the Baptist, the stern ascetic in the wilderness, he who announced the great and fearful day of God (Matt 3:1-12), might have perceived in Jesus the "ram of God," the warlike Messiah, the awaited liberator. At that time, in the circles influenced by apocalyptic ideas and in Qumran,[19] there was the belief in a warrior lamb, taken from the flock and defending its brothers by attacking and dispersing their enemies.[20] In Revelation, John describes Jesus, the Messiah, as a Lamb, victorious though slain. He has triumphed over all his enemies; he has preceded his own before God; he has redeemed with his blood persons of all tribes, tongues, peoples, and nations.[21]

But we should not forget that the blood of the lambs killed for Passover was poured (Exod 12) in Jerusalem, the very place where Isaac would have been sacrificed if God had not substituted a ram (Gen 22:13). We are reminded also of the oracle on the Suffering Servant, "like a lamb led to the slaughter or a sheep before the shearers"; of the just man, who "shall justify many and their guilt he shall bear" (Isa 53:7, 11).

To choose between these diverse meanings would amount to losing certain overtones of a specially rich symbolism.[22] On the contrary, we must hear them all in the words "Here is the Lamb of God who takes away the sins of the world" at the moment of Eucharistic communion.

Son of God

This title has a history. In the Bible, it first designates the person God has anointed to govern his people. The ritual of enthronement and crowning contained a covenant rite between God and the elect, adopted as his son: "The Lord said to me, 'You are my son'" (Ps 2:7).[23]

Among Christians, the title acquires a new depth after Jesus' resurrection; from now on, it expresses the unique intimacy between Jesus and his Father. The Fourth Gospel clearly asserts that the Son of God is also the eternal Word who was "at the Father's side" (John 1:18). After dwelling among humans, he filled his disciples with his fullness, grace in place of grace (John 1:14-16). After his resurrection, they recognized him as their Lord and their God.[24] Therefore, the words placed in the Baptist's mouth express the faith of the first Christian generations.[25] Matthew insists on the title "Son of God," already traditional in his time to designate Jesus.[26]

To See and to Witness

The prophets had seen from afar the features of him who was to come, the servant of God, the light of the nations. They related their visions in order that successive generations might keep and transmit them. In the course of the ages, the ancient outline became clearer by the light of current events and signs of the times, in the eyes of the little and humble ones not blinded by prejudices. In the simplicity of their hearts, they welcomed the word of the prophets, those bearers of hope that God sent them. They crowded the banks of the Jordan, where John gave them his baptism of repentance while announcing the very presence among them of the expected one. And, when pointing to a man who was coming towards him, the Baptist said "It is he," they accepted his testimony.

During the centuries of waiting, the Spirit was at work; he was opening the eyes of the great seers and preparing all hearts to receive their message of hope. It is the Spirit John saw descending upon Jesus, whom he did not know. Others have followed the Lamb of God, lived with the Lord, and preserved his teaching. They saw him healing the sick and giving sight to the blind; they saw him on the cross and, three days later, alive as he had foretold. Finally, they saw him ascending to the right hand of the Father. And they preached him.

Their testimony was transmitted to us in order that we, too, might believe, and recognize in Jesus the Son of God, and have life in him and through him. This testimony reaches us only if we let the Spirit act in us, because without the Spirit, no one can say, "Jesus is Lord" (1 Cor 12:3). Without the Spirit, the Gospel remains a dead letter; reading it leaves us as we are: blind, deaf, mute, lifeless. As it is impossible to make even one lump of dough, one loaf of bread, without mixing water with dry flour, we who were many could not become one in Christ Jesus without the water from heaven. And as the arid earth does not bear fruit without water, we who were only dry wood (cf. Luke 23:31) could never produce fruit without the generous rain from above (cf. Ps 68:10).[27]

It is the Spirit who allowed John the Baptist to see the Son of God in the man walking along the banks of the Jordan. It is the Spirit who, today, allows the believers to recognize the Lord's presence in the sacramental signs and his voice in the word proclaimed in the assembly. And it is the Spirit who validates the testimony of the Church when it announces the Savior to men and women of all races, tongues, and peoples.

> As you walked, Lamb of God,
> you crossed our path

and we followed you.
We want to see your home.
Welcome us today
near you
and to-morrow we shall proclaim:

Meeting you, LORD, is the dawn of life!
None can come to me
  unless the Father draws them.

Those who left everything to follow me
never know death.

Those who love me keep my word
And I dwell with them.[28]

Third Sunday

The Light of the Gospel Shines in the Darkness

A Great Light in the Darkness

On this Sunday, the liturgy opens with a particularly solemn proclamation of a prophecy from Isaiah. In God's name, the prophet announces that a glorious era is going to follow a shameful time, that the people of God "who walked in darkness" are going to see a resplendent light, and that this manifestation will take place in "the land west of the Jordan," in Galilee, "the District of the Gentiles" (Isa 8:23-9:3).

Like all similar prophetic oracles, this one was uttered in a definite historical context and concerned events that were to happen sooner or later, but in any case in a time to come. It is interesting and instructive to know the context of the prophecy and to relate it to historical vicissitudes. The exegetes look at these questions, but do not dwell on them[1] because the perspective of these prophecies—of that read today in particular—goes beyond; without a doubt, it is messianic. In fact, the Christian tradition has read this prophecy by the light of Christ's manifestation. The reason this text was chosen for this Sunday is that today's Gospel cites it verbatim.[2] Does it do so to show that Jesus fulfilled this prophecy? Undoubtedly. But this reference would be of limited interest if it answered only an apologetic preoccupation. On the other hand, the prophet's oracle becomes quite useful if it allows us to better understand the meaning and scope of the Lord's manifestation and, hence the situation that is ours today. And this is precisely what happens. A text such as this does not look toward the past; it enlightens the present and the future, which the present fashions. In sum, it says, "Are you aware of the time in which you are already living? Are you aware of what God has done for you, of what is at stake in the present? Light has shone in the darkness; God has delivered us from our old slaveries. Sing for joy. Pray that you obtain the grace not to stray from the land of the living."

The LORD is my light and my salvation.

The LORD is my light and my salvation;
   whom should I fear?
The LORD is my life's refuge;
   of whom should I be afraid?

One thing I ask of the LORD;
   this I seek:
To dwell in the house of the LORD
   all the days of my life,
That I may gaze on the loveliness of the LORD
   and contemplate his temple.

I believe that I shall see the bounty of the LORD
   in the land of the living.
Wait for the LORD with courage;
   be stouthearted, and wait for the LORD.
(Ps 27:1, 4, 13-14)

The Unity of the Community Gathered by Christ

The major letters of Paul, all addressed to existing communities, were written in response to particular situations and problems.[3] This is clearly the case of the First Letter to the Corinthians.[4] The passages we read from the Second to the Eighth Sundays of Year A[5] revolve around the subject of unity in the community, introduced in today's reading (1 Cor 1:10-13, 17).

To "the church of God that is in Corinth" (1 Cor 1:2), the Apostle addresses a stirring and pressing exhortation betraying anxiety: "I urge you . . . in the name of our Lord Jesus Christ, that all of you agree in what you say, and that there be no divisions among you, but that you be united in the same mind and in the same purpose." To designate these divisions, Paul uses the word schism, which is familiar to us, although its literal meaning, "tear," tends to be forgotten.[6] Faith, and not human considerations, is the foundation upon which Paul here, as in his other epistles, bases the demands of life and behavior that he presents: Christ is not divided. Here is what is at stake: Any assault on the unity of an ecclesial community undermines the indivisible unity of Christ. Thoughts, feelings, and actions are always evaluated in relation to him, his person. We cannot help but recall here another moral exhortation of Paul's, that to the Philippians, where again he pleads for unity. The Apostle concludes, "Have among yourselves the same attitude that is also yours in Christ Jesus" (Phil 2:1-5). And this appeal leads him to remind his correspondents of the beautiful and famed hymn, "Christ Jesus who though he was in the form of God. . ." (Phil 2:6-11).[7]

Scandal and Absurdity of Factions

When divisions occur in Christian communities, they are often caused by conflicts of personalities. Loyalty to so-and-so gives rise to parties, coteries that are rivals, even enemies. The persons to whom loyalty is given may have nothing to do with these rivalries; they may even deplore them. This must have been what happened in Corinth: "I belong to Paul" or "I belong to Apollos." There was even a group whose members stated "I belong to Christ." What did they mean? Perhaps by objecting to the other leaders, they pretended to be instructed directly by the Lord himself, which would indicate a certain gnostic tendency.[8] To all of these, Paul says "Nonsense!" And he retorts to his own followers: "Was Paul crucified for you? Or were you baptized in the name of Paul?" Such divisiveness bordered on the silly and the scandalous.

"Christ did not send me to baptize." This argument must not be misunderstood. It disparages neither the sacramental ministry nor baptism itself. But in the present case, Paul rejoices—"I give thanks," he even says—for having personally baptized only a few persons in Corinth: "Crispus and Gaius" and "the household of Stephanas." (These verses, 14-16, are omitted in the liturgical reading.) It is a good thing that no one can boast of having been baptized by the Apostle.

The passage ends with the absolute primacy of Christ's cross, the sole efficacious cause of salvation, "a stumbling block" for some, "foolishness" for others (1 Cor 1:23). The cross, however, is the good news of salvation; to announce it by means of "words taught by human wisdom" would be to empty it of its meaning.[9]

Christian Universality

The risk of disputes similar to those at Corinth in the past, still threatens Christian communities today. Paul, who calls himself "apostle of Christ Jesus" (1 Cor 1:1) gives us a timely reminder: no one possesses the gospel; no one should presume to selfishly monopolize Christ's name. To divide the Church into rival, jealous cliques would be to break apart the Body of him who came to unite all in his person. To follow a leader in a partisan way, to ban expressions of faith differing from our own would be to ignore the salvation that comes to us from the one cross of Christ. But the timeliness of Paul's advice concerns not only the situations in which divisions happen in ecclesial communities.

> [Ecclesial communities], being structured in a hierarchical manner, always have a shape of their own, recognizable among all other human communities. This singular stamp that each one owes both to its origin and its end, signifies that the gathering taking place in the Church, the communion realized there, overstep the boundaries that would exist in an assembly ruled by purely human decisions. The Church is the result of a ''convocation'' of God, according to the first sense of the biblical term. It cannot seek a kind of unity more restricted than that of God himself, that is to say, one including the entire human family. This stamp of divine origin, marking her and demanding, so to speak, an unceasing extension, forbids her to yield to the temptation of partisanship or sectarianism. Moreover, this stamp widens to infinity—God's very infinity—the space allowed for the blossoming of each believer's spiritual life.[10]

Jesus, the Good News at the Crossroad of Nations

On the Third Sunday of Ordinary Time in Year A, we open the Gospel of Matthew at the passage relating the beginning of Jesus' ministry. This passage constitutes a specially well-written introduction to the whole of the book that is read for thirty-three Sundays (Matt 4:12-23).

The twelve verses of this text contain a certain number of words and expressions that will often recur in Matthew; his Gospel will progressively reveal their meaning and scope: ''to repent,'' ''the Kingdom of heaven is at hand,'' ''to call,'' ''to leave everything in order to follow Jesus,'' ''to teach,'' ''to proclaim,'' ''to cure.''

It is noteworthy that the evangelist so clearly connects the beginning of Jesus' ministry with the end of that of the imprisoned John. Matthew likes to insist on the continuity in the unfolding of salvation; hence, his care in recalling the scriptures Jesus fulfills.[11] The text from the Book of Isaiah quoted here (Isa 8:23-9:1) highlights, in the first reading, the meaning of the fact that Jesus began his ministry in Galilee, ''the district of the Gentiles.'' It is in Galilee that Jesus found refuge after his stay in Egypt (Matt 2:23-25). It is to Galilee that Jesus summoned his disciples after his resurrection (Matt 26:32). And, finally it is after a last appearance in Galilee that he sent them to announce the gospel: ''Go, therefore, and make disciples of all nations, baptizing them in the name of the Father, and of the Son, and of the Holy Spirit, teaching them to observe all that I have commanded you'' (Matt 28:19-20).

From the outset of his ministry, Jesus resolutely confronts what he came to fight against: the darkness which covered the world and which his light would dispel, the shame, and everything that kept humankind in the sadness of slavery. That mission, which the Lord himself began in Galilee, "the district of the Gentiles," will also be that of the apostles and of the Church. We must never forget that spot where everything started, and we must unceasingly return to it.[12]

"Repent!"

The continuity between Jesus' ministry and the prophets' before him, is marked by the identity of their message, "Repent, for the kingdom of heaven is at hand." These are the very words with which we can summarize John the Baptist's preaching (Matt 3:1-2). It is also what Jesus will repeat, in different ways, with an insistence emphasized by Matthew. For him, the gospel is a "teaching to be lived," through a conversion to which the prospect of judgment gives urgency. The evangelist is so insistent because this preaching, with its demands, is timely, necessary in the community for which he is writing, a community in which there are "good and bad" and even "pretentious leaders"; all must repent without delay.[13] This situation remains that of the Church and of Christian communities. As we read it, we are struck by the obvious timeliness of the Gospel of Matthew.

"Come after me . . ."

As soon as he began preaching, Jesus surrounded himself with disciples called to become "fishers of men": "Simon, who is called Peter, and his brother Andrew," "James, the son of Zebedee, and his brother John."

Beyond the fact itself, the way it is reported must hold our attention. One characteristic of Jesus' words often stressed by Matthew is, from the beginning, thrown into relief—his authority. Jesus "orders," "enjoins," "commands."[14] The first four who were called and who "immediately" followed Jesus, leaving behind nets, boats, and parents, are models for disciples of all times. For the genuine disciple does not merely say, "Lord, Lord," but also does the will of the Father as taught by Jesus (Matt 7:23).

Jesus' Ministry Is Without End

The way in which Matthew presents the beginning of Jesus' ministry is particularly instructive. Jesus "went around all of Galilee, teaching in their synagogues, proclaiming the gospel of the kingdom and curing every disease and illness among the people." And he adds: "His fame spread to all of Syria, and they brought to him all who were sick with various diseases and racked with pain, those who were possessed, lunatics, and paralytics and he cured them. And great crowds from Galilee, the Decapolis, Jerusalem, and Judea, and from beyond the Jordan followed him.''[15]

Matthew willingly generalizes and amplifies the efficacy of Jesus' interventions:[16] ''all who were sick,'' ''every disease''; similarly, ''all of Galilee,'' ''crowds'' coming from all regions. This is not a sort of pet idea that would cause the evangelist to exaggerate. In Jesus' ministry in Galilee, Matthew sees the prefiguration and, in some way, the point of departure of the universal mission of the Church. When the evangelist was writing, the good news was proclaimed not only in Galilee and in the surrounding regions, but also to the ends of the earth, to all nations. We cannot forget that Galilee was the cradle of the universal mission. Therefore, we ''must know how to go back to Galilee, to recapture the moment of profound peace that was an encounter, and to begin anew to live it. . . . All of us, believers, possess somewhere within us Galilee, our own Galilee, in relation to God and to humankind. Let us return to Galilee; the forgotten certainty will become a certainty full of reality and untold possibilities. Then our faith will really be the assured belief in divine life, a certitude born of a rediscovered experience.''[17]

The Gospel in the Present
In the liturgy of this Sunday, everything turns us resolutely towards the present, from Isaiah's prophecy to Paul's plea for unity to the Gospel narrative of the beginning of Jesus' ministry. The prophetic oracle invites us to be more aware of the present situation of the world and of God's people. The time of shame and slavery has ended. Light has shone in the world, offering to each one the opportunity to escape the all-encompassing darkness. The good news of salvation has resounded throughout the whole world. All who have ears can hear it and come near the Lord who is here near them. No longer does an illusory salvation rest with humans, but true salvation is found in him who died on the cross for all. The gospel message is not human wisdom accessible only to the few. On the contrary, it is destined for the simple and all those who have a simple heart, for the crowd of obscure people. From now on, we must gather around Christ, as we do in the liturgy, the sacrament of the Body of Christ, who cannot be divided and gives the whole of himself to each.

> You came, Lord,
> into our night

to turn our ways towards the dawn;
your way however remains hidden,
only the Spirit uncovers for us
your passage.

To lead us to light
you took up a body
in the human shadow into which you come.
Many would want to see and understand:
will they recognize
your light?

We say to them: "See
the grain that dies;
no eye sees it,
but our hearts can divine
in the shared bread
his presence."

Then we carry to you,
like a cry,
the hope of today's men and women;
ripen the time, hurry the day,
and may it rise on earth,
Your kingdom.[18]

The Fourth and Fifth Sundays in Ordinary Time

Immediately after the overview of Jesus' ministry in Galilee (Matt 4:12-13—Third Sunday), Matthew inserted in his Gospel the first of Jesus' great discourses, the "Sermon on the Mount."[1] This inaugural or evangelical discourse contains three chapters. The first, which is the longest (forty-eight verses), is read in its entirety from the Fourth to the Seventh Sundays. On the Eighth and Ninth Sundays, we read excerpts from chapters 6 and 7 (Matt 6:24-34, 7:21-27).[2] This ensemble constitutes a unit well defined by two formulas: "When he saw the crowds, he went up the mountain . . . and he began to teach them" (Matt 5:1-2) and "When Jesus finished these words, the crowds were astonished at his teaching, for he taught them as one having authority, and not as their scribes" (Matt 7:28-29).[3]

The Fourth and Fifth Sundays in Ordinary Time, Year A, may be considered a sequence because the passages read there are a sort of introduction to the Sermon on the Mount.

Fourth Sunday

The Good News of the Master, Meek and Humble of Heart

Seek the Lord, You Humble Ones

The little Book of Zephaniah[1] supplies texts for the liturgy twice in Sunday Masses and twice in weekday Masses.[2] No doubt, this is because the prophet of the seventh century before our era (640–625 B.C.) speaks mostly of the "Day of the Lord" under its most dreadful aspect.[3] However, for all his unrelenting sternness, this prophet gives us here and there in his book passages that sound surprisingly evangelical; such is the brief excerpt we read on this Sunday (Zeph 2:3, 3:12-13).

The very fact that such verses happen in a series of threatening oracles deserves our attention. Whereas nothing seems able to stop God's arm, hope remains: "Perhaps you may be sheltered on the day of the Lord's anger."[4] God is not inflexible; God's mercy is always ready to manifest itself for the benefit of those who seek God, who seek justice and humility. To "seek the Lord" meant to go to the Temple in order to consult him through a priest, or in a wider sense, to render to the Lord the cult due him. But among the prophets, it meant above all to conform one's behavior to the demands of the covenant. Jesus will say likewise, "Seek first the kingdom of God and his righteousness" and all the things you need will be given you "besides" (Matt 6:33).

This hope is for the lowly ones, the little ones, the poor ones. They are a remnant that "shall pasture and couch their flocks with none to disturb them."[5] To designate these poor ones the prophet uses a word, *anawim*, a term that will become widely known. This word signifies those humble believers eager to welcome God, always ready to do his will, hoping in him alone. Their search for God and his justice will give rise to a current of admirable spirituality exemplified by the Virgin Mary, "the handmaid of the Lord."[6] And Jesus will say to the little group of his disciples, "Come to me, all you who labor and are burdened, and I will give you rest . . . for I am meek and humble of heart" (Matt 11:28-29).

Happy the poor in spirit;
the kingdom of heaven is theirs!

The LORD keeps faith forever,
  secures justice for the oppressed,
  gives food to the hungry.
The LORD sets captives free.

The LORD gives sight to the blind;
  the LORD raises up those that were bowed down.
The LORD loves the just;
  the LORD protects strangers.

The fatherless and the widow the LORD sustains,
  but the way of the wicked he thwarts.
The LORD shall reign forever;
  your God, O Zion, through all generations.
Alleluia.
(Ps 146:6-7, 8-9, 9-10)

The Sign of a Community Made Up of the Lowly

Paul wrote his First Letter to the Corinthians to help the community to take hold of itself. It was divided into rival factions. The Apostle begins by confronting this intolerable and absurd situation. These schisms are an insult to Christ and empty the cross of all meaning.[7] To refuse its "foolishness" amounts to seeking salvation in a so-called "human wisdom."[8] To illustrate God's way of bringing salvation, Paul invites the community at Corinth to examine the kind of people they are (1 Cor 1:25-31).

If God took into account human wisdom and power, noble birth, he certainly would not have looked for persons without influence, of modest origins, held in contempt in society, in a word, a paltry lot. Such is indeed the make-up of that community composed of slaves, petty merchants, unlearned men and women. Precisely, God has chosen this paltry lot. Here we have the proof that God's wisdom does not conform at all with human wisdom, that salvation is an absolutely gratuitous gift from God, since those who have nothing—who are nothing—can take advantage of it. Finally, we are confronted with Christ's cross, supreme manifestation of the paradoxical wisdom of God, foolishness and a stumbling block in human eyes.

This testimony and feeling is still with us today in communities made up of "lowly" people. In Africa, in many countries of the Third World, Christian communities whose membership consists only of simple folk, poor people lacking everything—possessions, power, education—are today the shining sign of the Spirit's action. They put to shame our own communities, rich in all sorts of human gifts.

Boasting in the Lord

We should not conclude from the preceding remarks that there is no place in the Church for those fortunate enough to enjoy gifts appreciated among humans: wisdom, knowledge, education, lofty religious and secular culture, etc. All these are valuable. We must be thankful to God for having received them, for having been able to acquire them. But above all, we must understand that all these do not give us any value in God's eyes; that, despite everything, we remain poor before him; that he—and he only—is our true treasure; that the gifts we have received create responsibilities and duties; that in no way can we boast of them. The communities that today resemble Corinth yesterday teach us to take pride in the Lord by giving thanks for the only valuable riches, given equally to all.

The Inescapable Way of the Beatitudes

Jesus begins his preaching of the "kingdom of heaven" being "at hand" after John the Baptist's arrest. Concerning the beginning of the Lord's ministry, Matthew limits himself to mentioning the theme of the inaugural preaching: "Repent." Then comes the call of the first disciples, then again a general mention of Jesus' teaching and cures. Then comes the first discourse, opening with the proclamation of the Beatitudes (Matt 5:1-12a).

From that time on, the Beatitudes have been understood as the compendium of the Gospel and the criterion par excellence of Christian authenticity. Whoever follow Jesus and try to live as disciples of the Master, "meek and humble of heart" (Matt 11:29), must seek, with God's grace, to make real the ideal of the Beatitudes.

> The foundation of our way to God is to advance on the way of life with great patience, humility, poverty of spirit, and meekness. All these lead us to justice—and by justice, we mean the Lord himself. The commandments that enjoin these virtues on us are like landmarks and signposts on the royal road that leads travelers to the heavenly city. For it is said, "Blessed are the poor in spirit. . . , Blessed are the meek . . . , Blessed are the merciful . . . Blessed are the peacemakers." This is what we mean by Christianity. Those who do not walk on this way wander where there is no way and they have set a bad foundation.[9]

Gospel of the Beatitudes According to Matthew

In the Gospel of Matthew, the Beatitudes, nine in number, are expressed in an original manner corresponding to the evangelist's own intention and to the needs of the community he is writing for.[10] As a rule, Matthew intends to show how Jesus fulfills the Scriptures, therefore how the "righteousness" he teaches continues the traditional teachings. On the other hand, we must not forget that apostolic preaching took place between the Sermon on the Mount and the written Gospel. The evangelists do not pretend to set down a shorthand version of Jesus' words. Neither do they distort them. They transmit them after having more deeply understood their meaning by meditation and preaching, both under the Spirit's guidance. Before leaving his apostles, Jesus told them, "the holy Spirit that the Father will send in my name—he will teach you everything and remind you of all that [I] told you" (John 16:13).

"Poor in spirit," "pure in heart"—this way of speaking of poverty and purity does not empty them of their concrete character. All through his Gospel, Matthew insists too much on the necessity of doing, of acting, to be suspected of "spiritualization." On the contrary, he wants to make clear that poverty and purity, as well as the other Beatitudes, have their roots in the depths of the human spirit—the human heart. For better or for worse, whoever looks at another with lust has already committed adultery in the heart (Matt 5:28). Everything comes from the heart (Matt 15:19). It is possible to be poor and eaten up by greed; rich and detached from possessions, always ready to share. Likewise, purity—in all the meanings of the word—is first, essentially "in the heart."

Finally, it is important not to take the Beatitudes in too material a manner, as though each one was closed upon itself. Matthew has a catechetical, a pedagogical aim. To reach it, he might, for instance, divide into two one Beatitude in order to better clarify its meaning and its scope, which a more condensed formulation might hide. At the same time, he might extend the meaning of a word and give it more precision. Thus, "the poor in spirit" must be understood as being also "the meek." Similarly, he gives a more concrete and detailed meaning to "persecuted for the sake of righteousness" by adding that this persecution will bring insults and calumnies.

"Blessed!"

The first word of each Beatitude might be confusing or shocking if ill understood. The people in question are in a painful situation, even one of unjustly inflicted violence. On the other hand, the reward is placed in an undetermined future. In brief, we would judge it more normal to say,

"You are persecuted, you will be blessed; the kingdom of heaven will be yours." But instead, we hear, "Blessed" right now!

To accept and understand this paradox, we must first turn to Jesus. It is he, the poor in spirit, the meek, the afflicted, the one who hungers and thirsts for justice, the merciful, the pure of heart, the peacemaker, the persecuted—unto death—for righteousness, the reviled one. And he is exalted at the right of the Father, in glory. Therefore, those who share what he has been, who are identified with him in their poverty, already share in his glory: "Blessed." The reward is not delayed; it is already in this very identification. What remains to come is the manifestation of that bliss. This is suggested by the first Beatitude which sets the tone for the others and gives the key to their interpretation, "Blessed are the poor in spirit, for theirs is the kingdom of heaven." This does not mean that paradise is already established here below, but that the "poor in spirit"— and those described by the other Beatitudes—already possess the earnest money and, in some way, the title to happiness. So the Beatitudes are not on the moral but on the mystical plane. By contemplating Christ, we can understand who is happy and why.

> "This poor one called out" (Ps 34:7). By the use of the demonstrative pronoun, the psalmist reveals his thought. Speaking of the person who is poor, who is hungry and thirsty, who has no clothing—and all this according to God—he means the poor one who is the disciple of Christ. We can also apply this word to Christ. Being rich by nature, since all the Father's goods are his, he became poor on our account in order to enrich us by his poverty. Christ himself has initiated every action by which we strive for beatitude, giving himself as an example to his disciples.
>
> Coming back to the Beatitudes, examine each one and you will see that the teaching was preceded by action.
>
> "Blessed are the meek." How shall we learn meekness? He says, "Learn from me for I am meek and humble of heart."
>
> "Blessed are the peacemakers." From whom are we going to learn peace? From this peacemaker himself who reconciled two adversaries into one new human being and brought peace to heaven and earth through the blood of his cross.
>
> "Blessed are the poor." It is he who was poor and who emptied himself, taking the form of a slave in order that we might receive gift for gift from his fullness.[11]

Nine Times Blessed

The nine Beatitudes do not repeat one another by proclaiming blessed the same group of persons described by words nearly synonymous. However, we cannot make of these persons nine rigorously distinct categories of blessed ones. In other words, we must read and hear these nine Beatitudes as a whole.

"Poor in spirit" is a typically biblical expression; it transposes the idea of material poverty to the inner and spiritual realm. That poverty of spirit is, in fact, an inner attitude of humility.[12] "Meek" is in the same vein. Psalm 37 speaks of the meek in the same way as does the Beatitude of the "poor in spirit": "the meek shall possess the land" (Ps 37:11).[13] Matthew (Matt 21:5) has kept only meekness from among the three qualities, "just," "victorious," "meek," that characterize the Messiah in Zechariah's oracle (Zech 9:9). Finally, Jesus speaks of himself as "meek and humble of heart" (Matt 11:29). The first two Beatitudes, which complement one another, set the tone of the following Beatitudes and help us to understand them.

"They who hunger and thirst for righteousness," "they who are persecuted for the sake of righteousness"; here we easily recognize the language and teaching proper to Matthew. The poor, the meek, the humble are no pious dreamers; they ardently seek the kingdom of God and his righteousness (Matt 6:33), committing themselves entirely to this search, despite the risk of persecution.[14] The Beatitudes of the merciful and the peacemakers again concern Christians' behavior toward their brothers and sisters. Matthew insists on this point; we must produce fruit, especially in the domain of charity. We shall be judged on what we shall have done for others (Matt 25:31-46).

Thus, from the first to the ninth Beatitudes, the development of thought is remarkably coherent and the progression is self-evident. The beginning of Jesus' inaugural discourse, in Matthew, is really a summary of the gospel, of the model of life proposed to the disciple who wants to imitate the Master, "meek and humble" in heart. The tradition of the great spiritual authors did not fail to understand this fact.

> They who hear these words, "Blessed are they who are persecuted for the sake of righteousness," examine themselves to see whether they have been persecuted on account of a commandment of God, since "all those who want to live in Christ will be persecuted," as the apostle says. This is why Christ adds these words: "Blessed are you when they insult you and persecute you and utter every kind of evil against you falsely because of me. Rejoice and be glad, for your reward will be great in heaven." Why has Christ mentioned in the last place those who are persecuted and insulted and why does he give them, with authority, this order, "Rejoice and be glad"? It is because those who have sincerely repented of their faults and

thereby have become humble—to repeat the same thing once more—have become worthy to be afflicted everyday. They also have become meek, hungry, and thirsty with all their soul for the sun of justice, merciful and compassionate, having felt in themselves the suffering, the tribulations, and the weaknesses of all. By weeping and purifying themselves, they see God, they are reconciled to God, they become truly peaceable, they are judged worthy to be called children of God. Such persons are, therefore, able to bear with joy, with an ineffable exultation, to be insulted, abused, and reviled, to be called all sorts of evil things, for God our master has solemnly declared, "Rejoice and be glad."[15]

Thanksgiving to God, Gladness of the Poor

The whole prophetic tradition teaches that God is the unfailing defender of the poor, the lowly, the oppressed, the despised—all those without defense. It is their right to find an assured refuge in God, who is on their side. But since Zephaniah, poverty does not define only a social status. It is availability, welcome, openness to God's gift. Therefore, there is nothing depressing about poverty itself; much to the contrary; it assures salvation. Moreover, those poor ones constitute the nucleus—the "remnant"—on which rests the completion of the plan of salvation that God has revealed and to which God remains and will always remain faithful.

From the beginning of the Sermon on the Mount, Jesus takes his place within the lineage of this spiritual tradition of "the poor of the Lord" (Matt 4:17). Therefore, he proclaims "Blessed" from that very moment, the "poor in spirit" because they have the proper disposition to receive the promised riches and all the gifts that the kingdom brings. Let them rejoice and be glad.

Paul, for his part, reminds those Christians who might forget it, that the gospel is not a human wisdom laboriously acquired by their own efforts, or reserved for those who, by human standards, are considered the elite of society. Just by being aware of what we are, we recognize that the Church at large and each Christian community are made up of poor people deprived of everything in order to gain God's grace. With thanksgiving, as poor people, we welcome the mystery of Christ, "meek and humble of heart," and we boast of his cross, which is the revelation of God's supreme wisdom and God's love.

> Messenger of the Kingdom,
> Jesus,
> crowds followed you:
> poor among humankind,

you revealed their greatness
to the poor.

Blessed are the humble,
God's glory dwells in them.

Place your joy in the Lord,
he will fulfill your heart's desire.

The meek will possess the land,
they will enjoy an immense peace.

Better the poverty of the just
than all the wealth of the impious.

The salvation of the just comes from God,
their shelter in times of distress.[16]

Fifth Sunday

Salt of the Earth,
Light of the World—
to the Glory of the Father

Your Light Will Rise in the Darkness

One day or another, every community experiences times of crisis when nothing seems to work anymore. Some members are irritated, others are discouraged, others who were counted upon defect. All undertakings aimed at redressing the situation fail. Rivalries and confrontations arise. Liturgy itself reflects the turmoil; it becomes more or less formalistic. Old demons once exorcised reappear. The light emanating from the community undergoes a distressing eclipse; the future seems to be blocked; and there is no way of escaping the dead end. In this case, we have here a perfectly applicable text from the Book of Isaiah.[1] But the whole community must read and reread it because it specifies the necessary conditions for light to shine as the dawn and for strength to rapidly return (Isa 58:7-10).

To share one's bread with the hungry, to welcome the homeless, to clothe the naked—these are the concrete demands placed upon the people of God whom the covenant has freed from all servitude (Exod 4:22, Deut 5:6, John 8:33). This privilege entails duties of justice that the people of God cannot overlook without falling back into slavery (Jer 34:8-22). It can happen that a member of the community is obliged to serve a richer member. But that person must never be treated as a slave and must be freed at the end of the prescribed term.[2] In the community according to God's heart, even a menacing gesture or a hurtful word is avoided, and no one is hungry or in need. God recognizes this community as his own and answers its prayer by revealing that he is close: "Here I am."

Such a community will shine with God's very glory. The lives of its brothers and sisters will be a testimony, in action, to God, whom it claims for its protector, whose name it bears, for he is light and justice. Despite its weakness, this community has in itself a prophetic function. It denounces the ways of a world dominated by a competitive spirit with its accompanying injustices, egotisms, subjection of the weak to the strong and rich, fears. It announces instead the ideal of a loving and just world, shown to be both possible and precious.

The just man is a light in darkness to the upright.

The LORD dawns through the darkness, a light for the upright;
  he is gracious and merciful and just.
Well for the man who is gracious and lends,
  who conducts his affairs with justice.

He shall never be moved;
  the just man shall be in everlasting remembrance.
An evil report he shall not fear;
  his heart is firm, trusting in the LORD.

His heart is steadfast; he shall not fear.
  Lavishly he gives to the poor;
His generosity shall endure forever;
  his horn shall be exalted in glory.
(Ps 112:4-5, 6-7, 8-9)

Announcement of Jesus, Crucified Messiah

Certain personal experiences have a universal dimension. Paul's is among these. The Corinthians to whom he is writing have a disturbing tendency to be captivated by the flamboyance of the preacher or the preaching. They exhibit a strange eagerness for the so-called human wisdom, whereas most of them are simple folks. On the other hand, Paul has not forgotten that in Athens he suffered a bitter failure when he thought it opportune to talk like the philosophers and orators.[3] And above all, he remembers how his own pride was dashed to the ground on the way to Damascus.[4] As a consequence, he adopted very soon—and especially at Corinth—an apostolic manner of living and preaching that relies on God, on the power of the Word and of the cross (1 Cor 2:1-5).

The "sublimity of words or of wisdom" is ill adapted to the preaching of the mystery. How could words and wisdom lead anyone to accept Jesus, this crucified Messiah? What good would preachers be who would want to know—that is, to experience in their lives—anything other than the one they are announcing? The hearers' vanity might be disappointed or even affronted. Maybe they openly deride the preachers or maybe they politely give them to understand that they do not take them seriously—"We should like to hear you on this some other time" (Acts 17:32). It is to their loss. But at least the preachers have not duped their listeners by watering down or disguising the message. And the disciples their preaching makes, even though few in number, respond with authentic faith (Acts 17:34). They have imitated Jesus himself, who never sought to flatter his audience in order to win it over through demagoguery.

Conscious of the transcendence of the message and the mystery they are announcing, the preachers cannot show any conceit or self-confidence, whatever their forcefulness or the strength of their conviction. They present themselves "in weakness and fear and much trembling," knowing the sophisticated language of wisdom would not be convincing.[5]

> What this discourse cannot gain, since it provokes only a growing resistance, the Word can, since, sacrificed, it exhausts itself drop by drop on the cross and finally is engulfed in that frightful, inarticulate cry in which all is summed up: what had been said; what has remained unsaid; and what, in the divine communication, was incommunicable. No one could finish speaking ("the whole world would [not] contain the books that would be written"). Action only is the final period. But neither would actions have any end; the last word is suffering and death, in which human beings sum up themselves before the Father. It is the last will and testament, the testimony to and the seal upon life.[6]

Responsibility of the Lowly and the Poor of the World

Right after the Beatitudes in the Gospel of Matthew, Jesus calls the disciples "salt of the earth" and "light of the world." At first sight, this juxtaposition might be surprising. The Beatitudes insist on the inner disposition of the disciples, "poor in spirit," "meek," "afflicted," "hungry and thirsty for righteousness," "merciful," "clean of heart," "peacemakers," "persecuted for the sake of righteousness," to whom is promised a "reward" that "will be great in heaven." And now Jesus invites them to become aware of their dignity and of the responsibility entrusted to them before the world (Matt 5:13-16).[7]

On closer inspection, we see that these two texts are far from being in opposition, still less in contradiction to one another. They have been intentionally connected in Matthew's plan. The literary form underscores this: "Blessed are you . . . You are the salt of the earth . . . the light of the world." Those whom Jesus declares "blessed" already possess the kingdom, although in a hidden manner. However, they must make it shine upon the world according to what they are and what they do. Therefore, with the Beatitudes, this text acts as an introduction to the Sermon on the Mount, which will teach more fully what are the characteristics and the demands of conformity to the gospel.

Salt of the Earth

Mark and Luke report a saying of Jesus relating to the significance of salt. "Keep salt in yourselves and you will have peace with one another" (Mark 9:50). "Salt is good, but if salt itself loses its taste, with what can its flavor be restored? It is fit neither for the soil nor for the manure pile; it is thrown out" (Luke 14:34-35). In the first case, salt is the symbol of wisdom or of the spirit of sacrifice, indispensable to fraternal or sisterly relations among disciples. In the second case, the emphasis is on the possible loss of flavor of the salt, this alluding to what happens to those disciples who would not be courageous enough to pursue their Christian commitment to the end.[8] Despite a certain resemblance, Jesus' saying in Matthew is completely original. The question is no longer to have salt, nor to keep one's flavor, but to *be* the salt of the earth. What is the meaning of this metaphor?

The Bible records several uses of salt. As we do to this day, it is used to flavor food (Job 6:6). It is used to purify persons, sacrifices, lands taken from enemies (Exod 30:35, Ezek 16:4, Judg 3:45). When shared, it is the sign of friendship (Lev 2:13). It is also used to enhance the quality of manure spread in the fields (Luke 14:35).

It is impossible to be sure which one of these meanings is intended here. Certainly there is an allusion to some ability in the disciples that they must use for the service of others.[9] One could think of the disciples as having been a fertilizing influence upon humankind.[10] But because salt can lose its natural properties—literally "become mad" in Greek—we are led to the meaning of evangelical wisdom, of the work of the disciples in the world. Having received God's secrets revealed by Jesus, they must share with all the divine wisdom, of which they are the bearers. If they fail to do this, they will surely be despised and finally "thrown out," that is condemned on judgment day like the tree that has not produced good fruit (Matt 7:19), the worthless fish (Matt 13:48-50).[11]

The loss of flavor on the part of those who, in their life in the midst of the world, should bring added flavor to humankind, is a constant danger. Where Christians adopt a worldly spirit and manner, they have no longer anything to announce. Their watered-down message has lost any ability to oppose the powers of evil at work in humankind; therefore, they are rejected by the very persons they should have converted, and, by the same token, the gospel is rejected too.

Light of the World

In the biblical writings, the symbol of light is akin to a series of religious realities. The Bible often speaks of God as a source of light (Ps 104:2). The Law, too, is light (Ps 119:105). Israel must be a bearer of light to the pagans; a beacon-people, it must inspire the nations to believe in the only true God. In a way, the "Servant of the Lord" personifies that Israel, "light for the nations" (Isa 42:6, 49:6). The messianic dawn will rise upon the world as a light; and the mountain of Zion, with its temple, will draw peoples to its radiance.[12]

With Jesus, light rose on those who lay in darkness and the shadow of death (Matt 4:15-19, Luke 1:79). He is the light of the world in which God made himself visible to humankind.[13] As for the disciples, bearers and witnesses of this messianic light, they must act as children of light (Eph 5:8-14). They must shine as a focus of light by proffering the word of life to the world (Phil 2:15).

The three Synoptics agree in presenting Jesus' messianic ministry as a time when the full brilliance of the gospel does not yet appear (Mark 4:22, Luke 8:17). But they also announce a time when what was hidden will be revealed, what was said in darkness will be proclaimed in broad daylight (Matt 10:26-27). From now on, the light that the disciples bear cannot be hidden, anymore than a hilltop city, seen from afar, can be hidden.

The disciples' function can also be compared to that of a lamp placed on a stand so that it may shine on those in the house. This more familiar image alludes to the mission of Christians among their kin. Modest lamps, no doubt, but very necessary ones, they radiate light on all those present.

All Together

By saying, "You are the salt of the earth, the light of the world," the Gospel suggests that the disciples must fulfill together, as a Church, the mission entrusted to them. We recognize here the ecclesial viewpoint proper to Matthew. No matter how influential we are, none of us alone can be the "light of the world," of the whole universe.[14] On the other hand, a town built on a hill appears from afar at night only because of all the lamps burning in the houses. One isolated candle does not produce much light, but many little lamps together show the way. One Christian holding high his or her lamp can encourage the others, perhaps more timid, to also place their lamps on stands.

Thus, preached by a handful of people wholeheartedly given to Christ, the gospel set the world ablaze. However, entire nations, whole regions have been de-Christianized because many lamps have been extinguished, one after the other. The responsibility of Christians called to be "salt of the earth" and "light of the world" is incumbent upon us.

To Act Publicly for the Glory of God

By their behavior, the disciples of the Christ-light will themselves be the "light of the world." The introduction to the Sermon on the Mount ends with this command, revealing the general orientation of the Gospel of Matthew. He insists on this point: To believe is to act in conformity with one's faith; words are worthless without acts.[15] Vatican II reminded us of this: "Laymen have countless opportunities for exercising the apostolate of evangelization and sanctification. The very witness of a Christian life, and good works done in a supernatural spirit, are effective in drawing men to the faith and to God; and that is what the Lord has said: 'Your light must shine before others, that they may see your good deeds and glorify your heavenly Father" (Matt 5:16)[16] But is there not a contradiction between this precept to act "before others" so that they may see what the disciples are doing and what is read elsewhere: "Take care not to perform righteous deeds in order that people may see them" (Matt 6:1)?[17]

First, we must observe that in the latter text, the topic is almsgiving, prayer, and fasting, which are to be practiced without proud ostentation. These are works of piety done by individuals who may succumb to the temptation of seeking attention. Second, we consider the good done by the community as a whole. It is true that there, too, we must guard against a form of ostentation that would smack of publicity for the group. Therefore, this last advice is fundamental; we must act in such a way that, by seeing the good done by the community, people may give thanks to the Father, who is in heaven.[18] Neither the glory of the community nor even that of the Church is sought, but always and solely that of God.

In Today's World

In most countries, the Christian communities are minorities, even marginal groups, small flocks in the midst of peoples who practice other religions or none at all. We are through with triumphalism, which caused too much harm to be viewed with any nostalgia. Secularized societies will not tolerate—and rightly so—Christian communities acting as pressure groups. But must we therefore, willy-nilly, withdraw snugly within ourselves as if the Church and Christian communities, waiting for better days, had nothing more to say? Certainly not. Such a response would be totally unlike that of Paul, arriving at Corinth "in weakness and fear and much trembling." The situation of the believer and of the Church in today's world brings Christians back to a proclamation of the gospel based on a "demonstration of spirit and power," and not on human wisdom and schemes. It remains true that Christians and the Church, "salt of the earth" and "light of the world," must assume a vital role, today as yesterday—one could say more than ever.

> Christians are not distinguished from others by country, language, or clothes. They do not dwell in cities of their own; they do not use some extraordinary tongue; their lifestyle has nothing singular about it . . . They follow local customs in matters of behavior, while exemplifying the extraordinary and truly paradoxical laws of their spiritual republic . . . They discharge all their civic duties . . . They marry like everybody else; they have children . . . They are in the flesh, but do not live according to the flesh . . . They obey the established laws, and their manner of living is more perfect than the laws . . . In brief, Christians are to the world what the soul is to the body.[19]

Let Christians act according to what they are, as if naturally. Then their lives will speak for them; and by acting like faithful disciples of Christ, they will be "salt of the earth," "light of the world." Seeing the good they do, all will give glory to their Father, who is in heaven.

> The disciples of the gospel
> have reflected before all
> your light,
> Jesus,
> and the world glimpses
> the face of the Father.
>
> *Little by little,*
> *the fire of love repels the night.*
>
> Blessed are those who see in each one your light:
> In their houses, they are sources of light.
>
> Blessed are those who are forgiven:
> In their turn, they radiate peace.
>
> Blessed are those who open their hands and give:
> The joy of God shines upon them.[20]

From the Sixth to the Ninth Sunday in Ordinary Time

The Sermon on the Mount, the introduction of which has been proclaimed on the two preceding Sundays (Matt 5:1-12, 13-16), constitutes the framework of a new ''sequence'' made up of the Sixth, Seventh, Eighth, and Ninth Sundays. First, chapter 5 of the Gospel of Matthew is continued to the end (Matt 5:17-37, 38-48). Then comes the last part of chapters 6 and 7 (Matt 6:24-34, 7:21-27).[1]

The tone is a little different from that of the introduction, but the line of thought remains the same. We must keep in mind the beginning of the Sermon on the Mount in order to understand well what follows. Sometimes this development has been called a catechism for the use of the Christian contemporaries of the evangelist. This is a misnomer. On the one hand, this ensemble of instructions given to the disciples does not form a complete whole, only a series of general teachings illustrated with some concrete examples. On the other hand, the tone and the style do not correspond to those of a catechism, deliberately dry and abstract. What we have here are not lessons to be memorized but vibrant exhortations confronting the audience so that everyone may feel that the general principles and their practical applications concern them. The aim is to arouse in the hearers new concepts of the Law and morals. But we should not make any mistake; this teaching with its unending demands ''is not rigorous and intransigent, is not an observance to maintain at all costs, but a call which urges us on farther and farther and which is increasingly identified with the deepest part of our personality. The most compelling demand ends up being that of freedom.''[2]

The Gospel of Matthew is addressed to believers who have already experienced the good news. They know they are called to live, like Jesus, under the eyes of him they name ''Our Father'' and to become ''perfect'' as their heavenly Father is ''perfect'' (Matt 5:48). Therefore, to remind them of the demands of their discipleship makes good sense.

The Sermon on the Mount is well constructed,[3] a fact that the Lectionary respects in its way of dividing the text. The first part shows how Jesus' teaching renews and fulfills the ''justice'' and the precepts of the Law (Matt 5:17-37, 38-48, Sixth and Seventh Sundays). The second part deals with the spirit in which we must accomplish the traditional good works. The Gospel of the Eighth Sunday gives us the end of this development. We must choose between God and money; trust must pervade the behavior of the children of the kingdom (Matt 6:24-34). Finally the third part records three admonitions of Jesus. The liturgy has kept the last of these: if they want to firmly build their Christian life, the disciples must act and bear fruit, their eyes upon Jesus, their model (Matt 7:21-27, Ninth Sunday).[4]

Last of all, from the Sixth to the Eighth Sunday, we continue the reading of the First Letter of Paul to the Corinthians. On the Ninth Sunday, we begin reading the Letter to the Romans, which will supply important texts until the Twenty-fourth Sunday.

Jesus, Wisdom of God, Law of the Christian

Choose Faithfulness

Freedom and responsibility are two prerogatives of the human person. While being the most strongly stated and claimed, they are also contested and recognized as curtailed by an ensemble of psychological, social, and other factors. The human being is free, but free of what, and up to what point? How is this freedom expressed and exercised? Is it by the possibility—and the right—to choose everything and anything? These are some of the serious questions that arise as soon as we speak of the freedom and responsibility of a human being. Simple and final answers soon run into objections, into experiences that call everything into question. The debate bounces back and forth again and again.[1]

Moreover, if we take into account God and his action, the problem worsens. In order to resolve it—or to get rid of it—two ways spontaneously open. According to the first alternative, God is really responsible for human choices, either for good or evil; this is determinism, negating in fact all human freedom. According to the other, radically opposed to the first, human freedom is so total that it can hold in check every initiative and influence of God on personal choices; in fact to deny God, to reduce God to an abstraction. In both cases, the mystery is not really confronted. Human freedom or God's freedom is eliminated, that is all. These two ways are dead ends.

Biblical wisdom could not avoid this serious problem. It does not approach it in a theoretical manner, on the level of philosophical reflection, but as always, in concrete fashion. Thus it joins the wisdom of all ages: we must assert at once that everyone is free and that nothing escapes God's power, in particular the freedom that humans received from their Creator, who has made them in his image.[2] The passage from Sirach, the sage, which we read on this Sunday deals with the first one of those two propositions (Sir 15:15-20).[3]

The human person has the responsibility of choosing between good and evil, "fire and water," "life and death." But how shall we evaluate what is at stake in the options offered? Is the human person again left with only free determination, with the tragic risk of erroneous judgment? No, because there are commandments revealed by God so that we may freely choose to obey them. This does not mean that we practically abdicate our freedom of choice to become slavishly, blindly obedient to a law external to us.

To be free is to decide knowingly. Freedom is diminished, impaired when judgment is canceled, disturbed. The sage, endowed with a sure judgment, does not hesitate concerning what is true or false, good or bad; he does not choose the false, the bad, death; if he does, he is guilty.[4] "Those who fear the Lord" share in his wisdom. Therefore, they follow his commandments, his law conveying divine wisdom, freely, with a freedom like God's. This is why the sages never cease to rehearse the wonders of the Law, their love of divine commands, and their attachment to their God's precepts.[5]

> *Happy are they who follow the law of the LORD!*
>
> Happy are they whose way is blameless,
>   who walk in the law of the LORD.
> Happy are they who observe his decrees,
>   who seek him with all their heart.
>
> You have commanded that your precepts
>   be diligently kept.
> Oh, that I might be firm in the ways
>   of keeping your statutes!
>
> Instruct me, O LORD, in the way of your statutes,
>   that I may exactly observe them.
> Give me discernment, that I may observe your law
>   and keep it with all my heart.
> (Ps 119:1-2, 4-5, 33-34)

Paradoxical Wisdom of God's Mystery

The gospel message can only shock human wisdom. It proclaims that salvation cannot be gained on one's own, but must be received from another and, to top it all, another who died on a criminal's cross. The cross, a sign of salvation for all humankind, is a mystery more accessible to the lowly—those without pretense—than to those who pride themselves on their intelligence and knowledge. According to Paul, who dwells on this paradox, the cross is foolishness and a stumbling block, but it is even more; it is the wisdom proclaimed by the gospel (1 Cor 2:6-19).

The wisdom of the world, Paul writes scornfully, is nothing to brag about. To what does it lead "the rulers of this age"? To self-destruction, for they vainly exhaust themselves in their efforts to acquire the knowledge that brings salvation. And where do they get their wisdom? From other sages as benighted as they. Our wisdom is that of God's mystery. It was "hidden . . . predetermined before the ages for our glory" and revealed to us. None "of the rulers of this age knew, for if they had known it, they would not have crucified the Lord of glory." The gospel proclaims "what eye has not seen, and ear not heard," moreover, "what has not entered the human heart." For this wisdom is inaccessible. Only God can reveal it to those who love God. God's love reaches where human intelligence is absolutely unable to ascend. This is done through the Spirit, who "scrutinizes everything, even the depths of God."

This wisdom has nothing in common with a knowledge—a gnosis—of unknown origin, secretly transmitted in some circles jealously keeping their mysterious doctrine. It is broadcast and all may have a share in it. Anyway, it is not intellectual in nature but experiential. The life of union with Christ disposes us to gradually receive it, for it is always beyond what has already been acquired. "You see the partial lights that have enlightened us. You see also the approach we should have to 'theology,' neither sudden revelation nor prolonged withholding. The former is awkward, the latter impious; the former can shock strangers, the latter alienate our own people. The Savior had showered his disciples with a multitude of teachings, but he kept secret certain teachings that, he said, could not be borne at the moment, without doubt for the reasons I have indicated. And he added that everything would be taught us at the coming of the Spirit."[6]

Come Not to Abolish But to Fulfill
The prologue to the Sermon on the Mount has been proclaimed on the preceding two Sundays. Now the liturgy is going to let us hear the continuation, beginning with a statement of intent and a general principle. Jesus' words and positions, as recorded by Matthew, answer in fact the twofold question: What attitude should we take concerning the traditional commandments and what is the relationship between "righteousness" taught us by what we call the Old Testament and that preached by Jesus? (Matt 5:17-37)[7]

Jesus states with the utmost clarity that he has come not to abolish the law or the prophets, "not to abolish but to fulfill." And he solemnly adds: "Amen, I say to you, until heaven and earth pass away, not the smallest letter or the smallest part of a letter will pass from the law, until all things have taken place. Therefore whoever breaks one of the least of these commandments and teaches others to do so will be called least in the kingdom of heaven. But whoever obeys and teaches these commandments shall be called greatest in the kingdom of heaven." Without question, the law is perennial, but its future is not that of a sealed text, of a dead letter. Jesus has come[8] so that all its potential may unfold, that it may be understood and observed in the Spirit that enlivens it more and more, and in order to "fulfill" it, to take it to its completion. From now on, whoever rejects one of the least commandments of the Law and teaches others to do so will be last in the kingdom of heaven. On the contrary, whoever observes the least commandments and teaches them to others will be declared great in the kingdom of heaven.

This judgment must be understood in connection with the Beatitudes and in the general context of the Gospel of Matthew.[9] Jesus says to those he addresses as blessed, "Your reward in heaven is great." This does not mean that the privileged, the violent, those who do not care for justice or for others will also have a reward, albeit a small one. Furthermore, throughout his Gospel, Matthew insists on the necessity to act according to what has been taught. It is the indispensable condition for entering the kingdom. The way in which the evangelist describes the judgment scene strikingly sums up this teaching (Matt 25:31-46). We must also remember this terrible saying, "Whoever causes one of these little ones who believe in me to sin, it would be better for him to have a great millstone hung around his neck and to be drowned in the depths of the sea" (Matt 18:6).[10] To give a bad example by contemptuously disobeying a commandment, even a "little" one, is a scandal. Worse still is to teach others to do the same. The warning addressed by Jesus to scribes and Pharisees is directed also to all the disciples of Christ and, in the first place, to community leaders.[11] The practice of justice specified by the Law, down to its least commandments, is the condition of entrance into the kingdom of heaven.

You Have Heard . . . I Say to You

In saying, "You have heard that it was said . . . But I say to you . . . ," Jesus seems to announce more than the change of a letter or a part of a letter in the text of the Law. Claiming his sovereign authority—"I have come"[12]—doesn't Jesus replace what "was said to" the "ancestors," revealed by God, with a new teaching?[13] This would contradict Matthew's constant thought. He never speaks of a "new" law, of a "new" commandment. For him "it is the old that becomes new and the new has worth only inasmuch as it expresses afresh the old."[14] We must have a closer look.

Jesus cites three "commandments" forbidding murder, adultery, and oaths. But he says that to be angry with brothers or sisters, to insult them, deserves judgment at the bench; to curse them makes one liable to the fire of Gehenna. To look at someone with lust is already adultery. To utter any oath is not only useless but comes from the evil one, since "Yes" or "No" must mean "Yes" or "No."

Obviously, there is no contradiction with what "was said to" the "ancestors." Jesus teaches that evil actions have their roots in the heart and that it is not sufficient to evaluate actions alone.[15]

Charity Between Brothers and Sisters

To be angry with one's brothers or sisters is to attack them. To insult them is to wound them and diminish them in the eyes of others. To curse them is to deliver them to evil. All this partakes of homicide. In any event, charity is damaged. The gravity of these feelings and actions is such that it bars access to worship. Before presenting our offering at the altar, we must go without delay to be reconciled with the brother or the sister who has something against us. Even though, for our part, we have nothing against them, there is no need to inquire who is in the wrong. When we remember, even at the last minute, a failure of charity, we must take the first step. The offering can and must wait.[16]

This teaching gives its full meaning to the sign of peace before communion. This brother or this sister whom I do not know, but who is there by me, represents in his or her anonymity all the others with whom I acknowledge to be at peace. But if my "opponent" were in the assembly, I could not receive communion without "first" going to exchange with him or her the sign of peace, which is not and must not be sheer formalism.

Conjugal Fidelity

What Jesus says concerning adultery is not only the application of the principle stating that the evil desire carries the germ of the culpable action. The question here is about a man "who looks at a woman with lust." According to the Law in its strict sense, only the woman could be guilty of adultery.[17] For his part, by consorting with a married woman, a man was only guilty of an offense against another's property, not against his own wife (Exod 20:17). There is no need to be scandalized by this ancient legislation. But the comparison with what Jesus says speaks for itself. For him, there is no difference between woman and man: the same duties bind the one as the other.

And Jesus adds: "If your right eye causes you to sin, tear it out and throw it away. It is better for you to lose one of your members than to have your whole body thrown into Gehenna. And if your right hand causes you to sin, cut it off and throw it away. It is better for you to lose one of your members than to have your whole body go into Gehenna." This manner of speaking attests to the price one must pay not to fall into temptation; it should not be taken literally. Anyhow, self-mutilation would not be sufficient to eradicate evil desires and lust. But it is sometimes necessary to resort to mutilations no less radical and painful in order to eradicate tendencies, feelings, desires that are a part of our very heart. For what is in question is the heart.

"It was also said, 'Whoever divorces his wife must give her a bill of divorce.' But I say to you, whoever divorces his wife (unless the marriage is unlawful) causes her to commit adultery, and whoever marries a divorced woman commits adultery." What is said here poses an insolvable problem of translation and interpretation. One thing is certain: The Christian law forbids the repudiation of one's wife, whereas the Law foresaw and regulated it.[18] But then what does the parenthetical phrase (on the case in which the husband would be allowed to divorce his wife) mean? That depends on the sense given the Greek word *porneia.* Usually this word means "prostitution" or "immoral behavior." If we accept such a reason for divorce—though a grave one—we contradict the principle of the indissolubility of marriage that the Gospel of Matthew strongly affirms (Matt 19:3-12).[19] But the Lectionary translation "unlawful union" is not satisfying either. If the union is unlawful, there is no legitimate marriage; separation is mandatory by definition.

Without going into the maze of innumerable discussions trying to elucidate this word recorded by Matthew,[20] we can be sure of one thing: Jesus goes farther than the Law. For him "divorce is like adultery with forewarning."[21] We must therefore reject everything that could lead to it, beginning with lust and evil desires.

Truth in Words

People have always been fully aware of the importance and of the weakness of language—their privilege—as a means to express themselves and communicate. Mastery over words is the foundation of human wisdom in general, of biblical and Christian wisdom in particular.[22] But everyone knows how deceitful human words can be. Therefore, people have always sought ways to guarantee the truth and credibility of words. Hence the recourse to the oath that appeals to God's witness, as it were, and implies a divine punishment for lies.

In itself, the oath is implicitly a profession of faith in God, in whom there is neither dissimulation nor lie; in God, who will not fail to react in case of untruthfulness. Therefore, the Bible expressly forbids swearing by gods other than the Lord, which would be idolatry. It condemns false oaths, which would be blasphemy. It also discourages the multiplication of oaths, which would show a lack reverence towards God. In order to avoid this fault, people resorted to swearing by the Temple, heaven, the altar, Jerusalem, which in fact was calling upon God without naming him. These forms of oath led people to the habit of distinguishing between this oath and that oath, through subtle casuistry. Some oaths were binding, others did not entail real obligations. Jesus did not fail to denounce such abuses.[23] He goes further, "But I say to you, do not swear at all." Indeed, human beings realize how easily they lie, and sometimes catch themselves lying to themselves. How then could they dare place their own word on a par with the most holy God?[24] God's intention when he endowed humans with the ability to speak is what must regulate our use of language. This is the only way to render homage to God and, at the same time, to bring to others the guarantee of truthful words. "Let your 'Yes' mean 'Yes,' and your 'No' mean 'No.' Anything more is from the evil one." Anything more is, indeed, playing the evil one's game, he who is "a liar and the father of lies" (John 8:44). The disciple must, on the contrary, imitate Jesus, for "Jesus Christ . . . was not 'yes' and 'no,' but 'yes' has been in him" (2 Cor 1:18).[25]

Adults in Faith

God never considered human beings, whom he created, children incapable of discernment. By creating them in his image, God willed them free and responsible (Gen 1:26). From the beginning, God judged them capable of freely and wisely choosing the peaceful and happy future the Creator placed within their reach (Gen 2:16). When they sinned by listening to the tempter and making a bad decision, God revealed commandments to serve as markers on the road of life. God constantly encouraged but did not force them to remain faithful.

That God-given law is not like a code fixed once and for all in its letter by a faraway lawgiver. It is an expression and a transmission of divine wisdom. Those who meditate on it and live accordingly acquire that wisdom which is not of this world, which leads them into God's very mystery. As centuries rolled on, prophets warned against the ever renewed temptation to reject divine wisdom in favor of human wisdom. Every time the people yielded to the temptation disaster struck. Falling under the power of the rulers of the world, God's people knew shame and humiliation, instead of the better condition they had hoped to gain. Then the people cried to God, "Come back! Make us come back to you!" And the merciful God heard, patiently educating the people into the freedom meant for them.

Jesus, anointed by the Spirit, who "sees the depths of everything, even God's," has brought all former revelations to their fulfillment. With an unequalled authority, he teaches righteousness according to God. He reveals the true relationship that human beings must have with the Law, purified of all legalism, a law that demands a commitment of the whole being, and of its center: the heart.

> Our hand still reaching
> toward a tree of life,
> wants to possess the fruit,
> seize the knowledge,
> fix the law that gives stability.
> But the foolishness of God foils our wisdom
> by the raised sign:
>
> *Jesus crucified,*
> *Wisdom of God!*
>
> The Law is fulfilled in Christ,
> Salvation of every believer.
>
> Wiser than human beings
> is the folly of God.
>
> One sole glory:
> the Cross of the Lord.
>
> Here is the new commandment:
> to live in love.[26]

Human Holiness, Reflection of God's Holiness

I Am Holy; Be Holy Also

The first reading for this Sunday is a fine excerpt from Leviticus, from which the liturgy borrows only rarely (Lev 19:1-2, 17-18).[1]

The title of this book indicates that it is concerned with the Levites, who were in charge of temple worship. In it, rules and customs are recorded with many details and minutiae concerning the ritual of sacrifices (1:1-7:37), the ordination of priests (8:1-10:20), the clean and unclean (11:1-16:34). This legislative body is only of historical interest to us today.[2] The fourth part (17:1-26:46), commonly called the "Code of Legal Holiness," is different.[3] It comprises, like the other parts, numerous prescriptions and prohibitions, ritual and moral; but the motivation, more clearly stated than in the first three parts, points to a timeless teaching concerning the foundation, meaning, and implications of worship and daily conduct, and their connection. Indeed, "I am the Lord" occurs like a refrain, often together with the reminder of God's holiness.[4] This is especially the case in the text read this Sunday. The deep reason why we must conform to the Lord's commands is expressed with the utmost clarity.

"Be holy, for I, the Lord, your God, am holy." The "Holy," the "All-Other," who resides in a sacred universe that is dangerous to approach, such is God in most religions. The Bible states God's transcendence with a special force. It prohibits most explicitly everything that could lead one to believe it possible to break in upon God, as it were, or to constrain God, for instance through magical rites. The remarkable originality of the Bible is that it affirms the extraordinary nearness of God. God does not direct the world and history from afar, but by getting involved in them. He does not decree laws and precepts from his throne in heaven; he makes a covenant with his people and deals with them as a partner. God does not remain entirely hidden in a cloud of unknowing. He reveals his name and the people can say "you" when speaking to him. God does not jealously monopolize holiness but invites his creatures to share in it. Finally, God does not cease to promise to come even nearer in the person of a mysterious emissary. Speaking in God's name—"oracle of the Lord God"—the prophets keep hope alive. There is no contradiction in this twofold affirmation, much to the contrary; for this nearness comes from the sole initiative of God, this nearness reveals God's transcendence rather than detracts from it. "Be holy for I, the Lord, your God, am holy" is the ever renewed affirmation to which the cry of faith responds, "Holy, holy, holy is the Lord!" At the same time, it is the revelation of the dignity to which God calls his creatures, of the future open to them, of the meaning and scope of obedience to God's laws. We are called to no less than participation in the holiness of God thrice holy.

In concrete terms, the Code of Holiness is the Lord himself. "You shall not bear hatred for your brother in your heart" because the holy God does not entertain hatred. "Though you may have to reprove your fellow man, do not incur sin because of him"; be like God, who reproves sinners so that they may repent and live. "Take no revenge and cherish no grudge against your fellow countrymen," since the Lord is merciful. "You shall love your neighbor as yourself;" here is the golden rule that everywhere and always binds anyone who believes in God, who is love in himself and in everything he does. Indeed, to believe is to act in conformity with one's faith.[5] Finally, the fact that this text is part of a book dealing with worship must attract our attention. Participation in worship implies a holiness beyond a simply legal and ritual purity. It is not enough to say, "Lord, Lord!" (Matt 7:21). To get near God by celebrating the liturgy, to praise God's holiness, to give thanks for God's love, means to commit oneself to be, like God, tenderness and compassion.

> *The LORD is kind and merciful.*
>
> Bless the LORD, O my soul;
>   and all my being, bless his holy name.
> Bless the LORD, O my soul,
>   and forget not all his benefits.
>
> He pardons all your iniquities,
>   he heals all your ills.
> He redeems your life from destruction,
>   he crowns you with kindness and compassion.
>
> Merciful and gracious is the LORD,
>   slow to anger and abounding in kindness.
> Not according to our sins does he deal with us,
>   nor does he requite us according to our crimes.

As far as the east is from the west,
    so far has he put our transgressions from us.
As a father has compassion on his children,
    so the LORD has compassion on those who hear him.
(Ps 103:1-2, 3-4, 8, 10, 12-13)

The Community, God's Temple of the Holy Spirit

From the Third to the Sixth Sundays, we have read four passages from the beginning of the First Letter to the Corinthians, in which Paul reproaches his correspondents for their scandalous and silly divisions. He entreats them to place themselves in front of Christ, who is not divided and who alone has saved them by dying on the cross. He invites them to consider their social status, a modest one, even contemptible in the eyes of the world, for it reveals that God chose them in order to manifest his humanly unattainable wisdom. Therefore, their faith rests on the sole power and wisdom of God, revealed to them by the Holy Spirit. Now, Paul comes back to the community (1 Cor 3:16-23).

This community is "the temple of God" where "the Spirit of God dwells." The Apostle mentions this in passing, for it is unthinkable that the Christians of Corinth have forgotten it.[6] The Fathers of the Church, for their part, have developed this doctrine.

> In that building which is the Church, we need also an altar. So, I believe that Jesus builds his altar with those among you who, "living stones," are able to become part of the altar. They are determined to pray assiduously, to offer their pleas night and day, to present their entreaties like sacrificed victims. It is with those that Jesus builds his altar . . . sacrifice to his Father. But we also on our part, must endeavor "to agree in what [we] say" (1 Cor 1:10), to have "the same mind, thinking one thing," to "do nothing out of selfishness or out of vainglory" (Phil 2:3), but to remain "in the same mind and in the same purpose" (1 Cor 1:10), in order to become stones for the altar.[7]

For anyone to destroy God's temple would be grievous; God would destroy that person.[8] To introduce the "wisdom of this world" into the community would destroy this temple. Its very foundation would be shaken. Its fate would be worse than that of the house built on sand (Matt 7:26).

You Are Christ's, Christ Is God's

We must know and remember that the Christian community is the temple of God where the Holy Spirit dwells if we want to correctly understand and rightly live as brothers and sisters, with each one shouldering his or her responsibilities in the community. This is not a mere formula attempting to sublimate concrete problems, to dissolve them in a mystical nebula. Such is certainly not Paul's intention or thought. He continues, reaching ever higher, "All belong to you, and you to Christ, and Christ to God."

"All belong to you." The community belongs to no one, to no preacher, no apostle, whether Paul, Apollos, or Peter. These are sent to be at the service of the community, of the building of "the temple of God." By reason of the responsibility entrusted to them by the Lord, they will have to give an exact account of what has happened to the construction that they were charged to further.[9]

"All belong to you," even the world and "life and death, present and future." The ecclesial community is already in the bud what it will become at the end of time. It should be viewed in the context of the ultimate fulfillment of all things referred to by Paul when he says, "you to Christ and Christ to God." This fulfillment, called eschatological, is the focus of God's plan from the beginning and of God's work of salvation realized in the world by Christ through the gathering of the ecclesial community. To keep this focus constantly in mind has nothing to do with daydreaming. On the contrary, it is the only way to measure the objective and relative value of everything. It gives us the only sure criterion for acting without missing the goal. It keeps before our eyes the plan according to which everyone of us, each in our own place, must build "the temple of God," exercise the function given us, verify and, if need be, correct the way in which we discharge it. Thus, in a concise formula easy to remember, Paul places in God the source of unity in the community, of wisdom, and of the practical conduct—the spirituality—that flows from that source.

> When three are assembled in your name,
> they already form a Church.
> Keep the thousands here gathered:
> their hearts had prepared a sanctuary
> before we set our hands to build it
> to the glory of your name.
> May the inner temple
> be as beautiful as the stone temple.
> Deign to dwell in the one and the other;
> our hearts like these stones
> are marked with your name.
>
> God almighty
> could have erected a house

as easily as, with one gesture,
he created the universe.
Instead, he built human beings
so that they might build for him.[10]

From the Law of an Eye for an Eye to Nonviolence

In the first part of the Sermon on the Mount, Jesus speaks with the authority of him who came to bring the Law to perfection: "You have heard that it was said . . . But I say to you . . ." First, he proclaims that righteousness is not measured only by acts; it takes into account the purity of the heart's intentions.[11] Now he comes to the demands of charity (Matt 6:38-48).

"Eye for eye, tooth for tooth" (Lev 24:17-20) is the way one usually quotes the *lex talionis,* the "law of the talion."[12] Today, it appears to be harsh and implacable. But in fact, it went a long way then, toward restraining the arbitrary nature of individual revenge that often led to the escalation of reprisals.[13] Although fallen into disuse, as was already the case in Jesus' time, its spirit often persists, even today, in certain ways we conceive of and exact punishment for culprits.[14]

However, Jesus does not stand on the level of penal or criminal justice codes. We cannot claim his words in order to disqualify all regulation of penalties meted out to offenders. He addresses himself to individuals, not to society or to those who exercise legislative or judiciary power. He asks the disciples never to return violence for violence. And he illustrates this general principle with four examples: "When someone strikes you on your right cheek, turn the other one to him as well"; "If anyone wants to go to the law with you over you tunic, hand him your cloak as well"; "Should anyone press you into service for one mile, go with him two miles"; "Give to the one who asks of you, and do not turn your back on one who wants to borrow." Literally applied, these examples could give rise to behaviors not only unreasonable but sometimes full of grave consequences for others, for the common good. What Jesus is teaching his disciples is a deliberate decision to act nonviolently even toward those who unjustly wrong them. Such a determination will at times lead them to the "extremes" quoted above. We can even say that the nonviolence of the heart is true only if we accept, when the occasion arises, to offer the other cheek, to give up the cloak, to give to the borrower. This is not a call to heroism or a counsel reserved for the few. It is a commandment of the Lord, directed to each of us personally. It does not require that we behave with naiveté, that we yield to injustice and violence, but that we be peacemakers, in actions as in words.

The Law of Limitless Charity

The last part of this Gospel passage gives the key for the interpretation and the ultimate reason for the concrete demands just mentioned by Jesus.

"You have heard that it was said, 'You shall love your neighbor and hate your enemy.' " To tell the truth, nowhere does the Law order one to hate one's enemy,[15] even though it invokes anathema and extermination on what could endanger the holiness of God's people.[16] We must also remember that in the Aramaic spoken by Jesus, "to hate" does not have the strong meaning we give to this verb. It would therefore be a mistake to understand that we owe love to neighbors, but not to enemies. It is possible, too, that Jesus is here quoting a popular saying of his time. In any case, this saying reflects a timeless state of mind that expresses itself, for instance, in phrases such as "We must love those who love us, our relatives, our friends. As to the others . . ."

"But I say to you, love your enemies and pray for those who persecute you." On the one hand, Jesus rejects the distinction between the neighbor and the others, but he goes further. He speaks of enemies we must love, of persecutors we must pray for.[17] Then, and only then, will we behave as sons and daughters of the Father in heaven, imitating Jesus, who on the cross asked forgiveness for those who crucified him (Luke 23:34). Such is the perfection of the law taught by Jesus.

> Only through a creative love of enemies can we be children of the Father in heaven; love and forgiveness are of absolute necessity for spiritual maturity. Comes the hour of trial. Christ, the innocent Son of God, is hung on a raised cross, in a painful agony. Is there still any room for love and forgiveness? How is Jesus going to react? What is he going to say? The answer to these questions bursts forth with a majestic splendor . . . "Father, forgive them, they know not what they do." It is Jesus' most beautiful hour.[18]

Be Perfect, Like the Heavenly Father

What Jesus asks of his disciples does not conform to the criteria that normally guide human behavior. He does not exhort them to act as well or better than sinners and pagans, those who do not believe or do not claim the gospel as a rule of life. A certain number of them conduct themselves in an admirable manner. We must recognize this fact with thanksgiving to God, without patronizing them.[19] Such examples can stimulate. Thus, in the monastic breviary before Vatican II, an antiphon from the office of St. Martin (November 11) placed these words in the mouth of Christ, "Martin, while still a catechumen, clothed me with this cloak."[20] In all times, preachers have had recourse to non-believers' examples in order to shame believers, rekindle their zeal, refresh their memory concerning the demands of their discipleship and faith. However, at bottom, it is not a competitive spirit that must animate Christians. The point is not to seek to outdo others in perfection—be they pagans, sinners, exemplary brother and sisters—but to be perfect as the heavenly Father is perfect. What Christians seek is a transcendent perfection that is communion with the most holy God. What they seek is to follow Christ, the perfect human.

Become What You Are

Through his words and his acts, through his whole life, Jesus taught us very concretely what is the fulfillment of the Law. Its bases, like its scope, are theological in nature. It was given to humans to bring them to God's very holiness, not to lead them on the way of human perfection, even a very high one. The evangelical ideal, clearly stated by Jesus, belongs to the mystical order; it goes much further than a search for moral perfection, as many masters teach. Christian righteousness is verified by the observance of the commandments without any exception (Matt 5:19). But this observance is centered on the fundamental duty of love of neighbor and mercy shown in acts, because God is love and mercy.[21] Whoever act in this manner, even if ignorant of Christ and the gospel, will be admitted into the kingdom. On the other hand, whoever act without charity, even though they have prophesied, expelled demons, worked miracles in the Lords's name, will not enter the kingdom (Matt 7:22-23, 25:31-46). Moreover, this active charity and mercy efficaciously contribute to the building, even here below, of a world of justice and harmony between human beings. No one is able to evaluate the effects of concrete gestures of peace, mercy, and charity accomplished by individuals and especially by communities whose sole aim is the building of the temple of God.

> Day against night,
> tenderness against hatred,
> attention against forgetfulness,
> hope against all hope,
> you, against death.
>
> *You are life*
> *and we are yours,*
> *Jesus Christ!*

We were told, Don't let people take advantage of you.
You, you tell us, Everyone is a child of the Father.
We were told, Fight your enemy.
You, you tell us, Be children of your Father.
We were told, Do not forgive!
You, you tell us, God is love . . .[22]

Eighth Sunday

Since God Is Our Father . . .

God Never Abandons Any of His Children

The first reading of this Sunday is a brief oracle from the Book of Isaiah.[1] It is addressed to those who have reached the point of thinking that, in spite of God's repeated promises, he forgets them in their trial (Isa 49:14-15).

It is a consolation[2] for an oppressed, exiled people to hear that liberation is near at hand. But when this does not happen, impatience increases, anguished questions arise, terrible doubts surface with desperate cries, "My way is hidden from the LORD and my right is disregarded by my God" (Isa 40:27); "The LORD has forsaken me; my LORD has forgotten me" (Isa 49:14). Nothing indeed is more painful when one is in trouble than the impression of being abandoned by the very person who had promised to intervene and whom, day after day, one awaits in vain.[3] When the expected helper is God, faith and hope are shaken. The words meant to restore force and courage, to cause a surge of energy, to help one get up again, wound the heart instead, causing it to fall into a weariness akin to despair. The disappointment would not be so painful had not God spoken as he did when he said: "Do you not know or have you not heard? The LORD is the eternal God, creator of the ends of the earth . . . He gives strength to the fainting; for the weak he makes vigor abound. They that hope in the Lord will renew their strength" (Isa 40:28-31). This reminder of the power of God, which is not doubted anyway, only intensifies anguish: "Really, since God does not do anything for us, he has actually forgotten us."[4]

"Can a mother forget her infant, be without tenderness for the child of her womb? Even should she forget, I will never forget you." Such is God's answer. This "word of the Lord" reveals in concrete terms who God is in his innermost depths. No commentary is needed; it would detract from the meaning and scope of this word. Every man and, even more, every woman knows from experience that it is enough to say "the child of my womb." To forget one's infant would be to negate oneself, to cease to be what one is. It remains nevertheless that no man and no woman could have imagined a God moved by such a love for his creatures.

The Bible often speaks of God's tenderness for his own, especially in the prophetic oracles.

> When Israel was a child I loved him,
>   out of Egypt I called my son . . .
> . . . it was I who taught Ephraim to walk,
>   who took them in my arms;
> I drew him with human cords,
>   with bands of love;
> I fostered them like one
>   who raises an infant to his cheeks;
> Yet, though I stooped to feed my child,
>   they did not know that I was their healer . . .
> How could I give you up, . . .
>   or deliver you up, . . .
> My heart is overwhelmed,
>   my pity is stirred.
> I will not give vent to my blazing anger.
> (Hos 11:1, 3-4, 8-9)[5]

Most often, the texts in question describe what we could call God's inner debate between his love and his just anger. God even seems surprised to see himself incessantly disarmed by his tenderness: "Is Ephraim not my favored son, the child in whom I delight? Often as I threaten him, I still remember him with favor; my heart stirs for him" (Jer 31:20).[6] The explanation is that "God is love" (John 4:16). What John will explicitly say is already clear in God's ways attested to by the whole Bible. The Gospels are the direct prolongation of this tradition; Jesus, by his words and acts, has manifested the Father's tender and compassionate love. He, the Son, knows the Father (Matt 11:27) and through the Spirit sees "even the depths of God" (1 Cor 2:10).[7]

Words fail the believers to express their unshakable trust in God. Images come in multitudes to express as adequately as possible faith in God. God is, only God is "my salvation," "my rock," "my stronghold," "my glory," "my refuge," "the rock of my strength." This litany is inspired by the wonderful experience of an immense love totally undeserved.

Rest in God alone, my soul.

Only in God is my soul at rest;
    from him comes my salvation.

He only is my rock and my salvation,
  my stronghold; I shall not be disturbed at all.

Only in God be at rest, my soul,
  for from him comes my hope.
He only is my rock and my salvation,
  my stronghold; I shall not be disturbed.

With God is my safety and my glory,
  he is the rock of my strength; my refuge is in God.
Trust in him at all times, O my people!
  Pour out your hearts before him.
(Ps 62:2-3, 6-7, 8-9)

The Lord Is My Judge

From the beginning of the Church, the role and the place of the ministers of the gospel has been misunderstood. This is the case in Corinth. Some claim to follow Peter, others Apollos, still others Paul, or even directly Christ. Hence, cliques, insufferable factions to which Paul vigorously reacts. "Is Christ divided?" "Do you forget that you are the temple of God, which divisions tear apart?" "Having known God's wisdom, are you now going back to human wisdom, sham and unsubstantial?" "Consider your own calling—simple, unlearned folks—and remember I announced the gospel in weakness." The scandal of divisions is so grave in a Christian community that the Apostle devotes a good portion of his letter[8] to this question. Paul then scrutinizes himself to see how he fulfills his ministry and what sort of example he gives (1 Cor 4:1-6).

"Thus should one regard us: as servants of Christ and stewards of the mysteries of God. Now it is of course required of stewards that they be found trustworthy." Each of us must place the gifts, qualities, and charisms we have received at the service of this mission. When he returns, the Master will demand an account from his servants, and he will judge them on the faithfulness with which they will have discharged the task entrusted to them.[9] Only the Lord is qualified to judge.

"It does not concern me in the least that I be judged by you or any human tribunal," Paul writes. One sometimes hears the remark, "I owe an account only to God and my conscience." Such speech is often suspect because it is tantamount to making oneself the only judge of good or evil, just or unjust, opportune or inopportune. This is not what Paul says. "I am not conscious of anything against me, but I do not thereby stand acquitted." He entrusts himself to God's judgment, which he does not take lightly. On the contrary, he knows that on that day, the workman's work will be tested through fire; it will be determined whether it is made of gold, silver, precious stones, wood, hay, or straw (1 Cor 3:11-15).[10]

Paul also knows that the preoccupation with being well regarded by those to whom we are sent can cause all manner of damage. "Servants" and "stewards" would be tempted to behave in order to please or not to displease, rather than to be faithful at all costs. By the same token, they would hurt those to whom they are sent. And, willy-nilly, they would cause cliques and divisions that would surely compromise the unity of the community.

A bishop of the fifth century claims Paul's authority to comment on the Lord's words when he says, "Who, then, is the faithful and prudent steward whom the master will put in charge of his servants to distribute the food allowance at the proper time? Blessed is that servant whom his master on arrival finds doing so" (Luke 12:42-43).[11]

> But who is the steward who must be both faithful and wise? The apostle Paul tells us when he says of himself and his companions: *This is how one should regard us, as servants of Christ and stewards of the mysteries of God. Moreover, it is required of stewards that they be found faithful.*
>
> But this does not mean that the apostles alone have been appointed our stewards, nor that any of us may give up our duty of spiritual combat and, as lazy servants, sleep our time away, and be neither faithful nor wise. For the blessed Apostle tells us that the bishops too are stewards. *A bishop,* he says, *must be blameless because he is God's steward.*
>
> We bishops, then, are the servants of the householder, the stewards of the Master, and we have received the portion of food to dispense to you. If we should wonder what that portion of food is, the blessed apostle Paul tells us when he says: *To each according to the measure of faith which God has assigned to him.*[12]

Attitude of the Disciples Toward Material Goods

On four Sundays, from the Fourth to the Seventh, we have read the first part of the Sermon on the Mount, which ends with this command: "So be perfect, just as your heavenly Father is perfect."[13]

The second part, chapter six, begins by showing in what spirit the disciples must accomplish traditional good works. "Take care not to perform righteous deeds in order that people may see them."[14] Then comes the passage read today (Matt 6:24-34).

The topic introduced here remains, and always will remain, one of burning timeliness, our relationship to material goods, a problem no one escapes. Whatever it may be, this relationship is governed by laws, principles, self-imposed, unwillingly received or willingly accepted. This relationship entails a certain viewpoint on the world, its meaning, its immediate and ultimate future. It also entails a viewpoint on society, material goods, and the relationship of each one of us to them. The Gospel, in particular in this passage from Matthew, teaches us on what principles the Christian attitude and behavior are founded.

God or Money

The first, and general, principle which applies in everything and every time, is unequivocally stated, "You cannot serve God and mammon." Money is personified under the name of Mammon, as a power that enslaves humankind and the world when they adore it, as a Moloch that devours his very worshipers. Everyone experiences this. But we must not be content to note the power of money all around us, in society, etc. Jesus addresses his disciples, who must personally question their concrete, daily attitude toward that idol which often hides itself or wears deceptive attire.[15] And we must not forget that our passive complicity, our silences, contribute to strengthening and expanding its tyranny or stopping others' efforts to resist it.

What is more, the point is not only moral conduct but also service of the Lord, which is incompatible with that of money. "Servants" of God and of Christ describes the disciples' attitude. It must be single-minded. The Gospel compares the kingdom to a precious stone; one must leave everything behind to acquire it (Matt 13:44-46). The service of God and of Christ demands freedom from all other attachments, renunciation of all possessions.[16] There is no room for the "yes . . . but," for a part-time commitment, and still less for an occasional one. It is also unacceptable to devote one segment of one's life to God—churchgoing for instance—and the rest, or most of it, to money.

"No one can serve two masters. He will either hate one and love the other, or be devoted to one and despise the other." Probably we have here a saying based on common experience. It is indeed an uncomfortable position to have two masters at once, especially if their demands conflict. Is it possible to hate one and love the other or be devoted to one and despise the other? This can happen when the behavior of one is obnoxious, harsh, unjust, despicable, and contrary to that of the other—humane, just, pleasant.

It is also possible to benefit by their antagonism of character and conduct and to exploit them to one's advantage.[17] But Jesus is not speaking of human masters when he quotes this saying. He is speaking of God and money. Devotion to either one leads to loving that one. The prophet Amos illustrates the point in a striking and concrete manner, showing us greedy people grumbling against religious festivities that curtail their opportunities to get rich.

> "When will the new moon be over," you ask,
> "that we may sell our grain,
> and the sabbath, that we may display the wheat?
> We will diminish the ephah,
> add to the shekel,
> and fix our scales for cheating!
> We will buy the lowly man for silver,
> and the poor man for a pair of sandals;
> even the refuse of the wheat we will sell."
> (Amos 8:5-6)[18]

Finally, and most importantly, we must not forget that God is not a master among others. In the Gospel of Matthew, the title "Master" is used to distinguish Jesus; he is "Master" in such an exclusive sense that the title is tantamount to "Lord."[19] This being the case, the dictum cited by Jesus takes on a very strong meaning, "You cannot serve at once the Lord and money which usurps the title of Master." One frees, the other enslaves. "Supreme alternative: either to exclude from ourselves all will other than ours or to give ourselves to the being that we are not, as to the only one who brings salvation. Humans long to play the god. To be god without God and against God, to be god through God and with God—this is the dilemma."[20]

Why So Much Worry?

That we must choose between serving God and serving the idol of money is easily conceded, at least in principle; however, we perceive that such a choice of God entails costly renunciations. On the other hand, what follows seems from the first to be totally unrealistic. We willingly cite these words but without seeing in them real practical rules of life. "Do not worry about your life, what you will eat, or about your body, what you will wear . . . Do not worry and say, 'What are we to eat?' or 'What are we to drink?' or 'What are we to wear?' " We tend not to take seriously the comparison with the birds of the sky, the grass of the fields, poetical as it is. On the other hand, when we think of poor people, these words hurt. Maybe all these reactions are as many reasons to read with attention and understand without prejudice this Gospel passage.

First of all, we have here a development of the principle just stated: "You cannot serve God and mammon." And immediately Jesus adds, "Therefore I tell you, do not worry about your life . . ." The emphasis is on the "worry," which in daily life betrays this very attachment to money that Jesus denounces as capable of becoming idolatry. The "worry" the disciples must guard against is that of seeking principally, if not exclusively, material things, symbolized by food and clothing, elementary needs. That worry monopolizes attention and even upsets the right scale of values. "Is not life more than food and the body more than clothing?" Jesus pronounces here a word of wisdom, similar to the saying "We must eat to live and not live to eat."

Here the supreme value to which it is indispensable to relate everything else is "the kingdom of God and his righteousness." Here is what must be and must always remain the dominant "worry," the principal and, in the last analysis, the only true preoccupation. This demand is an integral part of the gospel and is clearly laid upon every disciple of Christ. "Worldly anxieties and the lure of riches choke the word" and prevent human beings from bearing fruit (Matt 13:22).[21] For his part, Paul wishes the Corinthians to be "free of anxieties" in order to be "attached to the Lord without distraction." He presents voluntary celibacy as a proof of this exclusive attachment to Christ and the kingdom (1 Cor 7:32-35). "For the world in its present form is passing away" (1 Cor 7:31).[22]

Therefore, we must live "free of all worry," our eyes fixed on the end of all things, an eschatological perspective. This has nothing in common with some lazy or fatalistic waiting, a sham trust in Providence, which in fact would be idleness or refusal to take pains to earn one's living and share with others. Paul clearly teaches this: "We hear that some are conducting themselves among you in a disorderly way, by not keeping busy . . . Such people we instruct and urge in the Lord Jesus Christ to work quietly and to eat their own food" (2 Thess 3:11-12). And he writes to Timothy: "Tell the rich in the present age not to be proud and not to rely on so uncertain a thing as wealth but rather on God, who richly provides us with all things for our enjoyment. Tell them to do good, to be rich in good works, to be generous, ready to share, thus accumulating as treasure a good foundation for the future, so as to win the life that is true life" (1 Tim 6:17-19). These precepts do not contradict what Jesus says; there is nothing that allows us to qualify or weaken his words, to take them with a grain of salt as if they were a hyperbole, similar to those used in wisdom maxims. What is in question here is faith at its most fundamental. God pursues the establishment of the kingdom, which will be fully secured on the day of Christ's return, his parousia. The disciples must live even now, looking for this fulfillment of all things, as do God and his Christ.[23] Every "worry" that obscures this vision is therefore a lack of faith. It is unthinkable that God should forget his creatures and not think, even for an instant, of the completion of his plan. "Look at the birds in the sky . . . Learn from the way the wild flowers grow . . ." "All these things the pagans seek."

> Let us be careful to lean neither on our friends' power or favor nor on our possessions nor on our wit nor on our prayers nor even on the trust in God we feel we have nor on human means nor on any created thing, but on the sole mercy of God. This does not mean that we must not make use of all these and contribute all we can to conquer vice, to grow in virtue, to conduct and complete the affairs God has placed in our hands, and to acquit ourselves of the obligations pertaining to our position. But we must renounce all the support and the assurance that we could derive from all those things and depend on the pure kindness of our Lord. In consequence, we must take pains and work for our part as if we expected nothing from God and nonetheless we must not rely on our own care and labor any more than if we did nothing at all, but expect everything from the sole mercy of God.[24]

First of All, the Kingdom and His Righteousness

One of the most noteworthy characteristics of the Gospel of Matthew is its realism. We see this in the precept "Seek first the kingdom of God and his righteousness." "First": the priority is what is important. Besides, the search for the kingdom goes hand in hand with the search for his justice. This is to say that "to seek the kingdom" does not mean escape from this world by drifting into pious daydreaming. "Righteousness," "justice," as the whole Gospel of Matthew affirms, is nothing else than the active conformity to God's will. It is identical with the life of holiness that the Sermon on the Mount concretely describes.

The rest "will be given you besides." Jesus is no dreamer. He does not say that food and clothing are useless, that the things of ordinary life are due to us or will be freely and effortlessly guaranteed for us.[25] But they are "besides," a bonus, as it were. "Sufficient unto the day is the evil thereof." This proverb confirms, using other words, what was just said. Everyday we must labor for food and clothing, but we must always seek the kingdom of God and his justice, even while we are engaged in earning our living. Furthermore, the search for God implies, as a natural consequence, a total trust in the Providence that feeds the birds in the sky and lavishly clothes the lilies of the field. It is why we ask God first that his kingdom come, and only then that he give us today "our daily bread."[26]

God, Our Father

The Liturgy of the Word on this Sunday focuses attention on the prayer which "our Savior gave us," and which we so often recite, especially in the course of every Eucharistic celebration.

"Our Father." This name is an act of faith in God such as he progressively revealed himself; it is a cry of trust and a surrender into the hands of him to whom we pray. God cannot forget any of his children; he watches with solicitude and tenderness over every one of us; he knows what we need; we have the assurance that he will fulfill our needs.

"Hallowed be your name, your kingdom come, your will be done on earth as in heaven." This is what we desire "first," and what we want to devote our lives to with the help of his grace and according to our possibilities. Everything else is "besides."

"Give us today our daily bread." Does a mother forget to give her infant the indispensable daily food? "Even should she forget, I will never forget you," says our heavenly Father.

"Blessed are you, Lord, God of all creation. Through your goodness we have this bread to offer, which earth has given and human hands have made."[27] You give it to us, but "by the sweat of our face, for our own sustenance and for our sharing with brothers and sisters." Then, "humble and poor," we can present it to you at the altar: "It will become for us the bread of life."[28] We give thanks to him for having entrusted us with these mysteries and "for counting us worthy to stand in your presence and serve you."[29]

> Look:
> God weaves beauty into the flower of the field.
> Look:
> God gives food and joy to the bird.
> Each day he clothes us with tenderness,
> he satisfies our hunger with love.
>
> *Father,*
> *how could you forget your children!*
>
> The Lord is good,
> those who fear him lack nothing.

The Lord listens,
He relieves the poor of their anguish.

The Lord opens his hand,
he kindly feeds all that lives.

Near is the Lord,
near those who call on him in truth.[30]

"Blessed Are Those Who Hear the Word of God and Observe It"

Keeping the Commandments—a Question of Life and Death
Certain books of the Bible look like compilations of laws and command-ments given by God to his people. Among others, this is the case with Deuteronomy, which is a collection of sayings attributed to Moses. In fact, it is a rereading of the Law, enriched with oral traditions developed over the centuries, and adapted to the condition of the people now settled in the Promised Land.[1] From many points of view, this code of the Second Law proves to be very close to other legislative texts of the time.[2] The covenant is couched in terms found in the treaties signed between powers of the ancient Middle East. This historical foundation of Deuteronomy explains its characteristics and originality, well expressed in the text we read on this Sunday (Deut 11:18, 26-28, 32).

Here we have laws and commandments as in other similar codes and written in the same juridical style. But these prescriptions were revealed to inspired authors. Moreover, they look beyond organizing a society by justly balancing the rights and duties of individuals in view of the com-mon good. In a word, God's laws and commandments aim at establish-ing here below a society founded on God's justice by leading each person in God's ways. The stakes are high: either blessing or curse, salvation or utter loss.

The commandments of God demand more than a purely legalistic obe-dience. "Therefore, take these words of mine into your heart and soul. Bind them at your wrist as a sign, and let them be a pendant on your forehead."[3] This is to say that God's law is all-encompassing; one is never through with its dictates; it requires a consent of the whole being to its very depths. What is at stake is choosing God or rejecting him in order to follow false gods.

This choice is upon us "today," that is, every day.[4] God acts within the daily life of his people and of all humankind. We find him there, and we must walk in his ways every day. The greatness of the people of the covenant consists in its call to freely respond to God's initiative and follow his commandments, which mark out the way. "Choose life" (Deut 30:19), God repeats unceasingly, exhorting his people to practice the Law. Having received the word, the assembly sings its faith, its thanksgiving and its trust in the saving God.

> LORD, *be my rock of safety.*
>
> In you, O LORD, I take refuge;
>   let me never be put to shame.
> In your justice rescue me,
>   incline your ear to me,
>   make haste to deliver me!
>
> Be my rock of refuge,
>   a stronghold to give me safety.
> You are my rock and my fortress;
>   for your name's sake you will lead and guide me.
>
> Let your face shine upon your servant;
>   save me in your kindness.
> Take courage and be stouthearted,
>   all you who hope in the LORD.
> (Ps 31:2-3, 3-4, 17, 25)

Righteousness Through Faith

From the Ninth to the Twenty-fourth Sundays, we read, this year, the Letter to the Romans.[5] The Apostle writes to the Christians in Rome to expound the contents of his preaching, in broad outline;[6] hence, the tone of the letter which has a more rigorous structure than his other letters.[7] One of the core ideas of Paul's doctrine regards the salvation of all humankind through God's grace, granted to those who believe in Jesus Christ. The text read on this Sunday opens the development of this theme (Rom 3:21-25, 28).[8]

None of us can boast of our own righteousness, not even that coming from the Law. There is only one true righteousness, different from human righteousness; it comes from God and is received through faith (Rom 1:16–3:20). "All have sinned." The Law of Moses only brought consciousness of sin. It pointed, of course, in the right direction, signaled wrong ways and dead ends, but left all humans on their own. Humankind would have been without the hope of salvation but for the fact that "the righteousness of God has been manifested apart from the law . . . through faith in Jesus Christ for all who believe." This is really good news, gospel. The only condition for receiving God's righteousness is faith. All human beings can equally share in this salvation which is a partaking of "the glory of God," that is, of God himself.[9]

But let us not be mistaken. This participation in "the glory of God" is not acquired; it is received as a free gift. For righteousness comes from God in Jesus Christ, "forgiveness for all those who believe in him."[10]

True Disciples

In a few words, the end of the Sermon on the Mount clarifies in what spirit and with what aims we must receive Jesus' teaching (Matt 7:21-27).

"Not everyone who says to me 'Lord, Lord' will enter the kingdom of heaven, but only the one who does the will of my Father in heaven." No one could be any clearer. Jesus proclaims a teaching that is to be put into practice. This already stands out in the whole of this inaugural discourse, as Matthew records it. Matthew, throughout his Gospel, stresses the point: words are not enough; actions are necessary.[11] And to drive the lesson home from the beginning, Matthew already alludes to the judgment that will be the subject of Jesus' last teaching (Matt 25:31-46).[12] But here, it is the judgment of the disciples themselves that is in question.

For Jesus addresses himself directly to the disciples, since he speaks of those who call him "Lord, Lord." In the Gospel of Matthew, it is the only fitting title for addressing Jesus, the title used by his disciples, whereas others say, "Rabbi, Master."[13] Therefore, to speak of those who say "Lord, Lord" does not refer only to those who might think that prayer or celebration of the liturgy will assure them of a place in the kingdom of heaven. The warning has a more general scope; it is addressed to all disciples, to all who recognize Jesus as "Lord." In other words, orthodoxy is insufficient if it is not accompanied by right practice.[14]

Here this "practice" means evangelical righteousness taught by Jesus, having its source in the heart (Matt 5:20-37).[15] It concerns all disciples without exception, whatever their condition, their function and rank in the community, their natural or supernatural gifts. Special mention is made of some of these gifts: prophecy, power to expel demons and to work miracles.

Matthew insists on the power of Jesus that manifests itself particularly in his miracles. The evangelist even tends to generalize and emphasize the efficacy of Jesus' interventions.[16] He sees there signs which authenticate Jesus' mission and which we must recognize as such.[17] Matthew also reports that Jesus explicitly commands the apostles not only to proclaim the good news of the kingdom, but also to expel evil spirits, to heal all disease and infirmity, to raise the dead, to cleanse lepers (Matt 10:1, 8). Although precious and useful in the community and as a buttress for preaching among unbelievers,[18] charisms have only a relative value. On the one hand, we must not seek them for their own sake; on the other, they are and must remain subject to the practice of charity.[19] On Judgment Day, the disciples will not be able to claim glory for having prophesied, expelled demons, and worked miracles in the name of the Lord. The judgment they will hear then will be terrible. "I never knew you. Depart from me, you evildoers."[20]

Building One's House on Rock

The Sermon on the Mount ends with the very stern warning that the disciples will be brought to judgment. Jesus insists by showing in a parable[21] that the sentence rendered will reflect the evidence plainly seen by all.

The unleashed elements—the driving rain, the raging torrents, the fiercely blowing wind—conjure up the dreadful cataclysms of the end of time. The image of the house built on rock or sand is self-explanatory. The rock is Jesus' word on which we build when we put his teaching into practice. Lacking this, nothing can withstand a violent storm. For a time, the two houses may appear similar. The latter may even look more attractive because of the painted exterior, the outside appearance having been kept up. But it does not resist the assault of rain, torrents, and driving winds. Nothing is left once the tornado has passed, not even a heap of stones. Everything is carried away; it is a complete disaster.

The evangelical comparison has parallels in rabbinical literature. "To what should we compare a man of many good works and an assiduous student of the Torah? To a man who lays the foundation in stone and then uses bricks. Even though abundant waters bathe the walls, they do not dislodge the stones. But to what should we compare a man who studies the Torah but is without good works? To a man who first builds with bricks and then with stones. Comes a little flood and the stones immediately collapse."[22] This comparison is interesting because it highlights Jesus' authority. No longer is it the Law that must be practiced, but what Jesus says, the Sermon on the Mount, "these words of mine."

The serious warning, the great discourse taught by Jesus with surprising authority to the crowds (Matt 7:28-29), does not aim at frightening the disciples but at reassuring them; they have the Lord's word, an unshakable foundation. Duly forewarned of the coming of the devastating storm, they can act "like wise men." To act otherwise would be not only sinful but foolish.

> To me, coming near you with faith
> and hearing the word of Life,
> grant the grace to build as is right
> on you, the firm Rock,
>
> So that, when the winds of Evil blow
> and the torrents of trial come,
> the foundations of my house may not be shaken
> like those of the fool, built on sand.[23]

Our Actions Judge Us

Humans can turn away from God, since they are created free, but, try as they may, they cannot reach on their own the righteousness that only God possesses, he who is the Holy One. They must recognize this: they become just through faith; sinners, they can only receive the pardon gained by Christ on the cross on which he, the Just One, has offered his blood for those who believe in him, the Savior.

But it is not enough to proclaim in words that God is God, that Jesus is the Lord, that we are his disciples. We must act in such a way that on Judgment Day we may be recognized by the one to whom we claim to belong. We must build our own lives on the rock of the word, put into practice.

Legalism has nothing to do with this undertaking. The law is not a dead letter, a set of rules with which we must comply. It marks out the road that leads to life. Since the coming of Christ, he is the Way we must follow. By listening to his teaching, we have the revelation of the Father's will. By acting as he did, we have the certitude of acting according to truth. There is no other law than he, no other access to life. He is the object of faith and the warranty of hope.

> Still a little time,
> and the Lord will be here . . .
> Will he find in us
> the faith that he expects?
> If we have built
> our houses on sand
> when we should have dug
> into the rock of truth,

shall we be able to withstand
the onslaught of the torrent?

Still a little time,
and the Lord will be here . . .
Eucharist of joy
that saves the world.
If we have felt
his look of tenderness
finally illuminate
the abyss of our hearts,
we shall be able to celebrate
the eternal Pasch.[24]

It is fortunate that the Sunday Lectionary has given so much space to the Sermon on the Mount, which is proclaimed almost in its entirety from the Fourth to the Ninth Sundays. Every Christian should read and reread, unceasingly meditate on this inaugural discourse recorded in the Gospel of Matthew. Indeed, it reveals the spirit of the good news, its demands, its scope, its newness, couched in the tradition brought to its fulfillment. To live according to this teaching is to often follow a difficult way, but one that goes from joy to joy. It is the way of happiness that nothing can spoil. For all along this journey of perfection, we hear the cry ''Blessed.''

The Sermon on the Mount projects its dazzling light on the liturgy and its celebration. The liturgy is the great prayer of the Church, its intercession with the God of mercy and forgiveness, its petition for daily bread. But through all these, it is thanksgiving to the Father coming from a people whom the Son has proclaimed ''Blessed,'' and the Spirit makes fruitful unto eternal life.

The Tenth and Eleventh Sundays in Ordinary Time

In the series of Sundays in Ordinary Time, the Tenth and Eleventh form a small unit—a short sequence—centered upon God's mercy and revealed by two of Jesus' initiatives. The Gospel of Matthew records the call of the tax collector named Matthew, who did not hesitate one instant to follow Jesus, and the meal taken by the Lord with "many publicans and sinners" (Tenth Sunday). The other Gospel passage (Eleventh Sunday) narrates how Jesus selected those whom we name the twelve apostles. In both cases, it is mercy that inspires the Lord's initiative.

The texts from the Old Testament chosen in connection with the Gospels are drawn from the Book of Hosea (Hos 6:3-6—Tenth Sunday) and from the Book of Exodus (Exod 19:2-6a—Eleventh Sunday). The first text contains the pronouncement of Jesus, "It is love that I desire, not sacrifice." The second reminds us of how, through Moses' mediation, God entrusted a universal mission to the chosen people.

Two passages from the Letter of Paul to the Romans round out these liturgies. What Scripture says of Abraham's faith must be understood of the faith of all believers. By trusting in God's promise, Abraham was justified. By believing in God, who has raised Jesus, our Lord, we today obtain justification (Rom 4:18-26—Tenth Sunday). The death of Christ for the sinners we once were reveals in full light the infinite love and mercy of God (Rom 5:6-11—Eleventh Sunday).

All Are Welcome—Even Sinners

It Is Love That I Desire, Not Sacrifice

The first reading of this Sunday is an excerpt from the Book of Hosea, from which Jesus, according to the evangelist, quotes a sentence to justify his way of dealing with sinners: "It is love that I desire, not sacrifice" (Hos 6:3-6).

In the Gospel, this formula is taken by itself, as a general principle. In the Book of Hosea, it is part of a large ensemble of several chapters that are a series of oracles on the sins and punishment of the people.[1] The Lectionary has chosen one of these small units, which must be taken at face value in the celebration.[2]

These four verses resemble the plan of a penitential service in two parts: first, the intervention of the assembly; and second, the answer-challenge of God. We could also see in it a sort of interior monologue on God's part. God wonders how sincere are the confessions of his people, what pedagogy he should use to obtain what he desires—love, not sacrifice. But, in the end, it does not matter whether this text was written according to these literary devices or to another, whether the declarations of the people are sincere or not. The significance of the piece is not affected by any of this, at least for us today.

The knowledge of or learning about God is a religious awareness of the ritual and moral demands to which we must submit in order to benefit by God's faithfulness. This meaning is indeed traditional in the Bible. But the knowledge of God takes on a deeper and wider meaning in Hosea, where it occupies an important place.[3] To know God, that is, his commands, in order to conform to them, is not the result of a bookish knowledge acquired by studying the Law, remembered more or less confusedly, forgotten in smaller or greater measure. It is an experiential knowledge of the goodness and the love of God, pondered unceasingly in one's heart and urging one to a life of faithfulness to God. This knowledge implies both an intimate relation with God and a deep, indeed vital, perception of his interventions and his will. "I know what pleases him, what he desires; to do it is my joy." Nothing could be more opposed to this loving knowledge than a fleeting, fickle love. The two terms are contradictory.[4]

True love—the only love God can desire and accept—is not a superficial feeling that vanishes like dew under the first ray of the sun. It is firm, unshakable. It creates indissoluble bonds of unity. Without such a love, of what use are sacrifices and holocausts? Empty rites, despicable, insulting, blasphemous make-believe. God would not be God, would not have any dignity, if he did not reject these pretenses. But he does not despair of changing the heart of his people by pursuing them with his reproaches, in order to incite them to know him and love him.

Since the time of the prophet Hosea, the forms of worship have changed. But the prophetic oracle has not lost any of its relevance. The sacrifice we offer today is that of Christ, a perfect sign of the Father's love and mercy. How can we celebrate it if it does not really express the love and the knowledge that God desires, if we do not walk in the Lord's footsteps to give him glory?

> *To the upright I will show the saving power of God.*
>
> God the Lord has spoken and summoned the earth,
>   from the rising of the sun to its setting.
> "Not for your sacrifices do I rebuke you,
>   for your holocausts are before me always.
> If I were hungry, I should not tell you,
>   for mine are the world and its fullness.
> Do I eat the flesh of strong bulls,
>   or is the blood of goats my drink?
> Offer to God praise as your sacrifice
>   and fulfill your vows to the Most High;
> Then call upon me in time of distress;
>   I will rescue you, and you shall glorify me."
> (Ps 50:1, 8, 12-13, 14-15)

Justified by Faith in God, Who Raised Jesus

In his Letter to the Romans, Paul illustrates his thesis of justification through faith by the example of Abraham. Today we read the end of this development (Rom 4:18-26).[5]

The question of justification is of the gravest importance and never ceases to confront us. Simple and reassuring answers have been proposed. Thus, it was said in succession, "Outside of Judaism . . ."; "Outside of the Church, there is no salvation." In other words, "To participate in salvation, one must be a member of the Jewish community through circumcision, or of the ecclesial community through baptism. All others are pagans.''[6] Paul rejects this dichotomy. Jews and Gentiles are all under the law of sin. All equally need to be justified; and they can be, but only through faith.

Having strongly posited this (Rom 1:18–3:31), the Apostle deals especially with the question of how the members of the people of God can have access to salvation. This he does by choosing the example of Abraham, the first one to have received the promise of the covenant and the father of the people of God. Abraham himself was justified through faith (Rom 4:1-8), independently of circumcision (Rom 4:9-12) and the Law (Rom 4:13-17). This supremely significant example elucidates in a decisive way the situation of Christians and their justification.

Abraham was justified because he believed in God's promise, because he totally trusted the sole power of God. He knew that he and his wife Sarai were too old to have children, but he did not doubt for one instant that God had the power to give life to the dead, to call what is not into existence (Rom 4:17).

The same is true of Christians. They know themselves to be sinners, unable to become a "fresh batch of dough" because they are "the old yeast" (1 Cor 5:7). But they confess God's power that raised Jesus, our Lord; they believe in God who promised to give them everlasting life, through and in Christ. Whatever the necessity of belonging to the people of the redeemed, they can receive justification only through faith in God and in the dead and risen Lord.

Christ's Pasch, which is the object and the content of faith, is behind us. But we are waiting for the realization of the full justification he gained by delivering himself up to death. Faith is the foundation of hope; on the other hand, hope is the normal blossoming of faith; it expresses faith and, so to speak, verifies its vigor and its authenticity. We are helpless, radically unable to do anything. But through faith, we are empowered by Jesus Christ, our justification, as Paul wrote to the Philippians (Phil 4:13).

Not the Just, but the Sinners

Jesus taught us by his actions and his words the necessity of faith, the condition of justification that works cannot procure. Matthew's calling is a particularly significant illustration of this teaching (Matt 9:9-13).

Although extremely concise, the account of this calling speaks volumes. Jesus calls a tax collector and includes him in the group of disciples chosen to follow him. This tax collector[7] immediately leaves his post, without the slightest hesitation, in order to follow the Lord. A publican, regarded as a public sinner because of his very occupation, this man cannot boast of any personal righteousness; on the contrary.[8] The unconditional choice of such a sinner, without any demand for a sign of conversion other than his immediate response to a call, must appear as an aberration, a scandal to most people. In fact, Jesus' behavior is humanly inadmissible. Whoever would recruit a sinner to make of that person a disciple of choice should rightly be considered lacking in the most elementary common sense and discernment. In order to accept Jesus' initiative, we must recognize that he is not of the common run but is privileged to speak and act outside the norms that bind other humans. He himself has sufficient authority to say to someone, whether sinner or not, "Follow me," and at the same time the power to elicit as total a faith response in the one called. In other words, what Jesus did when he "saw" Matthew sitting at the customs post, was a revelation. A revelation, too, was the meal he took "in [Matthew's] house," where "many tax collectors and sinners came and sat with Jesus and his disciples." Therefore, beyond the reaction provoked by Jesus' behavior at the time, what the evangelist records must be understood as a challenge addressed to each of us. "Do you understand why Jesus ate with sinners and publicans?" Yes, we understand if we listen to Jesus' answer: "Those who are well do not need a physician, but the sick do." We understand if we comprehend what this word of the Book of Hosea means: "It is love that I desire, not sacrifice." We understand if we recognize in Jesus him who "did not come to call the righteous but sinners." It remains to understand correctly who the "righteous" are in this saying, and what all this means.

What is meant by the "righteous" are those who do not need a physician; being thankful for their good health, they should not be surprised— even less, scandalized—to see the doctors go to those who need their services. This is so natural that, without a doubt, Jesus has other "righteous" in mind. He thinks of those who esteem themselves righteous because of their own efforts; who attribute to themselves the merit of their good health and consider others—"sinners," the "sick,"—to be lost, irrecoverable, not worthy of care.

These righteous are deluded as to their state of health. They do not realize that it is, in fact, precarious, illusory; that they, too, need the physician who can give them true health, unfailing health that blossoms into eternal life. In other words, proud of their respectability, they remain practically ignorant of God's mercy, which alone, with faith, can give justification. This is why they are surprised to see Jesus go to publicans and sinners and, what is worse, eat at the same table with them.

For they are aware of what this table sharing means. Any meal evokes for them, and rightly so, the banquet of the kingdom. Either the sinners are excluded from the eternal feast—and thus Jesus has acted in a blasphemous way—or they are admitted to it, as Jesus says by his action. And this is what these righteous ones cannot accept. For them, the only way for sinners to enter the banquet hall is to be converted and become "righteous" like themselves. "No," says Jesus; "you must be open to God's mercy and follow me." To know ourselves to be sinners is the only way to see the Physician-Savior come to us, bringing God's mercy. It is, in sum, a whole concept of religion, of righteousness, which is at stake in the account of Matthew's call and of Jesus' meal with publicans and sinners.

> One has seen the incredible play of grace penetrate a bad soul, even a vicious one, and one has seen what seemed lost saved. But one has not seen what was varnished absorb water, one has not seen what was waterproof become wet, one has not seen what was formed by habit become pliable . . . The consequence is that the efficacy of grace miscarries so often, that having won unhoped-for victories in the souls of the greatest sinners, it often remains without effect with good people. Precisely the best people, or at least those we call such and who love to call themselves such . . . do not present this openness made by a dreadful wound, an unforgettable distress, an unconquerable regret, a suture forever ill-fastened, a mortal anxiety, an invisible hidden motive, a secret bitterness, a collapse perpetually disguised, a scar never healed. Sin is essentially an entrance for grace, and they are without sin. Because they are not wounded, they are no longer vulnerable. Because they lack nothing, no one brings them anything. Because they lack nothing, no one brings them what is everything. Even the charity of God does not bandage what has no wounds. Because there was a man lying on the ground, the Samaritan picked him up. Because Jesus' face was dirty, Veronica wiped it with a cloth. Those who have not fallen will never be picked up and those who are not dirty will never be wiped clean.
> "Good people" are impervious to grace.[9]

At the Heart of the Gospel Is the Mercy of God

God's mercy forms the framework of the whole history of salvation and of the covenant from their beginning. It is the object of faith, hope, and thanksgiving, of which the psalms sing. The psalms are the inspired prayers which believers of all times have made their own and which they repeat always with fervor.

This divine mercy Jesus taught by any means, not only in words. He is the living image, the incarnation of it. His way of welcoming sinners, going to them, sharing in the intimacy of their meals has revealed the God of mercy to the eyes of all. To believe in him is to find again the unfailing hope in the coming of salvation offered to all, because Jesus, our Lord, delivered himself up for our faults and rose for our justification.

The Church, which is the community of sinners to whom God was merciful, must in its turn announce this good news and exemplify it by its behavior, its attitude towards other sinners and publicans.

Proclaimed during the celebration of the Eucharist, the Scripture passages of this Sunday are set in relief and resound like an urgent challenge. At the moment of communion—"Happy are those who are called to his supper"—we repeat, "Lord, I am not worthy to receive you." It is not enough to say it. We must behave according to what we are by acting as the one we receive, the Body of Christ, who ate with sinners and publicans, who keeps open house for the sinners and publicans that we are. To say, "Amen," when receiving Communion, is to respond to the invitation: "Follow me. Be a witness and an apostle of my mercy in the Church and in the world."

> The table is ready for sinners,
> Jesus invites, he waits for us.
> Let us draw near the Master of life,
> he only can heal us,
> give back the joy of being saved.
>
> *With you, O Lord*
> *is abundant forgiveness!*
>
> I came to call not the righteous,
> but sinners.
> If you hear my voice,
> do not close your hearts.
> To those thirsting for it
> I offer deliverance.
> Today the announcement of salvation
> resounds in your ears.[10]

Eleventh Sunday

One Shepherd, Few Workers

Universal Mission of the People of God

After coming out of Egypt, the people of God walked from oasis to oasis. This first part of the journey of those freed from slavery by God is briefly described in the Book of Exodus.[1] On the other hand, the writer dwells at length on the coming to Sinai.[2] The text read today is the beginning of this part (Exod 19:2-6a).

The leg of the journey that is centered upon Sinai marks a turning point in sacred history and a beginning for the fulfillment of the plan of salvation. Mount Sinai is, indeed, the place where God took the initiative of offering his people a covenant by which he solemnly pledged his own unchanging faithfulness. At the same time, he proposed that his people be faithful in order to have access to the life and freedom of the redeemed, the saved. This is why the Old and New Testaments, like the liturgy of the Church, unceasingly speak of that always timely Covenant, to remind us of its stipulations, to celebrate it so that the community of believers may enter more and more resolutely into the dynamic movement, into the way of salvation that God has revealed and opened up.

Moses is the prototype of messengers and prophets of the Lord, chosen to make known to the people God's initiative and commands, expressions of his love and a source of life.[3] Because of the solemnity of his investiture and the amplitude of his mission, Moses is the image of Christ, who will promulgate the code of the new covenant: "You have heard that it was said . . . But I say to you . . ." (Matt 5:38-48—Seventh Sunday).

The Lord charges Moses with saying to the people, "You have seen for yourselves how I treated the Egyptians and how I bore you up on eagle wings and brought you here to myself." "You have seen"—this word is addressed not only to the direct witnesses of the marvels of the Exodus but to all believers of all times. They become contemporaries of the wondrous deeds of God when they recall them—*anamnesis*—by listening to the stories and, even more so, when this Liturgy of the Word flows into the sacramental liturgy, for example, when we say in thanksgiving after the proclamation of the resurrection Gospel:[4] ". . . in this Easter season when Christ became our paschal sacrifice."[5]

I "brought you here to myself," to this place from which I am speaking, but also to this "now" in which my voice resounds, this assembly that gathers you to listen to what I tell you through the word and through the ministry of those who speak in my name. "Therefore, if you hearken to my voice and keep my covenant, you shall be my special possession, dearer to me than all other people."

The divine election of a people or a prophet—and singularly that of Christ—is always in view of a mission. Among all others, the people of God, "a holy nation"—that is, a sanctified nation—has been assembled in order to witness to the sanctity of God most high. The people are "a kingdom of priests" in order to offer the whole of creation to the master of the whole earth. The Church, taking to itself the words of the Book of Exodus, has understood its universal mission in the same terms.[6] To hear the voice of the Lord and to keep his covenant, is to allow oneself to be led by him on the paths of life towards his house, all doors wide open to welcome all peoples. It is to walk in faith, hope, and thanksgiving, inviting all others to take the same path.

> *We are his people: the sheep of his flock.*
>
> Sing joyfully to the LORD, all you lands;
>   serve the LORD with gladness;
>   come before him with joyful song.
> Know that the LORD is God;
>   he made us, his we are;
>   his people, the flock he tends.
> The LORD is good:
>   his kindness endures forever,
>   and his faithfulness, to all generations.
> (Ps 100:1-2, 3, 5)

Because God Loves Us

To those who believe and are justified through faith, the gospel guarantees salvation and glorification. This assurance rests on God's love manifested through Christ and on the efficacy of the paschal mystery (Rom 5:6-11).

For Paul, this is self-evident and needs only to be stated for anyone to become aware of it. To give one's life for someone is the supreme proof of love; but it is not enough to be convinced of it and say in a rapture of love, "I shall give my life for you." To act upon the conviction is difficult; one can hesitate; it is heroic. But it is much more heroic to die for a sinner.[7] And yet that is what Christ did for us.

That death made us into just persons; it reconciled us with God. How would we not be saved? Christ is risen. How would his life not give us salvation? By delivering his son to death for us—the just one for sinners— God manifested that his love is stronger than his legitimate anger. Since he liberated the crucified just one from death, how could we doubt that he is able and willing to give, through him, with him, and in him, immortal life to those whom he redeemed?

All these pronouncements are not cold certitudes. We "also boast of God through our Lord Jesus Christ, through whom we have now received reconciliation." Boast, that is pride, joyful and deep assurance of a future of which we already have the guarantee. We know that God loves us; we have the inexpressible proof of this infinite love that surpasses all imagination and expectation, that is absolutely without compare. We can only keep the unshakable certainty that God, having done all this for us, will never abandon us.

The Love of Jesus for All Is at the Heart of the Mission
The love of Jesus for those sinners ready to respond to his call is shown by his calling Matthew the publican and his sharing in a meal with numerous sinners and publicans.[8] The disciples must have been surprised by the initiative and nonconformist behavior of the Lord, although they probably were not scandalized like certain others. They have seen him showing his mercy by curing a woman who did not dare to publicly entreat him, by raising to life an official's daughter,[9] by opening the eyes of two blind men,[10] by delivering a mute man from a demon.[11] Now Jesus addresses himself directly to his disciples, urging them to share his pity for the crowds (Matt 9:36–10:2).

Jesus sees these crowds "troubled and abandoned, like sheep without a shepherd." They wander and exhaust themselves in search of food they do not know where to find. This pity is a very potent feeling that grips the guts of Jesus, who like God himself is moved by a motherly tenderness.[12] There is so much to do, and the time is so short. The image of the harvest spontaneously evokes the reaping of grain that must be done rapidly. But in the Bible this image classically designates God's great judgment.[13] The task Jesus speaks of must therefore be seen against the background of the imminent end-times that give to the present time its character of extreme urgency.

We must pray for "the master of the harvest to send out laborers for his harvest." The latter, after all, only contribute, without too much toil, to gathering in the fruit that Another has caused to germinate and grow to maturity.[14] This Other is more than the owner of a field who hires seasonal harvesters;[15] he alone knows how long the delays are before the grain is garnered (Matt 24:36).

The Call and Mission of the Twelve Apostles

Jesus himself no doubt prayed for the Father to send workers into the harvest. Luke explicitly mentions that Jesus spent the night in prayer before choosing, "when day came," the twelve disciples to whom he gave the name of apostles (Luke 6:12-13).[16] Matthew says that he immediately sent them on a mission with precise instructions.

Jesus gives, to these twelve, powers identical to those he himself has exercised during his own ministry: to expel evil spirits, to cure all disease and infirmity, to cleanse lepers, to raise the dead.[17] The message they must announce is the same as that of Jesus at the very beginning of his preaching: "Repent, for the kingdom of heaven is at hand" (Matt 4:17—Third Sunday).

The development of this original mission still remains limited: "Do not go into pagan territory or enter a Samaritan town. Go rather to the lost sheep of the house of Israel." The Lord will send the apostles to all nations at the moment of leaving them, when after his resurrection he will recover the full exercise of his power in heaven and on earth (Matt 28:18-19). This initial limitation of the apostles' field of action does not mean that Jesus first excludes Samaritans and pagans from sharing in the kingdom. On the contrary, he gives to understand that the proper time will come.[18]

His instructions given to the apostles for their first mission are consequences of the principle that Israel has the first place because it is the "beacon-people," the "witness-people." After the resurrection, the gospel will be preached to all nations, starting from Jerusalem (Acts 1:8). Paul himself, in the course of his preaching-journeys into foreign lands, will always address himself first to the Jews of the cities he enters.[19]

A People Witnessing to and Announcing God's Mercy

Mercy is the name of God's efficacious love. The misery of his own people grips him to the depths and irresistibly pushes him to take in hand—

"with a mighty hand and an outstretched arm" (Ps 136:12)—their situation and their fate. With the gathering of the people God chose, the Exodus remains the great epic adventure guided by God's mercy and to which the memory of believers unceasingly returns. The departure from Egypt, the trek through the desert toward the Promised Land, conjure up the image of the Shepherd-God. He leads his people, wards off dangers, procures food and drink, gives them rest in meadows of fresh grass, leads them to calm waters that revive them. His staff guides and reassures. With him they lack nothing and fear no evil (Ps 23).

Jesus will apply this image to himself when he solemnly declares that he is "the good shepherd" in the absolute sense—"I am" (John 10:11, 14). To gather the flock, he will give his very life (John 10:11) for the unruly and sickly sheep. He will bring back the lost ones, for such is the will of the Father who sent him (Matt 18:10-14). Such are the love and mercy of God that he should deliver his own Son, dead for the sinners we were, risen so that we may have life and, through him, be saved.

In order that this ministry might endure after his return to the Father, Jesus early on chose apostles to carry on his preaching. He does not call them shepherds or pastors, but workers in the harvest that sprouts from God's word. Indeed, there is only one Pastor, Christ (John 10:29).[20] No one can take the Lord's place, substitute for him, since he has not left his Church (Matt 28:10). On the contrary, from now on sitting at the Father's right hand, he watches over and leads his own from one end of the universe and of time to the other, so that there may be only one flock and one Shepherd (John 10:16).

The mission of the apostles and of the Church is, therefore, an ecumenical mission at the service of unity: "So that they may all be one, as you, Father, are in me and I in you, that they also may be in us, that the world may believe that you sent me" (John 17:21). Every time they celebrate the Eucharist, Christians pray for this unity to which the Church must witness, which she has the mission of announcing and promoting with all her strength.

Finally, she must, following the example of Jesus, the true Shepherd, have a preferential option for the poor, those who are most cruelly wounded by sin and its tragic consequences. If she should retire into her shell, she would no longer be the Church of Jesus Christ; her image of witness to God's mercy would be tarnished; she would not fulfil her catholic, i.e., universal, mission.

But we must not forget that the Church is the actual assembly of all believers. To each the call of the Lord is directed: "Freely you have received, freely give."

> Go, messengers of the feast,
> into the new wind that scatters you,
> into the burning wind that comes from God.
> Faced with darkness, do not falter,
> too many guests would be missing.
>
> Leave your parents' country,
> go beyond your boundaries,
> go where the Spirit of God goes.
> Do not fear: the whole earth
> will be promised land for you.
>
> Go to the faraway islands,
> break all the captives' chains,
> in all tongues announce God.
> Shout to the poor God loves them
> and only love creates justice.
>
> The peoples slumber in darkness.
> Be the voice that awakens them,
> Be the voice of the Son of God.
> Cry out that he calls them
> that the Church may be born in every place.[21]

From the Twelfth to the Fourteenth Sunday in Ordinary Time

The way in which the Lectionary proposes to continue the reading of the Gospel of Matthew suggests that we consider the Twelfth, Thirteenth, and Fourteenth Sundays as a new sequence in Ordinary Time, Year A. The Gospels of the first two Sundays are taken from what is called the "Apostolic Discourse" or the "Discourse on the Mission," which the evangelist has inserted after the sending of the apostles to "the lost sheep of the house of Israel."[1]

The third excerpt[2] is taken from the narrative section of the following part of the Gospel, which deals with the mystery of the kingdom of heaven.[3] But it also records Jesus' thanksgiving to his Father upon the return of those he had sent on a mission, and thus matches well what is read on the preceding two Sundays, and constitutes the conclusion of the sequence.

The Old Testament readings shed their light upon the Gospel readings. The first two remind us that, in all times, those whom God sends often know persecution, but at other times a warm welcome from those who receive them.[4] The reading of the Fourteenth Sunday sketches the features of the Messiah, meek and humble of heart.[5]

We continue with the reading of Paul's Letter to the Romans.[6]

God, Strength of Those Who Are Sent

The Lord Is with Me in the Midst of Trials

What has been called the "Confession of Jeremiah" expresses the inner drama lived by an authentic witness of God.[1] These texts are a real descent into the psyche of a man torn between the expression of his own limitations and that of the divine intervention that turned him into a prophet. They belong to the most painful period of the great prophet's life. He is suffering from persecution at the hands of his compatriots and of a king with little regard for the covenant.[2] Moreover, his God himself inflicts pain on him by entrusting him with an impossible mission for which he, being very timid and hypersensitive, feels himself totally inadequate. The fifth Confession of Jeremiah[3] has this drama for its subject and is the most moving of all. We read part of it on this Sunday (Jer 20:10-13).

The prophet experiences the divine inspiration as a devouring and inextinguishable fire. He must speak, in spite of his natural resistance to the one who sent him "to root up and to tear down, to destroy and to demolish" (Jer 1:10), because he knows the risk of hatreds, ill treatment, and even violent death. The prophet's distress expresses itself in moving language. God has duped him, raped him, as a seduced woman who does not know where to hide her shame.[4] And again he comes back to the persecutions directed against him, whenever the irresistible thrust of the divine word obliges him to shout, "Violence and plunder." Even those who seem friendly plot with his declared enemies. They mimic his usual threats.[5] They strive to find charges against him. Although Jeremiah knows that all this is the lot of the just[6]—a paltry comfort, he regrets ever having been born.[7]

But after this profoundly human cry of distress, faith prevails, stronger and more tenacious than the fear that would submerge the prophet: "But the Lord is with me, like a mighty champion: my persecutors will stumble, they will not triumph.''

Having the Lord of hosts at our side, how should we still fear the fighting? An absolute trust expresses itself here, in the midst of all sorts of dangers, like a song of victory in the heat of battle. We are reminded of other texts in the Old Testament[8]; of Paul exhorting his disciple Timothy to apostolic courage, ''I know him in whom I have believed and am confident that he is able to guard what has been entrusted to me until that day'' (2 Tim 1:12).

Thanks to this surge of trust, Jeremiah foresees that he will ''conquer overwhelmingly'' (Rom 8:37). He is sure of it; he will see the fulfillment of the promise that God made upon first calling him and expressed anew on the occasion of his second calling.[9]

May this valiant warrior who is by his side show his power, he who probes the mind and heart.[10] It is to him that Jeremiah entrusts his cause, and it is upon him that he places the too heavy burden which overwhelms him.[11] This cry toward God is prolonged by a thanksgiving in which we all are invited to share, each of us, personally and as a church.

Jeremiah is really the father of this spiritual posterity of the ''poor,'' those dependents of God who in their material or spiritual distress place their cause in God's hands.[12]

> LORD, *in your great love, answer me.*
>
> For your sake I bear insult,
>   and shame covers my face.
> I have become an outcast to my brothers,
>   a stranger to my mother's sons,
> Because zeal for your house consumes me,
>   and the insults of those who blaspheme you fall upon me.
> I pray to you, O LORD,
>   for the time of your favor, O God!
> In your great kindness answer me
>   with your constant help.
> Answer me, O LORD, for bounteous is your kindness;
>   in your great mercy turn toward me.
> ''See, you lowly ones, and be glad;
>   you who seek God, may your hearts be merry!
> For the LORD hears the poor,
>   and his own who are in bonds he spurns not.
> Let the heavens and the earth praise him,
>   the seas and whatever moves in them!''
> (Ps 69:8-10, 14, 17, 33-35)

Freed from Sin and Death

Gained by Christ, redemption abolishes sin and at the same time insures salvation unto eternal life. This is what grounds our hope.[13] Now Paul comes to the confrontation—begun in this Sunday's text—between Christ's work and Adam's (Rom 5:12-15).

". . . just as through one person sin entered the world, and through sin, death, and thus death came to all, inasmuch as all sinned." This is a brief reminder of the original fall and its consequences (see Gen 2:17). How is this possible? How can we explain the involvement of all in death, the effect of Adam's sin? What is the connection between the sins that all commit and Adam's? What does the word "sin" mean when there is no law to sanction it? These questions, unavoidable when we read what Paul wrote, are not answered in the text.[14] The Apostle does not justify his statements; he does not explain them. If, through literal exegesis, we sought to elucidate the thought that the author himself did not well define, we would come to dead ends, or at least conclusions too divergent to be useful.[15] In a hurry to get to the effects of redemption through Christ, he is content, in his impetuosity, to allude to the disastrous effects of Adam's sin, the prototype of all sins. Without laboring the point, Paul says enough to emphasize that "the gift is not like the transgression."

Not only does Christ repair the catastrophic state that had its origin in Adam, he initiates a new, an incomparably better state. Through the sin of one "the many died." How "much more did the grace of God and the precious gift of the one person Jesus Christ overflow for the many." Let us turn our eyes toward him. In him we find our hope; through him the universe has become "a new creation" (see Gal 6:15) into which faith and baptism integrate us.

Do Not Be Afraid

The Discourse on the Mission in Matthew's Gospel reaches far and wide; it is directed, beyond time, to all who place and will place themselves at the service of Christ and the gospel. Those sent by the Lord must not let themselves grow fearful when faced with the contradictions, persecutions, and violent reactions that their ministry is bound to elicit.[16] No doubt the gospel is good news, but it also radically calls into question a world built without recognition of God and upon values foreign or even contrary to his law. Confrontation is unavoidable. A gospel that bothers no one and questions nothing is no longer the gospel.

But the impact of the good news is not always apparent—far from it. Christians very often seem to fight a losing battle. Being a little flock, they are submerged by the surrounding world, which sees them as despised and mocked dreamers, as dangerous challengers to be marginalized or suppressed. If they yield to fear, chances are that doubt will take over. "Therefore do not be afraid of them. Nothing is concealed that will not be revealed, nor secret that will not be known." "Take courage, I have conquered the world" (John 16:33). You, too, will share in this victory, through your faith (See 1 John 5:4).

In any case, why fear human beings? They can kill the body, but not the soul, what is deepest in humankind. It is well known and can often be verified that the worst aggressions against the body do not always succeed in reaching persons' inner core, what makes their greatness and dignity.[17] But this is not what Christ is speaking of, he who on the cross will remain, to his last breath, a man whose body, not soul, was slain. What he does is to contrast the fear of human beings with the fear of God, which has nothing in common with fear, even religious fear. Fear of God is consciousness of the transcendence and power of God, but also of his being the supreme good. It causes us finally to take seriously God's love and the real stakes of life.[18]

> The love which God pours in our hearts and which allows us to love him in return, banishes fear. Only a right and good trembling is left, caused no longer by fear but by fervor. A victory over fear, love shaking with fervor, a trust that is absolute yet always surprised, an ardent desire to correspond to God's gift and expectations by one's actions—the fear of God is all of that in turn and at one and the same time. It is, therefore, a beautiful and precious reality. It challenges both our fear and our laziness. It challenges our propensity for getting used to God and to his mercy, for confusing the high and demanding freedom of God's children with a vulgar familiarity, an easygoing, casual approach to God. It challenges this ability we have to comfortably settle even on Christ's cross, as Bernanos used to say.[19]

Only one thing should be feared—to be lost, "to perish in Gehenna," soul and body, for having cut one's self off from God's love. This latter sanction is not within the power of human beings, who can kill only the body. "What will separate us from the love of Christ? Will anguish, or distress, or persecution, or famine, or nakedness, or peril, or the sword? . . . No, in all these things we conquer overwhelmingly through him who loved us. For I am convinced that neither death, nor life, nor angels, nor principalities, nor present things, nor future things, nor any other creature will be able to separate us from the love of God in Christ Jesus our Lord'' (Rom 8:35, 37-39).[20]

Finally, ''do not be afraid,'' because you are precious to God. This divine solicitude is called providence. It extends to the least of creatures and even more to those who call God ''Our Father.'' They have been redeemed by the blood of Christ; God cannot let them perish.

''Proclaim Him''

Freed from fear, placing their trust in God, the disciples and the messengers of the gospel must proclaim from the housetops the good news that has been revealed to them, and boldly bear public witness to the one who chose them and whom they choose. To thus profess one's faith in words and actions, courage, sometimes even heroism, is needed. But Christ is present, whose Spirit is given so that we may speak and act without fear.

A mysterious and intimate solidarity exists between Jesus and the disciples. Those who make the Lord's cause their own will see him testify on their behalf on Judgment Day.[21] At that most dreadful moment, they will hear again, one last time, ''Do not be afraid.''

Humble Trust, Invincible Strength

The unconquerable strength of all—the prophet, the apostle, the Christian, the Church—is a gift from Almighty God, who never abandons his own, all appearances sometimes to the contrary. This strength is proportionate to the trust that believers place in the one whose cause they have espoused. When the tempest is at its worst, such trust manifests itself in praise:

> Sing to the Lord,
>   praise the Lord,
> For he has rescued the life of the poor
>   from the power of the wicked!
> (First Reading)

Christians indeed know that the grace of Christ has no common measure with sin; it has initiated a new world freed from death-dealing sin (Second Reading).

Therefore, it is with full assurance that they welcome and exercise their mission as witnesses to Christ and heralds of the good news. Joyful and proud to share with others the joy and trust that animate them, they guard against any form of arrogance or presumption, because they know that their strength is not their own (Gospel).

> Victorious love shouts to the four winds.
> You who follow Jesus,
> do not fear what leads to death,
> rather fear to yield to fear.
>
> *The joy of the Lord is our rampart.*
>
> The Lord is my light and my salvation,
> whom should I fear?
>
> Though an army encamps against me,
> my heart will not fear.
>
> I shall not die, but live,
> declaring the works of the Lord.[22]

Thirteenth Sunday

When the Love of Christ Has Taken Possession of Us

An Example of Hospitality Rewarded by God
The first reading of this Sunday is an excerpt from the narrative of Elisha's deeds in the Second Book of Kings (2 Kgs 4:8-11, 14, 16a).[1]

A wealthy woman from the country of Shunem invites Elisha to take his meals at her house whenever he passes by. The prophet accepts this generous hospitality with simplicity. She suggests to her husband that they build "a little room on the roof" for the "holy man of God." At his next visit, Elisha stays in this room. "Can something be done for her?" he asks his servant. "She has no son and her husband is getting on in years," is the reply. Called by Elisha, the woman goes upstairs and stands at the door. Elisha says to her, "This time next year you will be fondling a baby son."[2]

What we have here is an edifying story, similar to the *fioretti* (stories about St. Francis and his first followers), from which we may single out some traits that hold important lessons: the woman's generosity but also her discretion, for she does not overwhelm the prophet with her admiration, her excessive attentions, or her own sorrow; the simplicity of Elisha, who knows that the respect shown him is directed to God; his discretion as to the private life of his hosts; his desire to do something to express his thankfulness; and the naturalness with which he asks his servant, judged better advised than himself in these matters. We might be surprised that the narrator does not stress the legendary clearsightedness of Elisha with regard to what is lacking in the couple's happiness. But the prophet appears the closer to each one of us in his ignorance or lack of perspicacity, even if afterwards he regains his prophetic assurance.

This Shunemite woman prefigures the women of the Gospels who will help support Jesus and his disciples by supplying their goods, who will extend to them generous hospitality.[3] So many others, too, who afterwards will be, and still are today, such precious help to priests and Christian communities, through the humble and generous services they render.

Do they have a sufficient place in our personal prayer and in that of the community? This is also an opportunity to renew our sense and practice of hospitality. ''All guests who present themselves are to be welcomed as Christ, for he himself will say: 'I was a stranger and you welcomed me' (Matt 25:35). Proper honor must be shown 'to all, especially to those who share our faith' (Gal 6:10) and to pilgrims.''[4] Exercising hospitality enables us to manifest and welcome the love of the Lord so that we may be able to sing to him in all truth in the liturgy.

> *Forever I will sing the goodness of the LORD.*

> The favors of the LORD I will sing forever;
>   through all generations my mouth shall proclaim your faithfulness.
> For you have said, ''my kindness is established forever'';
>   in heaven you have confirmed your faithfulness.
> Happy the people who know the joyful shout;
>   in the light of your countenance, O LORD, they walk.
> At your name they rejoice all the day,
>   and through your justice they are exalted.
> For you are the splendor of their strength,
>   and by your favor our horn is exalted.
> For to the LORD belongs our shield,
>   and to the Holy One of Israel, our king.
> (Ps 89)

Baptism, Justification unto New Life

Justification and salvation are absolutely gratuitous gifts from God. Paul never tires of strongly affirming this, in particular by citing the example of Abraham, the father of believers.[5]

This doctrine could lead us into thinking that since everything depends on God, human responsibility plays no part. The extreme consequence of this would be to think it unnecessary to get rid of faults, since the more they abound, the more marvelous is the grace that blots them out.[6] Paul gives a first answer to this faulty reasoning in the passage from the Letter to the Romans that we read on this Sunday (Rom 6:3b-4, 8-11).[7]

In order to answer this difficulty, the Apostle says, ''Let us look at what happens in Baptism.''[8] Like his correspondents, Paul recalls clearly the baptismal rite as it was then practiced, by immersion into water. We ''were baptized into his death . . . buried with him.'' Such a manner of speaking reminds them of what has been concretely lived at the moment when they were immersed—buried—in the baptismal waters: the impression of dying and coming back to life.[9]

It is in Jesus Christ that we have ritually died and been buried. But we know that far from remaining a prisoner of death, the Lord has definitively conquered it. "He died to sin once and for all"; "he lives for God." The conclusion is self-evident; there is no need to formulate it. If we are purified, dead to sin, it is in order that we may lead "for God in Jesus Christ" a new life, a paschal life, under the Spirit's guidance.[10]

The meaning and the effect of baptism flow from the bond between the rite and the event-that-is-a-mystery of Easter. It is the central tenet of the traditional profession of faith: "For I handed on to you as of first importance what I also received: that Christ died for our sins in accordance with the scriptures; that he was buried; that he was raised on the third day in accordance with the scriptures" (1 Cor 15:3-4).

> The foundation of our present condition is Adam. But for our future life, it is Christ our Lord. As Adam was the first mortal man and caused all humans to be mortal, Christ is the first one risen from the dead and he gave the seed of resurrection to those who followed. We come to the visible life through our bodily birth, and thus we all are corruptible. As to the future life, we shall be transformed into it through the power of the Holy Spirit, and thus we shall rise incorruptible. Since this transformation will be realized only later, Christ our Lord willed to transfer us today into new life in a symbolic manner, by giving us baptism and a new birth in himself. This spiritual birth is the present figure of the resurrection and of the regeneration that must be fully realized in us when we go over to that new life. This is the reason why baptism is also called regeneration.[11]

The Complete Detachment of Jesus' Disciples

The Discourse on the Mission ends with a series of sentences that are directed to all disciples of Christ, even though they are directly addressed to the apostles (Matt 10:37-42).[12] "The love of Christ must come before all else."[13] This precept translates what Jesus says: "Whoever loves father or mother more than me is not worthy of me, and whoever loves son or daughter more than me is not worthy of me."

One should neither deny nor gloss over the extravagant character of such a demand formulated without any nuance.[14] But we can understand it. There are indeed causes and circumstances in which similarly heart-rending choices tragically confront men and women. To go to the point of sacrificing the love for one's father, mother, son, or daughter is such a heroic act that no person, no cause is entitled to exact it, that no one is qualified to condemn the person who lacks the strength for such a choice.[15] But God can ask it because what is at stake is the supreme good—salvation—and because God is the strength of martyrs.[16] The annals of Israel have preserved the memory of the seven brothers who preferred death to apostasy and whom their mother herself exhorted not to fear the executioner (2 Macc 7:1-42). Others had to overcome their most profound and legitimate feelings. Thus it was with St. Perpetua, who suffered martyrdom in Carthage in 202, and whose child had been born in prison.

> One day in the middle of the meal we are dragged to court. We reach the forum. The news rapidly spreads in the nearby neighborhoods; soon a crowd assembles.
> We get up on the platform. Others are interrogated and they confess their faith. My turn comes, when suddenly my father appears, carrying my son in his arms.
> He takes me aside and says, "Pity the child."
> The procurator Hilarianus, who replaced the consul Minutius Timinianus after his death and had the power to wield the sword, insists in his turn: "Pity your father's white hair, your child's tender age. Sacrifice for the welfare of the emperors."
> I answer, "I shall not sacrifice."
> Hilarianus, "Are you a Christian?"
> I answer, "I am a Christian."[17]

These are extreme situations. But one day or the other, in one way or another, all believers know the heartbreaks that Jesus announced: "Do not think that I have come to bring peace upon the earth. I have come to bring not peace but the sword. For I have come to set a man against his father, a daughter against her mother, and a daughter-in-law against her mother-in-law; and one's enemies will be those of his household" (Matt 10:34-36).

To Carry One's Cross, To Lose One's Life

That "the love of Christ must come before all else" can entail heartrending renunciations of the most legitimate affections. We are not speaking of demands resulting from a sort of total allegiance to a master who does not admit of competition. What is really at stake here is to receive God and salvation through communion with the mystery and the person of Christ. There is no salvation except through the cross, no savior except Christ dead on the cross and risen. We cannot be "worthy of him," be his disciples, without "taking up our cross." We must share in his mystery of death in order to have a part in his resurrection. The cross—"to lose one's life"—is the unavoidable step to gain life, but this step is taken "on account" of the Lord. Here we are really in the order of mystery, of love, and not in the order of some scheme or some condition arbitrarily imposed. For, by themselves, suffering and death—the cross—remain an evil whose signification only Christ has reversed by virtue of his resurrection.[18] Like Christian life, the gospel and its preaching carry the indelible mark of the sign of the cross.[19] The evangelist and his disciples have fully understood what Jesus wanted to say after his death and resurrection. "To carry one's cross," "to lose one's life to save it" take on a meaning both metaphorical—because the question is not to really reproduce Jesus' crucifixion—and realistic—because the trials to be endured are really crucifying.[20]

Welcoming Christ in Those He Sends

The last precept of the Discourse on the Mission deals with the welcome to be given to those the Lord sends, the just and the disciples.

"Receive this person whom I am sending to you as you would me." It is not rare for us to speak in this way in order to entrust someone to friends whose benevolence toward us has been proved. At the same time, it is proof of the esteem we have for the person with whom we identify. This is why we do not thus compromise ourselves lightly, for the benefit of anyone. What would the friends we called upon think if they saw a vagabond at their door or a person who has wronged them?[21] The friends would be surprised at the very least by such an identification; a strong friendship would be needed to take it seriously. But here we have Jesus himself identifying with every prophet, every just person, every disciple, be they the least. He even goes so far as to promise an eternal reward—that of the prophet, the just, the disciple—to anyone who receives him in their persons. To give a single glass of water will bring a reward. The scope of this command is broad, since it encompasses all disciples, not only the missionaries sent by the Lord. We must understand this by remembering that the door of the kingdom will be opened or closed according to what we shall have done or omitted to do for those who were hungry and thirsty, who were strangers or naked, sick or imprisoned: "you did for me . . . you did not do for me" (Matt 25:31-46).[22]

Such a word explains the high esteem in which the Church and the spiritual tradition have held hospitality. The reception of guests will take on quasiliturgical forms. "Once a guest has been announced, the superior and the brothers are to meet him with all the courtesy of love. . . . All humility should be shown in addressing a guest on arrival or departure. By a bow of the head or by a complete prostration of the body, Christ is to be adored because he is indeed welcomed in them. . . . Great care and concern are to be shown in receiving poor people and pilgrims, because in them more particularly Christ is received."[23]

Possessed by Christ

"I am a Christian," Perpetua indefatigably repeated to both her father and the Roman procurator, who were urging her to renounce her faith in order to save her life and to have pity on her family. Is it senseless obstinacy on her part or neglect of her duties as daughter and young mother? Her attitude was thus misjudged by those who were pressuring her through arguments and exhortations to change her mind. They did not realize that faith is a loving adherence to a person and not to a doctrine that one can shake off. They did not realize that the young Christian woman had been "taken possession of by Christ," according to Paul's expression (Phil 3:12). Perpetua despised neither her father nor her newborn child; on the contrary, she was torn to her depths by her filial and maternal love. Certainly these are extreme circumstances; the edifying narrative stresses the tragic element, avoiding cruelty or even a trace of sadism.[24] Still, it remains an exemplary illustration, inasmuch as all disciples must, at whatever cost, love Christ more than father, mother, son, or daughter, and consent to lose their lives in order to keep them. One day or another, this demand exacts real heroism, or else may require a whole life of daily renunciation.

To be Christians, must we be suicidal, unceasingly running to meet death, always choosing what goes against the deepest aspirations and feelings of human nature? Of course not. In a sense, Christians are dead, once and for all, but dead to sin. They are living, however, and they journey toward everlasting life.

They believe in Christ without having seen him, but they are given the grace to welcome him by welcoming those the Lord claims to be like himself. On judgment day, he will reward a hundredfold the least gesture of benevolence done for the little ones.

> To lose one's life
> in order to welcome Christ,
> to deliver one's self to Christ
> in order to meet the Father,
> to find one's self
> as a gift from God.
>
> *I shall follow you, Jesus,*
> *show me the way.*

Whoever loves father or mother more than me
is not worthy of me.

Whoever refuses to take up the cross
is not worthy of me.

Whoever loses life because of me
will keep it.[25]

Fourteenth Sunday

"Come to Me, All You Who Are Weary"

A Peaceful King for the Little Ones

"Rejoice heartily!"—dance wholeheartedly—"Shout for joy!"—utter acclamations—you who live in the holy city. These opening words of the Liturgy of the Word immediately place the celebration of this Sunday in a climate of popular rejoicing. They are taken from the Book of Zechariah, which is little used by the Lectionary.[1] Only two verses are read today (Zech 9:9-10).[2]

The one who is coming and entering his city is a king, "a just savior is he, meek, and riding on an ass, on a colt, the foal of an ass." What a marvelous and at once strange scene. It demonstrates a messianic hope, from now on strongly influenced by the spirituality of the "poor of Yahweh."[3] A "humble" king, he has nothing in common with the powerful of this world, who flaunt their glory and their warlike power, who ride impressive horses.[4]

This peaceful Messiah will do away with war chariots and war horses; he will break the war-bow. He will extend his dominion from the north—Ephraim—to the south of the country—Jerusalem—because with him[5] will be the strength of God, the only savior of his people.[6] And his dominion will extend not only to his people, since he "shall proclaim peace to the nations" and because his peaceful rule will reach "from sea to sea, and from the River to the ends of the earth."[7]

Upon hearing this scriptural text, we think of Jesus' entry into Jerusalem; Matthew, for his part, quotes from Zechariah (Matt 21:5). But in today's liturgy, this oracle has a more general scope. Jesus is this emissary endowed with singular power[8] and yet "meek and humble of heart" (Matt 11:28-30). When he began preaching, he proclaimed blessed the poor in spirit, the meek, the merciful, the pure hearts, the peacemakers, those who hunger and thirst for righteousness (Matt 5:3-12). He addresses himself to them with a preferential option, and they are the first to know him, to rejoice with all their strength, to shout for joy, and to sing their thanksgiving.

> *I will praise your name for ever,*
> *my king and my God.*

> I will extol you, O my God and King,
>   and I will bless your name forever and ever.
> Every day will I bless you,
>   and I will praise your name forever and ever.
> The LORD is gracious and merciful,
>   slow to anger and of great kindness.
> The LORD is good to all
>   and compassionate toward all his works.
> Let all your works give you thanks, O LORD,
>   and let your faithful ones bless you.
> Let them discourse of the glory of your kingdom
>   and speak of your might.
> The LORD is faithful in all his words
>   and holy in all his works.
> The LORD lifts up all who are falling
>   and raises up all who are bowed down.
> (Ps 145:1-2, 8-9, 10-11, 13-14)

From the Dominion of the Flesh to That of the Spirit

Through baptism, the believers have been symbolically immersed into the death of Christ—and thus freed from sin—in order to be reborn with him to a new life.[9] Paul pursues his reflection by showing how the Christians' lives are under the sway, under the dominion of the Spirit. This is the topic of the eighth chapter of the Letter to the Romans, which we begin to read today (Rom 8:9, 11-13).[10]

Everything rests on the antithesis "flesh—Spirit."[11] The "Spirit" is that which, after Christ, was poured out upon believers in the Church and the world. It is expressly identified "the Spirit of God," "the Spirit of Christ," "the Spirit of the one who raised Christ from the dead [who] dwells in you."[12]

On the other hand, we must understand the term "flesh" with the meaning Paul gives to it.[13] First of all, we must discard the meaning that would identify "flesh"—as we use the word today—with "body," with its physical, its bodily aspects. According to Paul's vocabulary, "flesh" designates everything that inclines human beings to sin: frailty, dullness of heart, opacity, and resistance to anything spiritual, to God. Therefore, Paul is able to speak of "human wisdom" (2 Cor 1:12), of "carnal body"

(Col 2:11). In the Letter to the Galatians (Gal 5:19-23) he best expresses his thought, because he concretely shows the contrast between "the Spirit" and "the flesh." Besides obviously sensual sins—"immorality, impurity, licentiousness, drinking bouts, orgies, and the like"—other sins are also attributed to the flesh—"idolatry, sorcery, hatreds, rivalry, jealousy, outbursts of fury, acts of selfishness, dissensions, factions, occasions of envy."[14] The meaning of the word "flesh" is further elucidated by the listing of what the Spirit produces: "love, joy, peace, patience, kindness, generosity, faithfulness, gentleness, self-control." The passage from the "dominion of the flesh" to the "dominion of the Spirit" changes human beings—bodies and souls—into new creatures belonging to a new world, the one that Christ established. From now on we owe nothing to the flesh, while we owe everything to the Spirit.

We must add this important point: the Spirit who dwells in us, having raised Christ, is the pledge of our future resurrection. Through the Spirit, the direction of bodily death is reversed; it becomes a passage—a pasch—to unending life. We cannot insist too much on the importance of these certitudes of faith that confer to our lives such an orientation for today and for the future world where what we are will appear in full light.

The Mystery of the Kingdom Revealed to the Little Ones

The fourth large part of the Gospel of Matthew is devoted to the revelation of the Mystery of the Kingdom.[15] According to his custom, the evangelist divides his writing into two sections, one a narration, the other a record of a long discourse of Jesus.[16] From the first of these sections, we read today a brief excerpt of particular importance. It sheds light on Jesus' teaching in general, on the teaching heard on preceding Sundays, and at the same time on Jesus' person (Matt 11:25-30).[17]

First of all, the evangelist records a prayer of thanksgiving pronounced by Jesus. It is likely that his experience as a teacher inspires this thanksgiving (Matt 11:1). He has stumbled against the lack of comprehension on the part of many who took offense at him (Matt 11:6). The cities along the Lake of Galilee, where he has performed so many miracles, have painfully disappointed him (Matt 11:20-24). But there are "the childlike," who have welcomed the revelation that remained hidden from "the wise and learned." The childlike are the disciples and all those whom Jesus has declared "blessed" (Matt 5:3-12). Their welcome compensates for the lack of understanding and the rejection to such a degree that Jesus exclaims, "I give praise to you, Father, Lord of heaven and earth."[18]

These little ones divine in Jesus the one who knows the Father and the mysteries of the kingdom. They see in him the one whom the Father himself has entrusted with words rich in revelation and they hear them with wonder. We have here an admirable manifestation of God's kindness and a proof of the absolute gratuity of the gift of faith.

Finally, this prayer expresses the special intimacy Jesus entertains with the one he calls "Father"; he is the Son of God, whom he reverently calls "Lord of heaven and earth." This prayer shows that to address God as "almighty" does not exclude the closeness expressed by the name "Father."[19]

Become My Disciples; My Burden Is Light

In the Gospel of Matthew,[20] the prayer of thanksgiving is followed by a pressing and warm call to become his disciples, to take his yoke that is said to be "easy" because he, Jesus, is "meek and humble of heart."[21]

This text is of prime importance from several points of view. Jesus addresses himself to those who "labor and are burdened," those childlike ones he has just mentioned. Probably Matthew keeps what Jesus has told them, while thinking of the believers afraid of the demands of the gospel, the Christians who find it difficult to carry them out, whose faithfulness remains fragile. Let them not be discouraged. They soon will realize that this burden is not as heavy as they thought; they will even find it light.

What does this mean? Must we understand that in the last analysis the gospel is demanding only in appearance, that it is enough to know how to deal with it so as not to feel its weight? Would Jesus all at once go back on the seriousness of what he exacts of his disciples? This is impossible, because the call to discipleship would no longer be credible. All the demands of the gospel come down to love of God and love of neighbor,[22] because we must imitate the heavenly Father who loves the little ones (Matt 5:21-48). Love entails demands; love is most demanding. But we certainly cannot say that it is painful.

Jesus is "meek and humble of heart." We must therefore not be afraid of becoming his disciples: he does not lay upon us crushing, intolerable burdens.[23] And above all, in the first place and far beyond, he has accomplished what he asks us to do with the help of grace. Matthew emphasizes Jesus' compassion; he is the opposite of a hard and stern master who would not take his servants' weakness into consideration. Indeed, the evangelist says that Jesus fulfilled in his actions "what had been spoken through Isaiah the prophet" (Isa 42:1-4). "Behold, my servant whom

I have chosen, my beloved in whom I delight; I shall place my spirit upon him and he will proclaim justice to the Gentiles. He will not contend or cry out, nor will anyone hear his voice in the streets. A bruised reed he will not break, a smoldering wick he will not quench" (Matt 12:17-20).[24] Such a reference to a prophetic oracle is a timely reminder that, in the Bible, "meekness" is the most remarkable quality of any one sent by God. Jesus embodied it in an exemplary manner.

> Why do the Scriptures, when praising Moses, leave aside all the miracles that he worked and only mention his meekness? For it does not say that Moses chastised Egypt; but it does say that he was alone before God in the desert, when God wanted to destroy Israel, and he asked to be destroyed along with the children of his people. He placed before God both love for humankind and sin by saying, "If you will not [forgive them], then strike me out of the book that you have written" (Exod 31:32). Thus spoke he who was the meekest man on the face of the earth (Num 12:3). . . . David, too, calls upon the virtue of meekness when he says, "Remember, O Lord, for David all his anxious care" (Ps 132:1). . . . Let us also acquire that meekness of him who said, "Learn from me, for I am meek and humble of heart" (Matt 11:29), so that he may teach us his ways and cause us to rest in the kingdom of heaven.[25]

With an Overflowing Heart

"I will run the way of your commands when you give me a docile heart" (Ps 119:32). This statement of the psalmist demonstrates the experience of those who apply themselves to God's law and its demands. Aware of the "humanity" of the Lord, the spiritual masters, for their part, keep before them the face and the teaching of Jesus—"meek and humble of heart"—when they propose a particular rule of life to answer the call of the Lord "seeking his workman in a multitude of people." Thus St. Benedict. He begins by saying, "What, dear brothers, is more delightful than this voice of the Lord calling to us? See how the Lord in his love shows us the way of life. . . . Clothed then with faith and the performance of good works, let us set out on this way, with the Gospel for our guide." Then, presenting the rule of the "school for the Lord's service" that he is founding, he writes: "We hope to set down nothing harsh, nothing burdensome. The good of all concerned, however, may prompt us to a little strictness in order to amend faults and to safeguard love. Do not be daunted immediately by fear and run away from the road that leads to salvation. It is bound to be narrow at the outset. But as we progress in this way of life and in faith, we shall run on the path of God's com-

mandments, our hearts overflowing with the inexpressible delight of love
. . . never swerving from his instructions. . . .''[26]

Yes, we are the subjects of a just and victorious king, humble and peace-
loving; we are the disciples of a master meek and humble of heart.
Through his death, he has delivered us from the dominion of the flesh;
through his resurrection, he has transferred us to the dominion of the
life-giving Spirit. In our weakness, he offers us food: the bread that ''for-
tifies the hearts of men'' and the wine that ''gladdens men's hearts'' (Ps
104:15), that is, his body delivered for us and his blood poured out for
us and the multitude. How could we hesitate to become his disciples,
to follow him on the road of life that, sent by God, he has opened in
front of us and on which he has preceded us?

The sequence that includes the Twelfth, Thirteenth, and Fourteenth
Sundays in Ordinary Time, Year A, thus ends in the joy and trust that
must fill the disciples' hearts when they hear and welcome his message,
his good news. ''Let us give thanks to the Lord our God!''

> Neither the violence of the powerful,
> nor the knowledge of the prudent,
> force the kingdom,
> but the weakness of the little ones
> and the patience of the humble
> fathom God's secrets.
>
> *Blessed are you, our Father,*
> *joy of the poor!*
>
> You listen to the cry of the unfortunate,
> you welcome and hearten them.
>
> You direct the humble toward righteousness,
> you teach them your way.
>
> You hold fast to those who fall,
> you draw straight the overwhelmed.
>
> You reveal your face to children,
> you teach them praise.[27]

From the Fifteenth to the Seventeenth Sunday in Ordinary Time

In the Gospel of Matthew, the "Discourse in Parables" constitutes a well-defined unit. "On that day;[1] Jesus went out of the house and sat down by the sea. Such large crowds gathered around him that he got into the boat and sat down, and the whole crowd stood along the shore. And he spoke to them at length in parables." Thus begins chapter 13. And at the end, Jesus asks, "Do you understand all these things?" It is rare enough to find in biblical books a whole so clearly recognizable as a unit.[2] This chapter is read in its entirety on the Fifteenth, Sixteenth, and Seventeenth Sundays in Ordinary Time, Year A; therefore we see an obvious sequence in this succession of Sunday liturgies.

The first readings shed their light on the gospel of each Sunday: efficacy of God's word (Isa 55:10-11—Fifteenth Sunday); God's power and patience (Wis 12:13, 16-19—Sixteenth Sunday); prayer of Solomon asking God for wisdom and discernment (1 Kgs 3:5, 7-12—Seventeenth Sunday).

And we continue with the reading of the important chapter 8 of Paul's Letter to the Romans.

Time of Sowing, Time of Birth

Creative Efficacy of God's Word

Nothing more fitting than the two verses from the Book of Isaiah that open today's Liturgy of the Word (Isa 55:10-11) could be placed as an epigraph to the sequence constituted by the Fifteenth, Sixteenth, and Seventeenth Sundays in Ordinary Time. Besides, these verses prepare us to understand well the parable of the sower.

"Words, words, words!"[1] Hamlet's exclamation aptly expresses human experience. How many vain words, lacking in substance, leaving those who pronounce them uncommitted! How many words that do not stand the test of time, forgotten as soon as spoken or heard! How many deceitful words that hide, distort or contradict truth! How many ineffectual words, how many hurtful or killing words!

God's word is totally other; it reveals and acts; it is truth and effectiveness.[2] The brief text we read today stresses this latter characteristic in the clearest and most precise way by using a particularly evocative image: "For just as from the heavens the rain and snow come down and do not return there till they have watered the earth. . . . So shall my word be that goes forth from my mouth. It shall not return to me void, but shall do my will, achieving the end for which I sent it."

The Bible unceasingly attests to the conviction that God means what he says. This conviction is the foundation of the people's hope in time of trial, in particular the trial of dispersion and exile.[3] It is impossible to doubt the efficacy of God's word, since it has created everything: "God said . . . And so it happened."[4] The wise men, the prophets, the psalmists never tire of reminding us of this: "By the word of the LORD the heavens were made; by the breath of his mouth all their host. . . . For he spoke, and it was made; he commanded, and it stood forth" (Ps 33:6, 9).[5]

Everything else flows from this: God's word creates history. At every instant, it has the power to create anew, to restore life—the power to save.

The seed that falls on good ground
will yield a fruitful harvest.

121

You have visited the land and watered it;
   greatly have you enriched it.
God's watercourses are filled;
   you have prepared the grain.
Thus have you prepared the land: drenching its furrows,
   breaking up its clods,
Softening it with showers,
   blessing its yield.
You have crowned the year with your bounty,
   and your paths overflow with a rich harvest;
The untilled meadows overflow with it,
   and rejoicing clothes the hills.
The fields are garmented with flocks
   and the valleys blanketed with grain.
They shout and sing for joy.
(Ps 65:10, 11, 12-13, 14)

Today's Sufferings, Birth Pangs

Christians are no longer under the sway of the flesh, but under that of the Spirit—through his Spirit, God will give life to our mortal bodies;[6] nonetheless, they know suffering and trials. How shall we reconcile and live this apparent opposition between the "already" and the "not yet"? It is the question Paul addresses now, beginning with a reflection on the "present time," literally the time of the "now" (Rom 8:18-23).

"The sufferings of this present time are as nothing compared with the glory to be revealed for us."[7] This statement may appear rather abstract and may seem to offer scant comfort even to those who know themselves to be "joint heirs with Christ" provided they "suffer with him so that [they] may also be glorified with him" (Rom 8:17). It is impossible to separate death and resurrection, whether in the Christians' pasch or in Christ's pasch.[8] So Paul describes very concretely what is happening in the "present time" with regard not only to believers but to the whole creation. He uses an image that is not simply a way of speaking but one that expresses reality.

The present time is that of giving birth; it is certainly painful, but it is assured of its happy end. After a grueling—sometimes excruciating—moment, an immense joy follows, such as makes one forget the pain that preceded it. "When a woman is in labor, she is in anguish because her hour has arrived; but when she has given birth to a child, she no longer remembers the pain because of her joy that a child has been born into the world" (John 16:21). Such is the present condition of creation. It is pregnant with the glory to come and about to see it come to birth. The pains it is undergoing are a guarantee of this result. The hour of its deliverance is at hand; it longs with all its strength for the moment that will usher in incomparable joy. The face, the radiance of the fruit that creation is carrying, lies hidden, but soon it will be revealed to the eyes of all.

"We know that all creation is groaning in labor pains even until now, and not only that, but we ourselves, who have the firstfruits of the Spirit, we also groan within ourselves as we wait for adoption, the redemption of our bodies."[9] We are quickened by Christian hope, not only by mere human hope. The latter allows one to wait, always with a touch of anxiety, for what one would like to see happen, but without having any guarantee. One speaks of a reasonable hope, of a certain hope, of a weak or a great hope, etc. But Christian hope rests on what one already has, and it guarantees the possession or the manifestation of what has not yet come but cannot fail to come. Christian hope is a word used without qualification. It has the pledge of God and Christ.

> When he comes back in glory,
> we shall know what we are.
> For the Lord will show us
> the Spirit that burns in our human lives.[10]

Jesus' Teaching in Parables

The integral reading of the Discourse in Parables, as it is called, is a good opportunity to further uncover the inexhaustible wealth and the variety of this teaching device that Jesus has renewed and perfected by using it to speak of the deepest and highest realities (Matt 13:1-23).[11]

The literary genre and form of teaching that we call parables are not found exclusively in the New Testament, but the Gospel parables are the best known. Although simple and familiar, these usually crisp and skillfully composed little narratives must not be taken lightly, as though they were pleasant but inconsequential stories. One feels that each is rich in meaning, even if this meaning is not immediately evident, at least not in all its depth. This is because the parables speak of the highest realities of faith, beginning with the mystery of Jesus' own person and of God. Parables unveil some of these realities but in halftone or in a subdued light. It takes time to understand exactly what Jesus means when he teaches in parables. He himself explains this: "Knowledge of the mysteries of the kingdom has been granted to you, but to them it has not been granted. . . . This is why I speak to them in parables, because they look but do not see, and hear but do not listen or understand.'' In order to understand parables, hearers must be attentive and open to the things of God.

Besides—and this is not their least original trait—parables are aimed at hearers who accept confrontation and questioning. Often, the story leads hearers to bare the depths of their hearts, to manifest how they spontaneously respond to the situation described in the story. They then become aware that by following their bent, they think, act, and react in a manner contrary to God. Finally, ''parables direct the listeners to their life experience and derive their efficacy from that experience which we must own. . . . But to understand them, we must allow ourselves to go through the personal experience of Jesus, to which they direct us . . . and endeavor to comprehend the manner in which Jesus spoke of himself . . . to see reality as Jesus saw it.''[12]

''A Sower Went Out to Sow''

Apparently the parable of the sower is very simple and does not raise any problem of interpretation. What it describes is commonplace; those who have seen people sow when the wind blows don't give too much thought to the soil on which the seed falls, trusting that a good proportion of the seed will fall on favorable ground.

And here is what is admirable. On this mixed soil, close to a path where the birds come to eat everything, on this field of stony outcroppings, where briers grow, one sees, a few months after the sowing, ears of wheat that have grown vigorously as soon as the seed found a little dirt. Really, the sower was right to sow liberally, without worrying much about the ground. The extraordinary potency of the seed has succeeded in producing fruit with an unusual yield—up to a hundredfold.

Jesus is this confident sower who has thrown his word, a seed of high quality, to the four winds. When we see the ''large crowds'' gathering around him, how can we help but be struck by the success of his generous sowing? But in this parable that underscores the fecundity of the seed, Jesus does not hide the fact that part of it is lost. We cannot avoid asking the question ''Why don't all receive the word so that it may bear fruit in them?'' The question was asked during Jesus' ministry, and even more afterwards, when his passion and death had swept everything away. Then, a handful of his apostles had to sow anew and without knowing the success of Jesus that had, at times, exhilarated them. Why? The question is not a theoretical one. It is a source of anguish for the indefatigable sowers, for the whole Church. The explanation given to the disciples is an answer, and the evangelical tradition has not forgotten it.[13]

"Hear, then, the parable of the sower"

In the parable of the sower, what is in question is the word of the kingdom. It is lavishly sown because the Lord wants to address all without discrimination. "Jesus said this to show that he was addressing everybody. The sower does not make distinctions between different soils; he simply throws the seed. Similarly, Jesus does not distinguish between rich and poor, learned and unschooled, careless and fervent, courageous and timid. His word concerns everybody. He does all he can, although he perfectly knows the future, so that he may say, 'What more was there for me to do?' (Isa 5:4)."[14] The explanation is clear: the word can develop its potentialities only if it falls on favorable ground. After the word has been heard, it must descend into the heart. Unable to take root or choked by the cares of the world and the inducements of riches, even though first received with joy, the word does not bear fruit.

Without reading more into the parable than what it does say, we shall keep in mind that it places the emphasis on the listeners' responsibility. The parable warns us against being "the person of one moment." What proves difficult is to keep on, to remain the man or the woman of all hours, all seasons, of an entire lifetime.

> I hardened myself like a rock;
> I became like the path;
> the thorns of the world have choked me
> and have made my soul unfruitful.
>
> But, O Lord, Sower of good,
> Make the seedling of the Word grow in me
> so I may yield fruit in one of these three:
> Hundredfold, sixtyfold, or even thirtyfold.[15]

A Time of Long Patience and Labor

Both creating history and playing a leading part in it, the word attests to God's obstinate faithfulness, long patience, and assiduous labor for the unfolding of salvation offered to all humankind. This word comes from God, who created human beings free, and who made with them a covenant of love. Efficacious, indescribably fecund, this word demands from human beings a willing response made of openness, conversion, and ever-renewed trust in him who speaks it. And this, in spite of appearances of failure, of trials besetting missionaries and all other believers, tempting them to lose trust and become discouraged.

In fact, everyone sees opposition, indifference, defections, etc., in the very places where the word should manifest its effectiveness. Jesus himself knew this fact, the disciples around him must have confronted it too; it remains the great test of believers and of the Church through all time when they hear it said, with sadness or irony, "Where is your God?" (Ps 42:11) We must then reread, study, and ponder the parable of the seed and the sower.

Yes, it is true, part of the seed is lost because the sower throws it by the handful to the four winds so that every nook and cranny may receive its share. And it is a fact that, thanks to the generous manner in which the seed is sown, we see the extraordinary fecundity of a single seed encountering a bit of good soil; it gives fruit "a hundred or sixty or thirtyfold."

Are these different yields due to chance or luck? Absolutely not, for it is in the human heart that the word is sown. Stones and thorns allude to the hardness of heart and the cares of the world that encumber it. If the seed remains on the surface, abandoned to the appetite of the birds of the sky, it is because we do not let it enter our beings. Therefore, if the word is not fruitful, it is due to the listeners' poor dispositions.

This urgent appeal to each one's responsibility must be welcomed with immense hope. Our time of long patience and assiduous labor, of sufferings also, is the time of "labor pains even until now"; they will soon end in the joyful hour of deliverance. Then what was hidden will come to light, and "the glorious freedom of the children of God" will be revealed, with that of Christ, who escaped from the shadow of the grave and will appear in the clouds in radiant splendor.

> The sower goes out
> to sow the good news.
> May the seed fall into deep soil!
> May the Spirit come!
> The word does not return
> without having borne its fruit.
>
> *Open our hearts to your call, Lord,*
> *open them to your promise!*
>
> When evil assails us
> and when the wind of doubt blows,

When hope falters
and our courage crumbles away,

When other joys fascinate us
and scatter our love.[16]

God Believes in Human Beings

God Judges with Indulgence and Governs with Restraint

Believers recognize and confess God's supreme power, which nothing or nobody can hold in check. They know that the Lord sees everything happening in the world, that no human action escapes him, that he sees the very secrets of the heart. They doubt neither God's justice nor his sovereign power. But when they consider what is happening, when they meditate on history—yesterday's and today's—these same believers cannot fail to ask: How is it possible that God intervenes so little to put order in the world? Why are so many crimes either unpunished or treated with so much leniency? Why, in sum, is there this sort of permissive attitude on God's part, as if he did not have the means to punish evil and check its spread? In other words, why this restraint on God's part? These are questions that the author of the Book of Wisdom already confronted. The text read today states the conclusions to which its author arrived after long reflection (Wis 12:13, 16-19).

Taken out of context, this conclusion proves to be particularly fruitful and stimulating for us and for all others who ponder similar questions.[1] He brings his contribution to the understanding of God's mystery and draws a lesson concerning the manner in which, in their turn, humans must behave. "There is [not] any god besides you who have the care of all, that you need show you have not unjustly condemned." No one can doubt this; all reflection must be based on indisputable certainties. On the other hand, we cannot demand that God give an account of himself; we cannot arraign God and address reproaches to him for his conduct (Wis 12:12). Should we then give up trying to understand? Absolutely not. Paradoxically, the answer to our questions lies in the fact that God is almighty and acts justly. Indeed, he can act with justice precisely because he is strong; he can show patience, indulgence, and moderation precisely because he has dominion over everything. In order to understand this, it is enough to observe human behavior. When human beings act brutally, they do so because they know that they are weak and unsure. They do not really have authority since they can assert themselves only by force. They oppress others when their weakness is detected or when they want to hide their frailty.

They must, as is said, make an example; and not being able to do this otherwise, they use terror to assert themselves. It is so true that people of that ilk bury themselves in their fortresses. For them, there exists no other argument, no other justice than brutal force; to show indulgence, consideration, would reveal their nakedness. God's justice and his patience manifest his supreme power and his universal dominion, these latter two being the origin of the former.[2] His example teaches that "the just must be human." The patience of God, holy and strong, imbues the believers with a "beautiful hope." Are they not themselves sinners who are helped by the divine mercy? So it is with a total trust that the Christian assembly prays to God, by calling upon the power of his mercy.

> LORD, you are good and forgiving.
>
> You, O LORD, are good and forgiving,
>   abounding in kindness to all who call upon you.
> Hearken, O LORD, to my prayer
>   and attend to the sound of my pleading.
> All the nations you have made shall come
>   and worship you, O Lord, and glorify your name.
> For you are great, and you do wondrous deeds;
>   you alone are God.
>
> You, O LORD, are a God merciful and gracious,
>   slow to anger, abounding in kindness and fidelity.
> Turn toward me, and have pity on me;
>   give your strength to your servant.
> (Ps 86:5-6, 9-10, 15-16)

The Inexpressible Cries of the Holy Spirit

With the whole creation, we groan in labor pains, expecting the promised glory; these pains are like those of a woman in labor.[3] Paul goes even further: "The Spirit itself intercedes with inexpressible groanings" (Rom 8:26).

"We do not know how to pray as we ought," because our prayer, albeit fervent, remains an impulse toward God, whom we cannot reach. At this point, the Spirit comes to our aid. It does not replace us, but it takes our prayer, translates it into inexpressible groanings that are not part of human language and directs it effectively towards God. By thus intervening, the Spirit fulfills with us the role allotted to it by the Father; it is the Paraclete—the Counselor—whom the Son has sent us.

Paul teaches us how to remedy what we lack through ignorance. To bring us healing, "the Spirit itself intercedes with inexpressible groanings. And the one who searches hearts knows what is the intention of the Spirit, because it intercedes for the holy ones according to God's will" (Rom 8:26-27). The Spirit, who, in the holy ones' hearts cries, "Abba, Father," knows perfectly well that the groanings of those who have sinned are, during this brief life, rather an added burden than a relief; so it intercedes with God with inexpressible groanings and, in its tenderness and benevolence, it takes upon itself our own groanings.

Its wisdom sees our souls dragged in the dust, prisoners of lowly bodies. The Spirit intercedes for us with God, not with groanings like our own but with "ineffable" groanings, "which no one may utter" (2 Cor 12:4).

Not satisfied with interceding with God, the Spirit increases its entreaties and its plea becomes more urgent. It leads to victory those who can say with Paul, "In all these things we conquer overwhelmingly" (Rom 8:37). It is probable that the Spirit intercedes for those who are content with conquering, without compromising their victory either by any defeat or by any further risks.

Corresponding to the text concerning the object of prayer, "We do not know how to pray as we ought, but the Spirit itself intercedes with inexpressible groanings," is another text, "I will pray with the spirit, but I will also sing praise with the mind" (1 Cor 14:15). Our intelligence can pray only if it is preceded by the Spirit and if it echoes the Spirit's prayer. Our intelligence can sing with measure, harmony, rhythm, and melody to the Father through Jesus Christ, only if the Spirit, who "fathoms even the depths of God," first praises and celebrates him whose depths it has fathomed and encompassed according to its power.[4]

Good Grain and Weeds in the Same Field

Today's Gospel records not one but three parables joined by Matthew himself, since they are followed by a single explanation. This explanation directly concerns only the first parable, the weeds among the wheat. But, placed at the end by the evangelist, this explanation concerns in some way the other two parables, the little mustard seed that grows into a large bush and the yeast that leavens the whole batch of dough (Matt 13:24-43).

Like last Sunday's parable, this one shows a man who has sown good grain in his field. Another person, his enemy, has followed him. "While everyone was asleep," he has sown weeds all through the wheat.[5] As the season progresses, the damage becomes apparent; there are among the wheat, growing along with it, these noxious weeds. But what we have here is a parable of the kingdom of heaven, in which Matthew certainly also sees a parable of the Church, that of his time and that of all times. It is obvious that there are bad and good people, including pretentious leaders.[6] To separate rightly the ones from the others is an impossible task for those who can judge only according to appearances. God alone, who sees what is in the human heart (Acts 15:8), has that power. He alone can, at every moment, remove the weeds without at the same time uprooting the least stem of wheat. But the parable contains another teaching.

"Let them grow together until harvest." God does not hurry to sort the weeds from the wheat; he will do that at harvest time. Until then, it is the time of growth and hope. God has, if we may say so, a longer experience than his servants. He knows that in the field of the kingdom, vigorous weeds may disappear before reaching maturity, that some wheat seeds germinate later than others, that certain wheat plants develop their ears just before harvest. But he also knows that wheat plants which have rapidly sprouted may dry out, that others, never growing beyond the stem stage, will not succeed in forming ears, and that some of the ears in ripe wheat grains are poor. The parable of the seed and the different places where it falls[7] has reminded us that all of this is not the result of unpredictable weather. We can blame neither the quality of the seed, uniformly perfect, nor some mistake on the sower's part; his enemy, not he, has scattered weeds in the field. Responsibility lies in the human heart that welcomes weeds, that allows the seed to fructify or prevents it from doing so.

God's patience and delay taught by this parable arise from his perspicacity, from his mercy that never loses hope, and finally from the fact that, until the harvest, he gives to each the grace that can work miracles.[8]

A Tiny Seed That Grows into a Tree
The evangelist places side by side the parable of the wheat and the weeds and another parable that, in a picturesque way, stresses the potency of the gospel seed; tiny—hardly the size of a pinhead—it develops into a small tree.

We have here an appeal for faith and hope. The kingdom of heaven has begun in a very small way; Jesus sowed the word by preaching for three years, in a tongue regarded as barbaric, to humble people in a restricted geographical area of no value in the vast Roman empire.[9] Nonetheless, from this minuscule seed a large bush develops, modest no doubt, but where "the birds of the sky come and dwell in its branches."

This last remark is not just a way of emphasizing the size of the large bush. The symbolism of the tree in which the birds nest evokes the ultimate and great eschatological gathering of all the peoples into the kingdom.[10] The large bush of the parable is large not only in size, without common measure with "the smallest of all the seeds" from which it came. What is stressed is the infinite disproportion between the insignificance of the beginning of the kingdom and the unimaginable greatness of the completed kingdom. We shall understand this point better if we do not linger on the intermediate period, when a frail sprout germinates, then imperceptibly grows until it reaches full maturity. The parable invites us to consider first the tiny seed, then the final stage at the end of its development.[11] We could say that here faith and hope coalesce, because we are invited to look at the seed and its final development in a single glance. When one of these tiny seeds is sown, the kingdom of the last times is already present. Between the moment when the seed falls into the earth and the moment when the birds can take refuge in the branches of the tree, there is certainly a delay. But one hardly notices it, because of the dramatic contrast between the smallness of the seed just sown and the size of the small tree that can soon be admired in the field.

A lesson for all disciples can be drawn from this pondering, through faith, on the assured growth of the kingdom from such a modest beginning. This teaching could be thus worded: "Do not neglect any opportunity to sow, in the field where you are, even a single one of these tiny seeds. What you should look at is not the smallness of the seed but the bush which you cannot doubt will grow from it."

A Pinch of Yeast; the Whole Dough Rises

The third parable conveys the same teaching as the first two, through a comparison taken from daily experience. But it contains an emphasis and two significant features. Again we have a contrast: a woman puts a little yeast in three large measures of flour, and the whole batch rises. The emphasis is placed on the rapidity with which the effect is produced. The first new feature is that the yeast mixed with the flour is not at all separate from the dough it raises. This is a trait commonly set forth; Christians are "the yeast in the dough."

The second significant feature is precisely this: what raises the dough is a little dough that one has left out to ferment. But in this parable, the yeast designates the leaven of the kingdom—again the word, the gospel—and not the disciples. It is their responsibility to mix with the dough this good yeast that they themselves are not. For there is some bad yeast, which we must guard against (Matt 16:6, 22)[12] or even clear out (1 Cor

5:7). This bad yeast is an agent of corruption. This last parable is related to the first one, that of the wheat and the weeds. It is not surprising to find its explanation last of all.

"Explain to Us the Parable of the Weeds in the Field"

Jesus speaks in parables to the crowd in order that all may have the opportunity to understand that his teaching is a key to "things hidden from the beginning." To gain access to this revelation, we must go beyond this imperfect intuition; we must recognize in Jesus the one who personally and uniquely knows the secrets of the Father. "Explain to us the parable of the weeds in the field," is an act of faith and not just an expression of curiosity.

"He who sows good seed is the Son of Man." When one has "ears that hear" (Matt 13:16),[13] one has already understood this. "The field is the world"; this widening of perspective would not have occurred to us at first. We must avoid understanding the parable in too narrow a sense, as if it concerned only the Church. No, the Church is not an enclosed yard where the Son of Man concentrates his activity. He sows the good seed everywhere in the world, in the middle of which is the Church. Everywhere, there are "children of the kingdom," since the good seed designates them. But everywhere, too—and therefore also in the Church—there are weeds, that is, "children of the evil one." Finally, everywhere the devil—the enemy—is at work during the night. We do not have here just an allusion to the underhanded character of his pernicious action. In the Bible, the night designates the present time, in which the seed sprouts and grows (Mark 4:26-28).[14] On the day of the harvest, that is, of the judgment,[15] "at the end of the age," when he will come back to collect the fruit of his sowing, the Son of Man will separate the wheat from the weeds, which will be thrown into the fiery furnace.

In the explanation of the parable, Jesus says that the weeds designate "all who cause others to sin and all evildoers." These will be rejected for having behaved without bothering with any law, in contradistinction to the just ones.[16] But those "who cause others to sin," who are they, if not those through whom scandal happens and whom Jesus has so vigorously denounced (Matt 18:6-9)? The Son of Man has received "all power in heaven and on earth" (Matt 28:18); he will judge all nations (Matt 25:32). What is said here concerns not only the Church. But Matthew did write for Christians; they, too, will be judged. Woe to those who will have lived in contradiction with the gospel, to those who will have caused the fall of their brothers and sisters inside or outside the community. Let all always have in mind the prospect of judgment! [17]But let them at the same time bear in mind the glory with which "the just will shine as the sun in the Father's kingdom."

This explanation of the parable of the weeds in the field also throws light on the parables of the mustard seed and of the yeast in the dough. These last two in their turn shed light upon the first. In the world today, the kingdom is like a seed sown in the earth, a pinch of yeast buried in the dough. This sowing and this leavening will not fail to produce effects well nigh miraculous, if we consider the disproportion between the smallness of what has been sown or mixed and the magnitude of the result. But we cannot conclude from these comparisons that it is enough for us to passively wait to see what is going to happen. For the parables use images that need to be correctly understood. We have our share of responsibility in what comes to pass. Good seed gives wheat; but the enemy sows weeds in the field already sown. The bush that we are must be willing to grow and blossom. The dough, as bakers know, does not always rise well despite the quality of the yeast. Small quantities of flour untouched by the yeast are still visible. The Son of Man will judge these results some day and will call each one of us to account. In the meantime, our patient God refrains from intervening in an untimely manner and does not anticipate the time of judgment.

"Whoever Has Ears Ought to Hear"
We cannot afford to listen distractedly to this Sunday's three readings, because they carry too important a teaching. They reveal what is in God's heart and the deep reason for his apparent inaction. Our conception of justice is sometimes offended: "Does God not see what is happening?" We do not dare go so far as to say, "Is he not weak, if not even conniving with evil?" We must keep these words from passing our lips. In any case, we do not see how we could imitate God's attitude. However. . . .

> If we ask that the criminal go unpunished, it is not because crime pleases us, but because, considering the person, we detest in him the crime or the vice. The more vice displeases us, the more we desire that the guilty one may not die before mending his ways. It is easy—and it is even a natural tendency—to hate evil persons because they are evil. But it is good—although rare—to love them because they are human, so that we at once blame the sin and show compassion for human nature in the same person. Without any doubt, many, to their loss, take advantage of this divine indulgence

and kindness. . . . Because the evildoers persevere in their misdeeds, will God not persevere in his patience?[18]

To speak in this manner is possible only if the Spirit comes to the aid of our weakness, makes us pray as we ought, makes us will what God wills.

Following the sower's steps,
another came stealthily, at night,
to scatter weeds.
Master of the field,
you take the risk of being patient:
seeds of life and seeds of death
will grow together.

On the last day
the just will be resplendent in the light.

The day of the Lord will come,
do not judge before the time.

Do not despise God's patience:
His kindness calls you to repentance.

When God's judgment is revealed,
He will render to all according to their works.[19]

Seventeenth Sunday

Acquiring the Only Worthwhile Treasure

Ask the Lord for the Gift of Wisdom

On this Sunday, the Liturgy of the Word begins with the prayer that Solomon addressed to the Lord, who was saying to him, "Ask something of me and I will give it to you" (1 Kgs 3:5, 7:12).

The Bible presents Solomon as the ideal king according to the heart of God. Jesus himself recalled his glory when speaking of the splendor of the lilies of the field (Matt 6:29). He also recalled what made this king's extraordinary reputation: "The queen of the south . . . came from the ends of the earth to hear the wisdom of Solomon; and there is something greater than Solomon here" (Matt 12:42).[1]

Whatever truth there may be to the proverbial wisdom of Solomon, it is worth rereading and pondering the prayer recorded in the First Book of Kings. It contains precious teachings that are perfectly appropriate to this Sunday, the very reason why the liturgy chose it.[2]

What are we to ask God to help us discharge the vocation he has given us, the task incumbent on us? More concretely, what would we ask, here and now, if he were to say to us, "Make your desires, your wishes known to me; I shall grant them."[3] Perhaps we would be at a loss. Solomon did not hesitate. "Give your servant . . . an understanding heart to judge your people and to distinguish right from wrong."

"An attentive heart," "an intelligent and wise heart" is acquired through meditation of the Lord's law that leads us to judge and act with security and assurance, according to the truth God reveals. Psalm 119 profusely celebrates this: "Happy are they . . . who walk in the law of the Lord." "Your decrees . . . are my counselors." "I will run the way of your commands when you give me a docile heart." "I will walk at liberty." "Through your precepts I gain discernment." "You despise all who stray from your statutes . . . ."[4] We have here as many expressions of faith in God, whose light can only illumine human judgment and direct human steps on the road of truth and life.

136

"To distinguish right from wrong" is a divine prerogative that no one can usurp without sin.[5] Solomon knows this; he humbly asks to share in the divine wisdom, precisely because he is aware of his weakness. Such consciousness pleases God, who grants his request.[6] One day, Jesus will give thanks to the Father, who gives wisdom to the little ones, "I give praise to you, Father, Lord of heaven and earth, for although you have hidden things from the wise and the learned you have revealed them to the children" (Matt 11:25), who are attached to the Lord's law.

Lord, I love your commands.

I have said, O Lord, that my part
   is to keep your words.
The law of your mouth is to me more precious
   than thousands of gold and silver pieces.
Let your kindness comfort me
   according to your promise to your servants.
Let your compassion come to me that I may live,
   for your law is my delight.

For I love your command
   more than gold, however fine.
For in all your precepts I go forward;
   every false way I hate.

Wonderful are your decrees;
   therefore I observe them.
The revelation of your words sheds light,
   giving understanding to the simple.
(Ps 119:57, 72, 76-77, 127-128, 129-130)

All Things Work for Good for Those Who Love God

The present time, the time of waiting and groaning,[7] is also the time of hope assured of reaching its goal. "We know," Paul writes (Rom 8:28-30).

Such a certitude is founded on the fact that God's plan for the world is "a design of his love," the steps of which are connected and call for one another: "For those he foreknew he also predestined to be conformed to the image of his Son, so that he might be the firstborn among many brothers. And those he predestined he also called; and those he called he also justified; and those he justified he also glorified." What an epitome and what a thrust in this passage, the vibrant crescendo of which ends with the proclamation of the glory that God gives to those whom "he foreknew." But, having read this hymn, we must return to some expressions to understand their whole meaning.

At the center of this process of salvation and glorification is the Son, "Light from Light, true God from true God,"[8] "image of God" (2 Cor 4:4), "image of the invisible God" (Col 1:15). We are reminded of what God said on the sixth day of creation, "Let us make man in our image, after our likeness" (Gen 1:26). When rereading this word by the light of their faith in Christ, certain Fathers of the Church have commented that God created humans "in the image of his image," thus seeing in the act of creation a still-veiled announcement of what God would do through his Christ in due time.

If the term "image" should appear weak—contrary to its biblical meaning—it should suffice to relate it to what, in Paul's text, makes it explicitly realistic. Conformity to Christ,[9] whose image we are, makes believers into brothers and sisters of the "eldest Son," "the firstborn of all creation" (Col 1:15). It raises them to the rank of sons and daughters in the Son.[10] The rest, especially glory, is a necessary, unfailing consequence of such conformity. Nonetheless, it is a cause of inexpressible wonder on our part.

> Thou art not only His creature (though for the very sparrows He has a care, and pitied the "much cattle" of Nineveh), thou art man redeemed and sanctified, His adopted son, favoured with a portion of that glory and blessedness which flows from Him everlastingly unto the Only-begotten. Thou art chosen to be His, even above thy fellows who dwell in the East and South. Thou wast one of those for whom Christ offered up His last prayer, and sealed it with His precious blood. What a thought is this, a thought almost too great for our faith! Scarce can we refrain from acting Sarah's part when we bring it before us, so as to "laugh" from amazement and perplexity. What is man, what are we, what am I, that the Son of God should be so mindful of me? What am I, that He should have raised me from almost a devil's nature to that of an Angel's? that He should have changed my soul's original constitution, new-made me, who from my youth up have been a transgressor, and should Himself dwell personally in this very heart of mine, making me His temple? What am I, that God the Holy Ghost should enter into me, and draw up my thoughts heavenward "with plaints unutterable?"[11]

Therefore, "we know that all things work for good for those who love God." It is what God has done for his Son in whom we love the Father. "All things," even trials and tribulations (Rom 8:18-23, 35-39).

When One Has Found the Treasure Beyond Price

Jesus has successively compared the kingdom of heaven to a sower gone out to sow,[12] to a field sown in wheat into which an enemy has scattered weeds, to a mustard seed, and yeast kneaded into three measures of flour.[13] Today, we hear another three parables and the conclusion of this long discourse (Matt 13:43-52).

First, there are two very short parables, or rather a twofold parable.[14] The first one presents a man who happens to find a treasure hidden in a field. In the second, we see a merchant who, in search of precious pearls, finally discovers an invaluable one. Both hasten to sell all their possessions in order to buy the field or acquire the rare pearl.[15] The lesson is clear: the kingdom of heaven is a treasure beyond price; we must renounce all we possess in order to acquire it.

The Net Filled with Good and Bad Fish

The seventh and last parable of Jesus' discourse comes back, in another guise and with new nuances of meaning, to the second one—the field in which wheat and weeds have grown together.[16]

In the crowds Jesus drew, there were all kinds of people. Nobody could exactly say what their motivations and intentions were or distinguish the good from the bad. It is true that Jesus could have sorted them out, and certain people thought that the Messiah, upon coming, would set the good people apart and condemn the others. Even John the Baptist seemed to have found it difficult to accept that Jesus was not making such a judgment.[17] He has thus described the one more powerful than he who was coming after him: "His winnowing fan is in his hand. He will clear his threshing floor and gather his wheat into his barn, but the chaff he will burn with unquenchable fire" (Matt 3:12).[18] Yes, the judgment will come in due course and the Son of Man will execute it. But Jesus does not forestall that day known only to the Father (Matt 24:36); he vigorously chided James and John, who wanted to have the inhospitable inhabitants of a Samaritan village chastised on the spot (Luke 51:56).

The Church and Christians must remember this. The present is fishing time. The net "collects fish of every kind." The sorting out will take place on the shore—then only. This delay is an opportunity for each of us.

> You dragged me onto the seashore
> with those gathered in the net;
> but at the time you chose the good,
> I was rejected with the bad.

> This is why in the same deep water
> I again went down into the foul mire;
> there the abysses that offer no exit
> have encompassed the powers of my soul.

But you can do everything—
ring me back again to the surface,
and deign to gather me with the elect
into the good and holy vessel.[19]

The Inexhaustible Reserves of the Scribe Turned Disciple

"Do you understand these things?" Do you understand what the parables of the kingdom mean? This question put by Jesus to the disciples around him when he told and explained his parables is today addressed to us. Would we dare to answer yes with the same assurance that the Lord's first hearers had? But, actually, what sort of understanding is meant here? How are we to acquire it?

The seven parables that the liturgy has chosen for us have for their unique subject the mystery of the kingdom of heaven: its revelation, its unfolding, the role reserved for us, the demands we must submit to in order to be admitted into it, its fulfillment at the end of time. To "understand all these things" is not a question of human intelligence—that of the sages and the smart ones—but of spiritual intelligence—that of the humble and the lowly, to whom God gives to understand "the mystery hidden from ages past" (Eph 3:9) and to act accordingly.

We can understand the parables and put their teaching into practice only in the light of the Spirit, in prayer and meditation; they teach us a way. Listen as they may, the crowds do not understand (Matt 13:14).[20] The disciples draw near to Jesus in order to receive from him the explanation of the parables. Only by being familiar with the one who pronounced the parables can we probe their meaning and, having become his disciples, be "like the head of a household who brings from his storeroom both the new and the old."

"A scribe" is a learned person and a sage, who has understood Jesus' teaching and shares the treasure discovered, the inexhaustible store. Scribes bring forth "both new and old" for the service of others. "The old" means what has been received from tradition and carefully preserved but at the same time perceived as ever new. "Scribe" disciples take after Matthew, who collected the teaching of the Scriptures and of Jesus and showed its timeliness for the Christian community of his time. The gospel is not a sealed collection of Jesus' words, acts, and judgments, the untouchable memory of which is transmitted. It is the good news announced today. Certainly this preaching must scrupulously respect the authenticity of Jesus' message, without changing any letter, "the smallest part of a letter" (Matt 5:18). But such preaching is not a material repetition; it must read and announce the message in the "todayness" of the kingdom.[21] We learn to profit, with wisdom, from all that befalls us, which God himself causes to contribute to the good of those he loves.

> Pearl of great price,
> wisdom,
> precious treasure,
> the kingdom!
> Happy are those who discover them
> and in their joy sell all their goods,
> Their hearts are free to love.
>
> *To those who look for the kingdom,*
> *everything will be given.*
>
> Seek and you will find;
> ask and it will be given you.
>
> Where your treasure is,
> there too is your heart.
>
> Share with the poor,
> You will have treasure in heaven.[22]

The Discourse in Parables in the Gospel of Matthew is inexhaustibly rich. Jesus' teaching, given in a simple and familiar form, proves to be accessible to all, particularly to the little ones and the simple, close to the daily realities they experience. Far from being surprised that the Lord should use these realities to teach the mysteries of the kingdom, they marvel, "Here is language we understand!"

For its part, the Letter of Paul to the Romans stimulates the zeal and enthusiasm of believers by reminding them that God's plan of salvation, which is definitely in progress, leads to the glory that is their destiny.

The sequence constituted by the Fifteenth, Sixteenth, and Seventeenth Sundays is really a particularly remarkable stage in the itinerary along which the Sunday liturgies take us during Ordinary Time in Year A.

From the Eighteenth to the Twentieth Sunday in Ordinary Time

"When Jesus finished these parables, he went away from there" (Matt 13:53). This formula indicates that we are coming to a new part in the Gospel of Matthew. The preceding one was centered on the mystery of the kingdom of heaven. This one is concerned with the community of the disciples—the Church—which will be built after the Lord's resurrection. In this ensemble, we can again distinguish a discourse of Jesus (Matt 18) that is preceded by a narrative section (Matt 13:54–17:27). The Sunday Lectionary has taken five excerpts from this section and grouped them in two sequences. The first is composed of the Eighteenth, Nineteenth, and Twentieth Sundays. In the Gospel readings for these days, the central topic is faith in Jesus, who multiplies the loaves (Matt 14:13-21), who comes to the aid of his own when their boat is tossed about by the storm (Matt 14:22-33), who answers a foreigner's prayer (Matt 15:21-28).

A People Gathered and Nourished by God's Love

Come to Me and Listen: You Will Be Satisfied

We always marvel at reading biblical texts that seem to have been written for us because they address our deepest longings and anxieties. This is the case with today's first reading, an excerpt from the conclusion of the "Book of Consolation" (Isa 55:1-3).[1]

Like all prophetic oracles, this one was written for a people who were in a situation that is no longer ours.[2] However, sometimes to our great surprise, these oracles are most timely.[3] The promise of an abundance of "good things" is a consolation when one is hungry for food and thirsty for water. But to be well supplied with material goods does not—quite the contrary—prevent one from suffering a thirst and a hunger for other "good things" that are cruelly lacking: inner peace, real reasons for living, hope, love. These are examples of heartrending wants in a society and a time of material abundance. So the prophetic oracle finds in us a painful echo when it says, "Why spend your money for what is not bread; your wages for what fails to satisfy?"

At the same time, it invites us to turn to him who alone can fulfill our deepest desires, "Come to me heedfully, listen that you may have life." We are seeking reasons for living; it is life that is offered to us, an eternal covenant that will confirm the benevolence, the love of God who is compassionate toward those he chose.

> The hand of the LORD feeds us;
> he answers all our needs.
>
> The LORD is gracious and merciful,
>   slow to anger and of great kindness.
> The LORD is good to all
>   and compassionate toward all his works.
> The eyes of all look hopefully to you,
>   and you give them their food in due season;
> You open your hand
>   and satisfy the desire of every living thing.

143

The LORD is just in all his ways
  and holy in all his works.
The LORD is near to all who call upon him,
  to all who call upon him in truth.
(Ps 145:8-9, 15-16, 17-18)

Who Will Separate Us from the Love of Christ?

In his letters, Paul often punctuates or concludes his expositions on the Christian faith and dogma with songs of thanksgiving, prayers springing from his believing heart.[4] Such upwellings of a lyricism that cannot contain itself manifest how inspiring faith is for the Apostle. It has nothing of a mere, cold, inner conviction. At the same time, these hymns allow us to understand the true nature of the often arduous doctrinal developments found in Paul's writings.[5] In order not to let ourselves be "tossed by waves and swept along by every wind of teaching arising from human trickery . . ."[6] Christians must be aware of the ins and outs of their faith—indispensable to the Church—that are by no means cold, intellectual speculations with which one can entertain one's self. The conclusion of the chapters that the Letter to the Romans devotes to salvation doctrine admirably expresses this (Rom 8:35, 37-39).

"For Christ, while we were still helpless, yet died at the appointed time for the ungodly."[7] We are therefore assured that we "have now received reconciliation" by the life of the risen Christ (Rom 5:6, 11). If, at baptism, "we have died with Christ, we believe that we shall also live with him" (Rom 6:8).[8] "The Spirit of God dwells in [us]" (Rom 8:9).[9] We are living in the painful expectation of our adoption and the redemption of our bodies. The Spirit utters "inexpressible groanings," revealing our hope for the full manifestation of our condition as children of God (Rom 8:26, 23).[10] When we encounter trials, we know that "all things work for good for those who love God" (Rom 8:28).[11] Having recalled all these truths, Paul can no longer contain himself; he sings his assurance based on the love that God bears for us in his Son. Nothing will be able to separate us from the love of Christ. He takes a kind of pleasure in enumerating obstacles of all kinds that can confront us: "anguish, or distress, or persecution, or famine, or nakedness, or peril, or the sword"; "neither death, nor life, nor angels, nor principalities, nor present things, nor future things, nor powers, nor height, nor depth, nor any other creature." "In all these things we conquer overwhelmingly[12] through him who loved us."

"The bird on the branch, the lily in the fields, the hart in the forest, the fish in the sea, the innumerable crowds of joyous human beings proclaim with cheerfulness: God is love! But beneath and, as it were, supporting all these voices, as the booming bass under the light sopranos, one hears, *de profundis*, the voice of those who have been sacrificed: God is love!"[13]

In the enumeration of the possible obstacles to our salvation, we might be surprised to find angels and principalities along with height, depth, and other creatures, unspecified and mysterious. In the pagan world and in certain Jewish circles of the time, angelic or demonic, astrological or cosmic powers were believed to influence the destiny of the universe and humanity. Are these beliefs of another age absent from modern societies and Christian communities? Whatever our opinion on the eventual influence of cosmic or other forces on human destiny, Paul tells us that God has despoiled "the principalities and the powers"; "he made a public spectacle of them, leading them away in triumph" by the cross (Col 2:15).[14] We cannot doubt that nothing "will separate us from the love of Christ" because "stern as death is love . . . its flames are a blazing fire. Deep waters cannot quench love, nor floods sweep it away" (Cant 8:6-7).

A Vast Crowd in a Deserted Place

The apostolic tradition has attached a great importance to the sign of the bread multiplied by Jesus to feed the hungry crowds: the Gospels record six accounts of this miracle.[15] The first of Matthew's two narratives occupies a significant place in his Gospel (Matt 14:13-21).

The reader's attention is focused on the tired crowds and on Jesus' attitude toward them. The crowds "followed him on foot from their towns" when they heard that Jesus had withdrawn "in a boat to a deserted place by himself." They made a long detour to catch up with him. One gets the impression that a new people is gathering, taking the place of preceding audiences who did not take Jesus' preaching to heart. "When he disembarked," he sees all these people waiting for him. "His heart was moved with pity for them, and he cured their sick."[16]

The disciples, too, find themselves in great distress, shown by their dialogue with Jesus. "When it was evening," there was an evident need to send away all these folks. Let them "go to the villages and buy food for themselves." There is nothing else to do. As if the disciples were not yet conscious enough of their poverty, Jesus tells them, "There is no need for them to go away; give them some food yourselves.'' The inventory of their supplies is quickly done; maybe the approaching end of the day had led them to wonder what there was for their own use. A pitiful amount, five loaves and two fish—they are in no better position than the people themselves. But by having them recognize their radical helplessness—for they know well that they themselves cannot give food to the crowds—does not Jesus want to lead his disciples—those of yesterday and those of today—to turn to him, understanding that he is able to feed many peoples and that "moved with pity" he does it? It is as though he were saying: "You have only five loaves and two fish. This is nothing indeed to feed the crowd that is following me. But it is much more than needed if, in faith, you turn to me. For, with me, you will see the bread multiply in your hands. Remember, by obeying the Lord's order, Moses fed a whole people in the desert (Exod 16); Elisha nourished one hundred men with twenty barley loaves (2 Kgs 4:42-44); and God said, 'Come to me and you will live' (Isa 55:3)."

In all of this part of Matthew's Gospel (Matt 14:1–18:35), we see Jesus endeavoring to form his disciples' faith in prevision of their role in the ecclesial community. There is no doubt that the evangelist recorded Jesus' acts and words, basing himself on his experience of the life of the Church in his time. We must therefore, today, read and understand them in this same perspective in order to seek and find in them a light for our life in the believers' community. What Jesus said and did is for the benefit of our faith.

> In my opinion at least, the Lord uses these loaves to fortify the disciples' faith, which was still weak. For the same reason he raises his eyes to heaven. The disciples had already seen many other miracles, but not yet this one. Taking the loaves, the Lord broke them and entrusted to the disciples the honor of distributing them: he wanted not only to honor them, but also to convince them of the truth of the miracle, so that they might not forget it afterwards, since their very hands would be its witnesses. As to the crowd, Jesus first lets them feel hunger; he wants the disciples to come to him and ask questions. He uses them as intermediaries to make the people sit down, to distribute the loaves, in order that all may attest to the miracle by their acts. He receives the bread from them, thus multiplying the witnesses of the miracle and the circumstances destined to remind people of it.[17]

Loaves Multiplied for the Multitudes

The multiplication of the loaves and fishes is recorded by Matthew with an extreme economy of words. Obviously, he wants three things to be noticed and remembered: Jesus' authority over the crowd, his gestures, and the overabundance of the food that the disciples are charged with distributing.

Jesus orders the crowd to sit down. This emphasis on his authority is characteristic of Matthew.[18] The Lord's power efficaciously acts in all domains. It is with authority that he speaks and teaches, cures the sick and expels demons, gathers the crowds and makes of them a seated congregation in the attitude of disciples whom he nourishes with word and bread.

"To take" the bread and fish, "to look up to heaven," "to say the blessing," "to give" to the disciples: these hieratic gestures spontaneously bring to mind the Last Supper (Matt 26:26-27) and the Eucharist. It is impossible for a Christian to read this account of the multiplication of the loaves without perceiving its Eucharistic signification, especially when the proclamation of this Gospel takes place in the celebration of the "Mystery of Faith."

The same is true of what follows. On Jesus' order—"Do this in memory of me"—we bring "this bread . . . which earth has given and human hands have made"[19] and the Eucharist is distributed to all by those who are commissioned for this ministry. These give it to the crowd, but it is actually the Lord who gives it to them. It is he who by his word makes of this bread and of this wine his Body and his Blood.

Finally, Christian tradition saw a sign, very early on, in the overabundance of the multiplied loaves and the twelve baskets filled with leftovers. Our Eucharists sacramentally perpetuate the gesture of the multiplication of the loaves. In the course of the centuries, we receive there the food that Jesus gave to the hungry crowds; it will never fail.

Give Us This Day Our Daily Bread

God addresses his call to those whom earthly foods disappoint and whose hunger they do not satisfy. "Come to me! You will be filled. I offer you free of charge and in abundance what can relieve your hunger and your thirst. It is a food that makes you live fully and unto eternal life. It leads you into my covenant and keeps you there forever."

In days of distress, when we are in the wilderness, along our way, Jesus is there, inviting us to sit down and receive the viaticum of his word and his bread. The daily praying of the Our Father is our first response, in faith, to this urgent invitation. The celebration of the Eucharist is the ecclesial gathering where the word and the bread are distributed to the disciples by those whom the Lord has entrusted with this service. "Mystery of Faith," memorial of Christ's death and resurrection, it remains, until the second coming, the sacrament of the infinite and merciful love that the Father has revealed through his Son in the Spirit. Strengthened by this love from which nothing can separate us, we are made capable of bearing anything in order to follow the Lord and announce to the whole world the good news of the "love of God in Christ Jesus our Lord."

> Toward whom, Lord, should we walk
> if not toward you?
> You alone speak of life
> and give it to us.
> Make us worthy of the table
> where your Father calls us today.
>
> *See our hunger, Savior of the world!*
> *Share with us your word and your bread.*
>
> I am the bread of life,
> those who come to me will never hunger,
> those who believe in me will never thirst.
>
> Here is the word of my Father:
> those who believe in the Son
> have eternal life.
>
> Those who eat my flesh and drink my blood
> have eternal life
> and I will raise them on the last day.[20]

A People Convinced of the Lord's Presence

Stand Before the Lord Because He Is Going to Pass By

When we speak of the Old Testament prophets, we spontaneously think of those men invested by God with a mission to the people and its leaders; we think of those inspired ones especially endowed with the gift of foreseeing the future, who have given their names to the prophetic books of the Bible: the four major[1] and the twelve minor[2] prophets. The term prophet has, however, a wider meaning, and it applies to others: Moses, in the first place, but also Samuel, Elijah, Elisha, David. It also applies to women such as Miriam, Moses' sister; Deborah; and Anna, who, along with Simeon, was the first to recognize the promised Messiah in Jesus. Elijah towers above all of these; he did not leave any writing, but the Bible abundantly speaks of him,[3] especially of his prestigious miracles.[4] The New Testament mentions Elijah and his mission several times.[5] Finally, the Christian mystical tradition—especially that of the Carmelites— has made a special place for Elijah because of his walk of forty days across the desert and his meeting with God that today's text recounts (1 Kgs 19:9a, 11-13a).

Horeb is the other name of Mount Sinai, where God gave the Law to Moses[6] and also revealed himself. Moses had begged the Lord, "Do let me see your glory!" God answered, ". . . My face you cannot see, for no man sees me and still lives." And he added: "Here . . . is a place near me where you shall station yourself on the rock. When my glory passes I will set you in the hollow of the rock and will cover you with my hand until I have passed by. Then I will remove my hand, so that you may see my back; but my face is not to be seen" (Exod 33:18-23). This is an admirable text, which one does not tire of pondering. God's sanctity—his glory—is so transcendent that it would blind and even kill a human being. However, in his mercy, God revealed some of it to Moses, letting himself be seen "from the back" in the luminous trace left by his passage.[7] It would be difficult to give a better inkling of the mystical ex-

149

perience of God with which some persons have been favored. The vision Moses was granted remains its prototype. Usually it occurs after a long solitary walk in the desert, the dark night through which faith travels, when everything seems to be confused for lack of signs on which to rely.[8] Elijah knows this trial.[9] Then the word of the Lord is addressed to him, "Go outside and stand on the mountain before the Lord; the Lord will be passing by." But how is God going to manifest himself? In order to answer this question, Elijah can refer only to experiences recorded by tradition when describing God's manifestations in "a strong and heavy wind" that "was rending the mountains and crushing rocks," in "an earthquake," in a "fire."[10] But God is not in any of these terrifying and grandiose manifestations of the forces of nature. Then "there was a tiny whispering sound." Elijah "hid his face in his cloak." And right away he feels comforted. He comes out of the cave where he had hidden himself, ready to assume his mission with a renewed trust in God.

We do not have here a story from the past, edifying for some, disconcerting for others, but that does not really concern us, i.e., does not present any interest in our day. Elijah's experience on Horeb contains, on the contrary, a teaching to be remembered. Except for sin, God does not consider anything as ever being finished. Far from meaning he is absent— and still less, dead—silence is the place of his presence, and also the place where we encounter him. The "dark night of faith" purifies us from too sensible representations of God and from the resulting illusions.[11] What believers may and must ask the Lord is that he manifest his love and grant us his salvation "in [the] tiny whispering sound" of ordinary days of life and faith, rather than in the clash of frightening theophanies.

> LORD, *let us see your kindness,*
> *and grant us your salvation.*
>
> I will hear what God proclaims;
>   the LORD—for he proclaims peace.
> Near indeed is his salvation to those who fear him,
>   glory dwelling in our land.
> Kindness and truth shall meet;
>   justice and peace shall kiss.
> Truth shall spring out of the earth,
>   and justice shall look down from heaven.
> The LORD himself will give his benefits;
>   our land shall yield its increase.
> Justice shall walk before him,
>   and salvation, along the way of his steps.
> (Ps 85:9, 10, 11-12, 13-14)

The Children of Israel, Our Brothers and Sisters

At the end of his reflection on the Christians' life in the Spirit,[12] Paul has proclaimed that nothing "will be able to separate us from the love of God in Christ Jesus our Lord."[13] This assurance, which fills Christians with joy, cannot make them forget the Jews, their brothers and sisters. Today we read the beginning of what Paul wrote in the Letter to the Romans on the place of Israel in the economy of salvation (Rom 9:2-15).[14]

We are conscious of having the Holy Spirit dwell in us and of having been freed from any debt to the flesh (Rom 8:9, 11-13).[15] We are conscious of having been justified by God (Rom 8:28-30).[16] And lastly, we are assured that nothing will be able to separate from the love of Christ those who believe in him (Rom 8:35, 37-39).[17] All this could lead us to regard the others as cursed—the Jews especially. The Church and Christians have not always avoided the temptation of anti-Semitism, whether latent or so violent it has led to persecution.[18] Paul, proud to be a Jew (Acts 22:1-5; 26:4-5), was, after his conversion, persecuted by his own, yet he never disassociated himself from them. On the contrary, he is ready to undergo everything, even, if it were possible, to see himself "accursed and separated from Christ for the sake of [his] brothers, [his] kin." On this point, his conscience bears him witness with the holy Spirit. He cannot forget that "theirs [are] the adoption, the glory, . . . the patriarchs, and from them, according to the flesh, is the Messiah." One could not say with more vigor or even more passion that Christians are spiritual Semites. Would that we could convince ourselves of this and publicly acknowledge it. What benefits and graces we might derive!

When scrutinizing the mystery of the Church, the Council recalls the bond that spiritually unites the people of the New Testament with Abraham's lineage.

> The Church of Christ acknowledges that in God's plan of salvation the beginning of her faith and election is to be found in the patriarchs, Moses and the prophets. She professes that all Christ's faithful, who as men of faith are sons of Abraham (cf. Gal. 3:7), are included in the same patriarch's call and that the salvation of the Church is mystically prefigured in the exodus of God's chosen people from the land of bondage. On this account the Church cannot forget that she received the revelation of the Old Testament by way of that people with whom God in his inexpressible mercy established the ancient covenant. Nor can she forget that she draws nourishment from that good olive tree onto which the wild olive branches of the Gentiles have been grafted (cf. Rom. 11:17-24). The Church believes that

Christ who is our peace has through his cross reconciled Jews and Gentiles and made them one in himself (cf. Eph. 2:14-16).

Likewise, the Church keeps ever before her mind the words of the apostle Paul about his kinsmen: "They are Israelites; theirs the adoption, the glory, the covenants, the giving of the law, the worship, and the promises, theirs the patriarchs, and from them, according to the flesh, is the Messiah" (Rom. 9:4-5), the son of the virgin Mary. She is mindful, moreover, that the apostles, the pillars on which the Church stands, are of Jewish descent, as are many of those early disciples who proclaimed the Gospel of Christ to the world.

As holy scripture testifies, Jerusalem did not recognize God's moment when it came (cf. Luke 19:42). Jews for the most part did not accept the Gospel; on the contrary, many opposed the spreading of it (cf. Rom. 11:28). Even so, the apostle Paul maintains that the Jews remain very dear to God, for the sake of the patriarchs, since God does not take back the gifts he bestowed or the choice he made. Together with the prophets and that same apostle, the Church awaits the day, known to God alone, when all peoples will call on God with one voice and "serve him shoulder to shoulder" (Soph. 3:9; cf. Is. 66:23; Ps. 65:4; Rom. 11:11-32).[19]

Take Courage, It Is I; Do Not Be Afraid

Like Mark and John,[20] Matthew attaches the narrative of Jesus' walk on the water to that of the multiplication of the loaves, thus establishing a link between the two episodes (Matt 14:22-23).[21]

The miracle of the multiplication of the loaves, in spite of its extraordinary nature, touches us without doubt because of its Eucharistic resonances. On the contrary, the story of Jesus and Peter walking on the sea disconcerts us. We find it difficult to grasp the relation that the Gospel means to establish between these two miracles. But on closer look, we readily see that in both cases the disciples' faith is the point. At the multiplication of the loaves, they had to trust Jesus, who had said: "No need to dismiss the crowds. You yourselves give them to eat. Bring me these five loaves and two fish which you have. Now, distribute this food to the crowd." They were lacking everything, as were all the people who had followed Jesus to "a deserted place." "They ate and were satisfied." The disciples even gathered twelve baskets full of remaining fragments.

Here, too, the disciples find themselves in a critical situation. "The boat, already a few miles offshore, was being tossed about by the waves, for the wind was against it." To make matters worse, the disciples are alone in the midst of the storm, without Jesus, who had remained, no one knew exactly where, "on the mountain by himself to pray." He had forced them to embark and precede him to the opposite shore. They are alone and in some way abandoned. How can they help but be "terrified" when they see Jesus coming to them walking on the sea? "They cried out in fear." They say, "It is a ghost." They cannot believe that it is really Jesus; that he can be there, so near, whereas they had left him on the shore from which they are already "a few miles" away. It cannot be he coming to them walking on the stormy sea.

However, Peter, divided between doubt—"Lord, if it is you,"—and his deep faith, speaks up. He says, "Command me to come to you on the water." He proclaims his faith in the sovereign authority of him whom he calls "Lord"[22] and who "commands."[23] Moreover, when Peter becomes frightened because of the wind and begins to sink, he cries, "Lord, save me!" He doubts, it is true, and Jesus points this out to him. But he surmounts the doubt, "Lord . . . command . . . save me."

And the story ends with a kind of brief liturgy when calm returns. "Those who were in the boat did him homage, saying, 'Truly, you are the Son of God.'"

Matthew has a significant manner all his own to show how we must address Jesus. One approaches him, conscious of the distance that separates him from his disciples. One prostrates oneself, saying, "Lord," and acknowledging in faith his being "Son of God."[24] These are as many elements of a liturgy already present in the Gospel of Matthew, attesting to an already very elaborate Christology.

The Paschal Community: Icon of the Church

Although it first disconcerts us, the narrative we have just read soon unveils its whole ecclesial and paschal significance.

In the boat "tossed by the waves, for the wind was against it," tradition very early saw an image of the Church, fighting the tide of evil. It is in the dark of night, in Jesus' absence, that we must reach the other shore. These details describe well the situation of the Christian community in the time of faith.

Besides, we cannot fail to put side by side this episode and the birth of paschal faith. The disciples, too, have known a "night" in which they found themselves at a loss. When, having risen, he appeared to the women who in the morning had found the tomb empty, Jesus must also have told them, "Do not be afraid" (Matt 28:10). And when the disciples "went to Galilee, to the mountain to which Jesus had ordered them . . . they worshiped, but they doubted"—still (Matt 28:16-17).

Finally, Peter appears as the typical disciple, whatever his preeminence may have been in the community gathered by Jesus. Faith has its ups and downs. If it looks to Jesus and leans on his word, it dares everything and can do everything. But if it lays itself open to doubt, it can only falter and all that is left, then, is a total trust in the mercy of Jesus, the Savior.

> "Take courage, it is I; do not be afraid." Hearing these reassuring words, perhaps there will be one among us animated by a greater ardor, a Peter, walking toward perfection but not yet perfect, who will get out of the boat, knowing he has escaped the trial which was shaking him. First of all, in his desire to meet Jesus, he will walk on the water, but, his faith still being insufficient, he still doubting, he will grow afraid and will begin to sink. However, he will escape this misfortune, because he will call Jesus with great cries, saying, "Lord, save me!" Hardly will this other Peter have finished speaking and saying, "Lord, save me!" than the Logos will stretch out his hand, will help him, and hold him when he begins to sink, reproaching him for his lack of faith and his doubts. Note however that he did not say, "Unbeliever," but "Man of little faith." It is written, "Why did you doubt, for you had a little faith, but you swerved in the direction opposite to that faith."[25]

In the Silence of the Desert and the Storms of the World

"God exists, I Have Met Him": This title of a book, in which the author tells of his sudden conversion and of what it radically changed in his life, gives a perfect definition of faith.[26] In like terms, Andrew brought his brother Simon to Jesus, and Philip spoke to Nathanael, "We have found the Messiah" (John 1:41, 45). Like love, faith is indeed an encounter. Certain persons can date it and situate it with precision: on the day following the one when John the Baptist designated Jesus as the Lamb of God, "[it] was about four in the afternoon" (John 1:35-39); the day after (John 1:43); on the way to Damascus (Acts 9:3); Christmas day 1886 in Notre-Dame de Paris, during the singing of the Magnificat, behind the second pillar;[27] at the age of twenty, "having, by chance, gone into the chapel of the Latin Quarter at ten minutes after five to find a friend."[28] Others have, one fine day, recognized him whom they had long known, or always known.[29] Still for others . . . . Whatever the circumstances, the journeys, faith is an encounter that makes one exclaim, "It is he!" From that time on, one knows the Other is, and will always be, there. Having given one's faith to him, one knows one can always rely on him. This does not preclude moments of hesitation and even doubt, which do not lessen deep faith: "He is late in showing himself. When will he give a sign, and in what way?"

On the brink of despair, Elijah the prophet goes into the wilderness to the mountain where God had formerly spoken to Moses. Does he know exactly what he is expecting of this return to the sources of revelation? Does he imagine that God can come without stupendous manifestations, storm, earthquake, fire? Invisibly present in "the dark night" of faith, the Lord goes by as "a tiny whispering sound." One catches a glimpse of his back, and one recognizes his passage by his luminous footprints.

The disciples' experience after the multiplication of the loaves is completely different. Still marveling at what happened, embarked with assurance to cross a familiar lake, here they are battling a contrary wind. Why did Jesus not come with them instead of remaining at prayer? He comes to them. But is it really he, this man walking on the sea? Yes, they recognize him, do "him homage, saying, 'Truly, you are the Son of God.'" We have here another fleeting manifestation of God's presence in a situation reminding us of the Church's: between two shores, it is sailing on an often stormy sea, but her Lord watches over her; tossed by the waves, Peter's boat will not founder.

Such an assurance must not lead us to forget those who have not embarked on the same crossing, but to whom we owe so much: the covenants, the Law, the promises of God, Christ born of their race, the forms of our worship, in prayer and the Eucharist. We make a memorial of all these when we celebrate the liturgy in which we draw near to the Father, through Christ, in the Spirit into which we have been adopted.

> Lord, you are not a God who saves easily.
> But as the mountain guide,
> you give us assurance . . .
> Make us firm in this Love.
>
> Lord, when the winds are contrary
> at sea, and when night adds to our trouble . . .
> May your cry reach us:
> "Take courage, it is I; do not be afraid."
>
> Lord, to each of us
> you say, "Come."
> Speak a little louder . . .
> Command that we go to you.[30]

Twentieth Sunday

A People Without Frontiers

The Lord's House Is Open to All

History creates situations that are always new and unexpected. It raises questions that did not exist before. This was the case for Israel, exiled to Babylon and then returning to its own country. Exile had immersed the people in pagan nations. Deprived of the Temple, this people had sought to preserve its national identity by remaining grouped around its priests and scribes, but without closing in upon itself. Of course, all were dreaming of returning to their land and restoring the old order. But the most lucid among them felt that nothing would be totally as before; generations in contact with a world unknown to their ancestors would have to ask new questions. Moreover, having returned to their country, they found foreigners who had been deported to Israel and had been settled there for years. What should the returning exiles' attitude be toward these foreigners? An oracle from the Book of Isaiah answers this question (Isa 56:6-7).

> The foreigners who join themselves to the LORD,
>   ministering to him,
> Loving the name of the LORD,
>   and becoming his servants—
> All who keep the sabbath free from profanation
>   and hold to my covenant,
> Them I will bring to my holy mountain
>   and make joyful in my house of prayer;
> Their holocausts and sacrifices
>   will be acceptable on my altar,
> For my house shall be called
>   a house of prayer for all peoples.
>   This is the Word of the LORD.

The principle is clear, and we have here a "word of the Lord" that begins by recalling the obligation to observe what is right and to do what is just. The attitude God prescribes for his people does not mean that they should abdicate their religious identity and embrace either some sort of syncretism or that kind of indifference that even the Lord's servants may succumb to, saying, "In the last analysis, one religion is as good as any other."[1]

Without aggression, without a proselytism bent on conquest, the people of God—the Church—must, on the contrary, remain firmly anchored in its faith in God and in Christ, who revealed God. If this is well understood, Isaiah's oracle proves to be more timely than ever.[2]

We live and shall be living in a society of diverse races, cultures, and religions. This poses many questions to Christians and to the Church. How will God make of his house a "house of prayer for all peoples"? No one can tell. But certainly it will not be by reversing the course of history. Therefore, to dream of a return to what we call Christendom is both vain and fraught with serious risks: a retiring into one's shell, a closing into a ghetto; a more or less fanatical fundamentalism, tinged with xenophobia, ostracism, and intolerance; sterilization of the missionary activity of Christian communities. More than ever, therefore, the Church is, so to speak, forced to give witness by its life and preaching, at once assured and humble. Then, without exerting pressures which no one countenances nowadays and which in any case prove short-lived, it truthfully serves the plan of God, who wants the salvation of all. Every Christian community, even though it be reduced to a handful in the midst of surrounding multitudes of all countries and religions, proclaims this faith and this hope.

> *O God, let all the nations praise you!*
>
> May God have pity on us and bless us;
>   may he let his face shine upon us.
> So may your way be known upon earth;
>   among all nations, your salvation.
> May the nations be glad and exult
>   because you rule the peoples in equity;
>   the nations on the earth you guide.
> May the peoples praise you, O God;
>   may all the peoples praise you!
> May God bless us,
>   and may all the ends of the earth fear him!
> (Ps 67:2-3, 5, 6, 8)

Mercy for All

The spiritual condition and the salvation of his fellow Israelites were the great preoccupation of Paul, who was, fully conscious, however, of having been elected to be "apostle of the Gentiles." One could say that he wanted to verify at every opportunity the authenticity of this vocation and reassure himself that it really came from God. Wherever he went, he began by announcing the gospel to the Jews. It was only when he met with their refusal that he went on to the Gentiles.[3] But he did not spend much time analyzing the reasons for this rejection of his message. He preferred to persuade himself that this disobedience would not last forever. And here again, he was thus reassured not by having recourse to human reasoning but by relying on God, especially his mercy (Rom 11:13-15, 29-32).

God has not entirely rejected his people. Paul, himself an Israelite, has encountered Christ (Rom 11:1). A good number of Jews and proselytes[4] welcomed the gospel.[5] Israel stumbled, it is true. But it will rise again (Rom 11:11). Paradoxically, the conversion of the Gentiles gives a guarantee that the Jews will stand up again and even allows us to speak of the marvelous resurrection that their expected reintegration will bring about. The reason for this is simple. All human beings, Jews and Gentiles, have disobeyed God. If the pagans, to whom Paul has turned, have been reconciled, it is because of the divine mercy. But "the gifts and the call of God are irrevocable." We cannot doubt that the others, too, will obtain mercy.

Is this problem obsolete or too theoretical to concern us? Certainly not. All human beings, whatever they may be, are entirely helpless when faced with the mystery of justification. Why was I born into a Christian family? How have I deserved the gift of faith; the call, at some point, to respond more fully to the grace of divine choice? These are questions that elicit the consciousness of being unworthy and the conviction that the wholly gratuitous love of God enters at the very heart of our poverty. In the light of faith, we can be assured that even when God reproves us, he does it through mercy. When we know that everything has a meaning in the unfolding of our lives because God freely loves us and is supremely free in distributing his gifts, we are encouraged to work with confidence and enthusiasm for the coming of his reign, without excluding anyone.

The Table of the Word and the Hunger of the Pagans

Jesus has sown plentifully, and to the four winds, the good grain of his word, unceasingly teaching the multitudes who thronged to him.[6] At Capernaum, he cured the Roman centurion's son[7] and all the sick presented to him, expelling with one word the spirits that tormented the possessed, "to fulfill what had been said by Isaiah the prophet: 'He took away our infirmities and bore our diseases.' ''[8] He called the publican Matthew and shared the sinners' meal.[9] He went all over Galilee[10] without respite. But as far as we know, he did not go beyond the narrow limits of his country;[11] when his controversies with the Pharisees[12] take a bad turn, he is obliged to withdraw to the region of Tyre and Sidon,[13] but still within the boundaries of Israel. Then a Canaanite woman,[14] perhaps from a neighboring territory, draws near him, crying: "Have pity on me, Lord, Son of David! My daughter is tormented by a demon" (Matt 15:21-28).

Here we do not have an ordinary episode, just another cure among others. In this woman, who follows after Jesus with her cries, the disciples seem to see only a nuisance to be silenced by sending her away after granting her request.[15] Jesus seems not to hear her cries. In truth, for him, the problem is elsewhere: "I was sent only to the lost sheep of the house of Israel." This question is none of the woman's concern. We are reminded of Cana. Jesus answered his mother, who was asking him to do something, "Woman, how does your concern affect Me? My hour has not yet come." There, too, it was a question of Jesus' faithfulness to his mission. Mary, relying on her son, simply said to the servants, "Do whatever he tells you" (John 2:4-5).[16] The Canaanite's attitude resembles Mary's. She thinks only of her daughter, "tormented by a demon." She knows that Jesus can cure her. This pagan woman's attitude and the way she addresses Jesus are remarkable. She "comes" to him, "does him homage"; she calls Jesus not only "Son of David" but "Lord"; she says, "Have pity on me" and "Lord, help me." This is exactly the way in which, according to Matthew's Gospel, the disciples approach Jesus and speak to him.[17]

Therefore, according to Matthew, the phrase "It is not right to take the food of the children and throw it to the dogs" certainly does not merely intend the scornful denotation that shocks us, especially in Jesus' mouth. The phrase emphatically reminds us[18] that Israel—"the children"—has been entrusted with the goods of the covenant signified by "the bread."[19] But the woman has understood—"Please, Lord, for even the dogs eat the scraps that fall from the table of their masters"—that pagans do not usurp others' goods. They will have their share. Today the crumbs, but tomorrow . . . All hopes are allowed, since Jesus has acknowledged the "great faith" of this woman who has come to him by crossing the boundary of pagan territories.

"Make Disciples of All Nations"

Revelation and salvation history develop in sudden outbursts, sometimes expectedly, even foretold, yet always surprising. The prophets' role is to show or at least to give us an inkling that the present is pregnant with a future that will exceed all hope. For their part, the sages ponder the past and help us to understand that it contained the germ of the present. Prophets and sages thus inspire us to live and act today by consciously entering the dynamic relation of what was, what is, and what will be tomorrow.

The way of behaving toward "the foreigners who join themselves to the Lord, ministering to him," is placed in the perspective of the day on which God's house "shall be called a house of prayer for all peoples."

Jesus' ministry was limited to the "lost sheep of the house of Israel." But the welcome of the Canaanite woman already announces that the day will come when pagans will be able to eat "the bread of the children" and not only "the crumbs falling from the table of their masters." In fact, the risen Christ will commission the eleven to go and bring the good news to all nations. Having gone back to the Father, he will exercise, through his disciples, the power given to him in heaven and on earth and he will be with them "until the end of the age" (Matt 28:16-20).

No one is excluded from this salvation that continually expands. The Apostle of the Gentiles attests to his assurance (one that all Christians must share) that God's mercy reaches all, Jews and pagans. But it is not enough just to know this.

On the very day after Pentecost, the idea of pagans sharing in the grace of salvation gave rise to many hesitations and bitter controversies.[20] Since apostolic times, the Church has displayed an intense and admirable missionary activity from one end of the world to the other. But Church history also reveals a degree of persistent discrimination not only toward Jews but also toward those it evangelizes, a practice from which it must unceasingly purify itself. For example, until recently it compelled believers to use a liturgy in a foreign language[21]—fortunately this era is over. We even see young Churches cause, among those who brought them the gospel, a kind of "envy" that Paul hoped the conversion of the pagans would bring about in his fellow Jews. May this envy rejuvenate and revive our communities! May it also remind all of us that sitting at the table of the children is a grace, a wonderful and undeserved gift and never a right we could claim or guard as a privilege.

As earthly joys call for a feast,
may joy unite us at God's table!
As wine makes the guests merry,
may the Spirit of Christ inebriate the living!
As a wedding gathers a crowd of friends,
may people come from the four corners of the world
to the banquet of the Lamb![22]

Like the Church at large, every Christian community, even a small one, even a very homogeneous and particularized one, is catholic, that is, open to universal values, especially when it is assembled for the liturgy, and particularly the Eucharist.

It owes this mark of identification to God's love, which constitutes and nourishes it; to the presence of the Lord, whose power extends over the whole universe—a love and a presence which know neither discrimination nor boundary; which encompass past, present, and future.

Beyond all differences, it is the same faith that from one end of the earth to the other, leads believers to Christ, before whom they bow while calling him Lord.

The liturgy is thus the sacrament of the gathering of that "great multitude, which no one could count, from every nation, race, people and tongue" which the Seer of Revelation contemplated, which the Christians and the Church must keep before their eyes.

As this broken bread, scattered on the mountains,
was assembled to be one,
may your Church be likewise gathered
from the extremities of the earth
into your kingdom.[23]

The Twenty-first and Twenty-second Sundays in Ordinary Time

The Twenty-first and Twenty-second Sundays form a new sequence. We read two excerpts from the Gospel of Matthew, in which for the first time we see Peter occupy a special place in the band of disciples gathered around Jesus. In the episode of the calming of the storm, we saw in him the typical disciple whose generous faith is imperiled if the Lord does not reach out his hand.[1] Now he speaks up in order to express the disciples' faith by declaring that Jesus is "the Messiah, the Son of the living God." In his turn, Jesus entrusts him with an unexpected responsibility in the community (Matt 16:13-20—Twenty-first Sunday). But immediately afterwards, the evangelist records how this same Peter finds it hard to accept that Jesus must undergo his passion, announced here for the first time (Matt 16:21-27—Twenty-second Sunday).

We continue to read the Letter to the Romans. The liturgy offers for our meditation Paul's hymn to the merciful wisdom (Rom 11:33-36—Twenty-first Sunday) and his comments on spiritual worship (Rom 12:1-2—Twenty-second Sunday).

Although brief, this sequence has a great importance for our understanding the mystery of both the Church and worship.

Peter's Ministry in the Church

A Trusted Steward Given Authority by the Lord

In itself, the episode briefly recorded in the first lesson of this Sunday has no real interest for today's Christians; it is a news item about the kingdom of Judah in the eighth century before our era. We care little about knowing who exactly were this Shebna and this "Eliakim, son of Hilkiah," who succeeded him as master of the palace. That this palace revolution may interest historians is understandable.[1] But why should it be recalled in the liturgy (Isa 22:19-20)?

Actually, the whole interest of this oracle resides in the words used and in the expressed hope that the day will come when God will finally establish over his people a trustworthy steward. This steward will not be a potentate acting on his whims and using his power for his own benefit. "He shall be a father to the inhabitants of Jerusalem and to the house of Judah." He will be trusted with "the key of the House of David . . . when he opens, no one shall shut, when he shuts, no one shall open." One cannot hear these words without noting their messianic significance. One remembers also the antiphon sung in the liturgy as Christmas draws near: "O Key of David, O royal Power of Israel controlling at your will the gate of heaven: come, break down the prison walls of death for those who dwell in darkness and the shadow of death; and lead your captive people into freedom."[2] The opening vision of Revelation shows Christ holding "the keys to death and the netherworld" (Rev 1:18), whereas the letter to the church of Philadelphia quotes the very oracle from the Book of Isaiah (Rev 3:7).

Shebna and Eliakim, along with so many others, have left few traces in history. On the other hand, all through the course of sacred history we see God pursuing with his initiatives the work he has begun, the gathering of a people in which and through which salvation occurs. In every age, he wants trustworthy stewards who, in his name and according to his intentions, administer the house of which he is and remains Lord. When celebrating his faithfulness and his wisdom, we entreat him to continue with his work of love.

LORD, *your love is eternal;*
do not forsake the work of your hands.

I will give thanks to you, O Lord, with all my heart,
   [for you have heard the words of my mouth;]
   in the presence of the angels I will sing your praise;
I will worship at your holy temple.
   we will give thanks to your name,
   because of your kindness and your truth:
When I called, you answered me;
   you built up strength within me.

The LORD is exalted, yet the lowly he sees,
   and the proud he knows from afar.
Your kindness, O LORD, endures forever;
   forsake not the work of your hands.
(Ps 138:1-2, 2-3, 6, 8)

Unfathomable Depth of God's Wisdom

At the end of his long exposition on the mystery of salvation, a hymn to God's wisdom spontaneously wells up in Paul's heart. "For from him and through him and for him all things are. To him be glory forever" (Rom 11:33-36).

This way of passing from a sometimes most arduous teaching to the praise of God deserves attention.[3] Whatever its dogmatic or even philosophical content, whatever the resources of intellect or wisdom called upon to better understand and communicate it, Christian doctrine is distinguished from all others: it is a revelation received from God, a knowledge of God towards whom it turns and to whom it binds.[4] In other words, theology and catechesis are activities of the believer who investigates—and expounds—things pertaining to faith. They normally lead, as if spontaneously, to prayer, contemplation, and praise.[5] In this, Paul is a model for the believer. The liturgy uses the same approach. The Word of God is announced in order that we may better understand its meaning and its scope. This proclamation also has a catechetical value, but it is not a mere, and still less, cold catechesis. The teaching it dispenses is of the same order as preaching. It aims at the conversion of hearts, based on a better knowledge of God and his mystery. This is why the proclamation of the Word leads to prayer and the Eucharist, the thanksgiving par excellence. Therefore, what Paul writes here, appears as the pattern or the summary of that contemplation and that praise without which theological discourse, catechesis, personal reflection, and study remain unfinished approaches.

Oh, the depth of the riches and wisdom and knowledge of God! How inscrutable are his judgments and how unsearchable his ways!
"For who has known the mind of the Lord
or who has been his counselor?"
"Or who has given him anything
that he may be repaid?"
For from him and through him and for him are all things. To him be glory
forever. Amen.

This is also a text to be freely pondered by dwelling on each word, each
expression.[6] It is a text which opens on infinite vistas which the Spirit
progressively uncovers for those who enter this contemplative, dynamic
movement and—why be afraid to say it?—this mystic process.[7] The point
is for us to let ourselves be drawn, without resistance, by the love of God,
who reveals himself and wants to lead beings created in his image to share
his bliss, to plunge without fear into the depth—the abyss—of his riches,
wisdom, and knowledge.

This eternal and supremely lovable beauty so desires human friendship that
it made a book for the sole purpose of winning such friendship, by revealing both its own excellence and the longing it has for human love. This
book is like the letter of a lover to her loved one, to gain his affection. Its
desires for the human heart are so fervent, its search for human friendship
is so tender, its calls and wishes are so amorous that upon hearing that
language, you would think that the divine beauty is not the sovereign of
heaven and earth but that it needs human beings in order to be happy.[8]

Who Is Christ?

Matthew inserts the "confession" of Peter at Caesarea Philippi and his
being made head of the Church (Matt 16:13-20) in the framework of Jesus'
teachings regarding the Church.

We are here at a turning point in the composition of Matthew's Gospel.[9]
Jesus has left Galilee. He avoids the crowds to devote himself almost exclusively to the Twelve, to whom he is going to reveal the mystery of
his passion. The person of the suffering and humiliated Messiah becomes
the center of his preaching and, for us, at this stage of Ordinary Time,
of our celebration. By the same token, faith appears the more necessary
to those who want to follow the Lord.

"Who do people say that the Son of Man is?" In the best scenario, a
new John the Baptist, a prophet. But what do today's people say about
Jesus? No need for an opinion survey to know the answer. The most contradictory views are expressed in a thousand ways in the press, literature, movies, theater; through attitudes, untroubled indifference, or

contempt. What Christians hear sometimes offends their faith but cannot fail to present questions to them. Yesterday, when Jesus was there, one could blame his contemporaries' incomprehension. Today, what people think and say relates to Jesus as presented and shown by believers. It is a matter not only of teaching and preaching orthodoxy, but also and chiefly of behavior, of witness in daily life and, let us not forget, in the liturgy, which contributes in the highest degree to the expression and manifestation of "the mystery of Christ."[10] Among the causes that blur Christ's image and explain the multiplicity of opinions about him and, no doubt, the indifference of many, the divisions of Christians into churches and denominations separate from and sometimes rivals to one another certainly hold a large place. Therefore the question Jesus asks his disciples and that is today addressed to all believers, urges us to take seriously, as soon as we assemble for the liturgy, the invitation to recognize our sinfulness.[11]

"You Are the Messiah, the Son of the Living God"

Our awareness of contributing more or less to the distortion of Christ's image, whether as individuals or as a Church, must not keep us from humbly but firmly confessing, especially during the liturgy, "You are the Messiah, the Son of the living God." Jesus says to us, as he said to Peter, "Blessed are you . . . For flesh and blood has not revealed this to you, but my heavenly Father."[12] Faith is a gift for which we thank God. It was transmitted to us through human intermediaries to whom our gratitude is also directed. To openly profess faith in the Son of God implies no pride, no arrogance.

Son of God: the mystery of the person of Jesus was revealed only progressively to the disciples, as the Gospels show.[13] Since then, the Church has never ceased to probe it and to perceive the implications of Peter's affirmation, the full content of which no one will ever exhaust. Thus when we proclaim, "Jesus is the Son of God," we know full well that our faith is always and necessarily imperfect. We know, too, that intelligence and knowledge—theology and biblical studies—cannot uncover what God reveals to the little ones (Matt 11:25). However, we believe and proclaim our faith with words and, if words fail us, by our way of living, and by the sacraments and liturgical actions, which are the work of the whole Church in which we take part.[14]

Finally, we must note that faith in the Son entails faith in God; to know the Son is to know the Father (John 14:7). In fact, today many still say they believe in God, but do not recognize him as the Father of our Lord Jesus Christ.

Simon, Established Rock of the Church of Christ

Like the faith of the little ones (Matt 11:25-26), Simon Peter's faith arouses Jesus' admiration and thanksgiving, "Blessed are you, Simon son of Jonah." "To you, man among others, my heavenly father has revealed who I am." But the narrative does not stop here. Solemnly, Jesus adds: "And so I say to you, you are Peter, and upon this rock I will build my church, and the gates of the netherworld shall not prevail against it. I will give you the keys to the kingdom of heaven. Whatever you bind on earth shall be bound in heaven; and whatever you loose on earth shall be loosed in heaven."

Here we have an investiture, a "nomination"; Jesus calls Simon and surnames him Peter. The play on words (Peter = rock) is clear in Aramaic: Simon is designated—instituted—as the rock upon which Jesus will build his Church. Do we not have here the fulfillment of the prophecy in the Book of Isaiah?

> . . . See, I am laying a stone in Zion,
> a stone that has been tested,
> A precious cornerstone as a sure foundation;
> he who puts his faith in it shall not be shaken.
> (Isa 28:16)

This oracle is explicitly quoted at the conclusion of the parable of the murderous tenants (Matt 21:42); the stone, therefore, is Jesus himself, the sole foundation (1 Cor 3:11). No one can replace Christ; he is, he only, the invisible rock on which the Church, as everything else, rests.[15] But Simon is, by the solemn designation of the Lord, the visible rock of the building, the stone solidly set upon the unique foundation, joined to it by the mortar of the faith that the Father has given Peter.[16]

Unshakable Church and the Power of the Keys

We might wonder whether Jesus places the emphasis on the person or on the faith of Peter, when he chooses him. But the answer to such a question would have only a mediocre interest. Peter, himself, and his successors remain men with their limitations and their foibles, in spite of the singular function conferred on them by Christ. If Jesus can and wants to lean on them, it is by reason of the strength that comes from above. On the other hand, the promise made to the Church is quite explicit, "The gates of the netherworld shall not prevail against it." Again, it is the person of the Lord that is in the foreground and, here, his paschal victory over death and all the powers of evil.[17] The guarantee of the life of the Church, and not only of its survival, is the risen Christ. In spite of his hesitations and doubts, his slowness to believe,[18] Peter is the steward, the major-domo of this faith in the Son of God forever living.

"I will give you the keys to the kingdom of heaven." This power, expressed in a picturesque formula, concerns the function of teaching and governing, of declaring something licit or illicit, of absolving or condemning, given to Peter for the benefit of the community.[19] It goes without saying that we are not speaking here of a discretionary power but of a pastoral power.[20] Such power can be that of a trusted steward only if it is exercised according to the example and in the spirit of the Lord.

At the end of this conversation, Jesus gives his disciples the mandate "to tell no one that he was the Messiah." The Lord still has many things to say; he has in particular the difficult task to help his own people, beginning with the closest, to understand and accept that to be really the Messiah, the Savior, he must undergo death in order to rise and return to his Father. At the time Matthew was writing his Gospel, the order of secrecy had been removed by Jesus himself when, after his resurrection, he had sent his disciples to preach to the whole world (Matt 28:16-20). However, the evangelist recorded the order given by the Lord "to tell no one that he was the Messiah." This discretion is obligatory at any time, therefore today. It is important to unfold a catechesis that takes its time in leading people to discover the mystery of Christ, the Messiah no doubt, but crucified and living forever.[21]

Peter's Ministry in the Church

Every time God has given a trusted steward to his people, he has done so within the continuity of the development of the plan of salvation. God's initiative may have appeared to be a short-term one; but people realized that it concerned a very long-term future—the messianic future. It would be endless to recall these interventions of God, who chooses human beings at every step for the fulfillment of his promises. Some are remembered; others have not left such a mark on history. But all have been the object of an election on God's part and, without divine aid, no one among them could have assumed the mission assigned to them.

Having come to proclaim the kingdom of God close at hand (Matt 4:17), Jesus is the emissary whom all others variously foreshadowed. Son of

God, to accomplish his mission, he received from the Father unprecedented authority and power, which he remains the only one to possess and exercise in an inalienable manner. He surrounded himself with a group of disciples to whom, before returning to his Father, he entrusted the mission to announce the good news of salvation to all peoples, teaching them to observe all that he commanded them and baptizing them in the name of the Father and of the Son and of the holy Spirit (Matt 28:19-20). Jesus made of the apostles the nucleus of the universal gathering announced from the beginning of salvation history, the nucleus of a Church whose head he is. And he entrusted Simon Peter with the keys of the kingdom of heaven, which is being built in this intermediary time from Christ's Pasch to his return. This Church will know crises, persecutions, and storms, but the "gates of the netherworld shall not prevail against it," because its leader is the Risen One, who has definitively conquered sin and death.

Peter underwent martyrdom, and the other apostles have disappeared along with the first disciples and the converts of successive generations. But the Church remains, and the keys given to Peter have been transmitted to his successors.

Whatever the concrete exercise of the papal ministry, the development brought to it by Christian reflection and practice, the vicissitudes it has known, this ministry draws its legitimacy from the investiture of Peter, on whom Jesus built his Church.

> The audible voice of the Church is the Pope. The voice of the Church cannot be a book, even an inspired book. Like a painter's works that seem to be alive, books keep a solemn silence if you ask them a question. Divine discretion and the mystery of the inspired book expose it the more to contradictory interpretations. When man is too young, his voice is indistinct. But the more the organism grows and gains strength, the more his voice becomes expressive and takes on a personal timbre. We have here all the reason and all the history of the progressive exercise of papal authority in the Church, formal and uninterrupted from the beginning.[22]

This choice of a frail and sinful man is not one of the least reasons for the admiration of the sovereign wisdom of God, whose judgments are inscrutable and whose ways are unsearchable. "To him be glory forever" through his Son, unique rock that saves us.

> Stone chosen to bear the building
> where God gathers his children,
> Simon, strengthen this Church
> upon the rock where you yourself rest!

Jesus, Son of the living God,
unique rock that saves us!

Who is the rock, if not our God?
He is the God who fills me with courage
and shows me a way beyond reproach.

Come near the living stone
rejected by humans
but precious in God's sight.

You yourselves, living stones,
form a building in the Spirit
to present your sacrifices to God.[23]

Twenty-second Sunday

Losing Everything— Even One's Life— to Follow Christ

The Irresistible Force of God's Call

Jeremiah is a striking example of the irresistible force of God's call, the seduction of which a person does not succeed in escaping (Jer 20:7-9).

Nothing prepared Jeremiah for the mission he received. Extremely sensitive, timid, deeply attached to his fatherland and kin, he becomes a prophet of doom, obliged to antagonize the powerful and foretell ruin to those he loves. He certainly is not cut out for this mission. How, then, has he come to assume this role?

The whole initiative was from God, who chose him before his birth. He protested, "I know not how to speak; I am too young." But God brushed aside his objections:

> Say not, "I am too young."
> To whomever I send you, you shall go;
> whatever I command you, you shall speak.
> Have no fear before them,
> because I am with you to deliver you. . . .
> See, I place my words in your mouth!
> (Jer 1:7-9).

Jeremiah allowed himself to be seduced. God's word is a "devouring fire."[1] Jeremiah is painfully experiencing that it is impossible from now on for him to evade his mission, whatever persecution he undergoes.[2]

And this is how weak and frail persons become capable, under the Spirit's impulse, to speak "on God's part" (2 Pet 1:21). No one can understand this without having experienced, at the very center of the torment, the invincible attraction exerted by God.

> *My soul is thirsting for you, O LORD my God.*
>
> O God, you are my God whom I seek;
> for you my flesh pines and my soul thirsts

171

like the earth, parched, lifeless and without water.
Thus have I gazed toward you in the sanctuary
  to see your power and your glory,
For your kindness is a greater good than life;
  my lips shall glorify you.

Thus will I bless you while I live;
  lifting up my hands, I will call upon your name.
As with the riches of a banquet shall my soul be satisfied,
  and with exultant lips my mouth shall praise you.
(Ps 63:2, 3-4, 5-6)

The Whole Life an Offering to God

For the most part, the Letter to the Romans is an exposition of salvation through faith.[3] Copious excerpts from it have been read over twelve Sundays. Now comes an exhortation to live out our daily lives according to the gospel.[4] This exhortation begins by regarding the Christian's moral life as worship of God (Rom 12:1-2).

In the Old Testament, prophets often denounced moral conduct contradicting the worship that honors God. How do we dare to come before the Lord when we live a life contrary to faith?[5] Vain is the worship offered by persons with corrupt hearts and morals.[6] The prophets' position is diametrically opposed to a worship that condones a ritual formalism without any relation to moral life. This having been said, moral life necessarily and clearly remains distinct from worship.

Christ rendered a perfect worship to the Father by his filial obedience throughout his life and in his death on the cross. From this point on, true worship is offered to God in his risen body—the new Temple not made by human hands. The only valid worship is in reference to the new life that the Lord communicates to his disciples through baptism. Paul views things from this angle. Like the Lord, with him and through him, they say, "Behold, I come to do your will, O God" (Heb 10:5; Ps 40:7-9).

For all that, rites are not eliminated.[7] But worship is so intimately bonded to life that it forms with it an indissoluble unit. The Eucharist is both source and expression of the charity that builds the Church.[8] The Fathers never tired of praising this spiritual worship.

> You want to see his altar? This altar is made of Christ's own members, and the Lord's body becomes an altar for you. Venerate it. It is more august than the stone altar on which you offer the holy sacrifice. Do not be scandalized. The latter is venerable on account of the victim you are offering; the former is made of the very victim. The latter is venerable because, although made of stone, it is consecrated by the body of Christ, which it

receives; the former is the very body of Christ. And you, you honor the altar which receives the body of Christ and you despise the one which is the body of Christ. This altar—it is possible for you to contemplate it in the streets and in the squares, and at every hour you can offer sacrifice.[9]

The Christian's moral life becomes, henceforth, an unceasing search for conformity to God's will, a way of perfection in the footsteps of Christ. "Become what you receive: the Body of Christ," said St. Augustine when he distributed Communion.

A Crucified Messiah

In Caesarea, Simon Peter, speaking in the disciples' name, confessed his faith in Jesus, "You are the Messiah, the Son of the living God." In his turn, Jesus declared: "Blessed are you. . . . For flesh and blood has not revealed this to you, but my heavenly Father. . . . I will give you the keys of the kingdom of heaven."[10] This event marks a turning point in Matthew's Gospel and also in the series of Sundays in Ordinary Time, Year A. After Peter's confession, "Jesus began to show his disciples that he must go to Jerusalem and suffer greatly from the elders, the chief priests, and the scribes, and be killed and on the third day be raised." From this Sunday on, we are invited to look more intently toward the cross when we listen to the word and celebrate the Eucharist (Matt 16:21-27).

We are accustomed to the cross of Christ. It is found everywhere: in churches and cemeteries, at crossroads, and in our houses. We carry it on our persons as an object of veneration, as a badge, or as a jewel. The Lord is shown on it in glory, peacefully sleeping in death, sometimes with his body broken by suffering. For Jesus' contemporaries, the cross was the infamous wood of punishment, the mere mention of which made one shudder. Who would not understand Peter's violent reaction? How could the Messiah, the Son of God, be subjected to violent pain, then killed, in Jerusalem, by the religious leaders of the people? "God forbid, Lord! No such thing shall ever happen to you." How, indeed, could we accept even the idea of such an end for him who manifested in his teaching and his acts an authority and a power never seen in a human being? If we admit so readily that Christ must suffer his passion, is it not because we do not dwell—except once a year, on Good Friday—on this scandalous reality?

Jesus feels Simon Peter's reaction, though it is a human and spontaneous one, as an intolerable temptation coming from him. It reminds Jesus of Satan's in the desert; he insidiously suggested to Jesus that he deviate from the way marked out by the Father (Matt 4:1-11). "Get behind me, Satan! You are an obstacle to me. You are thinking not as God does, but as human beings do." In effect, "How can you say such a thing after the revelation you received from the Father?" Yes, how was this possible? Because Peter remained a human being. This sincere and enthusiastic faith of the typical believer had to confront—as must our own faith—in a harsh battle, the scandal of a Messiah suffering and put to death. This faith of Peter's knew the humiliation of denial during his Lord's passion. One would think that Peter did not listen to the end of what Jesus was saying, that he missed the announcement of the resurrection "on the third day." In fact, the disciples were surprised on Easter day. The day after the sabbath, Mary Magdalene and the other Mary went to the sepulcher to complete the embalming of the crucified one (Luke 24:1). Their discovery of the empty tomb troubled the apostles; and Peter, who ran to verify their story on the spot, remained amazed (Luke 24:12). The appearance of the risen one disturbed the eleven. As at the quelling of the storm, they thought they were seeing a ghost (Luke 24:31). But on Pentecost day, they at last understood that Christ had to suffer much and be killed in order to rise on the third day. Then Peter boldly proclaimed, "God has made him both Lord and Messiah, this Jesus whom you crucified" (Acts 2:36). To come to this faith, we must—and this is not accomplished in one instant—go from human thoughts to God's thoughts.[11]

Losing One's Life

But the Gospel does not stop here. Having announced his passion, Jesus immediately speaks of his disciples' destiny. "Whoever wishes to come after me must deny himself, take up his cross, and follow me." "To carry one's cross" has become a standard expression of Christian language to mean "to bear trials with courage and faith."[12] Paul viewed in this manner the trials that were rife in his apostolate; he saw in them a sharing in the sufferings of Christ and in his passion (Col 1:24). But what Jesus says here is more precise and has a more general import. He addresses the disciples and no longer only Peter. "To take up one's cross" and "to follow Jesus" go hand in hand. Whatever the circumstances of their existence, all disciples must, on account of Jesus, lose their lives to save them. This means that we must lose possession of ourselves in order to gain life, to seek the realities above, where Christ is seated at the right hand of God, and not the earthly realities. For we have died with Christ, and our life remains hidden in God. When Christ our life appears, then we, too, will appear with him in glory. What Paul wrote to the Colossians (Col 3:1-4) is a commentary on and the application of Jesus' words to his disciples. For whom and for what do we live? The answer to this question resides in what we do; either we follow Christ, as Peter finally did, or else we remain as an obstacle in his way.

Seduced by God and His Christ

"Love cannot be discussed." We can give reasons for being attached to someone with our whole being. But none of these reasons, not even all of them taken together, are the reason that explains love. So much so that love and faithfulness remain even after the disappearance of what could have explained them. The same is true—even more so—when we give our faith to God. This is the experience attested to by Jeremiah, in whom all believers can recognize themselves. He was deeply conscious of not having the makings of a hero that were necessary to confront difficulties so contrary to his nature. He fights. He goes so far as to reproach God for his behavior. But he must admit to being defeated by God's irresistible force acting within him. "You seduced me, and I allowed myself to be seduced."

How, indeed, could we resist God's tenderness when it manifests itself? We want to devote to him our whole life, our whole person; we want to offer our lives to him to please him, thus responding to his love by a lifelong sacrifice of adoration.

Jesus has opened the way that leads to a more perfect union with God, up to the sharing of his glory with Christ. It is a disconcerting way because it goes through suffering and death in the footsteps of the Messiah, the Son of God. We do not set out on this way without hesitation, even diffidence. But we know that to lose one's life is to save it. The Eucharist, the memorial of the death and resurrection of the Lord, is a profession of faith in action, while we await the day when Christ will come with his angels in the glory of his Father and when the Son of Man will render to all according to their actions.

> You go up to Jerusalem,
> as appointed by the Father.
> Humans reject you:
> outside the city, you will be crucified.
> From Jerusalem will come the news:
> "Christ is risen!
> Day dawns on the city."

Day dawns on the city.

Disciples of a Master on his way,
we are seeking the city to come.

Companions of a crucified Lord,
we shall enter into his Pasch.

Witnesses of the risen Jesus,
together we shall go through
the gates of glory.[13]

The brief sequence formed by the Twenty-first and Twenty-second Sundays of Ordinary Time, Year A, places disciples at the heart of the mystery of the Church, founded upon Christ, and in which its members must grow and blossom.

This community is assured it will not be conquered by the powers of evil and death. It is made of men and women whose faith remains fragile, imperfect believers who nevertheless remain attached to him who has seduced them.

From them Jesus has chosen stewards, with Peter as their leader. He gave him the keys of the kingdom of heaven that he might exercise among his brothers and sisters the ministry of unity, that he might be the humble and watchful guardian of faith in Christ, the Son of the living God, who suffered, was put to death, and rose on the third day.

From the Twenty-third to the Twenty-fifth Sunday in Ordinary Time

The eighteenth chapter of Matthew's Gospel is commonly called the "Discourse on the Church" because it collects Jesus' teachings that directly apply to the life of ecclesial communities. First, we find in it Jesus' words on who is the greatest in the kingdom of heaven,[1] on scandal,[2] and on the shepherd's behavior toward the lost sheep.[3] Then come the teachings on fraternal correction and prayer in common (Matt 18:15-20), and on the forgiveness of offenses (Matt 18:25-35). These two Gospel passages are read on the Twenty-third and Twenty-fourth Sundays. On the Twenty-fifth Sunday, the reading is the parable of the workers sent to the vineyard (Matt 20:1-16). It contains both a promise and a warning for Christians.

We also hear two vibrant exhortations of Paul on charity (Rom 13:8-10; 14:7-9) and the passage of the Letter to the Philippians in which he proclaims, "For to me life is Christ" (Phil 1:20-24, 27a).[4]

Therefore, this new sequence reminds the faithful assembled for the liturgy that "they hold fast in their lives to what they have grasped by their faith."[5] They celebrate the love and mercy of God who gathers them into one community of forgiven persons. They are called to live in Christian charity and benevolence towards all human beings for whom Christ offered himself in sacrifice.

Twenty-third Sunday

A Community of Forgiveness Based on Mutual Love

Sentinel-Prophet in the Community

During Ordinary Time, the reading from the Old Testament is chosen in conjunction with the Gospel. Taken outside of its historical and literary context, such a passage has been selected for its own intrinsic meaning and for the additional meaning it receives from being inserted into the liturgical montage.[1] This is the case with Ezekiel's oracle read on this Sunday (Ezek 33:7-9).[2]

The image of the sentinel speaks for itself; the lookout has the task of watching for what is brewing afar so that the others may be warned in time and may not be taken by surprise.[3] Therefore, the prophet is a watcher, albeit a very special kind.

Prophets have the duty of warning the wicked of their impending fate if they persevere in their evil ways: "You will die." But prophets have another responsibility that goes farther than that of ordinary watchers. These often give the alarm. If they fail to do it, they will be condemned for not discharging their duty. However, they are not responsible for the use, judicious or not, made of the objective information they transmit. Sentinel-prophets do not speak of what they see with their human eyes; they will never be able to excuse themselves by pleading a defect in their eyesight or poor conditions of visibility. Nor are they neutral watchers: they speak on the Lord's part, and the object of their mission is identical with the intentions of God, who does not wish for anyone's death but wants all to be converted and live (Ezek 18:32). God wants to make of all persons new creatures (Ezek 36:26-27), wants them to come out of the graves where they are imprisoned (Ezek 37:14). Sentinel-prophets have a pastoral mission toward everyone. A grand but fearful mission—those who receive it will answer with their own lives for the death of those they were sent to.

The New Testament has not forgotten this; the term used to designate those accountable for the churches,[4] *episcopos*—today, "bishop"—means overseer, watcher ''. . . admonishing everyone and teaching everyone with all wisdom, that we may present everyone perfect in Christ'' (Col 1:28). ''I am writing you this not to shame you, but to admonish you as my beloved children'' (1 Cor 4:14). Paul wishes that all faithful share in this ministry, being ''able to admonish one another'' (Rom 15:14). Tradition, too, speaks in the same manner as Ezekiel, and with the same severity, of all those who exercise a pastoral charge among their brothers and sisters in the Christian communities.[5]

In the Christian community gathered for the liturgy, during which God's word resounds through the sentinel-prophets and those who have received a similar mission, we exhort one another to open our hearts to the voice of the Lord.

If today you hear his voice,
harden not your hearts.

Come, let us sing joyfully to the LORD;
   let us acclaim the Rock of our salvation.
Let us greet him with thanksgiving;
   let us joyfully sing psalms to him.

Come, let us bow down in worship;
   let us kneel before the LORD who made us.
For he is our God,
   and we are the people he shepherds, the flock he guides.

Oh, that today you would hear his voice:
   ''Harden not your hearts as at Meribah,
   as in the day of Massah in the desert,
Where your fathers tempted me;
   they tested me though they had seen my works.''
(Ps 95:1-2, 6-7, 8-9[6])

The Debt and Law of Mutual Love

Before concluding his Letter to the Romans, Paul directs a last exhortation. Last Sunday, we read the beginning of it, where the Apostle urges Christians ''to offer [their] bodies as a living sacrifice, holy and pleasing to God'' because that is ''spiritual worship.''[7] Today, we read another passage from the same part of the letter; it has lost nothing of its timeliness (Rom 13:8-10).[8]

We could sum up what Paul says here in the following manner: charity is a debt from which no one is ever free; keystone of all commandments, it elevates them to a mystical plane.

To pay off one's debts is a demand of justice. But when it comes to mutual love, this rule does not apply, because love is not a possession that one receives or gives in an exactly measured quantity. Therefore, everyone of us, try as we may, remains and will always remain in the debt of others as to the love that is due them. This is particularly true for Christians, who must love as God loves them.[9] Lacking the infinity of God's love, the disciples' love toward others must still be without measure. Therefore, in this matter, it is impossible to ever be without debt with regard to anybody. And the less so as this love, "like God's," includes all, without any distinction.

> Every man is, after God's image, an absolute. We do not lose our time when we love the least of men as a brother, as if he were alone in the world. Whatever his moral degradation, I make bold to say that he is as worthy of love as God himself. Jesus desires that you be devoted to the love of your brothers. Your refusal to sacrifice the fraternal quality of a friendship to productivity and efficiency will be, on the level of charity, a witness to the way Jesus never ceases to love everyone of his brothers, and an active participation in this love. (This does not mean that we condemn the use of the most sophisticated technical resources, provided it be done in a Christian manner).[10]

That charity should be a "duty" of justice—a "debt"—the fulfilling of a "law," a strict "commandment" may seem contradictory; if there is anything that cannot be decreed, that no law can impose, it is love! No doubt about it. But here we are talking of a commandment of God's law. Being a gift of his love, it establishes those who receive it in a filial relation with their Lord. He does not "order" us to love him; he asks for our love because he loves us humans. His commandments mark the road of charity and freedom in the universal love of brothers and sisters.

"The one who loves another has fulfilled the law," says Paul. Then he cites four commandments: "You shall not commit adultery; you shall not kill; you shall not steal; you shall not covet." Even though he adds that the law is not limited to these, we hardly suppress a first reaction of surprise. The four precepts quoted by the Apostle are in the purview of a rather elementary morality; not to do harm to others, whether in their possessions or their lives. Can we say we love them when we content ourselves with not wronging them? No, without any doubt. But this is not what Paul means. In his great hymn to charity (1 Cor 13:1-13), he also states negative precepts: "Love . . . is not jealous, . . . is not pompous, it is not inflated"; it does not do anything dishonest; etc. But he also affirms that, without love, heroic deeds or acts showing the highest form of self-sacrifice, faith itself, have no value. To wrong no one is therefore a demand of charity and not simply a demand of worldly justice. Contrary to what is sometimes said, there cannot be any conflict between justice and charity, since we must evaluate justice according to charity.

> "All manner of life that allows one to practice more sincerely the love of God and, for his sake, the love of neighbor—whatever the habit and the observances—is also more agreeable to God. Everything must be done or not done, changed or not changed on account of charity. Charity is the principle by which and the end toward which everything must be guided. There can be no sin in what is accomplished, in all truth, for it, and according to its spirit." [11]

"Love is the fulfillment of the law." "Christ is the end of the law for the justification of everyone who has faith" (Rom 10:4). Elsewhere, Paul writes that Christ is his law (1 Cor 9:21). The love of others is, therefore, imitation of somebody and not simply conformity to an external law. Thus, the debt of mutual love is transformed into a mystical reality. "For the love of Christ impels us" (2 Cor 5:14) and sends us to our brothers and sisters. "Far from liberating us from the demands of the Law, love of brothers and sisters inspires us to discharge our duties towards others. More than that, it constitutes in our eyes our first duty, the debt that is never paid off." [12]

When a Brother or Sister Sins

Chapter 18 of the Gospel of Matthew constitutes a distinct literary unit that gathers Jesus' teachings directly concerned with the life of his disciples' communities. In today's passage, the topics are fraternal correction and prayer in common (Matt 18:15-20).

The community for which Matthew collected and presented the Lord's teachings was already a motley group. There were brothers and sisters who did not behave in an evangelical manner toward the little ones. There were leaders concerned more with honors than service. There were even disciples who lived in sin, publicly and scandalously. What to do about them? What should be the means by which they could be helped to become aware of their disorderly ways and be converted? Certainly there was no question to prematurely separate the weeds from the good grain (Matt 13:24-30). [13] But in some cases, it became necessary to expel from the community brothers and sisters whose conduct could not be tolerated. These questions are still with us. The Gospel of Matthew shows us how to address them.

The concrete modalities of the procedure outlined in Matthew cannot be followed to the letter, but we must remember their spirit and perspective. The sins of brothers or sisters cannot leave their kin and other members of the community indifferent. Charity and the spiritual welfare of others demand that we exert ourselves to bring back onto the right path whoever has wandered off. The parable of the lost sheep (Matt 18:10-14) immediately precedes Jesus' words on charitable correction. The art of reprimand is certainly among the most difficult and the most delicate; yet this is no reason for us to evade our duty. To withhold assistance from a person in moral danger is a serious sin. Each one of us can remember examples of the dramatic consequences such an omission has had. But each one of us also recalls, no doubt, what we owe to the helpful intervention of a sister or brother even if, at the time, we did not welcome it.

Charitable correction is inspired by mercy and must be done with tactfulness and humility. First of all, we must speak privately to our brothers or sisters, in order to help them to become aware of the peril they are incurring. We must speak as a sinner to a sinner, and not as a judge—or a "pure one"—to a guilty person. We know that only God's grace can change hearts and effect conversion. An initial failure must not discourage us. We must model our behavior on God's trust and patience, such as Jesus revealed them, for instance, in the parable of the gardener who did not despair to see the fig tree produce fruit after being cultivated and fertilized (Luke 13:6-9).[14] We must also accept *not* to see the result of our efforts. It does not matter if others reap where we have sown (John 4:37-38). Our frame of mind is very different from the self-importance that would lead us to say: "Here, I have warned you. Now, it is up to you. Too bad for you. I wash my hands of the whole thing." Christians never resign themselves to their brothers' or sisters' misconduct. Eventually, the recourse to two or three witnesses and to the Church community is inspired by pastoral zeal; it is not tantamount to an appearance before a court of the first instance, then before a court of appeals. The exclusion itself—if things should come to such a pass—remains a measure dictated by the hope to see the guilty ones realize the seriousness of their faults and, with God's grace, to repent. "Treat [them] as you would a Gentile or a tax collector." But Gentiles and tax collectors are excluded neither from the pastoral solicitude nor from the prayer of the Church. "Those who are well do not need a physician, but the sick do. . . . I did not come to call the righteous but sinners" (Matt 9:10-13).[15]

"Whatever you bind on earth shall be bound in heaven; and whatever you loose on earth shall be loosed in heaven." The power given to Peter (Matt 16:19) is shared by the leaders of communities, but it is not a discretionary power. We must indeed exercise it with our eyes on heaven, with a conduct modeled after that of God and Jesus, who came not to judge but to save (John 3:17). The brother and the sister who refuse "to listen even to the church" are excluded from the community when human beings can do nothing for them. Then one leaves everything to God's mercy and to the power of his grace. The only intervention still possible is the prayer of the community for those who have excluded themselves from it.[16]

In spite of its somewhat juridical aspect, the perspective of evangelical discipline remains that of forgiveness. A community is Christian in the measure in which all know and want themselves to be responsible for the good of each member. This concern about others' salvation must be at the heart of every cell of the Church, especially the heart of the family. This is why charitable correction is a duty that, although difficult, devolves on everyone.

> We must be saved together. We must reach God together. We must present ourselves to him together. We must not expect to find God without the help of others. We must all come back together into our father's house. We must also think a little of others; we must work a little for others. What would he say to us if we arrived separately?[17]

Prayer in Common, Prayer Heard
Whatever the disciples do on earth to "win" their brothers or sisters to safeguard true communion among them is assured the help and the approval of heaven. Therefore, we should not be surprised if the Father in heaven hears the petitions made on earth when the disciples—even only two of them—agree on a common prayer.

This promise of efficacy is not limited to liturgical prayer or to common prayer. It includes them of course, but the emphasis here is on charity between brothers and sisters. Prayer expresses this unity and contributes for its part to strengthening it, even to healing it when it has been wounded. To pray together with the same formulas and the same gestures is an insult to God if we are not at one in the communion of charity between brothers and sisters and between members of the same community. "Therefore, if you bring your gift to the altar, and there recall that your brother has anything against you, leave your gift there at the altar, go first and be reconciled with your brother, and then come and offer your gift" (Matt 5:23-24).[18] Then, and only then, can we be sure that the Father in heaven will give what is asked of him on earth.

Presence of the Lord Among His Own

"Where two or three are gathered together in my name, there I am in the midst of them." This applies to prayer. "Through Christ, your Son, our Lord" is much more than a ritual formula of conclusion. It is an act of faith in the Lord's presence that one invokes *(epiclesis)* and upon which one calls. Similarly, if the Lord were not here among his own, how could we understand that what is bound or loosed on earth is bound or loosed in heaven? Jesus' affirmation has a general purview. He is and always will be present in his Church. Matthew's Gospel begins with the announcement to Joseph of the birth of "God is with us" (Matt 1:23).[19] And it ends with this promise of the risen one to the eleven, "And behold, I am with you always, until the end of the age" (Matt 28:20).[20] All the demands of the Christians' lives, of the ecclesial communities, of the whole Church follow from this presence that is their joy and sustains their hope.

God, Through Christ, Leads His People

Like all other communities, the Church has its inner rule, and even its code of laws.[21] It also has different institutions charged with watching over discipline and procedures for reproving those whose conduct is reprehensible. At first sight, one could think that the Church is purely and simply a society among others, at least when it comes to hierarchy and authority.[22] The liturgy of this Sunday directs our gaze to the true nature of the Church. This is the more striking as the Gospel passage we read concerns the way to deal with delinquent brothers and sisters. Despite the juridical aspect of this sort of procedure, it is easy to see that we are dealing here with something other than a lawsuit. Charitable correction is inspired by the desire to help brothers and sisters mend their ways. It is animated by charity. It takes after Christ, who came not for "those who are well" but for "the sick" and who is present among his own. It is in his name that the "overseers" charged with safeguarding the community rebuke the sinners toward whom, as toward everyone else, all owe the debt of mutual love.

Therefore, gathered for the liturgy, the faithful celebrate, today as on every Sunday, God and his Christ, who guide the Church. They turn their eyes toward God and Christ when the Scriptures speak of the relations between the members of the body, whose head Christ is, he in whom heaven and earth are reconciled. In the mystery of his presence, "cause and center of the assembly, object of the faith, source of the efficacy of prayer and of pastoral authority, . . . the vertical line of divine filiation and the horizontal line of fraternity cross one another."[23]

> When one human being wins another,
> heaven rises on earth.
> When two or three agree
> to implore the Father,
> heaven surrounds them
> and unfolds at their bidding.
>
> *Earth and heaven are reconciled,*
> *Jesus is in our midst.*
>
> Love and truth meet,
> glory will dwell on our earth.
>
> Truth will sprout from the earth
> and justice will lean from heaven.
>
> God himself offers happiness
> and our earth will give its fruit.[24]

Twenty-fourth Sunday

Forgive Us Our Trespasses, As We Forgive . . .

Forgive Your Neighbor and Your Sins Will Be Forgiven

The Book of Sirach was written in Hebrew in Jerusalem about 190–180 B.C.; some fifty years later, it was translated into Greek in Egypt for the Jews settled there. From the time of St. Cyprian (d. 258), and until recently, the book was called *Liber Ecclesiasticus,* "Church Book," because it was used for instructing catechumens. Its traditional teaching remains indeed timely, as the passage read today demonstrates (Sir 27:30–28:7).

It deals with an important, even vital, question: that of the daily relationships between human beings. Alas, the experience of many centuries shows that egotism, the spirit of competition, jealousy, the recourse to brutal force, etc., constantly threaten to enmesh us in the homicidal gear set in motion by resentment and anger. In all times, the sages have endeavored to convince people of the pressing need to renounce these evils, destructive to one's self and others. Sirach, the sage, forcefully brands resentment and anger as "hateful things." We readily agree. It is sufficient to see the ravages wrought by resentment and anger; when they gnaw at the human heart, the whole life is gravely, even dangerously, disturbed. Being obsessed with them can lead to true madness. Human wisdom does not lack arguments to urge us to protect ourselves against the virus of resentment and anger. Sirach knows well this type of reflection, which is of benefit to everyone.[1] But here he does not appeal to such considerations. The obligation to avoid resentment and anger is strictly enjoined on those who know God and are conscious of their own need for divine mercy.

Judgment belongs exclusively to God: "Vengeance is mine, I will repay, says the Lord." Paul (Rom 12:19) recalls this word of Deuteronomy (32:35). To usurp this right is impious. But another consideration, a very concrete one, helps us to guard against the temptation to vengeance. God is not a pitiless and unfeeling judge; one can implore his pardon. He even desires to grant it for the asking, because he is slow to anger and rich

186

in grace.[2] If he kept a tally of sins, who would survive (Ps 130:3)? It would be a contradiction to hope for divine forgiveness while showing oneself merciless toward others. The day will come when everyone will be submitted to God's judgment. Could we then appeal to his tenderness after having been severe and intractable with others? On the other hand, if we are able to say, ''Forgive my faults, for I myself have forgiven those who wronged me,'' he certainly will pardon us. More than that, he will listen only to his heart, without our having to say anything.

> How could I give you up, O Ephraim,
>   or deliver you up, O Israel? . . .
> My heart is overwhelmed,
>   my pity is stirred.
> I will not give vent to my blazing anger,
>   I will not destroy Ephraim again;
> For I am God and not man,
>   the Holy One present among you;
> I will not let the flames consume you.
> (Hos 11:8-9)

As a matter of fact, the whole covenant is, from beginning to end, the story of God's mercy. It is impossible to appeal to this story, and even less to remain faithful to it, if we set ourselves outside the dynamic movement of forgiveness or—worse—if we act toward all human beings, sinners, in a way contrary to God's dealings with us.

> *The LORD is kind and merciful;*
> *slow to anger, and rich in compassion.*
>
> Bless the LORD, O my soul;
>   and all my being, bless his holy name.
> Bless the LORD, O my soul,
>   and forget not all his benefits.
> He pardons all your iniquities,
>   he heals all your ills.
> He redeems your life from destruction,
>   he crowns you with kindness and compassion.
> He will not always chide,
>   nor does he keep his wrath forever.
> Not according to our sins does he deal with us,
>   nor does he requite us according to our crimes.
> For as the heavens are high above the earth,
>   so surpassing is his kindness toward those who fear him.
> As far as the east is from the west,
>   so far has he put our transgressions from us.
> (Ps 103:1-2, 3-4, 9-10, 11-12)

In Our Life and in Our Death, We Belong to the Lord

Since the Ninth Sunday, we have been reading excerpts from the Letter to the Romans. Except for the Gospels, no writing of the New Testament holds our attention during so many consecutive Sundays. It is true that no other apostolic letter is of such length.[3] But this is not a sufficient explanation for the special place of the Letter to the Romans in the Sunday Lectionary. It has an unparalleled doctrinal importance on account of its subject—salvation through faith—and the ample and vigorous development of this fundamental subject, as is obvious from the fifteen excerpts read at the Sunday liturgies over a period of nearly four months. The believer will not have failed to notice how naturally Paul moves from doctrine to living practice, and how his exhortations retain a resolutely theological perspective and never lapse into moralism. Indeed, he constantly returns to the very heart of the mystery in which we participate (Rom 14:7-9): "None of us lives for oneself, and no one dies for oneself. For if we live, we live for the Lord, and if we die, we die for the Lord; so then, whether we live or die, we are the Lord's." Such is the central truth to which we must go back, in everything and always, in order to evaluate what we do, what happens to us and to discern how we must conduct ourselves. Everything must be judged, determined in relation to our belonging to Christ, a belonging sealed by faith and baptism and constantly honored and deepened. This principle entails endless demands, but it places us in a climate of freedom that no ethical legislation could create. It would be interesting to reread the fifteen excerpts of the Letter to the Romans read since the Ninth Sunday in the light of what Paul says here.

> But now the righteousness of God has been manifested apart from the law.
>
> It will be credited [to us] who believe in the one who raised Jesus our Lord from the dead, who was handed over for our transgressions and was raised for our justification.
>
> Since we are now justified by his blood, [we] will be saved through him from the wrath.
> The gift is not like the transgression.
>
> You must think of yourselves as [being] dead to sin and living for God in Christ Jesus.
>
> You are not in the flesh; on the contrary, you are in the spirit.
>
> I consider that the sufferings of this present time are as nothing compared with the glory to be revealed for us.
>
> The Spirit too comes to the aid of our weakness.

We know that all things work for good for those who love God.

Nothing will be able to separate us from the love of God in Christ Jesus our Lord.

I have great sorrow and constant anguish in my heart . . . [for] my kin according to the flesh.

God delivered all to disobedience, that he might have mercy upon all.

Oh, the depth of the riches and wisdom and knowledge of God! . . . For from him and through him and for him are all things.

I urge you therefore, brothers, by the mercies of God, to offer your bodies as a living sacrifice, holy and pleasing to God, your spiritual worship.

The one who loves has fulfilled the law.

This doctrine of salvation through faith, with all implications, is the foundation of a true and demanding ecumenism, first of all for individuals and then within each community, in the Church, between the churches. This doctrine allows us to understand and appreciate the diversity of legitimate traditions, whether theological, spiritual, or liturgical. These traditions can then be lived not as antagonisms but as contributions to a rich communion. This doctrine also dictates the attitude we must adopt toward the "weak in faith" (Rom 14:1–15:13). Anyway, is there anyone so strong as to be without weaknesses?

To Forgive as God Forgives—Without Counting
Last Sunday, we read in Matthew's Gospel how we must act towards brothers and sisters who persist in sin. The duty of Christian correction is in order. Their obstinacy can lead to their being excluded and regarded as Gentiles and tax collectors.

But it is not a question of the leader and the community sending people away simply because they are bothersome, because they have a difficult character, because they are perhaps out of place and because they made demands on us. The leader and the community must dismiss only those who in their hearts have cut themselves off from the community, those who are a real danger of scandal by inciting rebellion against legitimate authority and by undermining the confidence others have in it. These persons divide the community and cause it to deviate from its original goals. In this difficult domain of divisions and schisms, no rule can be set down, except that of patience, watchfulness, and firmness, that of respect for structures and channels of dialogue.[4]

In fact, it is in this spirit that the general law of the Church, the inner rules of diverse communities determine the procedure to follow and the manner in which those who have been excluded or excommunicated for their sins can be readmitted after having made amends.[5] But if a brother or a sister has committed a fault "against me," how many times must I forgive? Peter puts to Jesus this concrete question that comes to everyone's mind. "As many as seven times?" (Matt 18:21-35)

We would be ill advised to laugh at Peter's question and at his casuistical perspective on forgiveness. Who would dare to cast the first stone at him? To forgive up to seven times—is it not already a lot, a limit beyond which it would be unreasonable to go? We would risk showing weakness and, by the same token, encouraging the backslider.[6] All this applies when we remain on the plane of human justice and the settling of contentious matters. But one day Jesus said that he had not been appointed as judge to arbitrate that kind of dispute (Luke 12:13-21).[7] His answer, "I say to you, not seven times, but seventy-seven times," is given from another viewpoint—that of the kingdom of heaven.

From the beginning, it is obvious that the parable contains a teaching requiring the hearers' undivided attention. It shows a king to whom is brought a servant who owes him money.[8] The sum due exceeds all imagination. One does not see how a servant could be indebted to his master for such an enormous amount.[9] No one can owe such a debt to another person, even a king. Therefore, we know the parable is speaking of God, to whom we owe what we absolutely are unable to pay back. The servant is fully conscious of his dead-end predicament. For his part, the king knows perfectly well that the sale of this debtor and his wife and children will never reimburse the large debt. What the king says means that the servant has lost everything: his freedom and his life, as well as his family's.

The religious orientation of the parable is then emphasized by the servant's attitude; he prostrates himself before the king and implores his patience and pity. According to Matthew, this attitude and manner of speaking are appropriate when one addresses God or Jesus.[10] In fact, "moved with compassion"[11] on hearing his plea, the master forgives the servant the loan.

The parable could stop here. But it does not intend to leave us to figure out for ourselves the practical consequences of God's infinite mercy toward the insolvent servants we are. It confronts us in our conduct toward our brothers and sisters who owe us amounts ridiculously low in themselves and in comparison with the debt God forgives us. The servant, who just was the object of his master's generous pity, right away meets one of his companions who owes him one hundred silver coins, that is, a sum one can reimburse—an agricultural laborer's salary for one hundred days—without proportion to the ten thousand talents.[12] He throttles his fellow servant. Deaf to the request for a delay, formulated in the very terms he himself had used, this servant, himself freed from an exorbitant debt, now causes his peer to be put in prison until he pays back what he owes.

The parable is designed to arouse the hearers' indignation—graciously forgiven an enormous debt by his master, the servant must, in his turn, have mercy on his companion. His behavior is scandalous. We share the master's anger and we applaud his decision. This is exactly what Jesus has in mind when narrating this parable, to bring us to be ourselves the judges of this servants's shamefully pitiless conduct.[13] But Jesus is not giving us a lesson in magnanimity, albeit an elementary one; he is speaking of the kingdom of heaven, "So will my heavenly Father do to you, unless each of you forgives his brother from his heart."

We are no longer speaking of fellow servants but of brothers and sisters. We are no longer asked to pardon indefinitely, "not seven times but seventy-seven times," but from the heart. The parable is addressed, therefore, to the Christian community where all are brothers and sisters. Each one of us has received, and continues to receive all the time, the mercy of the Father in heaven, who has remitted the unpayable debt of sin. Our conduct toward our brothers and sisters who have offended us follows from the conduct of God toward us. To act otherwise is to incur rejection from the Father. The pardon must be given from the heart, like the pardon of God, who is not content to receive lip service from a people whose heart is far from him. He would tell us:

> In vain do they worship me,
> teaching as doctrines human precepts.[14]

Church of the Forgiving Forgiven

Whether they pray in the secret of their rooms or in common, in the beginning of each Eucharistic celebration or at the moment of receiving the bread of life and of drinking the cup of the Lord, Christians acknowledge their sinfulness before God. But this confession of their sins goes hand in hand with the confession of God's infinite mercy. These two confessions, along with intercession and thanksgiving, are the essential components of prayer and worship, of life in God, to whom we belong. Thus the Church is a community that must witness to the infinite mercy of

God toward all human beings for whom Christ suffered his passion and conquered death. She is the place of forgiveness generously offered to all. The daily prayer of Christians is the Our Father, which the Savior taught them and through which they do not cease to beseech God to forgive their sins as they themselves forgive the wrongdoing of their brothers and sisters.

> Some persons tremble at this thought, and when the people, with one voice, recite the Pater in church, they refrain from saying these words along with others, for fear of condemning, rather than exonerating themselves with their own mouths. They do not perceive that these are vain subtleties with which they try to hide from the eyes of the Sovereign Judge, who wanted to foreshow to those who pray to him the manner in which he will judge them. Not wanting to be found severe and inexorable, he has marked for us the rule of his judgments in order that we may judge our offending brothers and sisters in the way we want to be judged by him.[15]

We must unceasingly say the Our Father not because we always and spontaneously forgive our brothers and sisters from the heart, but because we desire to receive from God the grace to do so. Such a prayer takes its full meaning within the celebration of the Eucharist, before we receive the Body of Christ and share the cup of his blood after having exchanged with our brothers and sisters a sign of peace, of reconciliation in God.

> No other debt
> than love,
> no other truth . . .
> No love
> greater than forgiveness,
> no other source
> whence life is reborn.
>
> *Happy those who forgive:*
> *they welcome your forgiveness, Lord.*
>
> Love is known by this:
> the Son of God has given his life for you.
>
> The Lord has forgiven you,
> do the same in your turn.
>
> Love, love in truth,
> you will know God's peace.[16]

Twenty-fifth Sunday

Send Us to Work in Your Vineyard!

The Thoughts and Ways of a God Rich in Forgiveness

The manner in which God leads the people he has chosen and gathered—his Church—is often disconcerting for believers. Frequently, it submits faith to a severe trial. What can we answer to those who ask us "Where in the world is your God, who, you say, watches over you and guides you? If he exists, he is mocking you. What befalls you obviously shows that you delude yourselves by trusting your so-called God." To tell the truth, these objections do not necessarily come from outside ourselves; they spontaneously rise from our own hearts. We are then strongly tempted, if not to deny God, at least to settle for a more "reasonable" view of things. This is a deadly mistake says the Book of Isaiah (Isa 55:6-9).

Instead of turning away from God, we must seek him "while he is near," that is, before we have strayed too far from him. We must abandon the dead-end roads and the evil ways of human beings and go back to God. "Generous and forgiving," he will set us back on the right track. Understand, he tells us, that "my ways are above your ways and my thoughts above your thoughts." This should not cause us any surprise. Human eyes do not see beyond a limited horizon; they see distinctly what is directly before them, in the foreground, whereas the rest progressively grows blurred and becomes more and more confused, where it is difficult, even impossible, to evaluate the distance between persons, things, and events and their real proportions. Therefore, human calculations necessarily entail great risks of error. Humans do not see that an auspicious-looking road turns sharply beyond the horizon or even ends in a precipitous slope. Because of their short-sightedness, their thoughts often prove to be deadly wrong. God, for his part, takes in, with a perfect clarity, past, present, and future. His design, written in time's continuity over which he has perfect mastery, is not disturbed in its unfolding by external vicissitudes, which oblige humans to constantly alter or replace their plans, always provisional and subject to chance. Whatever the

193

detours, God's ways always lead to the goal he has appointed. There-fore, when God tells humans to let go of their ways and thoughts, he does not ask for blind trust but for wisdom, once they take all things into account. "Do not let yourselves be deceived by the prophets and diviners who are among you; do not listen to those among you who dream dreams. . . . For I know well the plans I have in mind for you, says the LORD, plans for your welfare, not for woe! plans to give you a future full of hope" (Jer 29:8, 11). "As high as the heavens are above the earth, so high are my ways above your ways and my thoughts above your thoughts" (Isa 55:9). Here is our faith, the sure foundation of our hope, what decides us to adopt God's views with the certainty that we shall not go astray.

> *The LORD is near to all who call him.*
>
> Every day will I bless you,
>   and I will praise your name forever and ever.
> Great is the LORD and highly to be praised;
>   his greatness is unsearchable.
>
> The LORD is gracious and merciful,
>   slow to anger and of great kindness.
> The LORD is good to all
>   and compassionate toward all his works.
>
> The LORD is just in all his ways
>   and holy in all his works.
> The LORD is near to all who call upon him,
>   to all who call upon him in truth.
> (Ps 145:2-3, 8-9, 17-18)

According to God's Will

The Letter to the Philippians is one of those that Paul wrote while in prison.[1] His trial is in progress and a sentence of death is a possibility; therefore, he sends to the Church of Philippi a sort of spiritual testament.[2] After the customary greetings and thanks found as a rule in the begin-ning of his letters, Paul explains his personal circumstances. He has been able to see that his arrest has not hindered the progress of the gospel. On the contrary, it has prompted most of the believers to preach the word with more boldness. The greater number have so acted to continue Paul's ministry and thus soothe the suffering caused by his enforced inaction. Some have acted out of less pure motives: jealous, they have grasped this opportunity to show that the community easily dispensed with him. What does it matter? In either case, Christ is announced. But what is going to become of him, Paul? How does he foresee the issue of his prison term (Phil 1:20c-24, 27a)?

His feelings are mixed. He would like "to depart life and be with Christ," but to "remain [in] the flesh" will allow him to pursue his ministry in the service of the gospel. So he does not know which to choose. He entrusts himself to God's grace. Many others, after Paul, have known similar hesitations. The example of St. Martin of Tours (ca. 316-317) is famous.

> Hard are the combats we must undergo in our bodies for your service, Lord; and I count enough struggles that I have endured up to now. But, should you order me to labor still more in order to guard your camp, I shall not offer as an excuse the exhaustion due to age. I shall devote myself to the task you will urge upon me; I shall serve under your banners as long as you yourself command it. No doubt, an old man would wish for retirement after a life of toil, but the soul is able to conquer the years and will know how not to yield to old age.[3]

But not only saints find themselves at a loss to know which of two options to wish for and even to pray for: the possibility of continuing the mission received from the Lord and the work undertaken or else the personal advantage offered by the end of labor and the return to the Father—"I am caught between the two." When this happens, we peacefully rely on God insofar as the motivation of our whole lives has been the sincere and disinterested search for God's will.

> The true, the only perfection is not to embrace such and such way of life; it is to do God's will. It is to lead the kind of life that God wants, where he wants, and in the manner in which he himself would have led it. . . . Whenever he leaves us free to choose, then, yes let us seek to follow him step by step, as exactly as possible, to share in his very way of life as the apostles did during his life and after his death. Love impels us to this imitation. If God leaves the choice, this freedom, to us, it is because he wants us to unfurl our sails to the wind of pure love. He wants that, moved by him, we should run after him, in the fragrance of his perfumes, in an exact imitation, like Peter and Paul. . . . Only here does perfection reside. . . : God's will, this will alone, to be where God wants us, to do what God wants of us, and in all states in which God wants us; to think, to speak, to act as Jesus would have thought, spoken, acted, if his father had placed him in the state that is ours.[4]

Paul does not speak otherwise: "Conduct yourselves in a way worthy of the gospel of Christ." The excerpts from the Letter to the Philippians to be read on the following three Sundays will give some concrete applications of what Paul means by these words.

God Hires Workers at Any Time of Day

In its method and aim, the parable of the workers in the vineyard is a particularly good example of Jesus' teaching. The method is a popular one: the parable tells a simple story; it shows ordinary persons in everyday situations; it appeals to common experience. Being thus constructed, the narrative incites the hearers to take sides, to adopt the position of such and such a person, of such and such a group of protagonists; in a word, to verbalize their spontaneous reactions to the circumstances described. Such reactions cause Jesus to react in his turn. He then says, "You think so. Well, you are in error." All see themselves directly and concretely affected by the teaching of the parable. This is why, even when we know a parable by heart, even if we have heard it a hundred times, it does not stop prompting questions in us. Finally, the parables show that Jesus knew how to announce the good news of salvation without seeking to systematically offend his hearers, without in the least watering down the demands of the gospel, and without showing any demagogic or even apologetic concern. There is a lesson here for the Church in its preaching, as well as for all Christians called to witness to the gospel and to preach it by their lives. We must, therefore, attentively reread the parable of the workers in the vineyard (Matt 20:1-16a).

The first part—the hiring of workers at dawn, around nine, noon, and five—could be read as a simple preamble necessary to introduce the scene in which every group of workers receives payment for the hours worked. Indeed, the master's behavior is the focus of the parable and contains its particular teaching. Jesus lingers a little on this hiring scene in order to arouse the hearers' curiosity and attention concerning what is going to happen in the evening when salaries are allotted. There is no reason to dwell on all the details in order to find in them an allegorical meaning. Certain Fathers of the Church have done so, interpreting the various times of hiring as successive phases of the history of salvation, the last one being our own era.[5] Preachers, for their part, have often utilized the different hiring hours to exhort latecomers to go and work in the vineyard: "It is never too late. The last-hired workers are also welcome."[6] It is possible to thus illustrate the appeal, "Oh, that today you would hear his voice: 'Harden not your hearts. . .'" (Ps 95:7d-8a). But the parable does not center on this moral exhortation, important as it is.

On the other hand, it is certainly not by chance that the parable speaks of workers sent to work in the vineyard. The image is a traditional one in the Old and New Testaments to designate God's people.[7] That it is used here emphatically shows that we are dealing with a parable of the kingdom of heaven.

We shall especially remember from this first part of the parable that this master, who goes out at any time to hire workers, behaves much like the shepherd who seeks the lost sheep (Matt 18:12-14).[8] God does not want that any of these little ones, for whom Christ came, be lost or without employment in the kingdom.

Human Justice and Divine Kindness

The way in which the master orders the payment of the workers' salaries is surprising, even shocking. Who would dare to begin with the last and finish with the first?[9] The latter, seeing that each of their companions receives a silver coin—the agreed upon sum for a whole day's work—could only expect to get at least four times that amount. But no. The master commands that they be given one silver coin, in spite of their having borne the day's burden and the heat. "It is not fair. It is even downright scandalous."

Certainly—and we know it—Jesus does not give here a lesson in justice or social equity. He intends to drive home what the kingdom of heaven is like. This, however, is not sufficient to make us accept as evident the teaching of the parable. Other and graver questions arise precisely because we are speaking of the kingdom of heaven. Would God make light of the requirements of justice and the payment of a just salary that he himself enjoined upon human beings when he gave them his Law? On the day of judgment, is he going to exercise a regal power based on his arbitrary good pleasure? The words put in the landowner's mouth answer these questions or rather show that they are not germane.

By giving to the workers the salary agreed upon, the master in no way wrongs the workers of the first hour. In any case, they do not dispute this. But they grumble because those who came last are given as much as they. And this is what the master reproaches them with, curtly reminding them that they receive their due. They are envious because the master is generous. Those workers at dawn were hired because the master is good. Through kindness, he offered them a silver coin for their salary. Therefore, they should not only be grateful to him, but also rejoice that others were called later and now receive the same pay. The parable of the workers in the vineyard is to be seen in the same perspective as that of the prodigal son and his older brother (Luke 15:11-32). In both cases, Jesus condemns the complaints of those who do not accept God's goodness. There is no room in the kingdom for the pursuit of a higher salary, since what we receive comes from God's liberality and not from our own merit. Through grace, we are given a share of his goods. If we do not see in this light the salary and God's service—the work in the vineyard—we go astray, failing to understand—and worse, to accept—that our relationship to God is one of love. "Everything I have is yours," says God to us (Luke 15:31). How can we not be overwhelmed by such generosity? How can we not rejoice when others also benefit by it? "Love is not jealous, [it] is not pompous, it is not inflated" (1 Cor 13:4).

> There are two kinds of training, there are two lineages, there are two races of saints in heaven.
> God's saints graduate from two schools.
> From the school of the just and the school of the sinner.
> From the tottering school of sin.
> It's a good thing the schoolmaster is always God.
> There are those who come from the just and there are those who come from sinners.
> It's a good thing there's no jealousy in heaven.
> On the contrary.
> There's the communion of saints.
> It's a good thing they're not jealous of one another. But all together, on the contrary, are close as the fingers of the hand.
> Because all together, they spend their whole time, their whole blessed day plotting against God.
> Before God.
> So that foot by foot Justice
> step by step may yield to Mercy.[10]

The Last First, the First Last

The sentence that concludes the parable in the Lectionary—"Thus the last will be first, and the first will be last"[11]—does not restrict its meaning to merely a teaching on the order in which God will render their dues to each one. To understand this word of Jesus, we must begin by discarding the meaning it has in ordinary life when it is cited as a proverb. It was necessary that the workers hired last be paid first; otherwise, the others would not have known that the master gave the latecomers the same salary as theirs, that which was agreed upon for one day's work. In the opposite case, the narrative would probably have mentioned, instead of the grumbling of those who saw themselves as unjustly dealt with, the latecomers' joy and astonishment. But this is not what Jesus wanted to speak of. Jesus' intention was certainly not to emphasize only—and rather uselessly—a secondary theme of the parable.

It would also be too skimpy and too simplistic to say that when pay-day comes, we who have arrived at the last hour shall go ahead of others.[12] Matthew is not bent on encouraging proud self-satisfaction among Christians. Throughout his whole Gospel, he appears, on the contrary, intent on vigorously warning them against such a fault.

God is just; he will not fail to give all workers what he promised them. In the parable, those hired last are paid first, and the first to be paid are those hired last. This is certainly not meant as a reward for the ones and a slight for the others. The point that must hold the hearers' attention is the piece of good luck that befalls the workers hired at day's end. The master does not discuss salary with them; nevertheless, they go to work in the vineyard, relying on the master's judgment and generosity, not worrying about the amount they will receive. In this, they are the models of God's servants who boast of nothing; they have done only their duty (Luke 17:10).[13] They are the first.

The others do not feel penalized. They have had the good fortune to be engaged at dawn. It is the master who mentions the wage and indicates its amount. He has nothing to reproach them with. But their behavior at pay time marks them as servants who are jealous of their companions and murmur because God, the master of the vineyard, is good. Those who resemble them will be the last, even though they will have borne the day's burden and heat.

The final saying does not explain any teaching in the parable. It is a general statement and concerns us all. We are God's servants—a good thing. But what kind of servants?

To Answer Every Call from God Unselfishly
In spite of similarities in vocabulary, the service of God and the salary he promises and gives have no equivalents among human beings. When he hires workers for his vineyard, he bestows a grace on them. When he pays them, not only does he exceed their deserts, but he grants what no labor could ever deserve. ''I do not refuse work in your service''; this is what true servants of God say, even when they legitimately long to enjoy rest at last. To answer God's call, to remain available for what he wishes is their joy and their reward.

> Happy those you call
> at first light;

their entire lives
are a work of love.
And blessed are you, Father,
for the evening workers:
is it ever too late
to work in your vineyard?

Here we are, Lord,
whenever you call.

No more first or last,
God himself is the pay.

Peace to you who were far,
peace to those who were near.

The Master's goodness is beyond measure,
he wants to make servants his friends.

May I sing to my God
the song of his love for his vineyard.[14]

As Christ, so the Church. It has a twofold nature: human and divine. Very human, because it is made up of men and women, as is every community, and because its members are exposed to the assaults of sin and allow themselves to be overcome. However, divine also, because it is the Church of God, to whom it belongs, because, for it, to live is Christ.

In order to remain what the Church is and become more so, it must unceasingly model its ways of seeing, judging and acting upon God's. There is no other justification for Christian and ecclesiastical ways. Neither are there any possible compromises with the vision, the logic, the morals of the world.

God is concerned about the least of his own who wander from the way and risk getting lost: the Christian community must do everything to bring back an erring member.

God indefatigably forgives: the Christian community must be the place where mercy is exercised.

God is good and generous and all his gifts are grace: there is no room in the Christian community for jealousy or laying claim to any privileges, as if they were deserved.

One single debt: that of mutual love. One single object of competition: to lead a life worthy of the gospel in the disinterested service of God, brothers, and sisters.

Not to us, O Lẑṟ, not to us
   but to your name give glory'' (Ps 115:1)

''May your will be done on earth as it is in heaven'': in your Church, in our community, by each one of us.

From the Twenty-sixth to the Twenty-eighth Sunday in Ordinary Time

"Every liturgical celebration, because it is an action of Christ the Priest and of his Body, which is the Church, is a sacred action surpassing all others. No other action of the Church can equal its efficacy by the same title and to the same degree."[1] "But in order that the liturgy may be able to produce its full effects, it is necessary that the faithful come to it with proper dispositions, that their minds be attuned to their voices, and that they cooperate with heavenly grace lest they receive it in vain."[2]

Matthew's Gospel—as we have seen time and again—is characteristically insistent on the necessity to harmonize the doing with the saying, practice with faith. Moreover, he unceasingly reminds Christians that they will be judged on their actions by the one they call "Lord";[3] hence those vigorous warnings to disciples to be on their guard against false securities that would lead to their loss. The three parables read on the Twenty-sixth, Twenty-seventh, and Twenty-eighth Sundays—the two sons (Matt 21:28-32), the wicked vinedressers (Matt 21:33-43), the wedding feast (Matt 22:1-14)—proclaim that faithfulness to the Lord cannot be a dazzling display of words; one must, following Jesus' example, do the will of the Father. It is a question of life and death.

Paul's Letter to the Philippians proclaims the same message: "Have among yourselves the same attitude that is also yours in Christ Jesus." "Keep on doing what you have learned and heard and seen in me." "I have the strength for everything through him who empowers me" (Phil 2:1-11; 4:6-9; 4:12, 14, 19-20).

This new sequence of three Sundays is also, for the Christian assembly, a reminder of the demands and implications of participation in the liturgy, "summit . . . [and] fount"[4] of the life of the Church and of each believer.

Twenty-sixth Sunday

Not Promises but Acts

The Lord's Behavior: Strange but Normal

There is nothing more fearsome and complex than the exercise of justice toward delinquent persons. Unwritten law or written codes have striven, since the earliest times, to resolve, as best they can, the contradictory demands to be reckoned with: not to yield to vengefulness, but to fit the punishment to the gravity of the offense; to take into account the circumstances and guilt, but to avoid the arbitrariness of too subjective evaluations; to consider possible extenuating circumstances and complicities, but to avoid wronging the victims and harming the innocent; to make the punishment exemplary, but not to exclude a possible reform of the guilty party, etc. Today's most sophisticated codes remain imperfect, a fact of which their authors are well aware. Therefore, we should not be surprised at the gropings and hesitations of the past, at the continuing evolution of the law, as attested by the Bible, that covers so many centuries. There was a time when the notion of collective responsibility caused a whole family to be condemned for the fault of one of its members (Josh 7:24) and descendants were also seen as sharing in the crime, which lead to the saying

> The fathers ate unripe grapes,
> and the children's teeth are set on edge
> (Jer 31:29).

Deuteronomy destroyed this logic: "Fathers shall not be put to death for their children, nor children for their fathers; only for his own guilt shall a man be put to death" (Deut 24:16). This principle of personal and individual responsibility was a progress that finally became the rule of law (2 Kgs 14:6). But what about divine justice? God knows everything; he alone can evaluate with exactitude and without hesitation each one of our acts. Should he not then immediately give reward or punishment for good or bad actions? Nothing of the sort. God behaves as a judge who would drag out cases indefinitely, without deciding upon a just sentence. Is this not strange behavior? "Is it my way that is unfair, or rather, are not your ways unfair?" (Ezek 18:25-28).

The oracle does not justify this manner of acting as it could: by pointing out, for instance, that God has time on his side and, at any moment, can intervene; neither does it mention that the delay in rendering a decision is not equivalent to dropping the case. The Lord does not remain indifferent to the good or the evil done by humans. But as long as they are capable of making a free choice, God gives them this possibility. The persons who have sinned are not saddled forever with their record of convictions. The "evil ones" are not labeled once and for all. God believes in their sincere amendment—"If a wicked man, turning from the wickedness he has committed, does what is right and just, he shall preserve his life." Such is God who never despairs of anyone, who never says to the sinner, "You will never amount to anything worthwhile; you are definitely unrecoverable."

But by the same token, it is a serious warning for the "just." It will do them no good to produce their certificates of good behavior acquired yesterday or recently. They must persevere in the practice of justice and remain humble. They must not look down with contempt upon the evil ones, whose misconduct quickens their watchfulness and makes them all the more zealous to seek to convert them. All of us must be converted again and again. God's patience and mercy—that every liturgy celebrates—are the basis of our hope and an appeal to our responsibility. Far from finding the Lord's conduct strange, we sing its praise. For, if God can—and wants to—forget our rebellions, the sins of our youth, then his love never forgets us.

Remember your mercies, O LORD.

Your ways, O LORD, make known to me;
   teach me your paths,
Guide me in your truth and teach me,
   for you are God my savior.
Remember that your compassion, O LORD,
   and your kindness are from of old.
The sins of my youth and my frailties remember not;
   in your kindness remember me,
   because of your goodness, O LORD.

Good and upright is the LORD;
   thus he shows sinners the way.
He guides the humble to justice,
   he teaches the humble his way.
(Ps 125:4-5, 6-7, 8-9)

Unity, Humility, Solicitude Toward Others

No Christian community is immune to internal dissensions, rivalries between persons, and slackening of mutual charity. Often these are petty things that would be considered ridiculous if they did not risk degenerating into more serious problems. As a consequence, it is important to be watchful and to uproot the evil. This is what Paul says in his Letter to the Philippians; its solemn exhortation always proves timely (Phil 2:1-11).

The Christian community is built upon three pillars: unity, humility, and solicitude for others, which must be kept free of cracks. According to Vatican II, "The universal Church is seen to be 'a people brought into unity from the unity of the Father, the Son and the Holy Spirit.' "[1] Paul wrote to the Corinthians, "The grace of the Lord Jesus Christ and the love of God and the fellowship of the holy Spirit be with all of you" (2 Cor 13:13). This beautiful and concise formula is taken up in the Missal at the beginning of the Eucharistic celebration. It means that the unity of the assembly directly flows from the Holy Trinity. In today's reading, Paul is less explicit, but it is possible to discover a Trinitarian flavor in the manner in which he speaks of the characteristics of the community in which "there is . . . encouragement in Christ," "solace in love," "participation in the Spirit." In any case, for Paul, the necessity of unity does not need arguments; it is absolute. It manifests itself in the fact that in the community, all have "the same mind, the same love,[2] [are] united in heart, thinking one thing." Intrigues and boastfulness undermine this unity. It is impossible to live a common life in unity if all do not vie with one another for true humility. Everywhere and always, the spirit of competition, the underhanded disparaging of others in order to win the first place for oneself leads to factions, rivalries, which are deleterious, even though they are not always fully obvious. Eaten from the inside, the pillar will crumble one day and suddenly the building will fall into ruin.[3] But, in a community where unity reigns and where all members desire to occupy the last place, there will be no room for self-preoccupation.

However, Paul does not launch into a moralizing discourse. For him, Christian morality can be centered only on theological truth: "Have among yourselves the same attitude that is also yours in Christ Jesus." Spontaneously, the remarkable text of a hymn, known to his correspondents, wells up, "Christ, who though he was in the form of God. . . ."[4]

To Say "Amen" Is Not Enough. We Must Obey the Father

The parable that shows us two sons asked by their father to work in his vineyard for the day is crystal-clear. The first begins by refusing the request. "Afterwards he changed his mind and went." The other immediately agrees, "Yes sir," but does not budge. There is no possible doubt; the first one does his father's will. What Jesus then declares is more unexpected (Matt 21:28-32).

"They say but don't do." How many times is this reproach addressed to Christians, to ecclesial communities, to "people of the cloth." Rightly or wrongly? Does this reproach target us or others? Are those who denounce the gap between the words and actions of Christians and the Church, simply accustomed to being scandalized? Could we not retort that first they should remove the beam in their eye? This sort of controversy leads nowhere; it only serves to harden positions in fruitless polemics and to reinforce self-satisfaction. Jesus himself confronts us here. In no way can we contest his right to do so and reply "And what about you?" "For the Son of God, Jesus Christ . . . was not 'yes' and 'no,' but 'yes' has been in him" (2 Cor 1:19).

He does not ask us to adopt a low profile or even prolong our confession of sin, to rue the denials shown by our actions, whereas so often, in private as well as in the liturgy, we say Amen. Time is pressing, and we have already lost too much of it. Let us go and work in the vineyard—the Lord will see our repentance.

Publicans and Prostitutes Enter Before You

As if the lesson were not already clear enough, Jesus adds a word introduced by the solemn formula "Amen, I say to you." "Tax collectors and prostitutes are entering the kingdom of God before you." Maybe we are too accustomed to this text to perceive all of its force and its shocking character. We must have recourse to explanations to understand why the term "publican" typifies sinners. But when it is associated with that of "prostitute," there is no longer any possible hesitation.[5]

Jesus reminds us of the reason why tax collectors and prostitutes precede others, the self-righteous who boast of their title of "just" because they never stop saying, "Yes, Lord." John the Baptist inveighed against Pharisees and Sadducees—those "pure" ones who flocked to his baptism: "You brood of vipers! Who warned you to flee from the coming wrath? Produce good fruit as evidence of your repentance. And do not presume to say to yourselves, 'We have Abraham as our father.' For I tell you, God can raise up children to Abraham from these stones" (Matt 3:7-9).[6] He was already proclaiming, "It is not enough to say; you must do; it is not enough to accomplish religious acts; you must accomplish what they signify and imply." All prophets have said the same thing, and Christian preaching does not stop repeating it. Because they listened to the Baptist, tax collectors and prostitutes turned to Jesus and received his teaching with joy.[7] But Matthew does not recall this simply to make sure his readers remember the attitude of these different persons when they heard John's preaching and Jesus' teaching.[8] He does not suggest either that we should look around us in order to appreciate, with satisfaction or incredulity, the impact of the gospel among today's publicans and prostitutes. What he does is give a serious warning to those who, seeing sinners unexpectedly converted, do not themselves repent and believe in the Lord's word. This word is proclaimed in the assembly gathered for the liturgy; and it is acclaimed, "Praise to you, Lord Jesus Christ!" After this vibrant "yes," do we hasten to go, this very day, to work in the vineyard? As we are about to leave the church, the Lord's call is repeated, "Go in the peace of Christ." To answer, "Thanks be to God," and then quickly go back home, would be to condemn one's self and, in a word, to mock Christ as well as the liturgy while becoming, besides, an occasion of scandal for brothers and sisters, believers and unbelievers alike.

Our Actions Judge Us

"Intention is as good as action," the proverb says. This is true when the genuine intention cannot be actualized because of an obstacle independent of one's will. However, actions usually prove the seriousness of the intention. In any case, the intention to convert, even if frequently repeated, is not itself conversion. In religious matters, to limit oneself to the declaration of intentions becomes scandalous and closes entry into the kingdom of God. When he comes back in glory, the Son of Man will recognize as disciples those who will have acted, even unknowingly, according to the gospel. The others will be cast far from him (Matt 25:31-46). If mention is eventually made of their multiple professions of faith, it will be as an aggravating circumstance, and rightly so. They will see tax collectors and prostitutes take the places they themselves should have occupied. This behavior of the Supreme Judge is not strange. But it arouses surprise among those who do not go past declarations of intention and imagine that it is enough to say "Lord, Lord!" Who do they think God and his Christ are?

For God did not just promise salvation—he accomplished it. He sent his own Son, who did not hesitate to empty himself of everything to the point of "death, even death on a cross" to obey the Father's will. There is no other salvation than obedient faith, faith showing itself in actions. In order to understand this, there is no need for reasoning; it is enough to look at Christ, to truthfully celebrate the memorial of his passion and resurrection.

> Life in the kingdom does not consist of in an inscription. Entrance into the kingdom requires a living and continual will, a constant and present acceptance of God's will for us. It is a "yes" constantly repeated. On the contrary, what is constant with us is our unfaithfulness. In particular, there is a way of escaping God's will while believing one is doing it. This is a frequent defect among intellectuals; it consists in confusing the reality of a thing with the plan, the thought, the idea of this thing. It is possible to think very profoundly of something, to taste this thing and make much of it in one's mind, and yet live in a wholly different manner. A certain deformation of our intellectual attitude prevents us from measuring the gap. However, there is no definitive settling in the kingdom of God. If we do not seek to enter it at every instant, we leave it without even noticing we have done so.[9]

A People Chosen to Bear Fruit

The Song of the Beloved to His Vineyard

Today, the Liturgy of the Word begins with the reading of a poetic lament found early in the Book of Isaiah (Isa 5:1-7).

> Let me sing of my friend,
> my friend's song concerning his vineyard.

Even today, the vine, wealth and pride of vine-growing regions, is the object of a sort of worship. One watches over it without ceasing. One takes continual care of it. One scrutinizes its blooming; but whatever the hope entertained, one must wait until the harvest to evaluate the quantity and quality of its fruit, because all can be ruined by disease or weather: a late frost, too much or too little rain, unpredictable sunshine. The vine is a curious plant. Its wood is not sightly and is good for nothing. It must be pruned so that only a few branches remain. The dry vine-shoots are burned. It is therefore not surprising that the biblical authors have taken the vine as a privileged image of the people whom God cultivates and from whom he expects beautiful fruit.[1]

In vine-growing regions, the grape harvest is the great yearly feast, especially when the yield is good; a day of bitter disappointment, when the fruit is mediocre; a day of mourning, when there is nothing worth picking.[2] Perhaps the memory of an elegy sung in one of those catastrophic years inspired Isaiah's poem. But here we are speaking of "the vineyard of the Lord of hosts," "the house of Israel," "the men of Judah . . . his cherished plant."

The Lord had done everything for his vineyard. He had planted "choicest vines" on "a fertile hillside" with a good exposure, carefully hedged it in to keep away trespassers and animals that might have damaged it; there was even a "watchtower." One could hope for the best: a "wine press" had already been hewed out. Alas! "Why, when I looked for the crop of grapes, did it bring forth wild grapes?" In his sorrow, the master appeals to the land's inhabitants as to witnesses: "Judge between me and my vineyard. What more was there to do for my vineyard that I have not done?"

God is justified in holding his vineyard responsible, because he has not withheld sunshine and rain. It should have borne abundant fruit of justice and righteousness, but it has produced only iniquity. It deserves to be punished: the "fertile hillside," abandoned to itself, without care, is going to lie fallow and produce only thorns and briers, to become an arid desert deprived of beneficial rain.

What a warning! May the Lord not prolong such a devastation. May he come and save his people.

> *The vineyard of the* LORD *is the house of Israel.*
>
> A vine from Egypt you transplanted;
>   you drove away the nations and planted it.
> It put forth its foliage to the Sea,
>   its shoots as far as the River.
>
> Why have you broken down its walls,
>   so that every passer-by plucks its fruit,
> The boar from the forest lays it waste,
>   and the beasts of the field feed upon it?
> Once again, O LORD of hosts,
>   look down from heaven, and see;
> Take care of this vine,
>   and protect what your right hand has planted
>   [the son of man whom you yourself made strong].
> Then we will no more withdraw from you;
>   give us new life, and we will call upon your name.
> O LORD of hosts, restore us;
>   if your face shine upon us, then we shall be safe.
> (Ps 80:9, 12, 13-14, 15-16, 19-20)

Last Advice from an Apostle in Prison

Sometimes the Letter to the Philippians has been seen as a collection of notes that Paul, uncertain of his fate, sent from prison to the community in Philippi. This is quite plausible, and if it is the case, we should thank those who had the excellent idea to save these messages that even today maintain their relevance. This applies to the short pieces of advice that make up today's second reading (Phil 4:6-9).

We all have our share of preoccupations of every kind: personal difficulties, concern over relatives or friends, community trials. We should not minimize these and fall prey to a smug optimism, thus proving ourselves to be either frivolous or unaware. This is not Paul's style. However, neither must we allow ourselves to be dominated and paralyzed by anxiety. "In everything, by prayer and petition, with thanksgiving, make your requests known to God." This is what Paul advises during his captivity. Prayer does not induce anaesthesia or euphoria; it does not cause us to rise above difficulties. But, whatever happens, it gives us, from God, an astonishing peace "that surpasses all understanding." This peace of mind and heart comes from Christ (John 14:27) because he himself is our peace (Eph 2:13-14). It is this peace we ask for at the moment of union with him in the sacrament of his Body and Blood.

Should we doubt this, we clearly see the realism of Paul's spirituality in what follows—Christian morality assumes what most human beings commonly regard as respectable. Paul uses this human morality as the foundation for Christians' behavior: "Whatever is true, whatever is honorable, whatever is just, whatever is pure, whatever is lovely, whatever is gracious, if there is any excellence and if there is anything worthy of praise, think about these things." They will be able to put into practice the gospel teachings that have been announced to them and to follow the example Paul himself gave them. To tell the truth, Paul does not consider himself as the highest model; he has always sought to imitate Christ. Whoever follows this way will have "the peace of God." The only true model is Christ. However, we need to see this imitation of Christ lived by men and women like us. Such is the saints' role and the reason for their veneration; in them, God gives us "[in] their lives on earth . . . an example; in our communion with them . . . their friendship; in their prayer for the Church . . . strength and protection."[3]

The Drama of Greedy and Murderous Vinedressers

The parable of the homicidal vinedressers begins with an echo of the "vineyard song" of the first reading. Here, however, we no longer have an elegiac poem inspired by disappointment at the low quality of grapes, but a drama in which the culprits are the vinedressers (Matt 21:33-43).

The story proves to be less unlikely than at first appears. There were in Galilee—and still are in certain countries—powerful landowners who, having acquired vast domains, are heard from once a year—to collect the produce of "their" land. It happened in Galilee—and still happens in certain countries—that *campesinos* revolted against the stockpiling landowners. The persons sent to gather the fruit of the farmers' labor are the first to be the victims of their rebellion. Woe to the landowner if, not coming in person, he dares to send his own son. Why should the rebels respect him? To kill him would insure their remaining masters of the land now in foreign hands. The adventure of these desperate workers always ends in tragedy, as is well known. Therefore, Jesus' hearers answer his question "What will the owner of the vineyard do to those tenants when he comes?" without hesitation: "He will put those wretched men to a wretched death and lease his vineyard to other tenants who will give him the produce at the proper times." The example and the memory of the heavy repression will prevent, for a long time, all attempts at a similar rebellion.

The parable told by Jesus could be read thus, remaining banal though dramatic. But it would be difficult to see what he meant to teach. Would he have described such a drama only to bluntly side with the owner as if the latter were the completely innocent victim of greedy and criminal persons? In this case, Jesus' position would raise—especially today—grave objections.[4] But we are warned at the very first that we have here a parable, that it speaks to the chief priests and elders and not to agricultural laborers or powerful landowners. Moreover—and especially—the reference to the vineyard song removes all danger of ambiguity. The parable turns into allegory; it concerns the kingdom.

In the framework of Jesus' ministry, this parable-allegory has a decidedly polemical aim against the religious leaders of the people.[5] Today, it is read without reference to this conflict-ridden context. In terms hardly disguised and very revealing, Jesus speaks of God's conduct toward his people and the malfeasance of the leaders he had appointed or even anointed. Not only have many been unfaithful to their mission as stewards, but they have often persecuted or even killed those whom the Lord had sent them.[6] This tragic story is told throughout the Bible. For those who still read the Scriptures, it remains a sobering subject for meditation. In the son "finally sent," Christians see Jesus put to death outside the city because his message was troublesome and because he never ceased to exhort his hearers to produce fruits of penance. For God did not send only his servants the prophets, but his own Son.

> Certain persons could imagine that God sent to humankind some subordinate—angel, ruler, one of the spirits in charge of terrestrial affairs, or one of those running the celestial government—but he actually sent the Craftsman and the Organizer of the universe. It is through him that God created the heavens, through him that he restrained the sea within its limits. It is he whose mysterious laws the cosmic elements faithfully observe; he from whom the sun has received the rule it keeps in its daily course; he whom the moon, shining at night, obeys; he to whom submit the celestial bodies that accompany the moon in its journey. It is by him that all things have been given order, limits, and hierarchy: the heavens and everything

which is in the heavens, the earth and everything which is on the earth, the sea and everything which is in the sea, fire, air, the abyss, the world above, the world below, and all the regions in between. This is the one God has sent to humankind.[7]

He is "[the] stone that the builders rejected" which "has become the cornerstone." The literal quotation of Psalm 118:22-23 turns Christian readers' attention no longer simply to the announcement of Christ's passion, but rather to the fate of the kingdom, to the admirable work God has done by raising his Son. But Christians cannot forget the consequences of the refusal of the vinedressers who have thrown the Son outside the vineyard. Neither do Christians forget what the Church of Christ owes to the Jews.[8] It does not read the parable of the wicked tenants with any aggressiveness toward anyone. The Church receives it as an admonition addressed to itself. It cannot fail to do so because Matthew has too consistently insisted on the necessity of bearing fruit. The Church will be faithful to its mission and election only if it welcomes the prophets whom God does not cease to send it, only if it practices the gospel of his Son, only if it remains faithful through everything. The vineyard song still resounds in today's Church.

O my Church,
how shall I love you more?
I have planted you as a choice vine,
for you my Son's blood has flowed,
new sap in your branches.
Where are the fruits I was hoping for?

Master of the vineyard,
do not reject the work of your hands!

If you mark faults, who will stand?
But with you is forgiveness.

Our sins are stronger than we are,
but you, you blot them out.

Visit this vine, protect it,
your right hand has planted it.

Your wrath lasts but an instant,
your mercy endures for life.[9]

Happy Are Those Invited to the Wedding of the Lamb

See What God Prepares for All Peoples

One of the characteristics of the Old Testament—and the source of its riches—is that it gathers writings of all kinds composed in the course of two millennia.[1] What is true of the whole of the ancient Scriptures is verified also in a good number of the individual books. Thus the Book of Isaiah is a collection of oracles set down from the eighth to the fifth century B.C. The text read on this Sunday belongs to the most recent part of this ensemble, which has come down to us under the name of a single author (Isa 25:6-9).[2]

The prophet's attention and reflection are directed to "that day" which will see the fulfillment of the work of salvation accomplished by God. To describe that day, the author has recourse to images suggested by the great royal celebrations that he has witnessed or of which he has heard tales magnifying their grandiose character. That day will be like a great banquet, not only organized by God but actually prepared by him. A banquet of all peoples gathered on the mountain that is the place of God's presence. A feast incomparably more sumptuous than wedding meals, sacred meals in the Temple, those which kings planned in order to display their magnificence,[3] but resembling in no way the orgies often censured by the prophets.[4] What is more, this great banquet is only an image describing the immense joy of the just, admitted on that day to God's table, into God's presence, into God's community of life.[5]

It will be the end of all bereavements, sufferings, humiliations: all that one will have endured will vanish. God will go so far as to destroy death for ever. In the Book of Revelation, John writes: "God himself will always be with them. . . . He will wipe every tear from their eyes, and there shall be no more death. . . ." (Rev 21:3-4). Today's Christians understand the prophet's oracle in this manner, and they know that victory over death has been gained by Christ's death and resurrection.[6]

That day, in which hope will be fulfilled, will be the time of endless

214

thanksgiving that our liturgies anticipate in songs, where are intermingled the "already" and the "not yet," the present and the future we already possess in promise.

> *I shall live in the house of the* LORD
> *all the days of my life.*
>
> The LORD is my shepherd; I shall not want.
>   In verdant pastures he gives me repose;
> Beside restful waters he leads me;
>   he refreshes my soul.
> He guides me in right paths
>   for his name's sake.
> Even though I walk in the dark valley
>   I fear no evil; for you are at my side
> With your rod and your staff
>   that give me courage.
>
> You spread the table before me
>   in the sight of my foes;
> You anoint my head with oil;
>   my cup overflows.
> Only goodness and kindness follow me
>   all the days of my life;
> And I shall dwell in the house of the LORD
>   for years to come.
> (Ps 23:1-3, 3-4, 5, 6)

God Gives Strength to Endure Anything

In the conclusion of his Letter to the Philippians, Paul thanks his correspondents for the material help they have thoughtfully sent him in prison. Today, we read an excerpt from this note[7] where, once more, we see the way in which Paul looks at the most ordinary things (Phil 4:12-14, 19-20).[8]

Paul has voluntarily renounced his right to their help by not demanding that the communities he was evangelizing provide for his needs. He has chosen rather to work with his hands to meet his daily necessities (Acts 20:34). He has not acted out of pride, in order not to owe anything to anybody, but to remain totally free in the exercise of his mission. This absolute unselfishness has often reduced him to penury, and he has known hunger (2 Cor 11:22-23). The apostolic ministry, today as yesterday, demands such a price that must be agreed upon with joy. Is it not the normal condition of the missionary of the gospel? "Without cost you have received; without cost you are to give," said Jesus to the Twelve he was sending on a mission (Matt 10:8). "Do not take gold or silver or copper for your belts," but he added, "the laborer deserves his keep" (Matt 8:9-10). "Eat and drink what is offered to you" (Luke 10:7). The Lord himself has lived this way, unattached, free of preoccupation for his daily needs, knowing how to be content with little. But he accepted the aid which some volunteered to give him. "Afterward he journeyed from one town and village to another, preaching and proclaiming the good news of the kingdom of God. Accompanying him were the Twelve and some women . . . : Mary, called Magdalene . . . Joanna, the wife of Herod's steward Chuza, Susanna, and many others who provided for them out of their resources" (Luke 8:1-3). In like manner, Paul has accepted the generous material help of the Philippians, and he is grateful to them (Phil 4:10-11, 15-18). But let no one be mistaken; he is not to be taken for a Stoic. If he can endure everything, it is with the one who grants him strength—Christ, who "for [our] sake became poor although he was rich, so that by his poverty [we] might become rich" (2 Cor 8:9).[9] And Paul rejoices to see that the Philippians—as their liberality proves[10]—take seriously the Lord's example and the gospel that has been preached to them. Let them return thanks to God for what he gives them the grace to accomplish.

> May God lure you with a taste for sharing
> and for humble service:
> You will transmit his justice
> without alloy!
>
> *Let us not waste this day,*
> *the just way is that of love!*
>
> May God lure you with a taste for living in him
> in humble silence:
> He will know how to tell you
> he is present.
>
> May God lure you with the taste for his work
> in humble patience:
> He will turn your trial
> into praise!
>
> And may he lure you with the taste for the feast
> in the play of his grace:
> You will prove that you are
> of his race![11]

The Parable of Those Invited to the Wedding Feast

After the parables of the two sons and of the wicked tenants, we have that of the people invited by a king who is celebrating his son's wedding. Several similarities between this and the preceding parable show a parallelism in their composition: two groups of servants are sent: in the one parable to collect the produce; in the other, to urge those invited to come to the feast. The second group of servants are mistreated, and even killed; punishment is swift and severe. But one also notices a dramatic progression from one parable to the other: not only are the murderers themselves put to death, but their city is burned down. Others are called to replace them and attend the wedding, in the same way the vineyard was to be leased to trustworthy workers. But this is not all. One of the guests is not wearing the wedding garment; he is harshly chastised.[12] Therefore, we must attentively read this Gospel passage to the final sentence, without evading its difficulties (Matt 22:1-14).

In Matthew's Gospel, the parable presents a king who celebrates his son's wedding.[13] This detail inclines us to an allegorizing interpretation. In this parable of the kingdom of heaven, the king immediately calls God to mind and, at the same time, the messianic nuptials at the end of time:[14] "Blessed is the one who will dine in the kingdom of God" (Luke 14:15); "Blessed are those who are called to the wedding feast of the Lamb" (Rev 19:9).

God has sent this invitation from the beginning; it has not ceased to be heard, more and more pressing. Servants in great numbers have been dispatched to human beings of all generations. Finally, Jesus has come announcing that the kingdom of God is at hand.[15] He has entrusted to his disciples the mission of proclaiming it (Matt 10:7). This message has already reached us since we are believers. We respond to the invitation each time we gather around the table to participate in the liturgy: "Happy are those who are called to his supper." We should not, however, imagine that the parable of this Sunday does not concern us. On the contrary, Matthew placed it in his Gospel because he was thinking of Christians of his time.[16] To tell the truth, the other evangelists recorded Jesus' acts and words with the same intention, as the conclusion of John's Gospel explicitly states (20:30-31). But this is particularly the case for the parable of those invited to the wedding of the king's son. Matthew appended to it another parable, that of the guest who was not wearing the nuptial garment. When he told this parable, speaking to the chief priests and the elders of the people (Matt 21:23), Jesus had in mind those of his contemporaries who refused his invitation and were about to put him to death. But this Gospel is read today to a Christian assembly. It would be an error to definitively relegate to the past the story of those who were first invited; to tell ourselves that they received what they deserved, that we have nothing in common with them since we have replaced them.[17]

The attitude of some among those invited in the first place will particularly hold our attention. They simply ignored the invitation, going "one to his farm, another to his business." "Worldly anxiety and the lure of riches" (Matt 13:22)[18] prevented them from taking seriously the Lord's invitation. "I don't have the time," "I am occupied with my business and my obligations" are excuses often proffered when the Lord's invitations reach us. "Not everyone who says to me 'Lord, Lord,' will enter the kingdom of heaven," Jesus proclaimed to the disciples gathered around him on the mountain (Matt 7:21).[19]

Holy Scripture shows us throughout that those God sent to invite guests to the royal wedding were mistreated or even put to death.[20] Jesus did not fail to warn us of the dangers in store for the messengers of the gospel: they will not be better dealt with than their master (Matt 10:16-25). As to those who refuse to receive the king and his delegates, they will know God's wrath through their own fault.[21] After this admonition, we concentrate our attention on the guests who have entered the wedding hall.

The Parable of the Guests and the Wedding Garment

The king sends his servants to the crossroads to assemble all passers-by that they may replace those who failed him. They soon are numerous enough, good and bad, to fill the banquet hall. What marvelous universalism—now the celebration is open to all, without condition.

As is often the case in parables, what follows holds surprises and shows that one must guard against hasty interpretations. The king enters "to meet the guests." But this is not an ordinary visit in order to enjoy his satisfaction at not having prepared the sumptuous banquet for nothing; he is coming to conduct an inspection. He catches sight of a man who is not wearing the nuptial garment, "How is it that you came in here without a wedding garment?" We would be tempted to answer in the guest's place, "Your servants so hurried us, I really did not have time to bother with it. What is surprising is that the others were able to get this festive clothing. Is it really that important?" But the man who is questioned remains silent. Therefore, he is conscious of having failed his duty, of being an intruder. The parable gives no explanation; it records only the king's sentence and the order given to the servants to execute the guest straightaway, which implies that the servants have no responsibility in this garment business. The sentence is terrible; it is the same as for the weeds sown in the wheat field by an enemy (Matt 13:42), for the bad fish caught in the net (Matt 13:50), for the unfaithful servant who will share the fate of the hypocrites (Matt 24:51). Therefore, what could appear incoherent in the structure of the parable is not so—far from it— to the eyes of the Christians for whom Matthew recorded it[22] and who read his Gospel from end to end as we ourselves have been doing from the beginning of this year's Ordinary Time. Under various forms, Matthew never stops preaching that faith—the first response to the Lord's invitation—is of no value if it does not translate into action. On the contrary, it is an aggravating circumstance: "Depart from me, you accursed, into the eternal fire prepared for the devil and his angels . . . you did not do. . . "(Matt 25:41).[23] The man who does not have the wedding garment evokes those who have been fruitless, who have not "put on the Lord Jesus Christ" or "the new self," to use Paul's words.[24]

Many Are Invited, but Few Are Chosen

Jesus' word placed here by Matthew says nothing about the actual number of the elect or about their proportion in relation to the others. This is a question that Jesus refused to answer. He came to teach humans the way of salvation and to exhort them to follow it (Matt 7:13-14).[25] "Many are invited, but few are chosen." We have here a solemn warning that underscores the timeliness of this parable with its unexpected turns.

Matthew can only rejoice at the sight of those who have responded to the Lord's invitation. But among them there are good and bad alike. It would be gravely wrong to assert, "We are safe." The Gospel says in effect: "No. Nothing is final before the day when the Lord himself will enter the banquet hall to see the guests. What cannot be discerned today will not escape his glance. Whoever will be found not dressed in the wedding garment will be thrown outside."

Invited Today to God's Table

On the eve of his passion, Jesus left us the sacrament of the feast prepared by God on his mountain for all peoples of the earth. Already today, God welcomes at his table those whom he wants to see, one day, fill the banquet hall for the wedding of his Son, the Church's Spouse. The Eucharist is both a sacramental celebration and a sacramental anticipation—through efficacious signs—of what will happen on that day. Our participation in that sign prepares and begins our participation in the banquet of the Jerusalem above, on the mountain of God. It is within the framework of the Eucharistic liturgy that the parable of those invited to the wedding of the king's son takes on its full meaning and directly affects us.

The Church, which has a foretaste of the heavenly banquet, must go to the crossroads in order to invite to the wedding feast all those it encounters, "bad and good alike," but also to teach them the demands of the kingdom of heaven. Christians assembled around the Lord's table have the heavy responsibility to "manifest to others . . . the real nature of the true Church"[26] and the meaning of participation in the Eucharist, the "summit toward which the activity of the Church is directed . . . [and] also the fount from which all her power flows."[27] Each one has the duty to act in such a way that most people become aware of the invitation to the Lord's meal, and many are moved to join them when they see Christians celebrating. This demands that Christians show themselves "having put on Christ" as attested by their good works.

Like the Church, the liturgical assembly is made of sinners. Therefore, there is no room for self-glorification because all know that their strength comes from God, beginning with the fruits of conversion which the grace of the Eucharist causes them to produce and which they offer with Christ's offering. The liturgy is the privileged place where Christians acknowledge their deafness to the Lord's call and turn to God, trustfully entreating him to bring them back to himself and give them a sincere and determined heart, in joy.

> You were hungry,
> you were thirsty,
> for you I have prepared
> the wedding feast.
>   So many other voices
> have drowned out your call,
> so many lies
> have ensnared our hearts.
>
> *Lord, call us back to your love!*
>
> Your days were spent
> far from my joy,
> for you I have prepared
> festive garments.
>   So many other joys

Scattered our desires,
so many mirages
fascinated our eyes.

Lord, call us back to your love.[28]

The celebrations of the Twenty-sixth, Twenty-seventh, and Twenty-eighth Sundays could be called "liturgies for times of crisis," when we must make serious decisions. Indeed, the Word of God proclaimed on these three Sundays in Ordinary Time vigorously reminds us of the urgency of these decisions. Today, we must obey God in action, not just in word. Today, his call resounds to share in the meal prepared by him for those he loves resounds everywhere. Today, we are given the opportunity to take to ourselves "whatever is true, whatever is honorable, whatever is just, whatever is pure, whatever is lovely, whatever is gracious, if there is any excellence and if there is anything worthy of praise" (Phil 4:8); to put into practice what we have learned and received when we welcomed the gospel.

Then, having celebrated the Lord's meal on earth, in truth and joy, we shall take our place, with the chosen, at the wedding banquet of the Lamb, in the kingdom.

From the Twenty-ninth to the Thirty-first Sunday in Ordinary Time

The Gospels of the Twenty-ninth, Thirtieth, and Thirty-first Sundays proclaim serious lessons that Jesus taught, not in the form of parables but within the framework of harsh confrontations with scribes and Pharisees. These teachings show in full light what characterizes the gospel and the life lived according to it, in opposition to die-hard religious conceptions and practices that to the present day threaten to distort Christian behavior into a caricature. "Is it lawful to pay the census tax to Caesar or not?" (Matt 22:15-21—Twenty-ninth Sunday). "Teacher, which commandment in the law is the greatest?" (Matt 22:34-40—Thirtieth Sunday). These are genuine questions that must be asked. But in what spirit are they asked? Is it with a sincere heart and in order to conduct oneself according to the gospel, or is it to find loopholes through which to escape its exigencies? Beyond this—and we see once again a constant theme of Matthew's Gospel—is our religion vain ostentation or loyal and sincere practice? Fighting against religious Pharisaism, Jesus speaks to us with a rare vehemence, the accents of which are unforgettable (Matt 23:1-12—Thirty-first Sunday).

At the beginning of this sequence, we start the reading of the First Letter to the Thessalonians, the earliest of the New Testament writings, dating back to the year 51.

Twenty-ninth Sunday

"Repay to Caesar
What Belongs to Caesar . . .
to God What Belongs to God

Without Me There Is Nothing

The first reading of this Sunday cannot fail to surprise, even to shock the modern reader. What is the meaning of a prophecy that proclaims a king, the great conqueror Cyrus, to be "anointed," "messiah"[1] of God? In fact, history has shown the cruel ambiguities and the dangers of bestowing a sacred character upon rulers and the aberrations that result from it.[2] How is it possible for this text from the Book of Isaiah to find a place in the liturgy (Isa 45:1, 4-6a)?

Cyrus, king of Persia from 550 to 530 B.C., left the memory of a deliverer in the minds of the peoples of the Near East. In the empire formed by his conquests, he practiced a conciliatory policy aimed at winning the conquered peoples by its tolerance, by the lessening of the burdens laid on them, by economic programs. Israel did not forget that Cyrus quickly brought to an end, as soon as 538, the deportation to Babylon. He gave back the utensils of gold and silver taken from the Temple by Nebuchadnezzar and, above all, he published an edict authorizing the rebuilding of the Temple.[3] Truly, Cyrus was, for Israel, a providential king; every reader of Sacred Scripture must concede it. This oracle from the Book of Isaiah says the same thing in its own way. It sees history as directed by God, its master, for the benefit of his people. Even if our conceptions are no longer exactly the same, we still believe that God dominates events, pursues his saving plan, and causes everything to work for the good of those who love him (Rom 8:28) and place their trust in him. Everything that is, even trials imposed by malice, the murderous madness of the powerful. All the more we believe that a leader's benevolence, which historians call political intelligence, comes from God. We must thank him for remembering his people. It would be unjust to take the prophet for a vile opportunist and to cite his example in order to sanction or, on the

223

contrary, to pillory leaders according to whether they favor or oppose the interests, the ambitions, the agenda of the group, the class to which we belong.[4] We must not mistake any god for God. "I am the Lord and there is no other, there is no God besides me." This proclamation is at the heart of the liturgy, as well as of faith.

> *Give the LORD glory and honor.*
>
> Sing to the LORD a new song;
> sing to the LORD, all you lands.
> Tell his glory among the nations;
> among all peoples, his wondrous deeds.
>
> For great is the LORD and highly to be praised;
> awesome is he, beyond all gods.
> For all the gods of the nations are things of nought,
> but the LORD made the heavens ·
>
> Give to the LORD, you families of nations,
> give to the LORD glory and praise;
> give to the LORD the glory due his name!
> Bring gifts, and enter his courts.
> Worship the LORD in holy attire;
> tremble before him, all the earth;
> Say among the nations: The LORD is king,
> he governs the peoples with equity.
> (Ps 96:1, 3, 4-5, 7-8, 9-10)

The Announcement of the Gospel, Power of the Spirit

Paul's First Letter to the Thessalonians is precious for several reasons. Written only some twenty years after Christ's death, before all other New Testament writings, it already contains the main doctrinal themes that are the riches of the Apostle's thought. It allows us a glimpse of the fervor and the level of Christian formation attained by a community founded in a pagan milieu.[5] On this Sunday, we read only the very beginning: address, salutation, and initial thanksgiving (1 Thess 1:1-5b).

Paul calls the community established in Thessalonica a "church"; this way of speaking is therefore very ancient.[6] The term goes back to the "assembly" of the Exodus desert, "convoked" by God to give it his Law and make of it his people (see Acts 7:38).[7] It possesses this quality "in God the Father and the Lord Jesus Christ," because it is convened by the Father and is gathered here around the Lord. It deserves this appellation because of the Thessalonians' active faith,[8] their charity that labors,[9] their strong and enduring hope.[10] Such are, we must remember, the marks of an authentically Christian community: adherence through acts to the

Christian message, practice of the "new commandment," assured trust in divine promises, and an ardent desire to see them fulfilled. "[We know], brothers loved by God, how you were chosen. For our gospel did not come to you in word alone, but also in power and in the holy Spirit and [with] much conviction." These two sentences give us matter for thought. Paul, Silvanus, and Timothy spent relatively little time in Thessalonica.[11] They had to leave this city in a hurry. And yet the time had been enough for them to establish a community—a Church—firmly secure in its faith. The same happened again and again throughout Paul's missionary journeys; he never sojourned more than three years running in the same city.[12] Of course, he was not the only one who preached; a small band of co-workers accompanied him. Still, the fact remains that in the space of a few months churches were founded, organized under local leaders, and developed on the foundation of an apostolic preaching of short duration. A similarly rapid evangelization happened again in the history of the Church, with the great itinerant missionaries who Christianized Europe, for example, or during the voyage of Francis Xavier (1506–1552) in Eastern Asia and in Japan. In Paul's case, the explanation is a simple one: the initiative comes from God, who—one does not know how—had prepared hearts. Then, the announcement of the gospel has not been "word alone, but also . . . power . . . in the holy Spirit."

> When the Church goes to a people who has not yet received the faith, it goes to meet a grace from God. For grace is at work in every human group and, within each human group, in every individual; it produces there first effects that can come to fruition only through the Church and in it. The Church does not go to a mere void in order to fill it. It is attracted by a call from God. Those it approaches are not conscious of this call. The Church, however, hears it because it is more perceptive in things human than humans themselves. . . . Despite the numberless failings and refusals, despite also the opacity that individuals cannot immediately dissipate, God's grace pursues this providential preparation, the outcome of which must be the adherence of this people to the Church, which will bring to it its original contribution and its own riches. Hence the imperious and sacred character of missionary activity (although it must always be conducted in patience). What is at stake is to "deliver" and to "perfect" a divine grace.[13]

Without doubt, the secret of the apostolate and of its efficacy resides here: to go boldly "to meet a grace from God," rather than to set too much store by human resources, techniques, and strategies. This, of course, does not mean at all that one will be able to escape weariness, labors, errors, even failures.

An Insidious Trap Brought to Naught by Jesus

"Give to Caesar what is Caesar's and to God what is God's." This axiom, borrowed from the Gospels, is still quoted today. Jesus pronounced it as an answer to a deceitful question put to him with the intention of tripping him up. Since then, people have often quoted the axiom in the case of conflicts between civil power and religious obligations. What is the exact state of affairs here (Matt 22:15-21)?[14]

The Gospel explicitly relates the occasion in which the question was posed and with what intention. The evangelists attest to the obvious bad faith and hypocrisy of Jesus' interlocutors. The Pharisees ("pure ones")[15] are plotting against him with the complicity of Herod's followers. The former are intransigent toward the usurpation of power by the occupying forces; the latter are members of the faction favorable to the Romans. The leaders of the Pharisees remain cleverly in the background. They send some of their disciples. They think that Jesus will be less distrustful if undistinguished people ask a question apparently sincere and without ulterior motive, especially if these delegates suspect that they are being manipulated. For, in effect, there was a problem of conscience for many. "Is it lawful to pay the census tax to Caesar or not?" In other words, "Does the Law order us to refuse obedience to the occupying forces or does it authorize compromises?" Without going as far as participating in armed rebellion,[16] must we not support that movement by at least being tax resisters? This is a serious debate. But those who had suggested the question addressed to Jesus have only one thing in mind: to fault him by presenting him with a dilemma. Whether he answers yes or no, he is lost. If he answers "Yes," he squarely opposes the popular sentiment and sides with the detested collaborators. His apparently merciful attitude toward tax collectors will seem to be complicity with their advantageous service to the Romans; he will seem obviously contemptuous of the Law. If he answers "No," Herod's partisans are ready to denounce his revolt against the established power; and by denying his testimony, the Pharisees will be rid of him. The trap is perfectly contrived; Jesus cannot escape. But these people with their clever calculations have overlooked the wisdom of Jesus, who reads the secrets of the heart.

" 'Show me the coin that pays the census tax. . . . Whose image is this and whose inscription?' They replied, 'Caesar's.' At that he said to them, 'Then repay to Caesar what belongs to Caesar and to God what belongs to God.' "[17] With this answer, Jesus avoids the trap that appeared to be inescapable. Moreover, he confounds those who want to find fault

with him and set him against both Pharisees and Herodians, whose relations must not have improved after such a misadventure. But is this all?
Must we be content with admiring Jesus' wisdom and skill that day, as
if his words did not contain any teaching for us today? Certainly not.

Serving God Wholeheartedly

People have often understood Jesus' reply to the Pharisees' delegates and
Herod's followers as stating a principle of compromise between duties
to God and obligations to temporal power. At certain times, thinkers
elaborated a theory—"of the two swords"—according to which the
Church, which held God's power while respecting Caesar's, exercised
a supreme jurisdiction, even over the princes of this world: it judged them
and they were to be submissive to it. In fact, the question was not whether
it was allowed to pay the tax to Caesar, but whether to pay it after having recognized the supremacy of the universal jurisdiction of the Church.
It was a principle that was to confine God's sovereign power, exercised
by the Church, and Caesar's subordinate power to their respective domains. This prevented neither minor quarrels over boundaries nor violent confrontations, especially when the Church also exercised a temporal
power, and when the Pope and the emperor were both strong personalities. But in any event, by declaring "Give to Caesar what is Caesar's and
to God what is God's," Jesus did not advocate a law of compromise between the two powers.

In modern times, the separation of Church and state, whether it is imposed or negotiated,[18] has become the rule. Nevertheless, the principle
"Give to Caesar what is Caesar's and to God what is God's" continues
in force, but with another meaning. Certain persons see in it the affirmation of the total autonomy of political power that has its own laws independently of God, of the gospel, and all the more, of Church and
clerics. Any interference on the part of Church or clerics is felt as an intolerable attack. Their sensitivity on this point is sometimes so acute that
they want to confine religious values to the private sphere, i.e., as the
slogan used to express it: "Priests, stick to the sacristy." Some Christians give to Jesus' word a similar meaning. For them, faith and its expression in actions—what they give to God—constitute a domain of their
life juxtaposed to the other—what they give to Caesar—which covers all
things political, but also all the rest: their social and professional activity,
sometimes even their family life. They consider themselves irreproach-
able if they fulfill their "religious duties," even at low cost and some-

times after much haggling. Jesus did not advocate this sort of dichotomy or this Manichaeism.

The Gospel does not underestimate the duty to give back to Caesar what is Caesar's. "Be subject to every human institution for the Lord's sake, whether it be to the king as supreme or to governors as sent by him for the punishment of evildoers and the approval of those who do good. For it is the will of God that by doing good you may silence the ignorance of foolish people. Be free, yet without using freedom as a pretext for evil, but as slaves of God. Give honor to all, love the community, fear God, honor the king" (1 Pet 2:13-17). This clear apostolic guideline was given at a time when public powers persecuted Christians and the Church. We must therefore discharge our duties to Caesar without hesitation *but* give back to God what is God's. Jesus directly teaches this: the duties toward God bind all, everywhere, always. He, and he alone, demands that we give back everything to him. The rest—the duties toward Caesar—do not come afterward but simultaneously, in the light of this absolute, "for the Lord's sake," because such is God's will. Jesus has not been appointed to settle our disputes over inheritances (Luke 12:13) or our political or other problems: these are our responsibilities. However, he has not left us to our own resources. "Give back to God what is God's." "Judge everything, take your responsibilities in light of this absolute that is laid down on the Church and on everyone, without possible compromise."

God's Effigy in Us

Isaiah was able to give the name "messiah," the anointed of the Lord, to a pagan king "Whose right hand [God] grasp[s], subduing nations before him and making kings run in his service," to deliver his people. By raising Cyrus to fulfill his plan, God showed that there is nothing outside him. Therefore, how can we conceive obedience to his laws in the same terms as obedience to kings, emperors, governors, and other earthly leaders? They can require our money, our services, a part of our time. To God alone we owe everything; to him we must give back our souls, because we are created in his image—stamped with it—and because faith has been put in our hearts by the power of his Spirit.

> In the same way as Caesar looks for his image on a coin, God looks for his in your soul. "Give back to Caesar what is Caesar's," the Savior says. What does Caesar demand from you? His image. But Caesar's image is on a coin, whereas God's is in you. If the loss of a coin causes you to weep because you have lost Caesar's image, would not any damage brought in you to God's image be for you a cause for tears?[19]

The Two Inseparable Commandments

Act Toward Your Neighbor as God Acts Toward You

In the Book of Exodus, as it has come down to us,[1] the text of the Decalogue is immediately followed by what is called today the "Covenant at Mount Sinai."[2] Written later, after the Exodus, it is a series of laws and prescriptions that follow from the Ten Commandments.[3] Today's first reading, chosen with the Gospel in mind, enunciates laws regulating behavior toward widows, orphans, and poor persons obliged to ask for a loan (Exod 22:20-26).

The prescriptions of the covenant are presented as transmitted by Moses at God's command. Therefore, they are qualified by this divine origin, distinguishing them from the codes put forth by humans to regulate relations between members of a society organized around respect for individual rights. By being explicitly related to the Decalogue, they are understood as part and parcel of the Law, upon which God's people is founded. However, they take into account the experience of the people that has resulted in a greater awareness of the extent and scope of the Law given on Mount Sinai. Here one sees at close range the fundamental characteristics of the laws of God's people. They come from him who remains close to his own, who watches personally the manner in which they are observed or disregarded, and who, moreover, is intimately involved in his people's faithfulness or unfaithfulness. In sum, there is nothing of the distant lawgiver about him. He personally watches over the observance of his law, in particular when it comes to behavior toward the poor and the weak.[4] To mistreat, to oppress, to intimidate them is to insult God, to act as if he did not exist, to render him evil for good. Should we forget all he did for his own when they were reduced to nothing in Egypt? In the immigrants, we must see brothers and sisters and act toward them as God has acted toward us or toward our fathers: we are all children of immigrants, freed by God from slavery.[5] The defenseless have God himself for defender and advocate.[6] Jesus aligns himself with the Law and fulfills it when he proclaims blessed the little ones, the poor, the hungry, the destitute (Matt 5:3-11), because they are assured they have God on their side.

Human beings have the tendency to take advantage of others' needs. They exact interest or a guarantee from those who have to borrow in order to live. We know to what abuses these practices can lead, although such practices are usual and supposedly honest. The rich grow richer by exploiting the want of the needy. In the first Christian community, there were no indigent, thanks to the sharing of goods (Acts 4:34-35). To lend at interest or with the guarantee of a pledge was unthinkable. The Old Testament never ceases to denounce this form of exploitation of the poor,[7] because God wants a people of free men and women. The borrower— whether individually or collectively—is always in some way under the lender's power. The ideal of loan without interest remains very difficult to realize, even within small societies like the family. In fact, today, this ideal is understood as almsgiving, an "act of charity,"[8] since in an economic system that is really based on money-lending, to lend without interest is to renounce the profit derived from the sum loaned. Is this sufficient reason to declare interest-free loans totally out of the question? In any case, the spirit of God's law must inspire our actions,[9] because it is a matter of faith.

"For I am compassionate." This word of God is decisive for the good understanding and practice of his law. The concrete principles that it states are only examples destined to guide the conduct of those who walk in his ways; they are not articles of a code that determine once for all what is to be done or avoided. God is compassionate, merciful. Sacred history has kept the memory of the great manifestations of his love. But everyone is at every instant, although in a less striking manner, the object of the Lord's tenderness. In general, we become aware of this after the event, as we reflect on our own life and look around. The Lord's laws themselves are manifestations of his love; they light our road and give us the strength to ceaselessly pursue our course and thus manifest our love for God and, after his example, for our brothers and sisters.

I love you, LORD, my strength.

I love you, O LORD, my strength,
  O LORD, my rock, my fortress, my deliverer.
My God, my rock of refuge,
  my shield, the horn of my salvation, my stronghold!

Praised be the LORD, I exclaim,
  and I am safe from my enemies.

The LORD live! And blessed be my Rock!
  Extolled be God my savior.

You who gave great victories to your king
  and showed kindness to your anointed.
(Ps 18:2-3, 3-4, 47, 51)

Radiance of a Church That Welcomes the Word

The announcement of the gospel is "in power and in the holy Spirit" and not "in the word alone"; it transforms pagans into believers who have a faith that works, moved by a charity that labors, sustained in their attachment to the Lord by a hope that endures. Paul has marveled at these virtues in the course of his preaching at Thessalonica.[10] Continuing his missionary journey, he observes the extraordinary radiance of this young church. Everywhere, people speak of the eager and joyous welcome that the Thessalonians have given to the word "in great affliction"[11]; they have become "a model for all the believers in Macedonia and Achaia" and "in every place" (1 Thess 1:5c-10).

Today, we are still surprised at the rapid and lasting success of Paul's preaching[12] in the capital of the Roman province of Macedonia, the first European city he set foot in. It was a flourishing commercial center where many foreigners, among them an important Jewish colony, crowded together. In this cosmopolitan city, Paul and his companions, Silvanus and Timothy, succeeded in implanting a Christian community both fervent and strong. It was like a new Pentecost: Paul knows full well that only the action of the Holy Spirit can explain the results obtained by his preaching.

Although the letter does not give any explanations, it is clear that the way Paul acted played a large part in the success of the mission. Does he allude to the courage he showed when announcing the good news? It is certain—he affirms it—that the Thessalonians have begun to imitate the preachers and, at the same time, the Lord they were announcing. The apostles' faith must have been contagious, because trials have not altered it but, on the contrary, have stimulated their ardor. People saw in them a convincing witness of Christ. If Paul, Silvanus, and Timothy had been preachers similar to so many others, seeking their own glory or human advantages, they could not have borne what they had to suffer for the Thessalonians' good. So it goes: the credibility of the message depends upon the witness of those who spread it.

What we then read reveals the content of Paul's preaching. He has exhorted the Thessalonians to abandon idols in order "to serve the living and true God" and wait for the fulfillment of the promises and of the Messiah's manifestation. These themes were already those of the Jewish preaching to pagans. Paul repeated them in Thessalonica where, on three consecutive Sabbaths, he discussed "from the Scriptures" in the synagogue (Acts 17:3), "expounding and demonstrating that the Messiah had to suffer and rise from the dead and that 'This is the Messiah, Jesus, whom I proclaim to you'" (Acts 17:3). Here is the message the Thessalonians welcomed in joy—whether born in Judaism or worshipers of God or Greeks who have relinquished their idols.[13] Jesus Christ, dead and risen, is the Savior. Believers are waiting for his return; he "delivers us from the coming wrath." Such is, briefly, the content of Paul's preaching, of his creed, and of our faith. Such is the message, the good news that the Church and each Christian must announce to the world.

> People of God, do not be ashamed,
> show your sign to this age!
> While traversing worldly times,
> seek your breath in the Spirit.
> Raise your hymn to his power,
> turn your leaning to his grace:
> so that he may dwell in your praises
> and be visible in his children.
> Hold his love, hold his trial:
> he entrusts to you in joy
> the whole burden of his work
> so that it may sing through your voice:
> do not withdraw within yourself
> as if God did so!
> When you love, God loves you,
> open you heart, act as he does.
>
> Go, draw from your inheritance
> and, without counting, share it;
> win the trial of this age,
> carry God's name everywhere!
> Let him shake you, let him wake you:
> you are his body, in his Spirit!
> People of a God who works wonders,
> be his wonder today.[14]

Two Commandments Really One

We have known for all our Christian lives Jesus' response to the scribe's question "Teacher, which commandment in the law is the greatest?" Therefore, we do not expect surprises when, once more,[15] we hear this Sunday's Gospel. But it is such an important text that we must listen to it with attention. At the time each evangelist was writing what he received from tradition, he took into account the needs and the situation of the Christians he was addressing. Accordingly, we must continue today to read within the context of the present time the witnesses of Matthew, Mark, and Luke as they have been transmitted to us.[16] We shall often be surprised to realize how much each reading, from one year to the next, resonates anew (Matt 22:34-40).

It is in order to test him that a lawyer asks Jesus to tell him which is the greatest commandment in the Law. This test is not an examination. The episode is part of the controversy aimed at tripping up Jesus (Matt 22:15).[17] The question was debated at the time,[18] and under one form or another, still is today. And let us recognize that our intentions are often objectively suspect when we ask this question or when we answer it.[19] For example, we seek to justify our behavior or our conception of our duties to God: "Am I not right with God, since I attend Mass every Sunday?" or "Is there not a quick or easier way, even a somewhat rough shortcut, to directly and unhesitatingly reach the goal?" Jesus' answer reveals a completely different perspective. We must welcome and understand it as the enunciation of the supreme law that obtains everywhere and always and not as a vague general principle brought forward to defuse—or abet—controversies.

"You shall love the Lord, your God, with all your heart, with all your soul, and with all your mind." Particular and detailed prescriptions derive from this first commandment written in the Law (Deut 6:5). But all together, they can neither limit nor even foresee all concrete applications. To love—with all one's heart, with all one's soul, and with all one's mind—has nothing to do with discharging a series of predetermined obligations. Love is constant attention to the other; it is inventive and does not let us ever consider ourselves free of its demands. With all one's heart, with all one's soul, and with all one's mind means that particular obligations jotted down on a calendar—for instance, the dates of birthdays, anniversaries, etc.—are mere reminders, not the bill of expenses to be paid so as to be released from all debts. God is not like a faraway person who keeps rigorous accounts of our actions and omissions.[20]

"The second is like it: You shall love your neighbor as yourself." We do not see God; the neighbor is . . . nigh. God, who loves all his children, judges the love we say we bear him by the manner in which we act toward brothers and sisters (1 John 4:12, 20). The second commandment, which is like the first, must be understood and practiced in the same perspective as the first. Doing what is contrary to our neighbor's good, in any domain whatever, never corresponds to God's will, to the love we owe him. Determining what must concretely be done at every moment is the business of everyone of us. We must ask ourselves what we would do or would like to do for ourselves in a similar situation. We must open ourselves to risk-taking by accepting the responsibility of an error. This is why the particular commandments are useful, even necessary as guides. This is why we must have the wisdom and the humility to have recourse to others' advice, not in order to have them make decisions for us but with their help, to act with discernment. We are not always certain of what is, here and now, good for us.

God's Law Without Legalism

In and out of season, Matthew's Gospel insists on the imperative necessity of an active faith. We cannot find in this Gospel the slightest support for a religion free of any law. On the contrary, for him, evil consists in living lawlessly. But his conception of law is diametrically opposed to a legalistic understanding of the practice that is inseparable from faith. He also vigorously insists on the fact that our attitude toward others verifies our belonging to Christ and opens access into the kingdom. What Matthew says in various ways throughout his Gospel finds its natural climax in the passage on the last judgment. The reprobate, rejected from the kingdom, and the just, introduced into it, are separated on the basis of what they have omitted to do or have done for their neighbors (Matt 25:31-46).[21]

Jesus' answer to the lawyer asking him about the greatest commandment is also a revelation concerning Father, Son, and Spirit. The Father, above us, nobody has ever seen; the Son has become our brother through his incarnation and we find him in our neighbor; the Spirit dwells in our hearts. Father, Son, and Spirit are one in the indivisible Trinity. It is impossible to find the Father in prayer and the Spirit in the secret of our hearts if we do not recognize and serve the Son in the brothers and sisters with whom he identifies himself. It makes no sense at all to look for what distinguishes the first commandment from the second or the second from the first.

> The love of God is the first in the order of precepts; the love of neighbor is the first in the order of practice. For he who prescribed this love in two precepts has not recommended neighbor first and God second, but God first and neighbor second.
>
> As for you, because you do not see God yet, you merit to see God by loving your neighbor. By loving your neighbor, you purify your gaze to see God. This is what St. John says very clearly, "For whoever does not love a brother whom he has seen cannot love God whom he has not seen."
>
> Here is what is said to you, "Love God." If you tell me, "Show me whom I must love," what shall I answer but what John says, "No one has ever seen God." But do not imagine that you are absolutely excluded from God's life. John tells us, "God is love, and whoever remains in love remains in God and God in him" (1 John 4:16). Therefore, love your neighbor; look within yourself whence this love of neighbor comes; there you will see God in the measure in which this will be possible for you.[22]

Thirty-first Sunday

All Are Humble Servants of God and His Christ

One Cannot Trifle with the Liturgy

The first reading of this Sunday comes from the Book of Malachi—a made-up name—that we can place around 480–460 B.C.[1] Today's oracle is a stern admonition to priests and, through them, to all those whose lives are in contradiction to God's sanctity celebrated in the liturgy (Mal 1:14b–2:2, 2b, 8-10).

"For a great King am I," "the Lord of hosts," "my name will be feared among the nations." Under one form or another, these are God's titles of which the prophecies remind us. In any case, this is the faith of the people to which he revealed himself: outside of him, there is no God, no King, no Lord. This profession of faith entails a commitment to honor God through a life consonant with his laws and to witness to the divine majesty among the nations. Then, the worship conducted in the splendor of the Temple will be truly meaningful. Being a celebration of the transcendence of the only God, the liturgy praises the incomparable glory of him who created heaven and earth, who chose a people from among all peoples in order to make it into a holy nation.

The prophet echoes God's indignation at the sight of a degenerate and perverted worship. Anything goes. As if God did not see, as if one could fool him by offering him what one has no use for: blind, lame, sick, unsound, or even stolen animals; polluted food fit for nothing but to be thrown away (Mal 1:7-14). Really, people scandalously mock God by dealing with him as they would not dare to deal with any worldly potentate. "Present [such offerings] to your governor; see if he will accept [them], or welcome you" (Mal 1:8).

Our liturgy is no longer that of the Temple with its animal sacrifices and its ritual offerings of first fruits. But transposed into today's context, the prophet's invectives are not—alas—untimely. They urge us to question the manner in which we celebrate the liturgy in our communities, the spirit and the seriousness that animate us, the image of God our celebrations project. The liturgy is "an exercise of the priestly office of Jesus Christ. It involves the presentation of man's sanctification under the guise of signs perceptible by the senses and its accomplishment in ways appropriate to each of these signs. In it, full public worship is performed by the Mystical Body of Jesus Christ, that is, by the Head and his members."[2] Although it "does not exhaust the entire activity of the Church,"[3] it is "the summit toward which the activity of the Church is directed; it is also the fount from which all her power flows."[4] "But in order that the liturgy may be able to produce its full effects it is necessary that the faithful come to it with the proper dispositions."[5] As a result, "the faithful take part fully aware of what they are doing, actively engaged in the rite and enriched by it."[6]

If we are convinced of all these principles, we shall not devote to the liturgy fragments of time good for nothing else;[7] we shall not consider it a chore to be gotten through, willy-nilly at the lowest cost possible; we shall not be unconcerned about the way it is celebrated. The oracle from the Book of Malachi directly addresses priests, who are officially responsible for the liturgy and who, through their ministry, are the guardians and promoters of its holiness. But we know well that priests are not the only persons involved: a real liturgy, living and fruitful, is everyone's responsibility. When worship becomes a ritual parenthesis in the life of believers and community, in the ministry and life of priests, it is a corruption of the covenant with the Lord, as the prophet says. True worship is incompatible with the bending of the law, since, on the contrary, it proclaims its exigencies, requires that they be met with joy, and renews the strength necessary to advance in the Lord's ways. "The liturgy daily builds up those who are in the Church, making of them a holy temple of the Lord, a dwelling-place for God in the Spirit, to the mature measure of the fullness of Christ."[8]

The holiness of worship is so much the responsibility of all in the community—and not only of the priests—that we betray one another when we desecrate this sign of the covenant. "Have we not all the one Father? Has not the one God created us?" It is not enough to proclaim this; we must help one another to live this one faith and to preserve the holiness of the liturgy that we celebrate together. Unfaithfulness toward God and unfaithfulness toward brothers and sisters go hand in hand.[9]

The assembly gathered for the celebration cannot hear this oracle of Malachi without shuddering. It has been selected in order to rudely awaken us from our slumber and to severely warn us to avoid the empty formalism and the corruption of a worship given the lie by our actions. We must recognize this as a constantly lurking danger. We must remember the humility with which we are to approach God, trusting in his tenderness, as the children who, feeling threatened, nestle against their mother, who rely on her to learn how to walk and find refuge with her after a fall.

> *In you, LORD, I have found my peace.*
>
> O LORD, my heart is not proud,
>   nor are my eyes haughty;
> I busy not myself with great things,
>   nor with things too sublime for me.
> Nay rather, I have stilled and quieted
>   my soul like a weaned child.
> Like a weaned child on its mother's lap,
>   [so is my soul within me.]
> O Israel, hope in the LORD,
>   both now and forever.
> (Ps 131:1, 2, 3)

To Give Oneself According to the Gospel Message

The manner in which Paul exercised his ministry is diametrically opposed to that of the priests Malachi inveighed against. It remains a model for all who, for one reason or another, must transmit the gospel (1 Thess 2:7b-9, 13).

Fearless, Paul acted in Thessalonica ''as a nursing mother cares for her children.'' There has never been on his part either a word of demagoguery or an ulterior motive, greed or any pursuit of his own glory. Everywhere he preaches the gospel God entrusted to him, careful to please not human beings but God, who tests our hearts. He does not boast of his title of Apostle of Christ to impress others with his importance. He renounces even the just salary to which he has a right (1 Thess 2:3-7a). To avoid burdening any of the members of the community, he provides for his own needs by working day and night.[10] Really, he does not spare his pains; he gives himself without reservation. But he does not attribute to himself the success of his preaching; he gives thanks to God, who has prepared the Thessalonians' hearts to receive God's word, always at work in the community in spite of the hurried departure forced upon him by external circumstances (Acts 17:7-10). Someone else might have bemoaned a premature relinquishing of one's apostolate with so much work left undone. But Paul knows that the future of what has begun to germinate does not depend on him any more than the sprouting of a seed. Humility and unselfishness give people to understand that Another speaks through the Apostle's mouth and is welcomed. "He must increase; I must decrease" (John 3:30): this testimony of John the Baptist remains the motto of every forerunner, preacher, catechist, witness of Christ. To give oneself, along with the message, without second thoughts of place of honor or self-glorification on account of the success of one's ministry—here is what makes Paul the model apostle.

The Bad Example of Vain Leaders

The historical value of the Gospels in undeniable: they faithfully transmit the teaching given by the Lord in words and actions. But they are not history books in the usual sense of the word. Thus, for instance, their purpose is not to describe the religious and political society in Jesus' time; to analyze its components; to expound the doctrines and positions of the groups, factions, or classes that composed it. What they say, among other things, concerning scribes and Pharisees agrees with what we know from other sources about the tendencies of these two groups. But it would be erroneous and unjust to conclude that all scribes and all Pharisees were like those whom the Gospels show in the controversies with Jesus.[11] Matthew himself, who is usually stern toward them, knows that Pharisees are faithful to praiseworthy practices, like fasting (Matt 9:24). He even records the word of Jesus that concludes the Discourse in Parables, "Every scribe who has been instructed in the kingdom of heaven is like the head of a household who brings from his storeroom both the new and the old" (Matt 13:52).

Moreover, to the Christians who were the first readers of Matthew's Gospel, scribes and Pharisees were already personages of the past to whom they gave little thought. But in the community to which Matthew spoke, there were "bad and good"[12] and even vain leaders.[13] How must their brothers and sisters act toward them? How must they themselves behave not to fall into the same defect? Matthew answers these questions by recalling what Jesus taught us when he stigmatized scribes and Pharisees whose behavior made him indignant (Matt 23:1-12).

In the Church and in Christian communities, the leaders do not have a role as teachers only; for this, competency based on knowledge would suffice. They must also exhort their brothers and sisters to live according to the gospel and incite them to walk in the Lord's footsteps. If they do not preach by example, their discourses sound hollow and their behavior misleads the wavering, the rebellious, and especially the simple. All, even the strong, need the twofold teaching of word and action. Therefore, a serious malaise settles in a community whose leaders' acts are in contradiction to their teaching and to the gospel's, which they announce. There is a great risk that many individual members of the community will fall and that even the whole group might go adrift.

"Therefore do and observe all things whatsoever they tell you, but do not follow their example. For they preach but do not practice." We must admit that to abide by this advice of the Lord demands great strength of character and serious Christian maturity. This only aggravates the scandalous conduct of the leaders Jesus has as a target. They will have to answer before God for their own sin, but also for others'. All must remember this grave warning of the Lord, whatever their responsibility to others in the community or among relatives. "Woe to the one through whom [scandals] come" (Matt 18:7).[14] But happy the many communities that can imitate their leaders as these imitate the Lord (1 Thess 1:6).[15]

Helping Leaders to Remain Honest and Humble

After having severely admonished those who betray their charge by conduct contradicting their preaching, the Gospel censures their vainglory: "All their works are performed to be seen. They widen their phylacteries and lengthen their tassels.[16] They love places of honor at banquets, seats of honor in synagogues, greetings in marketplaces, and the salutation 'Rabbi.'"[17] One easily falls into these faults as soon as one has some authority. This could be merely ridiculous. But in a Christian community, these worldly doings are seriously wrong; they run counter to the nature of the Church, where all are brothers and sisters, and to the nature of ministry: "The greatest among you must be your servant." Ecclesiastical careerism and the pursuit of honors are in contradiction to the gospel.[18]

But we must correctly understand what Jesus said lest we draw wrong conclusions. First of all, we do not have here a condemnation of the diversity and distinction of functions and services in the Church and ecclesial communities; these are indispensable to the smooth functioning of the community and of the liturgical assembly in particular. The Church is like a well-structured body that needs diverse members, each one fulfilling its role, without bragging about it (1 Cor 12:12-31).[19] Similarly, there is no radical condemnation here of all titles that usually designate those who exercise a ministry. But they must bear such titles as a demand and not as a mark of honor.[20] Finally, in the liturgical celebrations, the insignia of the various functions are not baubles; they show who is who and who does what, a proper thing for an assembly that must be visibly structured. The same is true of the attribution of places. Certain egalitarian demands forget that the assembly is not an amorphous crowd. They ignore what befits not only the good order that must prevail in the Church and the assemblies but also the elementary laws of the life of a group and the respect due to each one.[21]

But another remark is in order. We are prone to see in the charge bestowed on us an honor and a right to honors, as is customary in the world. However, we must also confess that often other people encourage this human tendency. Despite the respect shown them, we should help our Christian leaders to see themselves as brothers and sisters charged with a responsibility in the community. Finally, it is a matter of general climate, created and maintained by all, having their eyes turned toward their one Father, who is in heaven, and toward Christ, who gave us the example of becoming a servant—he, the Master (John 13:1-20)—and who was exalted because he humbled himself (Phil 2:5-11).

> One alone is our Father,
> God who so loved us
> he gave us his Son.
> One alone is our Master,
> Jesus, Son of God,
> the servant of all.
>
> *Your love, Lord,*
> *is the light of our steps.*
>
> Love one another,
> and you will glorify my name.
>
> Defer to one another,
> and you will be children of your Father.
>
> Carry one another's burdens,
> and you will fulfill Christ's law.[22]

We do not try to cheat where the gospel and Jesus are concerned. We do not ask questions of them with impunity, hiding our motives of finding support for petty calculations. To make dazzling discourses on the law of the Lord and put on devout airs does not do any good if our concrete actions belie these words and these airs. We fool ourselves if we hope to find a way of balancing the books with God, thanks to a list of duties defined once for all. This is what Jesus' words strongly say on the Twenty-ninth, Thirtieth, and Thirty-first Sundays.

Yes, we must attend to duties toward Caesar. But let us not forget that in all things we must serve God. To love God and to love one's neighbor are one and the same thing. "The whole law and the prophets depend on these two commandments." Every Christian community is a community of brothers and sisters who are one another's servants.

How can we hear these strong words without asking ourselves in what spirit we celebrate or what place the liturgical practice occupies in our personal and communal lives? "Become what you receive: the Body of Christ," St. Augustine said when he distributed Communion. And the Scriptures read on the three Sundays of the sequence just completed say to us: "Become the one whom you celebrate: the Servant Christ who emptied himself of himself to accomplish God's will."

The Thirty-second and Thirty-third Sundays in Ordinary Time

The topic of the last sequence in Ordinary Time, Year A—before the feast of Christ the King—is the Lord's coming at the end of time. The two Gospels are taken from the long discourse of Jesus on his coming (Matt 24–25), which in Matthew's Gospel immediately precedes the account of the passion and resurrection of Christ (Matt 26–28).

From this vast collection the Lectionary has selected the two parables that insist on the urgent necessity of an active watchfulness, since no one can say when the Son of Man will come (Matt 25:1-13—Thirty-second Sunday; Matt 25:14-30—Thirty-third Sunday).

The two passages of the First Letter to the Thessalonians also deal with the end times. One sketches the end's scenario in order to reinforce hope in the certainty of the Lord's return, a source of mutual consolation (1 Thess 4:13-18—Thirty-second Sunday). The other heralds a call to the watchfulness that must characterize the life of the Church and of Christians (1 Thess 5:1-6—Thirty-third Sunday).

The celebration of these two Sundays urges us to a fresh awareness of an essential and dynamic dimension of the believer's life as well as of the liturgy: "We are expecting your glorious coming. Come, Lord Jesus!"

Thirty-second Sunday

Keeping Watch
and Being Prepared

Seek Wisdom

The Book of Wisdom is the most recent of all the writings of the Old Testament.[1] The work of a poet and spiritual master, it can be read on several levels. The author explicitly addresses secular kings and judges: those who have responsibilities in government and discernment must go to the school of wisdom in order to obtain, as if from within, a profound understanding of human destiny and history. But beyond these immediate and official addressees, the sage proposes to all persons the result of reflections inspired by a long meditation nurtured by experience. Not satisfied with merely recording facts, he seeks their causes and consequences. At that level, the author shows himself a great master of human wisdom. But he is also a believer for whom wisdom is an attribute of God, who alone possesses it in its fullness and in which he allows us to share. So the author personifies Wisdom—the word is then capitalized. He describes her, resplendent and attractive. He speaks to her, hears her speak, shows her at work in the world near those who seek her and let her guide them. Reflection rises to the level of mystical meditation on God, who governs the world he created and assists human beings who walk according to his laws.[2] This Sunday's first reading treats of the quest for Wisdom, who allows herself to be found by those who seek her (Wis 6:12-16).

After getting an inkling of her beauty, we cannot rest until we find her. The author speaks of Wisdom as a lover speaks of his beloved, as do mystics in their most sublime flights of devotion. He sees Lady Wisdom more beautiful and attractive than any creature, endowed with all gifts of intelligence and heart. To receive the grace to contemplate her, we need eyes of extraordinary purity, full of a light that nothing carnal tarnishes, the eyes of a chaste love. Those who love her can easily contemplate her and she allows them to find her. She anticipates their desire; she herself seeks those who are worthy of her and awaits them, smiling, at the turn of the path. To think of her constantly brings freedom, because the mind and the heart are no longer encumbered with concern about worthless things.

Only the language of poetry and love is able to express the quest for God, the deep desire to find him and live from his spirit, his transcendence that brings him near those who seek him, the peace and joy with which his presence fills hearts.

> *My soul is thirsting for you, O* LORD *my God.*
>
> O God, you are my God whom I seek;
>   for you my flesh pines and my soul thirsts
>   like the earth, parched, lifeless and without water.
> Thus have I gazed toward you in the sanctuary
>   to see your power and your glory,
> For your kindness is a greater good than life;
>   my lips shall glorify you.
>
> Thus will I bless you while I live;
>   lifting up my hands, I will call upon your name.
> As with the riches of a banquet shall my soul
>   be satisfied,
>   and with exultant lips my mouth shall praise you.
> I will remember you upon my couch,
>   and through the night-watches I will meditate on you:
> You are my help,
>   and in the shadow of your wings I shout for joy.
> (Ps 63:2, 3-4, 5-6, 7-8)

Seeking God Together

Despite the undeniable threats weighing upon the future of our world and the questions concerning the chances of the survival of humankind, we certainly cannot say that the matters relating to the last times particularly worry Christians. Impressed, like everybody, with what is said on the risks of destruction threatening the planet and, we must hope, conscious of their duties as human beings to preserve the future, they, too, think that they will not see the apocalyptic catastrophes that have been foretold.[3] In any case—and it is fortunate[4]—they do not indiscriminately mix their faith with these reflections. However, the least we can say is that the perspective of the Lord's return is not at the center of their preoccupations as believers. But this ultimate manifestation of Christ, toward whom we are going, is an integral part of our faith. It is therefore important to attentively listen to what Paul wrote to the Thessalonians on this topic. Provided we understand it well, this teaching is relevant to our times.

Paul's correspondents are worried about the fate of "those who have fallen asleep." Their preoccupation is not exactly ours. Of course, human beings have always wondered about death, from which no one escapes. Does it definitively end human existence or is there a life—what sort of life?—after death? The Thessalonians also pondered this grave question. Paul repeats to them that faith in everyone's resurrection is based on Jesus' resurrection. This reminder of an essential article of the Christian creed is always timely. But the manner in which Paul depicts it already reveals the exact nature of the Thessalonians' question. Convinced that the Lord will come back soon, during their own lifetime, they worry about the dead: how can they participate in this event?[5] "Do not grieve like the rest, who have no hope," Paul answers. Everyone will be present at the rendezvous together: "The dead in Christ will rise first. Then we who are alive, who are left, will be caught together with them in the clouds to meet the Lord in the air."

To formulate his answer, Paul has recourse to ways of speaking and accepted images: the Lord's coming down from heaven is announced by a herald—the archangel—and the sound of the trumpet; there is a cortege of those who ascend on the clouds of heaven to meet him.[6] Paul's intention is not to disclose to us the scenario of the Lord's manifestation. He reminds us of the certitude based on faith: we will rise; when the Lord comes back, we shall share in his glory; all those who will have lived in the hope of this great day will be forever with the Lord.[7] It is good for us to regularly face this certitude and speak of it with others.

At the same time, Paul opportunely suggests that we must not speak of death as if it made us enter a world measured by time like ours. The story of each one of us ends with death whose date survivors can note on their calendars. These chronological landmarks are no longer adequate when we speak of the world beyond. Time is the measure of what is born, lives, and dies on this earth. We cannot help but speak of the time of eternity. But we should not have any illusion about the meaning of this expression that joins two contradictory terms.[8] We shall then avoid the trap of such objectively meaningless questions as: How long do the dead have to wait until we join them? What must absorb all our attention is the present, this time that is given us to live in the dynamic and trustful expectation of what, we hope, will happen.

Parable of the Bridesmaids Invited to the Wedding

The evangelical tradition is unanimous and explicit: Jesus has said," But of that day and hour no one knows, neither the angels in heaven, nor the Son, but the Father alone."[9] It is absolutely impossible to find in the Gospels anything to bolster speculations on the date of the end of this world or descriptions of what will come to pass. But Jesus did foretell the ruin of the Temple and of Jerusalem; the Gospels attest to this.[10] It was terrible—the end of a world[11] evoking the end of the world?[12] We must attentively read the great discourse found in Matthew's Gospel. It is addressed to Christians to exhort them to prepare themselves for this event in order to be saved. The three concluding parables—the Lectionary has kept two[13]—show clearly that this teaching on the end of time and the Lord's return has been transmitted by the evangelist for our instruction. These parables make us understand how we must live today in the perspective of the Day that will not fail to come, though we do not know its date: "Then the kingdom of heaven will be like ten virgins" invited to a wedding (Matt 25:1-13).

Like many others, this parable is based on a fact, a situation of ordinary life. It tells of a custom connected with the wedding celebration. The bridesmaids—the ten young girls—went to the bride's house, waiting with her until the bridegroom came to lead her to his home. Then people went in a cortege to the wedding hall. But it happens that unusual, even unlikely, traits are introduced into a narrative to make a point. There are several in our case: the interminable lateness of the bridegroom, who keeps people waiting until the middle of the night;[14] the errand of the five maidens wanting to buy oil, as if they thought it possible to find a shop open at that hour; the closing of the banquet hall door, so contrary to the customs of oriental hospitality[15] and so scandalous on the part of the bridegroom, who acted so thoughtlessly—his retort to the latecomers, "I do not know you." To these we could add the fact that the young girls who had taken a supply of oil are not reproached for refusing to share. It would be out of place to quibble with these improbable features of the story. A parable is not a narrative of an event, retold with exactitude down to its minutest details. Storytellers can legitimately put in exaggerated traits that fit their purposes. This is done knowingly and fools no one.

This being understood, the lesson of the parable is clear. We shall be kept waiting for the Lord's coming; unforeseeable, it will happen suddenly.[16] At that moment, everything will be lost for those who were taken by surprise. Others will not be able to help them. The improvident ones will find a closed door in the kingdom where the wedding of the Son of Man is celebrated.

Therefore, we understand why and in what sense the five maidens who had no extra oil are called foolish. They have demonstrated that folly, that utter lack of wisdom characterizes those who do not reckon with God. They have acted impiously:

> The fool says in his heart,
>   "There is no God" (Ps 14:1).

"You are invited to the wedding. Watch, for you know neither the day nor the hour of the Lord's coming."[17]

The lesson is a moral one. But it results from faith in Jesus, who is, who was, who is coming again, whom we have found, whose return we are expecting. This faith is at the heart of the Church's life. The liturgy, chiefly that of the Paschal Vigil and of the night office, reflects such a faith.

> All this time during which the ages flow is like one night. Throughout it, the Church watches, her eyes of faith intent on the Holy Scriptures, as on nighttime torches, until the Lord comes. This is what Peter the Apostle says: "We possess the prophetic message that is altogether reliable. You will do well to be attentive to it, as to a lamp shining in a dark place, until day dawns and the morning star rises in your hearts" (2 Pet 1:19). Therefore, in the same way as I have just come to you in the Lord's name and have found you watching in his name, may the Lord himself in whose honor this solemn feast is celebrated, find, upon coming, his Church watchful in the clearsightedness of the Spirit, so that he may awaken her also in her body, slumbering in many graves.[18]

The Heart on Watch

Far from producing anxiety, nervousness or, on the contrary, discouragement, carelessness, or sleepiness, the uncertainty about the day and hour of the Lord's coming stimulates watchfulness and arouses attention. Believers have vigilant hearts, like lovers who scrutinize the night in order to detect, at the least sign, the approaching beloved. The Church is the gathering of all those who are preparing to depart in a joyous cortege, their lamps in their hands, to meet the bridegroom. Every liturgical celebration is like the dress rehearsal of the great procession to the wedding hall. In any event, the Lord is already here; he comes for his own to whom he manifests himself under the veil of signs. Those who have preceded us in death also prepare themselves. With us and like us, they wait in hope for the signal, given by the archangel's voice, which will cause the great portals of the wedding hall to open wide.

> Wakefulness in our hearts,
> a lamp lighted by the Lord,
> renews itself at his flame
> as we sing our joy with one voice.

> May thanksgiving watch in us
> as the flower of the almond tree
> which, the earliest, glimpses from afar
> the coming summer and its harvest.

> May our love and his praise
> be the two wings of the morning
> which unfold in prayer
> and take us far from ourselves.

> Here is the Bridegroom calling us:
> let us run to the Lamb's nuptials!
> But how long the road seems:
> when will you dawn, last morning?[19]

Thirty-third Sunday

Keeping Watch While Working for the Lord

The Ideal Wife, Model of Wisdom

As its name indicates, the Book of Proverbs is a collection of maxims from various sources.[1] The reading of this Sunday's excerpt might surprise some and even cause a few smiles in the assembly. It is an encomium of the perfect wife, which does not exactly correspond to the modern image current in our countries.[2] However, we would be wrong-headed if we refused to hear this eulogy because we judge outmoded such an exaltation of the housewife, "the angel of the home" (Prov 31:10-13, 19-20, 30-31).

Whatever their author's viewpoint and the society they reflect, these proverbs are not read, in the liturgy, to advocate a particular status for women or to determine the tasks befitting them and within which they must immure themselves. This housewife is praiseworthy because she accomplishes her work to perfection. In the last analysis, appearances ("charm" and "beauty") do not matter. The one is deceptive, the other vain, without assiduous work, good judgment, generosity: "She reaches out her hands to the poor."

The conduct of the perfect housewife reveals her fear of God. This biblical expression designates what we would call the virtue of religion, that is, faithfulness to God's law, God's service. It is the foundation of Wisdom, finally of sanctity.[3] Therefore, here is a woman presented as the model for people faithful to God because she diligently fulfills the humble daily tasks entrusted to her. We must not seek perfection elsewhere than in faithfulness to everyday duties. To remind us of what the fear of God is, biblical wisdom has chosen—and it is significant—this example of a woman applying herself to humble works. We must all be humble handmaids of the Lord, humble servants of God in the fulfillment of the duties of our state.

Happy are those who fear the LORD.

Happy are you who fear the LORD,
  who walk in his ways!
For you shall eat the fruit of your handiwork;
  happy shall you be, and favored.
Your wife shall be like a fruitful vine
  in the recesses of your home;
Your children like olive plants
  around your table.
Behold, thus is the man blessed
  who fears the LORD.
The LORD bless you from Zion:
  may you see the prosperity of Jerusalem
  all the days of your life.
(Ps 128:1-2, 3, 4-5)

No Surprise in the Lord's Coming

Today we read the fifth and last passage of those chosen for the Sundays of Year A from the First Letter of Paul to the Thessalonians.[4] It is a new instruction on the coming of the Lord (1 Thess 5:1-6).

The unanimous evangelical tradition is perfectly clear: it is absolutely impossible to determine in advance the date of this coming; it remains God's secret.[5] Therefore, there is no room for uncertainty as far as Christians are concerned. They do not even dream of indulging in speculations or of listening to those who do indulge in them. "It is not necessary to speak about delays or dates: 'You know very well that the day of the Lord will come as a thief in the night.' "

The Day of the Lord has a long biblical past. In the Old Testament, it evokes the last manifestation of God, which will put an end to the present world. First it was seen as a day of blessing, happiness, and light when God's salvation would appear (Amos 5:18-20). Under the influence of the prophetic literature, this day took on a twofold connotation: salvation for the just, judgment for the evil ones.[6] In the New Testament, it is the day of the coming of the Lord on which the history of salvation will be completed. Then Christ will hand the kingdom to his Father (1 Cor 15:24).

Paul insists here on the sudden character of this manifestation (*parousia*) that will not have the same consequences for all. To explain this, Paul uses an image: "The day of the Lord will come like a thief at night."[7] For certain people, it will be catastrophic because, living heedlessly—in peace and quiet, as they see it—they will be taken unawares. For others who remain watchful, this coming will hold no surprise. It will happen in the night of the world; but Christians are not in darkness, for they are the "children of light." They behave as in full daylight; they remain at all times spiritually awake, ready to welcome the Lord as a friend they have waited for; to him, they will joyfully open the door (Rev 3:20).

> A cry will resound in the night:
> "Behold, the bridegroom!"
> The Master will come like a thief,
> at a time no one knows:
> on that Day, will you be ready?
>
> *Keep us vigilant, Lord,*
> *until the hour of your coming!*
>
> Mountains melt like wax
> before the Master of all the earth.
> Light dawns for the just
> and for the upright of heart, joy.
> When the Son of Man comes,
> will he find faith on earth?[8]

The Parable of the Servants and the Talents

The parable usually called "the parable of the talents" is often understood as an exhortation to make good use of our gifts of nature or grace, little or great. Such a commentary is far from exhausting the content of the parable (Matt 25:14-30).

The Lectionary rightly reminds us that Jesus was speaking to his disciples of his coming, the day and hour of which no one knows. Therefore, we must be alert, so as not to be taken by surprise at this event. Today's parable explains that we have a task to accomplish during this vigil. By the same token, it reveals the meaning and the importance of the time that elapses between the master's departure on his journey and his return "after a long time." Christians readily understand that Jesus is speaking of himself: "He ascended into heaven. . . . He will come again in glory to judge the living and the dead" (Creed). But he has not left the disciples, his servants, with nothing to do. He has entrusted them with his goods. The parable speaks of these when it mentions talents, a monetary unit used to handle large sums.[9] The servants, therefore, receive invaluable capital according to each one's capacity. The master's trust is unheard of. It exceeds the boundaries of reason and human prudence. The master relies on his servants' sense of responsibility. Obviously, only the Lord can act in this manner with his servants.

The parable does not say how the first two servants managed to invest profitably their master's capital. He congratulates them in the same terms and invites them into his joy; he praises them for having been faithful "in small matters" and promises them "great responsibilities." When one realizes that the allotted capital—"small matters"—was already enormous, one understands that the reward—"great responsibilities"—will be without measure. In truth, we are no longer dealing with a human being who demands accounts from others, but with God, who bestows his infinite riches upon his servants who have faithfully administered the portion of the capital entrusted to them.

The meaning and the extent of the parable are made more explicit by the appearance of the third servant and by the terrible punishment inflicted upon him: he is thrown "into the outer darkness, where there will be wailing and grinding of teeth," that is, into the place where the impious go (Matt 8:12). His conduct has been a truly mortal sin that deprives him forever from sharing in his master's joy. But what is this sin that is punished by such a rejection?

The narrative says that he buried his master's money in the ground in order to give it back intact when the master returned. Contrary to his companions, he did not understand that he had to profitably invest this fortune; he lacked initiative. We would understand that his disappointed master ceased to trust him. But here is the crux: we are dealing with a parable and not with a story of common occurrence among human beings; we are dealing with the coming of the Lord after a protracted absence and not with the return of a wealthy man after a long journey. We could rightly reproach such a man with his harshness and, even more, his injustice. What right has anyone to require from servants more than what was entrusted to them and, worse, what right has anyone to punish such servants? Everything changes when we are speaking of God and his servants. If we consider ourselves bound to God by a contract in human terms, if we regard religion as the strict fulfilling of a certain number of duties taken on through servile fear, we misunderstand who God is, we insult him, and we declare ourselves unworthy of entering his joy.

"Jesus was speaking to his disciples of his coming." On that day we all will be judged on what we shall have done, as Matthew's Gospel does not stop repeating in various ways. The time of the Lord's absence is, for disciples, the time of active waiting.

Trustworthy, Active, and Efficient Servants

God has no use for slaves who are timorous, devoid of initiative, and idle when the master is not present to watch them and stimulate them with carrot and stick. God wants his servants to behave in a responsible manner, to be enterprising and apply themselves to what they are doing. The master must be able to entrust his goods to them; they will know how to invest them profitably. He does not ask them to do great things but to assiduously discharge the tasks assigned to them. Grace, that inestimable good, is not something inert that we, for fear of losing it, can bury in the earth or hide under the mattress. If we have acted thus, let us hasten to take it out of its hiding place. Let us make the best of the delay granted us—we do not know for how long—to make it fruitful with God's help.

> I was like the unworthy servant
> who earned nothing out of his talents;
> and I even outstripped him,
> because I lost the gift of grace.
>
> I have neither doubled your talent
> nor made fourfold the two, nor tenfold the five,
> so as to be in complete mastery
> of the ten cities of the senses.
>
> But I buried in the ground the one talent,
> by wrapping it up in the shroud of vices;
> I did not put the money in the bank
> so that you might demand the interest,
>
> that is, I have not carried the word of your command
> to the ears of my mind,
> which are the spiritual bank
> of the wisdom of the Bread of Life.
>
> This is why I expect
> to be chastised in the darkness
> until you come to look for the talent
> which you granted me at the sacred font.
>
> But to you, O Savior of my soul,
> I want to weep and say:
> "Since it is still possible for me to do good,
> give me the grace to please you by acting rightly."
>
> Thus I shall hear the joyous sentence
> like the faithful servant:
> "Enter my celestial house
> in the joy of your Lord."[10]

The biblical readings of the Thirty-second and Thirty-third Sundays direct our eyes toward the coming of the Lord, the end and fulfillment of the whole history of salvation. The intent is not to make us evade the present but, on the contrary, to help us to fully live it in the light of its completion.

The Lord will come on the day and at the hour that no one knows, except the Father. Far from overwhelming us, disheartening us or, on the contrary, throwing us into careless living as a means of exorcising our fears, this uncertainty stimulates our hope and revives our fervor in the efficient service of God.

The Lord will come. This certitude is at the heart of the liturgy and animates it. Every time we celebrate the holy mysteries, we have a twofold experience: that of the presence of the Lord among us through signs, especially the Eucharist, and that of longing for another presence—a final one—that will fulfill our expectation.

Today is the time of lamps patiently replenished with oil and of fervent diligence in daily tasks.

Tomorrow will be the entrance into the banquet hall in the joy of the Lord.

Christ the King

A New Feast Instituted in 1925

The liturgical feast of Christ the King was established in 1925 by Pope Pius XI (1922–1939) in the encyclical *Quas primas*.[1] The decree of institution prescribed that it would be "celebrated in the whole world, every year, on the last Sunday of October which immediately precedes the feast of All Saints" and, moreover, that "every year, on this very day, Christians are to renew the consecration of humankind to the Sacred Heart of Jesus," already enjoined by Pope Pius X (1903–1914).

Pius XI, whose motto was "Christ's peace through Christ's reign," began this encyclical by recalling what he said in his first encyclical.[2] Asking himself what are "the causes of this deluge of evils submerging humankind," he blamed "the apostasy of a great number of people who have banished Christ and his most holy law from their individual and familial lives and from public affairs." And he added that there would be no hope for a lasting peace between peoples as long as nations and their citizens refused to affirm and proclaim the authority of our Savior. He then concluded, "We must look for the peace of Christ in the reign of Christ."[3]

The encyclical dwells at length on the doctrinal foundation of the feast before speaking of the advantages of its institution. Pius XI reminds his readers that liturgical feasts have been successively instituted to answer needs or provide spiritual benefits under the circumstances of the times. "For instance, it was a troubled time in which encouragement was called for. Or it was necessary to warn people against the snares of heresy. Or other motives required the urging of piety toward a mystery of our holy religion or thanksgiving for a special blessing of divine Providence." He also evokes the cult of martyrs "from the first centuries of the Christian era when the faithful were the object of furious persecutions"; the feasts in honor of confessors, virgins, and widows "to kindle the zeal for virtue not only in the days of persecution but also in time of peace"; "the liturgical honors offered to the most Holy Virgin," which "have had a salutary effect on Christian souls, even more than the feasts of saints," and from which the Church particularly received "a most efficacious aid in its age-old struggle against error and heresies." "Recent feasts have been instituted in the same spirit and for the same reasons as the old ones." The encyclical then cites the feast of Corpus Christi, instituted when devotion to the Eucharist had slackened; the feast of the Sacred Heart, "especially opportune at the time when the somber and forbidding doctrines of Jansenism had, as it were, frozen hearts and closed them to trustful love toward our divine Savior."

The encyclical then explains the usefulness and timeliness of the new feast.

> Through the institution of a feast in honor of Christ's kingship, we are convinced that we also are acting opportunely. This feast will be one of the great means of fighting against secularism, its errors and its tendencies; against this secularism which is the plague of our society. As you know, Venerable Brothers, this impious secularism did not grow up overnight, and it is easy to follow its progression in social life. First, Christ's authority over all nations was denied. Then, the Church was refused her right, derived from the divine rights of the Savior, to teach, legislate, and govern human beings in view of their eternal happiness. Then, the Christian religion was likened to false religions, and Catholic worship was shamefully equated with all other worships. Afterwards, the Church was declared subject to civil power and practically abandoned to the whims of princes and governments. A vague natural religion was preconized in place of the Catholic religion. Finally, things came to such a pass that representatives and leaders of several nations shook off every (any) religious conviction and sentiment, renounced every (any) duty toward God, and chose irreligion as state religion.

Repeating what he had written in *Ubi arcano Dei*, Pius XI evokes "the bitter fruit of this individual and social apostasy." "To sum up everything in one sentence, society is threatened with irremediable ruin because of its rebellion against God and his Christ."

The Pope hopes that the institution of the feast of Christ the King will awaken Catholics so that

> . . . they may actively work at preparing and hastening the ardently wished for return [of society to its Savior.] When the majority of Catholics clearly understand that they must fight without respite under Christ's banner, the fire of apostolate will be kindled in their hearts and all will find the necessary courage to devote themselves to the conversion of those who ignore and those who rebel against the divine king and to defend to the bitter end his imprescriptible rights. . . . The feast of Christ the King and its yearly celebration among all the peoples of the earth will work efficaciously against secularism in still another way. Secularism has caused the disastrous defec-

tion of nations from Jesus Christ. It is important to protest this defection and to repair it as much as possible. International meetings do not pronounce the beloved name of our Savior. The more shameful this lack of recognition, the louder our acclamations must rise toward him, the more energetic our affirmation of his royal authority and power.

The encyclical concludes with the vibrant evocation of the hopes the Pope places in the celebration of this feast.

> And allow us, Venerable Brothers, to conclude this encyclical by telling you what blessed fruit we firmly expect for the Church, civil society, and individuals from a public worship rendered to the kingship of Christ. As they give royal honors to our Lord, people, of necessity, will remember the rights of the Church; the fact that she has received from her divine Founder the nature and the form of a perfect society; the impossibility for her to renounce her independence from civil power; the fact that no outside authority can lord it over her in the exercise of her charge to teach, govern, and lead to eternal beatitude all the souls who belong to the kingdom of Christ. The religious orders of men and women must enjoy the same liberty from civil powers because they are precious auxiliaries of the shepherds of the Church. And they most efficaciously work for the extension and the prosperity of the kingdom of our Lord by fighting, through the three vows, against the triple concupiscence and by manifesting increasingly from day to day, through the practice of high perfection, that holiness which the Savior wanted to be one of the marks of the true Church. This feast will moreover remind the leaders of civil society that they too, as well as private individuals, must render public worship to our Lord and observe his commandments. It will bring to their minds the great day of judgment, that day when Christ will very severely demand an account not only from those who will have expelled him from social life and affairs of state, but also from those who will have insulted him by forgetting and neglecting him in the conduct of civil society. For his royal dignity demands that states obey his orders and Christian principles in lawmaking, in administering justice, as well as in educating youth. But who can tell the help the faithful will find in the celebration and meditation of Christ's kingship so that they may gain a true understanding and practice of Christian life. For if our Lord has received every power in heaven and on earth; if human beings, redeemed by his blood, now belong to him by a new title of authority; if his rule extends over the whole of nature and the whole of human life, we must obviously conclude that none of our faculties can be withdrawn from his empire. He must reign, therefore, over our minds: we must firmly and constantly believe his doctrine. He must reign over our wills: we must observe his laws and his commandments. He must reign over our hearts: we must rise above our natural affections and desires and love God with a unique love, above all things. He must reign even over our bodies and our limbs: we must use them as instruments or, as St. Paul says, as "weapons of righteousness for God" (Rom 6:13) for interior and spiritual perfection. What

an incentive would not the faithful find in the attentive consideration of these truths for the practice of all virtues!

The Pope who instituted the feast of Christ the King very distinctly affirms that it is rooted in the circumstances of the time of its institution, a time that he analyzes with great lucidity. The climate was one of very active secularism. The Christian structures of society were crumbling. The Church was losing the social role that history had imposed on it, which it had justified by doctrinal pronouncements, and which had come to be seen as natural.

We must not forget that the loss of papal temporal power, accomplished in 1870 under Pius IX (1846–1878), was considered an impious despoliation of the Church. Later on, from Pius IX to Pius XI, the popes styled themselves "prisoners of the Vatican." But on the very day of his election (February 6, 1922), Pius XI made it clear that he intended to escape from this imprisonment. To everyone's surprise, he gave his first blessing *Urbi et orbi* not from the inside balcony of St. Peter's Basilica, as had been his predecessors' custom, but from the balcony that opens onto the Piazza Bernini. He thus demonstrated, by a highly symbolic gesture, that he had decided to resolutely turn to the world to confront it and reconquer it by "fighting without respite under Christ's banner," as he later wrote in *Quas primas*. In any case, it is undeniable that, under his pontificate, the militant spirit of Christians was reawakened and even became combative.[4] Songs of the movements—the Young Catholic Workers in France *(Jeunesse Ouvrière Catholique)*, for instance—and popular hymns are proof of this pugnacious spirit. The words did not bother with nuances and the tunes were decidedly martial.

> We shall rechristianize our brothers;
> we swear it by Jesus Christ.

> *Christus vincit,* (Christ conquers)
> *Christus regnat,* (Christ reigns)
> *Christus imperat!* (Christ rules)

> Speak, command, reign:
> we are all yours!
> Jesus, spread your kingdom:
> be the King of the universe![5]

> Save, save France,
> in the name of the Sacred Heart![6]

Today, these expressions and others like them seem to imply an unorthodox collusion between faith and the temporal order, even the political order in the most partisan meaning of the term. We must place all this in the context of the time, especially in Western European countries. Secularism appeared as "irreligion," "individual and social apostasy," "defection of the nations from Jesus Christ," against which protest and reparation were called for. Hence, this movement aiming at consecrating families, states, and kingdoms to the Sacred Heart. It was also the time of vast gatherings, such as Eucharistic Congresses, whether diocesan, national, or international.[7] "All the discourses pronounced at the gatherings and ceremonies of these congresses, the hours of common adoration, the impressive processions do not fail to eloquently testify to the kingship of the Savior. It seems that the Catholic crowds, moved by an inspiration from on high, are going to meet Christ—whom the impious refused to receive when he came into his kingdom—in the silence and the mystery of the tabernacle, in order to carry him through the streets of large cities and to reestablish him in all the rights and honors of his kingship." Today these displays seem to us vitiated by exaggerated triumphalism, as well as being rather artificial, and in any case devoid of the expected results. Is it not because Christ's kingship is finally of another order and must be recognized in other ways?

In all events, the Pope of the Lateran Accords (1929) certainly did not conceive of the kingship of Christ as a return to bygone Christendom. Although manifestly embedded in the context of its time, the encyclical *Quas primas*, correctly read and understood, does not justify confusion between politics, partisan side-taking in secular matters, and religion; such confusion is even in our day placed under the banner of Christ the King. The concordats concluded under Pius XI, and under Pius XII (1939–1958) in particular, with numerous nations, no longer claim the privilege of state religion for Catholicism, even if it is the religion of the majority.

A New Situation
Nevertheless, under the influence of combined factors, the situation has considerably developed over the past thirty years or so. Of course, this does not mean that the Church has come to think of the gospel as neutral with respect to cultural, social, and political realities. But freed from the shackles of outdated models, ecclesiology has worked out healthy adjustments. At the same time, the distancing of cultural, social, and political realities from the tutelage of the Church has benefited the Church in many ways and has facilitated the preaching of the gospel to all peoples, whatever their political regimes. The current talk of inculturation reveals

a considerable reversal of perspective. Paradoxically, the interventions of the hierarchy—Pope, bishops—certainly have more weight and impact today than formerly, when they touch upon cultural and social questions.[8]

The encyclical *Pacem in terris*, published by Pope John XXIII on April 11, 1963, a few months before his death on June 3, attests to this evolution of doctrine and practice. What immediately strikes the reader and appears on every page is the new manner in which the Church places itself in relation to the world, here when speaking of *Peace on earth*. The Church exercises its ministry certainly with conviction, but also with humility, aware of the values of which human beings, including all who do not belong to it, are bearers and active agents. This encyclical is addressed not only "To the Venerable Brothers the Patriarchs, Primates, Archbishops, Bishops and other Local Ordinaries in Peace and Communion with the Apostolic See" but also "to the Clergy and Faithful of the whole World and to All Men [and Women] of Good Will."

Like Pius XI, John XXIII observes that Christians have too little impact on the building of the world. But he no longer exhorts them to aggressive action but to conversion.

> It is no less clear that today, in traditionally Christian nations, secular institutions, although demonstrating a high degree of scientific and technical perfection and efficiency in achieving their respective ends, not infrequently are but slightly affected by Christian motivation or inspiration.
>
> It is beyond question that in the creation of those institutions many contributed and continue to contribute who were believed to be and who consider themselves Christians; and without doubt, in part at least, they were and are. How does one explain this? It is Our opinion that the explanation is to be found in an inconsistency in their minds between religious belief and their action in the temporal sphere. It is necessary, therefore, that their interior unity be re-established, and that in their temporal activity faith should be present as a beacon to give light, and charity as a force to give life.[9]

Vatican II, convoked by John XXIII, will adopt the same perspective, especially in the Pastoral Constitution on the Church in the Modern World, *Gaudium et spes*. The Council "addresses not only the sons of the Church and all who call upon the name of Christ, but the whole of humanity as well, and it longs to set forth the way it understands the presence and function of the Church in the world of today."[10]

> In wonder at their own discoveries and their own might men are today troubled and perplexed by questions about current trends in the world, about their place and their role in the universe, about the meaning of individual and collective endeavor, and finally about the destiny of nature and

of men. And so the Council, as witness and guide to the faith of the whole people of God, gathered together by Christ, can find no more eloquent expression of its solidarity and respectful affection for the whole human family, to which it belongs, than to enter into dialogue with it about all these different problems. The Council will clarify these problems in the light of the Gospel and will furnish mankind with the saving resources which the Church has received from its founder under the promptings of the Holy Spirit. It is man himself who must be saved: it is mankind that must be renewed. It is man, therefore, who is the key to this discussion, man considered whole and entire, with body and soul, heart and conscience, mind and will.

This is the reason why this sacred Synod, in proclaiming the noble destiny of man and affirming an element of the divine in him, offers to cooperate unreservedly with mankind in fostering a sense of brotherhood to correspond to this destiny of theirs. The Church is not motivated by an earthly ambition but is interested in one thing only—to carry on the work of Christ under the guidance of the Holy Spirit, for he came into the world to bear witness to the truth, to save and not to judge, to serve and not to be served.[11]

The Celebration Today

Obviously, this whole evolution is reflected in the liturgy of the feast. To tell the truth, when the liturgical reform was in preparation, certain persons questioned the celebration of Christ the King. On the one hand, liturgists pointed out how abnormal was the celebration of a title of Christ. They added that the celebration of Epiphany already has for its object the manifestation of the universal kingship of Christ. On the other hand, pastors mentioned the difficulty of a feast that ran the risk of being misunderstood. One needed to furnish explanations so that the faithful would see that the kingship of Christ had nothing in common with the images of absolute power, luxury, splendor, and so forth, associated with the concept of king. In sum, they said, it was necessary to begin by insisting on what Christ the King was not.

The feast was kept in the liturgical calendar and was moved from the last Sunday in October to the last Sunday of the liturgical year, which it crowns. It is not just the title of Christ that is the object of the celebration but his person and the global mystery of the Risen One at the right hand of the Father, who came, who comes, and who will come. Before the liturgical reform, only two texts from the New Testament were read: Colossians 1:12-20 ("The Father [has] transferred us to the kingdom of his beloved Son") and John 18:33-37 ("Are you the King of the Jews? . . . My kingdom does not belong to this world"). It is worth noting that these two texts situate the kingship of Christ in its proper perspective and do not allow us to confuse it with a political and temporal power of whatever sort. In any case, the Lectionary now gives us, over the space of three years, four other texts from the New Testament and three from the Old. To these we must add the three psalms of meditation after the first reading. Therefore, the new liturgy borrows more liberally from Scripture in order to highlight the meaning and the object of the celebration.

The Preface has not changed, but the three prayers have undergone significant revisions.

Almighty and everlasting God, you willed to restore all things in your beloved Son, the King of the whole world; grant in your mercy that all the families of nations, torn apart by the world of sin, may become subject to his most gentle rule. (Opening Prayer, Formulary of 1925)

Almighty and merciful God, you break the power of evil and make all things new in your Son Jesus Christ, the King of the universe. May all in heaven and earth acclaim your glory and never cease to praise you. (Opening Prayer, Roman Missal, 1969)

We offer you, Lord, the Victim of man's reconciliation; grant, we pray, that he whom we immolate in our present sacrifice, may himself give to all nations the gifts of unity and peace, Jesus Christ, your son, our Lord. (Prayer over the Gifts, Formulary of 1925)

Lord, we offer you the sacrifice by which your Son reconciles mankind. May it bring unity and peace to the world. (Prayer over the Gifts, Roman Missal, 1969)

After receiving the Food of immortality, Lord, we pray that we who glory in our service under the banner of Christ the King, may come to reign forever with him in his heavenly home. (Prayer after Communion, Formulary of 1925)

Lord, you give us Christ, the King of all creation, as food for everlasting life. Help us to live by his gospel and bring us to the joy of his kingdom, where he lives and reigns for ever and ever. (Prayer after Communion, Roman Missal, 1969)

The revision is especially significant in the last prayer, the more so as this prayer is turned toward the time after the celebration and as it is inspired by the mystery that the liturgy has just presented to us and urged us to live by. No more triumphalism. No longer are we exhorted to do "service under the banner of Christ the King." We humbly ask God to "help us live by his gospel" and to be brought "to the joy of his kingdom." This is a prayer that places our Christian life of every day in the exact perspective of the feast of Christ the King.

Jesus vehemently defended himself against political expectations carried and exacerbated by a certain kind of messianism.

Christ, King of the Universe, neither dethrones kings nor seats the powerful of this world. No political regime or system can claim his approval to establish its authority and contest others'.

It is to those blessed by his Father that Christ, King of the Universe,[12] sitting "upon his glorious throne," will say, "Inherit the kingdom prepared for you from the foundation of the world" (Matt 25:34, Year A).

"You say I am a king. For this I was born and for this I came into the world, to testify to the truth. Everyone who belongs to the truth listens to my voice" (John 18:37, Year B).

" 'Jesus, remember me when you come into your kingdom.' He replied to him, 'Amen, I say to you, today you will be with me in Paradise' " (Luke 23:42-43, Year C).

Every year the celebration shows us an aspect of this mystery of Christ, King of the Universe.

Under the Staff of God, Shepherd of His People

In civilizations and cultures where pastoral experience is strong, the metaphor of the shepherd is very rich. This is the case in the Bible. Shepherds exercise an undisputed authority over their flock, but at the same time they are very close to their sheep, surround them with care and thoughtfulness, know whether each one of the ewes is doing well or not, drive them with much prudence. This is why the Bible compares leaders of the people, kings, and even God, to shepherds.[13] The passage from the Book of Ezekiel, read this year for the feast of Christ, King of the Universe, belongs to this tradition (Ezek 34:11-12, 15-17).[14]

God does not entrust to others the care of the flock he owns; like a good shepherd, he himself looks after it. All the verbs and all the expressions used to describe the model shepherd's activity refer to what God does for his people: "[I will] tend my sheep, I will rescue them from every place where they were scattered when it was cloudy and dark. . . . I myself will pasture my sheep; I myself will give them rest, says the Lord God. The lost I will seek out, the strayed I will bring back, the injured I will bind up, the sick I will heal [but the sleek and the strong I will destroy], shepherding them rightly." We must not overlook the last sentence, particularly important in the context of this Sunday's celebration: "As for you, my sheep, says the Lord God, I will judge between one sheep and another, between rams and goats." God, the Good Shepherd, will intervene to maintain order in his flock. He will not allow the weak to be bullied by the strong; he will push these away in order to protect the more vulnerable.

A certain iconography has popularized the image of a sweet Good Shepherd with soft features, devoid of any strength of character. Nothing could be farther from reality. Although full of tenderness for his sheep, a shepherd does not resemble in the least these mawkish representations. He is a man with a weather-beaten face and piercing eyes that are used to searching the horizon, a walker who is able to cover long distances and climb slopes at the head of his flock or in search of the lost sheep, often a sage who has the time to think and reflect in solitude. But he is also a strong person who does not take lightly the welfare of his flock, who raises his voice and acts threateningly in order to bring back to the right path the recalcitrant sheep. His almost motherly solicitude toward the lambs and their sick or tired mothers is the more touching. He thinks of himself only after the flock has entered the sheepfold or is settled in the pasture. Such is our God in whom we can have trust.

> The LORD is my shepherd;
> there is nothing I shall want.

The LORD is my shepherd; I shall not want.
  In verdant pastures he gives me repose.
Beside restful waters he leads me;
  he refreshes my soul.
He guides me in right paths
  for his name's sake.
You spread the table before me
  in the sight of my foes;
You anoint my head with oil;
  my cup overflows.
Only goodness and kindness follow me
  all the days of my life;
And I shall dwell in the house of the LORD
  for years to come.
(Ps 23:1-2, 2-3, 5-6)

Royal Power of Christ, the First of Those Who Are Risen

"Christ is risen": such is the central core of the faith, the basic content of the gospel. If this is questioned, everything crumbles; Christian life loses all meaning. Paul never ceases to repeat this, in various ways, at every turn, and especially when he broaches the questions that have a bearing on the moral conduct of Christians. In the brief passage from the

First Letter to the Corinthians that is read today, Paul contemplates the resurrection of the Lord within the unfolding of the salvation of humankind up to its fulfillment in God (1 Cor 15: 20-26, 28).

We are dealing here with a mystery, that is, a divine event that has happened once for all, but that has decisive consequences for the present and the future in the history of salvation in which believers share. The resurrection of Christ is not an event that concerns only him. "But now Christ has been raised from the dead, the firstfruits of those who have fallen asleep." "First" in the absolute sense because this personal resurrection makes of Christ the leader of a new humanity. We are humans and mortals because we are born of Adam's stock. We become new humans and are promised eternal life because we are reborn in Christ. The process of the resurrection of the dead is started by the resurrection of Christ. This is the first step, decisive and already effective, of the process that leads history to its term.

Children of Adam, human beings continue to die, but in order to live again in Christ. This second phase will take place when the living Lord comes back and leads the immense cortege of those who belong to him and who, glorious, follow him in their assigned ranks.

Then the apotheosis will come when, after everything is subjected to him, Christ offers his power in homage to the Father. Then "God [will] be all in all," in the kingdom finally established.

This majestic vision is not a sort of poetical and mystical reverie. Paul expresses the reality of the mystery better than all discourses and all explanations: "For from him and through him and for him are all things. To him be glory forever" (Rom 11:36). Christ, King of the Universe, has come to found this kingdom of God, and we have a part in it: "You [belong] to Christ and Christ to God" (1 Cor 3:23). Such is the kingship of Christ, totally transparent to that of God.

The liturgy celebrates and proclaims this kingship: "Through him, with him, in him, in the unity of the Holy Spirit, all glory and honor is yours, almighty Father, for ever and ever. Amen."

"Inherit the Kingdom"

There was no need for lengthy research to find in Matthew's Gospel the passage that was appropriate to the feast of Christ the King: the passage that concludes the great discourse of Jesus on his coming at the end of time was an obvious choice. It proposes for our contemplation the solemn intervention of the Son of Man when he "comes in his glory, and

all the angels with him." Taking "his glorious throne" in order to judge
all nations, he will appear as the king of the universe who has received
the power to give to those blessed by his Father the inheritance of the
kingdom, prepared for them "from the foundation of the world" (Matt
25:31-46).

This gospel passage sheds full light on the nature and the object of Jesus'
mission. He came to proclaim it: "Repent, for the kingdom of heaven
is at hand" (Matt 4:17). By his words and acts, he never stopped teaching that the kingdom has been prepared for the little and poor ones, to
whom God will do justice, and for those who are like them. "Rejoice
and be glad, for your reward will be great in heaven" (Matt 5:12). To
all, he gives this solemn admonition: "My disciples are not those who
say 'Lord, Lord,' but those who act in accordance with their faith, those
who are merciful toward others because the two commandments of love
of God and love of neighbor are one commandment." The judgment
scene, as shown in Matthew's Gospel, is the summit of this teaching and
further enhances it. Indeed, the evangelist shows that all will be judged
on what they will have done or not done for those who were hungry and
thirsty, strangers, naked, sick, prisoners, those whom from the beginning of his ministry Jesus declared blessed (Matt 5:1-12). "You did for
me . . . You did not do for me."

This will be the great surprise of the former, even if they did not know
that the Lord had identified himself with the little ones. As to the latter,
"these will go off to eternal punishment." They will have no excuse because they had been duly warned: "Not everyone who says to me, 'Lord,
Lord,' will enter the kingdom of heaven. . . . Many will say to me on
that day, 'Lord, Lord, did we not prophesy in your name? Did we not
drive out demons in your name? Did we not do mighty deeds in your
name?' Then I will declare to them solemnly, 'I never knew you. Depart
from me, you evildoers' " (Matt 7:21-23).[15] The works of mercy that we
shall have done or neglected to do—"almsgiving"—will judge us.[16]

> You are moved, I see, as I myself am moved. The thing is really admirable.
> And I sum up, as best as I can, the reason of this admirable thing to ex-
> plain it to you. It is written:
>   Water quenches a flaming fire
>   and alms atone for sins (Sir 3:29).
> It is also written:
>   Store up your almsgiving in your treasure house,
>   and it will save you from every evil (Sir 29:12).

It is also written: "Therefore, O king, take my advice; atone for your sins by good deeds, and for your misdeeds by kindness to the poor. . ." (Dan 4:24). There are, in the divine writ, many other examples demonstrating the destruction of sins. It is why God takes account only of almsgiving when he deals with those he is about to condemn, and still more, those he is about to crown. It is as if he said, "If I examined you and carefully weighed all your actions, it would be difficult not to find grounds for condemnation. But 'inherit the kingdom . . . For I was hungry and you gave me food.' If you enter the kingdom, it is not because you have not sinned but because through your almsgiving you have expiated your sins."[17]

King of the Little Ones, the Poor

Christ is King. But this title does not designate him as a powerful one among or above the powerful of the earth. In the tradition of the cultures of the Middle East, this title refers to the concept of God as Shepherd-King of his people, who tends the frailest sheep of his flock. The king is the one who does justice to the weak and the poor whom he protects against the powerful and the tyrannical power they exercise toward the defenseless and those threatened by injustice. God is this perfect king who acts with mercy, compassion and tenderness.

> For he shall rescue the poor man when he cries out,
>   and the afflicted when he has no one to help him.
> He shall have pity for the lowly and the poor;
>   the lives of the poor he shall save (Ps 72:12-13).

Jesus has revealed this divine kingship. He calls the little ones his brothers and sisters. He does so not because he belongs to their world by his birth and shares a sort of class kinship with them, but because he is the Son and the Image of the Father and shares the same sentiments. This is why he recognizes as his own those who act like him, are animated by the same effective charity, feed the hungry, see to the needs of the destitute, liberate prisoners.

When he comes back in his glory and gives his royal power in homage to God, he will introduce into his kingdom those who will have acted as he did.

> Your kingdom
> is not of this world,
> Lord Jesus,
> since you carry
> this world on your shoulders,
> as a shepherd
> his lost sheep.

To show your dominion,
no other scepter
than your cross.
No other strength
than your mercy:
no other right
than your victorious love.

You offer to us
your life in exchange
for our death,
because your power
wants to give us back to ourselves
and snatch us out
of the yoke of remorse.

Your kingdom
already inhabits us,
Lord Jesus;
at your word
the child in us rises,
you recreate it
almost unbeknown to us.

Everything
journeys in you
toward its beauty;
still frail,
joy touches the earth;
heaven is near,
near, its radiance.[18]

Postscript

As we read Matthew's Gospel, we are struck by its timeliness. On the one hand, it obviously envisions churches as ideal communities. On the other, it addresses a community strangely similar to our own, where bad and good are found side by side. Moreover, it shows a remarkable pedagogical concern through its composition organized around five great discourses.

Step by step, it helps us to discover in Jesus the one who fulfills the Scriptures, a man different from others, the Son of God who speaks and acts with sovereign authority. But in order to be his disciples, it is not enough for us to recognize and proclaim that he is the Lord, or to be content with multiplying acts of veneration toward him. It is all-important to put his teaching into practice, to act as he himself acted, to show others an efficacious charity like his. Matthew's Gospel is, par excellence, the Gospel of Ordinary Time, of Christian faithfulness to daily duties, of the everyday life of ecclesial communities, with their ups and downs, their crises that necessitate frequent revisions, their internal difficulties, and their constant need to keep free of the worldly spirit that threatens to insinuate itself into their midst and to cool their fervor.

Although it does not in any way water down the exigencies of discipleship, Matthew's Gospel is still a heartening message. Toward hypocrites, Jesus shows himself, if not harsh, at least pitiless. He denounces and stigmatizes all false pretenses. But Jesus, as presented by Matthew, also reveals himself as the Master, meek and humble of heart, compassionate toward the little ones whom he surrounds with his devoted solicitude and whom he leads in the ways of spiritual freedom. He does not weigh them down under the burden of multiple observances—far from it. He speaks to them in the language of the heart and opens them to a religion of love. Certainly loving is often costly and requires many sacrifices, but it cannot be said that it is painful. On the contrary, it is the source of all joys. Those who love constantly transcend themselves. The little ones understand this language and undertake with enthusiasm the gratifying adventure of the gospel lived without compromise. There are bad and good in every Christian community, conceited leaders who are more interested in being served than in serving. To recognize this fact is not resignation but a healthy realism that spurs true disciples to become perfect like the heavenly Father.

At the same time, Matthew's Gospel promotes a liturgy, a worship, closely related to daily life, to ordinary time, to the life of each one within the community. It manifests with a particular vigor that "the liturgy is the summit toward which the activity of the Church is directed; it is also the fount from which all her power flows."[1] It is not a pious—and vain—worshipful parenthesis, but a place toward which converge all the efforts of daily life offered to the Lord, who renews its energy. Matthew's Gospel reminds us that we must strive to live like Christians in order to truthfully celebrate the Christian liturgy and that we must celebrate it in order to live like disciples of Christ.

> Come to me, all you who labor and are burdened, and I will give you rest. Take my yoke upon you and learn from me, for I am meek and humble of heart; and you will find rest for yourselves. For my yoke is easy, and my burden light (Matt 11:28-30).

> "Do you understand all these things?" They answered, "Yes." And [Jesus] replied, "Then every scribe who has been instructed in the kingdom of heaven is like the head of a household who brings from his storeroom both the new and the old" (Matt 13:51-52).

NOTES

Ordinary Time—Pages 1–13

1. *Calendarium romanum*, editio typica (Vatican City, 1969) no. 43. Constitution on the Liturgy, *Documents on the Liturgy, 1963–1979* (Collegeville, Minn.: The Liturgical Press) no. 102.

2. It may happen that the Holy Family is celebrated during the week (on December 30) because Christmas falls on a Sunday. It will be so in 1994 and 2005.

3. Constitution on the Liturgy, no. 5.

4. *Calendarium romanum*, no. 22. It is called "a great Sunday" by St. Athanasius, Patriarch of Alexandria (ca. 295-373).

5. The following feasts will fall on a Sunday: Assumption (August 15) in 1993, 1999, and 2004; Birth of St. John the Baptist (June 24) in 2001 and 2007; Sts. Peter and Paul, Apostles (June 29 in 1997 and 2003); Transfiguration (August 6) in 2006; Triumph of the Cross (September 14) in 1997, 2003, and 2008; All Saints (November 1) in 1992 and 1998; All Souls (November 2) in 1997 and 2003; Dedication of St. John Lateran (November 9) in 1997, 2003, and 2008. The missals of the faithful contain the masses for all these feasts.

6. This is true even when they find in their vacation spots, as often happens, fine celebrations in the midst of assemblies larger and more "alive" than at home. True also even when they make of their vacation an opportunity for spiritual renewal.

7. The months of July and August correspond to the period occurring between the Thirteenth and Twenty-third Sundays in Ordinary Time.

Some of the readings from Matthew (Year A) assigned to this period are the parables of the weeds among the wheat, the mustard seed, and the yeast; the conclusion of the great "discourse in parables"; the multiplication of the loaves; the walking on the water; the Canaanite woman; Peter's confession; and the first prediction of the passion.

During Year B, the great sixth chapter of the Gospel of John is read from the Seventeenth to the Twenty-first Sunday.

During Year C, the reading of the central portion of the Gospel of Luke, which is termed "the journey to Jerusalem," begins on the Thirteenth Sunday.

It will be seen more clearly as we proceed that a series of Gospels tightly joined to what precedes or what follows constitutes a well-planned itinerary.

8. Constitution on the Liturgy, no. 51.

9. It is well known that there exists a Lectionary for Sundays and feastdays that can be celebrated on a Sunday and a Lectionary for weekdays.

One must add the Lectionaries for the sanctoral cycle (feasts and memorials of saints during the week), for celebrations for diverse intentions and circumstances, for votive masses for the dead, and, finally, for the celebration of the sacraments.

These Lectionaries are the source from which the missals draw the scriptural texts and integrate them into their proper place.

10. During Eastertime, the first reading is not taken from the Old Testament but from the Acts of the Apostles. During Lent, the Old Testament reading recalls an important stage of salvation history.

11. The "continuous" reading is not an "integral" reading. Rather we read the book in sequence, sometimes skipping one page or another. We must, however, acknowledge that the Lectionary has proceeded with great discernment; for instance, it omits in one Gospel a strictly parallel passage that will be read in another year. As we apply ourselves to the "continuous reading" proposed by the Lectionary, we realize how judicious this discernment is.

12. As the Gospel of Mark is too short to provide thirty-four readings, it is interrupted at the point of the multiplication of the loaves (Mark 5:30-34) on the Sixteenth Sunday. Instead, the Gospel of John is read, including Jesus' long discourse on the bread of life (John 6:1-69), from the Seventeenth to the Twenty-first Sunday.

13. Let us add that almost all texts from each of the Synoptics not used in the Sunday Lectionary are used in the Weekday Lectionary in the course of the year.

Thus, we read Mark almost in full from the first to the ninth week; the better part of Matthew from the tenth to the twenty-first week; and Luke from the twenty-second to the thirty-fourth week. As to John, we read a good part of his Gospel on Sundays and weekdays during Eastertime.

This is a considerable amount, since we also read the passion according to both John and one of the Synoptics each year.

14. Of course, this is also true if we include the fourth evangelist. But, as is well known, his testimony is distinct from that of the other three, called "Synoptics" because it is possible to arrange their texts into three parallel columns.

15. "Better a tacit than an obvious agreement" (Heraclitus, Greek philosopher ca. 540–480 B.C.). Father Lagrange used this maxim as an epigraph for his monumental work *L'évangile de Jésus Christ* (Paris: Gabalda, 1936).

16. See n. 10 above.

17. This expression means that we do not read the entire book, even with some occasional omission, but only large portions. Instead, we select more significant and topical passages, culled from such and such epistle.

Following this method, we read: During Year A, 1 Cor (Second to Eighth Sunday), Rom (Ninth to Twenty-fourth Sunday), Phil (Twenty-fifth to Twenty-eighth Sunday), and 1 Thess (Twenty-ninth to Thirty-third Sunday).

During Year B, 1 Cor (Second to Sixth Sunday), 2 Cor (Seventh to Fourteenth Sunday), Eph (Fifteenth to Twenty-first Sunday), Jas (Twenty-second to Twenty-sixth Sunday), and Heb (Twenty-seventh to Thirty-third Sunday).

During Year C, 1 Cor (Second to Eighth Sunday), Gal (Ninth to Fourteenth Sunday), Col (Fifteenth to Eighteenth Sunday), Heb (Nineteenth to Twenty-second Sunday), Phlm (Twenty-third Sunday), 1 Tim (Twenty-fourth to Twenty-sixth Sunday), 2 Tim (Twenty-seventh to Thirtieth Sunday), and 2 Thess (Thirty-first to Thirty-third Sunday).

18. There is clearly something abnormal in this omission of one of the readings; it is a kind of last resort. Therefore, we must endeavor to prepare the assembly by catechesis to receive the three readings offered by the Lectionary. On the other hand, we are surprised by the reasons put forward to retain—or reject—this or that reading. Some say, "The Old Testament is outdated." What does this mean exactly? In any event, the New Testament prolongs the Old and shows its dynamism within the uninterrupted continuity of God's design, realized in Christ and unfolding even today. To declare the Old Testament a dead end is, in fact, to negate it. Furthermore, on each Sunday in Ordinary Time, the text from the Old Testament has been chosen in correlation with the Gospel.

Others would prefer to omit the second reading, saying, "Peter was right; there are too many difficult passages in Paul's letters (2 Pet 3:16). They are incomprehensible to the majority of today's faithful."

To which one could answer with an argument *ad hominem*. These letters were written for recent Christians, sometimes for converts lacking any biblical formation, even more underprivileged than we from that point of view. But they had been seriously evangelized and catechized "not with the wisdom of human eloquence," desiring "to know nothing . . . except Jesus Christ, and him crucified" (1 Cor 1:17; 2:2). Perhaps we should not underestimate the capacity of today's Christians and the Spirit working in them. Besides, do we not deprive them of an important and precious part of the apostles' teaching?

19. One could object that the Gospel is the summit of Revelation toward which everything converges and from which everything flows. It is thoroughly traditional to read the Old Testament and the apostolic writings in the light of the Gospel. In that case, however, the reading should take in not one single passage followed by other readings but a whole group of texts, often brief ones, dispersed throughout the Bible. This is the appropriate method for the study of a Gospel passage in, for instance, a Bible class. It is the viewpoint of the commentary.

The viewpoint of the liturgy is different. It presents a "montage" made of three scriptural passages chosen from among many others, as one makes a montage with three slides. We should not retain only one detail from the first two readings.

20. In contrast to the other seasons, the liturgical celebrations in Ordinary Time do not fit into a well-defined context, as we have seen.

The liturgies of feasts present still another situation. Let us take, for instance, Christ the King, the Thirty-fourth Sunday in Ordinary Time. Here we have a sort of triptych, the central panel of which is the Gospel presenting Christ as king when he comes in his glory to judge all nations (Matt 25:31-46—Year A), when he appears before Pilate (John 18:33-37—Year B), when he opens his kingdom to one of the two thieves crucified with him (Luke 23:35-43—Year C).

21. During the other times of the liturgical year, we do not read one Gospel in sequence.

22. As we know it today, the division of the Bible into verses was done in the sixteenth century. Henri Estienne, a famous and erudite printer, is credited with having put the last touch to this work.

23. No matter how great the authors' erudition—and it is great—the division of the Gospels into chapters is often questionable. Based on a more sophisticated internal criticism, the modern Bibles propose large sections and subsections more trustworthy and at once more enlightening. Obviously, these do not always coincide with the division into chapters. Thus in Matthew, *The New American Bible* distinguishes seven sections: The Infancy Narrative (1:1-2:23), The Proclamation of the Kingdom (3:1-7:29), Ministry and Mission in Galilee (8:1-11:1), Opposition from Israel (11:2-13:53), Jesus, the Kingdom, and the Church (13:54-18:35), Ministry in Judea and Jerusalem (19:1-25:46), The Passion and Resurrection (26:1-28:20).

In Mark, it distinguishes four sections: The Preparation for the Public Ministry of Jesus (1:1-13), The Mystery of Jesus (1:14-8:26), the Mystery Begins to Be Revealed (8:27-9:32), The Full Revelation of the Mystery (9:33-16:20).

In Luke, it distinguishes eight sections: The Prologue (1:1-4), The Infancy Narrative (1:5-2:52), The Preparation for the Public Ministry (3:1-4:13), The Ministry in Galilee (4:1-49:50), The Journey to Jerusalem: Luke's Travel Narrative (9:51-19:27), The Teaching Ministry in Jerusalem (19:28-21:38), The Passion Narrative (22:1-23:56), The Resurrection Narrative (24:1-53).

These titles reveal the concern to mark out the text for the reader. Needless to say, all exegetes would not have made the same divisions and, above all, they often question certain subdivisions.

24. Even though all do not propose an identical arrangement for each of the Gospels, they concur with regard to the overall plan. Our own division into sequences does not compel us to choose among these plans and does not propose another one. On the one hand, our division does not concern the whole of each Gospel but only the texts found in "continuous reading" in the Lectionary. On the other hand, our different sequences fit into the great articulations upon which all exegetes agree.

25. This is not intended as a condemnation of those who follow in their missals the passage being proclaimed. Certain persons—and not just those with impaired hearing—need to follow the passage with their eyes in order to hear well the proclamation. But the attitude of those who are able to receive the word directly by listening to it is a totally different one. Moreover, this listening posture is highly symbolic; it signifies that the word comes from elsewhere, that its hearers must receive it personally, albeit in the assembly and not individually.

26. When we speak of the homily, we rightly refer to what Jesus did in the synagogue at Nazareth. He read the passage from Isaiah (61:1) probably assigned to that day. Then, having closed the book, ". . . he said to them, 'Today this scripture passage is fulfilled in your hearing' " (Luke 4:14-21—Third Sunday).

27. There is still another way of reading the Bible, done in the secrecy of our room or oratory for our spiritual benefit; it is called *lectio divina* in the monastic tradition. This reading is different from Bible study, although it is useful to have done the latter beforehand or else to have recourse to some commentaries. Such study allows us, in this sort of reading, to avoid the pitfall of an overly subjective interpretation and to place ourselves in the purview and spirit of a reading that must remain in union with the Church.

It is obviously completely different from the act of listening to God's word in the liturgy, if for no other reason than that the passage is freely chosen and pondered over at leisure.

This *lectio divina* will always benefit from being done as a prolongation of the liturgy, by reading either the texts heard there or others that add their resonance to the former.

28. They are called "green" because of the color of the liturgical vestments used during Ordinary Time.

29. This does not mean that exegetes restrict themselves to the cold and remote study of texts, that they treat them as any others that would remain foreign to them, etc. The exegetes are believers, looking at the Scripture not as a mere text but as God's word. However, like any believer, they distinguish between the technical study of a Bible passage and *lectio divina* or the act of listening to the readings during the liturgy.

30. This is succinctly taken from what L.-M. Chauvet develops in a remarkable fashion. L.-M. Chauvet, *Du symbolisme au symbole: Essai sur les sacrements (Rites et symboles 9)*, (Paris: Cerf, 1979) 142-52.

31. This psalm is called "responsorial" not only because it "responds" to the word, but also because it "plays" on the dialogue between the soloist who sings the verses and the assembly that sings the refrain.

32. When reference is made to a Sunday without further precision (Year A, B, C), it applies to a Sunday of Year A.

33. The weeks are therefore numbered from one to thirty-four, the Sundays from two to thirty-four. The reason for this is that on the Sunday following January 6—which normally would be the first Sunday—we celebrate the Baptism of the Lord.

34. Depending on the years, Easter falls between March 22, at the earliest, and April 25, at the latest. As a consequence, Ash Wednesday comes between February 4 at the earliest and March 10 at the latest.

In the first period of Ordinary Time, there are five Sundays in 1997, 2002, and 2005; six in 1994 and 1999; seven in 1993, 1996, 2004, and 2007; eight in 1992, 1995, 2001, 2003, and 2006; nine in 2000.

35. The week after Pentecost is the seventh in 1997, 2002, and 2005; the eighth in 1994, 1996, and 1999; the ninth in 1993, 1998, 2001, and 2006; the tenth in 1992, 2000, and 2003.

But after Pentecost Sunday, there is Trinity Sunday. Both have proper formularies. After these feasts, we resume the formularies of the Sundays in Ordinary Time at the tenth (1997, 2002, and 2005), the eleventh (1994), the twelfth (1993, 1998, 2004, and 2006), or the thirteenth (1996—because the Birth of St. John the Baptist falls on the Sunday following the Body and Blood of Christ—and 2000). The fact that the feast of Sts. Peter and Paul or of the Birth of St. John the Baptist can fall on the Sunday following the Body and Blood of Christ sometimes delays the resumption of the liturgies in Ordinary Time until the Fourteenth Sunday (1999) or even the Fifteenth (1992, 2001, and 2003).

36. Our intention here was simply to briefly answer the often asked question, "How are the Sundays in Ordinary Time counted? According to what principles?"

Let us note that the process was not any simpler before the liturgical reform. Quite the opposite.

There were six formularies assigned to the "Sundays after Epiphany" and twenty-four to the "Sundays after Pentecost." It was necessary to take the readings that had not been used between Epiphany and Ash Wednesday for the Sundays preceding the Twenty-fourth Sunday after Pentecost.

There were three, two, or one of these Sundays, termed "movable," depending on the date of Easter. Introductory rites, responsorial psalm, alleluia, preparation of the gifts, and communion utilized the same chants.

37. See nn. 13 and 17.

38. N. Berthet and R. Gantoy, *Chaque jour ta Parole. Le Lectionnaire de semaine. Notes de lecture, textes pour la prière* (Paris: Publications de Saint-André-Cerf, 1980) 8:73-106. This gives the table of all scriptural texts with the number of chapters and verses in each book, the number of verses used, and the percentage of the latter to the former.

39. Custom has lessened the strangeness of the adjective "ordinary." In Latin, this time is called "per annum," "throughout the year," which is not any better.

Ordinary Time A—Page 14

1. Chapters 26 to 28 are devoted to the passion and resurrection, from the plot against Jesus (Matt 26:1-5) to his appearance in Galilee, where he sends the eleven to teach all nations (Matt 28:16-20). The passion Gospel (Matt 26:14–27:66) is read on Passion (Palm) Sunday; chapter 28 during the Easter Vigil (Matt 28:1-10) and at Mass on Ascension (Matt 28:16-20). Only eight verses have been reserved for the Weekday Lectionary (Matt 28:8-15 on Easter Monday).

2. We must note, however, that from the Monday of the tenth week to the Saturday of the twenty-first, the Lectionary assigns a reading from Matthew (5:12–25:30). See N. Berthet and R. Gantoy, *Chaque jour ta Parole*, vols. 5, 6.

3. The "semi-continuous" reading goes from Romans 3:21 to 14:9. The Letter to the Romans contains 16 chapters divided into 433 verses. Ninety-seven of these are read on the Sundays in Ordinary Time. But in odd years, the Weekday Lectionary assigns 208 verses, which are read from the Monday of the twenty-eighth week to the Saturday of the thirty-first week.

4. In order to realize this clearly, one needs only refer to the titles and subtitles in *La Bible de Jérusalem*, editio major (Paris: Cerf, rev. 1973) 1631–42.

5. On account of the Baptism of the Lord, there is no formulary for the First Sunday in Ordinary Time. But the first week begins on the following Monday, or on the following Tuesday when Epiphany falls on January 7 or 8 and the Baptism is celebrated the next day.

Practical Plan of the Gospel of Matthew—Pages 15–16

1. There are no signs of punctuation. See note 23 in "Ordinary Time" concerning the present-day division into chapters and verses.

2. Several more or less obvious indications help us to locate these units: typical introductions and conclusions, geographical or topographical landmarks, changes in style, etc. However, it happens that exegetes disagree as to their meanings.

3. This alternation is clearly marked by the titles and subtitles of the *Bible de Jérusalem*: Matt 3–4 (pp. 1417–20) and Matt 5–7 (pp. 1420–4), Matt 8–9 (pp. 1424–7) and Matt 10 (pp. 1428–9), etc.

4. Topographical data corresponding to Jesus' life, formulas acting as guideposts ("Jesus began . . .": Matt 4:17, 16:21), general dynamic movement of the narrative, etc.

See introductions to the Gospel of Matthew. The more accessible are those of the *Bible de Jérusalem; La traduction oecuménique de la Bible, édition intégrale* (Paris:Cerf, rev. 1988); an article by J. Zumstein in *Cahiers Evangile*, 58 (1986); and "Matthieu, Evangile," *Dictionnaire encyclopédique de la Bible* (Paris: Brepols, 1987) 799–800.

5. In fact, we are following, in the main, the plan proposed by J. Zumstein in the article cited in n. 4.

6. Where the section contains but one chapter, we put the verses that constitute it in parentheses in order to highlight its length.

7. It is a fairly common custom to call chapter 18 "The Ecclesial Discourse" or "The Discourse about Community."

8. One usually says "The Eschatological Discourse," which means the same thing.

9. Among others, the *Bible de Jérusalem*, the *Traduction oecuménique*, *Cahiers Evangile* 58. For practical and immediate use, as the title indicates, see J. Dupont, "L'évangile de saint Matthieu: quelques clés de lecture," *Communautés et liturgies* 57 (1975) 3–40.

The Second and Third Sundays in Ordinary Time—Page 21

1. *Dominica II 'per annum' adhuc refertur ad manifestationem Domini quam celebravit solemnitas Epiphaniae.* "The Second Sunday in Ordinary Time is still a reference to the manifestation of the Lord which Epiphany has celebrated." *Ordo lectionum Missae*, ed. typica altera (Libreria editrice vaticana, 1981) no. 105 1, p. XLIV. See "Mystery of Epiphany," *Days of the Lord, Advent and Christmas-Epiphany*, vol. 1.

2. The same thing will happen in Year B. The Gospel of the Second Sunday (John 1:35-42) tells how the Baptist's testimony led Andrew and John, then Simon Peter to "discover" the Messiah. The reading of Mark starts on the Sunday following by recalling the beginning of Jesus' preaching "after John had been arrested" (Mark 1:14-20).

Things are different during Year C. On the Second Sunday, we read the "Sign at Cana" (John 2:1-11) in John's Gospel and, on the Third Sunday, the opening of the Gospel of Luke, followed by the passage that relates the beginning of Jesus' preaching (Luke 1:1-4; 4:14-21). In this year, the Second Sunday forms a separate unit.

Second Sunday—Pages 22–29

1. These four "songs," separated in the Book of Isaiah as we now know it, form an ensemble revealing a striking progression. The first song (Isa 42:1-7) emphasizes the Servant's election. The second (Isa 49:1-6) stresses the fact that the Servant will fulfill his mission only through failure and contradiction, although he is predestined by God. The third (Isa 50:4-7) shows with what constancy the Servant imparts a teaching that offends and provokes contradiction. Finally, the fourth (Isa 52:13–53:12) describes the Servant's passion, while hinting at his glorification by God. The first song is read on the Baptism of the Lord and on Monday in Holy Week; the second, on Tuesday in Holy Week; the third, on Passion Sunday and on Wednesday in Holy Week; the fourth, during the Liturgy of Good Friday.

2. Here is the text of the omitted verses: "Hear me, O coastlands, listen, O distant peoples. The Lord called me from birth, from my mother's womb he gave me my name. He made me a sharp-edged sword and concealed me in the shadow of his arm. He made me a polished arrow, in his quiver he hid me" (vv. 1-2). "Though I thought I had toiled in vain and for nothing, uselessly spent my strength, yet my reward is with the Lord, my recompense is with my God" (v. 4).

3. Thus with regularity the responsorial psalm (after the first reading) is a selection of verses or only a portion of the psalm as it appears in the Psalter. The liturgy has always done this. For the entrance and Communion antiphons, for the acclamation of the Gospel at Mass, for the antiphons of the Office, it has freely adapted the biblical text to which these chants refer.

4. "Sacred Scripture is of the greatest importance in the celebration of the liturgy. For it is from Scripture that the readings are given and explained in the homily and that psalms are sung; the prayers, collects and liturgical songs are scriptural in their inspiration; it is from the Scriptures that signs and actions derive their meaning. Thus to achieve reform, progress and adaptation of the liturgy, it is essential to promote that warm and living love for Scripture to which the venerable tradition of both Eastern and Western rites gives testimony." "The treasures of the Bible are to be opened up more lavishly so that a richer share in God's word may be provided for the faithful. In this way a more representative portion of holy Scripture will be read to the people in the course of a prescribed number of years." Constitution on the Liturgy, nn. 24, 51.

5. On the other hand, it is inadvisable to manipulate the texts to have them say the contrary of what they say, or to do violence to them in order to have them serve our "cause." It sometimes happens in the press, in motion pictures, or on posters that a photo becomes a lie because of the accompanying commentary or legend. In the same way, it is possible, by faking, to present a person in the company of another whom that person never met or in a place that person never visited. The liturgy never does anything of this sort.

6. These are questions for the exegetes' studies. Whatever their interest, they do not concern us here. Neither the understanding of the text nor its meaning in the liturgy depends on the solutions—often differing—proffered by the experts. See Cl. Wiémer, "Le Deuxième Isaïe," *Cahiers Evangile*, 20 (1977) 53–58: "Le Serviteur du Seigneur."

7. See *Bible de Jérusalem*, 1615–1634; *Traduction oecuménique de la Bible*; M. Quesnel, "Les épîtres aux Corinthiens," *Cahiers Evangile*, 26 (1977); E. Cothenet, "Saint Paul en son temps," *Cahiers Evangile*, 26 (1978); M. Carrez, "La première épître aux Corinthiens," *Cahiers Evangile*, 66 (1988).

8. Possibly that lesser authority is Paul's companion Sosthenes, "the synagogue official" in Corinth who was ill treated when Gallio, the proconsul refused to hear the reason why the Apostle had been dragged before his tribunal (Acts 18:12-17). If this is the case,

to mention a man well known to the addressees of the letter, a man who, furthermore, had publicly suffered for Christ in their city, was calculated to impress the Corinthians.

9. Acts 7:38; Deut 4:10, 31:30; 1 Chr 28:8; Neh 8:12.

10. St. John Damascene, bishop (ca. 650–750), *Exposé de la foi*, 1 (Migne, ed., *Patrologie grecque*, 95), 419.

11. This brief passage of the Gospel plays on the twofold meaning of the verbs "to know" and "to see," a meaning not unknown to us, and often used by John. The verb "to know" for John means less an intellectual act than an inner sense, an experience of God. Didymus states, "To know, especially in the Scriptures, does not always designate the act of knowing but the experience one has of something, the fact of being united to it." *Les épîtres de saint Jean*, (*Verbum Salutis* 226), (Paris: Beauchesne, 1936); cited by E. Viau, "Connaître Dieu: une expression johannique," *Vie Spirituelle* 77 (1947) 331–32. See also the article "Connaître," *Vocabulaire de théologie biblique* (Paris: Cerf, 1970) 202–03.

12. "It is remarkable that the Synoptics speak of John only as Precursor. Only the Gospel of John shows him to be a witness. On the one hand, this is due to the fact that John the Evangelist, a disciple of John the Baptist, has complemented and not repeated the Synoptic tradition on this point, as well as on others. On the other hand, this is due to the fact that the theme of witness is one of the most striking features of the Gospel of John." J. Daniélou, *Jean-Baptiste, Témoin de l'Agneau*, (Paris: Seuil, 1964) 109.

13. In the liturgy, indeed, the Gospel—as well as every word of God—is proclaimed. This proclamation has an authentic sacramental value. We listen to it personally, of course, but within the Church, in the assembly that is its visible, efficacious, sacramental sign. This ecclesial dimension of the hearing and receiving of the word must be present also when we read the Scripture in private in our room. This is why the Scripture reading in the liturgy is both source and summit of all the other forms of Bible reading.

14. See the Third Sunday in Lent, Year C, Exod 3:1-8a, 10, 13-15: *Days of the Lord, Lent, Year C*, Vol. 2.

15. Isa 32:15, 44:3, 49:11; Ezek 11:19, 36:25-29, 37, 39:29; Joel 3:1.

16. Jesus applied this prophecy to himself at his first preaching in the synagogue in Nazareth (Luke 4:16-21).

17. See J. Dupont, "L'évangile de saint Matthieu," 6-9.

18. Ibid., 7-9, 11-13.

19. Qumran, a dozen kilometers from Jericho, was the location of a community calling itself "Sons of Sadoq," "Sons of the Covenant," "Men of the Community" or "of the Covenant," "Sons of Light." The caves near the ruins have yielded, since 1947, a number of manuscripts of both biblical and other books belonging to the community. See "Qumrân" and "Morte, Manuscrits de la mer," *Dictionnaire encyclopédique de la Bible*; J. Pouilly, "Qumrân," *Cahiers Evangile*, Supplément au 61 (1987).

20. See the Latin translation of Isa 16:1 by St. Jerome: "Send, Lord, the Lamb, sovereign over the land." This is a messianic interpretation that claims the authority of a passage from the Book of Henoch (1 Hen 89:45-49, 90:6-20) and of another passage from the Testaments of the Twelve Patriarchs (Test. Joseph 19:8). Concerning these two apocrypha, see the articles in *Dictionnaire encyclopédique de la Bible*.

21. Rev 5:6-10, 6:15-16, 17:14.

22. See A. Jaubert, *Approches de l'évangile de Jean* (Paris: Seuil, 1976) 135-39, concerning these diverse possible meanings.

23. A variant of the Greek text clarifies the connection between the election of the king and his title "Son of God": "I was crowned on Zion, his holy mountain. The Lord said to me, 'You are my son, today I have begotten you.' "

24. John 2:11; 20:28, 31; 1 John 5:20.

25. See "Fils de Dieu," *Dictionnaire encyclopédique de la Bible*, 477-79.

26. See Dupont, "L'évangile de saint Matthieu," 17-21.

27. Saint Iraeneus, bishop of Lyons (ca. 135-202), *Contre les hérésies*, III, 17:2 (*Sources chrétiennes*, 211), (Paris: Cerf, 1974) 333.

28. Commission Francophone Cistercienne, *Tropaires des dimanches, Le livre d'heures d'En-Calcat*, (Dourgne: 1980) 50.

Third Sunday—Pages 30-36

1. See, for example, J. Ponthot "Un enfant nous est né. . . ," in *Assemblées du Seigneur* 10 (Paris: Publications de Saint-André-Cerf, 1970), 7-9.

2. Isa 9:1-6 is read at Midnight Mass on Christmas. See *Days of the Lord, Advent and Christmas-Epiphany*, vol. 1.

3. Paul's work comprises thirteen letters: nine are addressed to one Church (Rom, 1-2 Cor, Gal, Eph, Phil, Col, and 1-2 Thess), four to one particular person (1-2 Tim, Titus, and Phlm).

4. Let it suffice to read the titles and subtitles of the *Bible de Jérusalem* and the *Traduction oecuménique de la Bible*, of the plans offered by exegetes. See in particular *Cahiers Evangile* 66 (1988). The divisions and scandals in the community at Corinth (1:10-4:21), a case of serious misconduct (5:1-13), fornication (6:12-20), marriage and virginity (7), meats sacrificed to idols (8:1-11:1), behavior in the assemblies (11:2-14:40), the resurrection of the dead (15).

5. 1 Cor 1:10-3, 17 (Third Sunday); 1:26-31 (Fourth Sunday); 2:1-5 (Fifth Sunday); 2:6-10 (Sixth Sunday); 3:16-23 (Seventh Sunday; and 4:1-5 (Eighth Sunday).
Another series of excerpts, 6:13 to 11:1, is read from the First to the Sixth Sundays of Year B. Besides, the Weekday Lectionary draws readings from the whole epistle on odd years from Thursday of the twenty-first week to Saturday of the twenty-fifth, offering there the very passages not read on Sundays. In all, the First Letter to the Corinthians is contained almost in its entirety in the two Lectionaries, distributed over a period of three years.

6. "Schisma," from the verb *schizein*, to split. Paul uses this word only in 1 Cor, but three times (1:10, 11:18, 12:25).

7. Phil 2:1-11 is read on the Twenty-sixth Sunday. The hymn by itself (Phil 2:6-11) is read on Passion Sunday.

8. The "gnostic tendency" we are speaking of here consists in pretending to receive the knowledge (gnosis) of Christian truths through a direct revelation from Christ or, at any rate, without benefit of the mediation of the apostles' tradition. Those who claimed to be Christ's must have formed a party, a faction, as did the others.
The different groups must have set the teachings of Peter, Paul, Apollos, and Christ against each other, thus creating divisions.

9. In the following verses (1 Cor 1:18-2:16), Paul develops the opposition between worldly wisdom and Christian wisdom.

10. R. Marlé, *La singularité chrétienne* (Paris: Casterman, 1970) 151.

11. It is typical already in the "Infancy Narrative," organized around five quotations from Scripture: Matt 1:23; 2:6, 15, 18, 23. The same pattern continues throughout the rest of the Gospel, where there are forty-three quotations from the Old Testament and eighty-seven other cases where one can detect allusions to or words borrowed from it.

12. Galilee is thus what could be called a "theological place," more than a geographical or historical one.

13. See J. Dupont, "L'évangile de saint Matthieu," 21-32, 37, 39.

14. Ibid., 16-17. J. Dupont recalls in particular "the order" given to the apostles to cross the lake (Matt 8:18) and to Peter to come to him by walking on the sea (Matt 14:28). The

same is true of the preparations for the entry into Jerusalem (Matt 21:6, 26:19), the sending of the apostles to preach (Matt 11:1), and the end of the Gospel of Matthew (Matt 28:40).

15. The reading for the Third Sunday stops before these two verses, 24-25.

16. See J. Dupont, "L'évangile de saint Matthieu," 14-15.

17. A. Bloom, "L'expérience, le doute et la foi," *Lumen Vitae* 26 (1971), 25.

18. Commission Francophone Cistercienne, *La nuit, le jour* (Paris: Desclée-Cerf, 1973) 29 (Fiche de chant P LH 49).

The Fourth and Fifth Sundays in Ordinary Time—Page 37

1. Most exegetes agree that the Gospel of Matthew is organized into five books. Each of these contains a narrative section followed by a discourse. The whole is flanked with the "Infancy Narrative" and the "Passion and Resurrection Narrative." The five "booklets" are Matt 3-7, 8-10, 11:1-13:52; 13:53-18:35; 19-25.

2. These two chapters are read in their entirety from Wednesday of the eleventh week to Thursday of the twelfth.
There are complex questions concerning the composition of the Sermon on the Mount. See J. Dupont, *Les béatitudes*, 3 vols. (Paris: Gabalda, 1958, 1959, 1973); "Le message des béatitudes," *Cahiers Evangile* 24 (1978); "Lecture de l'Evangile selon saint Matthieu," *Cahiers Evangile* 9 (1974), 28-34; "Introduction aux Béatitudes," *Nouvelle revue théologique* 98 (1976) 97-108.

3. We find a similar concluding formula at the end of the discourse on the mission (Matt 11:1), at the end of the discourse in parables (Matt (13:53) and at the end of the discourse on the end of time (Matt 26:1).

Fourth Sunday—Pages 38-45

1. The Book of Zephaniah has fifty-three verses divided into three chapters. Only Jonah, Nahum, Haggai, and Obadiah (which the liturgy never uses) are shorter.

2. Besides this Fourth Sunday, these are the Third Sunday in Advent, Year C (Zeph 3:14-18a), the Tuesday of the third week in Advent, if that day does not fall on December 17 or 18 (Zeph 3:1-2, 9-13), and December 21 as an optional reading.

3. In the Middle Ages, his description of "the Day of the Lord" (Zeph 1:14-8) inspired the opening line of the famous *Dies Irae*, formerly sung at funeral Masses.

4. Amos (5:15) and Joel (2:14) speak in the same vein, under Zephaniah's influence.

5. This theme of the "remnant" made up of "lowly ones" is dear to Isaiah (see 1:9, 2:6-22, 4:3, 10:20, 28:5). See "Reste," *Vocabulaire de théologie biblique*.

6. The classic book remains A. Gelin, *Les pauvres de Yahvé* (*Témoins de Dieu* 14) 2nd ed. (Paris: Cerf, 1961), see especially "L'Eglise des pauvres de Sophonie aux psalmistes," 30-52, and "Marie et son chant de pauvreté," 121-32. See also "Pauvres," *Vocabulaire de théologie biblique*.

7. 1 Cor 1:10-13, 17 is the reading of the Third Sunday.

8. 1 Cor 1:18-25 is not read on a Sunday, but on Friday of the twenty-first week, in even years.

9. St. Macarius (ca. 302-392), *Homélies spirituelles: Le Saint-Esprit et le chrétien*, hom. 27,23, Trans. Pl. Deseille, (*Spiritualité orientale* 40), (Abbaye de Bellefontaine, 1984) 270-71.

10. In the Gospel of Luke (Luke 6:20-23) there are four beatitudes, to which one must add four "woes" (Luke 6:24-26) that are also in Matthew in a different form and in another context (Matt 23:13-32).

11. St. Basil, bishop of Caesarea (329-379), *Commentaire sur le psaume* (34:7), cited by J. Leclercq, "Il s'est fait pauvre: Le Christ modèle de la pauvreté volontaire d'après les Pères de l'Eglise," *Vie spirituelle* (1967) 503-05.

12. J. Dupont, *Les évangélistes*, (*Les Béatitudes*, 3), 385-419, has rightly noted this as a result of an extensive inquiry among ancient commentators of the first Beatitude.

13. The Qumran texts consider meekness, together with humility and patience, one of the components of poverty in spirit.

14. See J. Dupont, "L'évangile de saint Matthieu," 27-28. The word "justice" never appears in Mark and occurs only once in Luke (1:75). But it is found seven times in Matthew, five in the Sermon on the Mount (Matt 3:15; 5:6, 10, 20; 6:1, 33; 21:32).

15. Symeon the New Theologian (949-1022), "Examen de conscience sur les 'Béatitudes,' " *Catéchèse*, XXXI, (*Sources chrétiennes*, 113), (Paris: Cerf, 1965) 233-35.

16. Commission Francophone Cistercienne, *Tropaires des dimanches*, 55.

Fifth Sunday—Pages 46-52

1. The last chapters of Isaiah (Isa 56-66) were written for the community reassembled after the Exile. A few months after the return of the first caravans (shortly after 520), the altar of holocausts was restored at its former place and the normal offering of sacrifices was resumed (Ezra 3:3-5). Painstakingly, the prophets Haggai and Zechariah kept urging the people to rebuild the Temple. But would it become for the faithful people the spiritual center of which Ezekiel, priest turned prophet, dreamt of during the Exile (Ezek 37:26-28, 40-48)?

These expectations are soon frustrated. Material difficulties and the ups and downs of the restoration sow seeds of division and disenchantment. The lack of cohesion within a community of former exiles trying to integrate the people who had remained in their land does not favor a new, unequivocal beginning. Soon idolatrous practices and aberrant rites flourish anew (Isa 57:3-13, 65:3-11, 66:3-4). Religious hypocrisy is ready to reappear; it was often denounced by the prophets before the Exile (1 Sam 15:22; Isa 1:10-16, 29:13-14; Hos 6:6; Amos 5:21-27; Mic 6:5-8; Jer 6:20; Joel 2:13; Zech 7:4-6).

2. Exod 21:2-11, Lev 25:39-43, Deut 15:12-18).

3. This episode and Paul's fine speech are recorded in Acts 17:16-34.

4. Three accounts of this conversion: Acts 9:1-19, 22:3-16, 26:9-18.

5. Was Paul lacking in physical presence and eloquence as some seem to have reproached him for (2 Cor 10:10)? In any case, what he says remains true for all preachers, and he himself preaches without apparent effort an eloquence that shows personal experience and rings true. Biblical wisdom is above all a life according to God, culminating in the gospel of Christ. It is this wisdom that Paul opposes to the typical expressions of Greek intellectualism, in a discourse full of a barely restrained passion.

6. H. Urs von Balthasar, "Dieu a parlé un langage d'homme," *Parole de Dieu et liturgie* (*Lex orandi* 25), (Paris: Cerf, 1953) 90.

While speaking of the "mystery of God," the Lectionary chooses one of the possible meanings; other manuscripts speak rather of the "testimony of God." Paul uses the two expressions and the meaning remains the same: the cross reveals the mystery of God and, at the same time, witnesses to the fulfillment of God's plan (1 Cor 1:6, 4:1; 2 Thess 1:10).

7. These words of Jesus are also in Mark (Mark 4:21, 9:50) and Luke (Luke 14:34-35, 8:16, 18:33) but in another context and with different emphases. They are read on Thurs-

day of the third week in Ordinary Time (Mark 4:21), Thursday of the seventh week (Mark 9:50), Monday of the twenty-fourth week (Luke 8:16). See N. Berthet and R. Gantoy, *Chaque jour ta parole*, 4:36, 84; 6:66. See J. Dupont, *Les Béatitudes*, 1:82-93, 130, for a comparison among the three Synoptics.

8. The *Bible de Jérusalem* titles this text ''Not to lose one's flavor.'' Luke's text follows the sayings on the choice of guests (Luke 15:12-24), on the necessity to renounce what is dearest (Luke 15:25-27) and, in particular, all one's possessions (Luke 15:28-33).

9. This conclusion is based on the parallelism with ''light of the world.''

10. This role in indicated by Luke when he says that the salt which loses its flavor ''is fit neither for the soil nor for the manure pile'' (Luke 14:35).

11. See also 18:6-9 and 22:13: the fate of those who scandalize the little ones and those who have not put on the festive garment for the banquet.

12. Isa 2:2, 60:1-3, 19-20; Mic 4:1; Tob 13:11.

13. John 1:1-13, 8:12, 9:5; 12:46, 14:19. See 2 Cor 4:6.

14. The ''earth'' and the ''world'' are synonymous in English. But the Greek word used for world is *kosmos*, whence we get ''cosmic.''

15. See J. Dupont, ''L'évangile de saint Matthieu,'' 21-32.

16. Vatican Council II, Decree on the Apostolate of Lay People, *The Conciliar and Post Conciliar Documents*, ed. Austin Flannery, O.P. (Collegeville, Minn.: The Liturgical Press, 1975) no. 6.

17. This Gospel (Matt 6:16, 16-18) is read on Ash Wednesday.

18. This remark is similar to that of the text on almsgiving, prayer, and fasting: ''Your Father who sees in secret will repay you'' (Matt 6:4, 6, 18).

19. *Epître à Diognète* (beginning of third century), trans. H. Marrou (*Sources chrétiennes* 33), (Paris: Cerf, 1951) 63-64.

20. Commission Francophone Cistercienne, *Tropaires des dimanches*, 58.

Sixth to Ninth Sunday in Ordinary Time—Pages 53-54

1. Matt 6:1-6, 16-8 is read on Wednesday of the eleventh week; Matt 6:7-15 on Thursday; Matt 6:19-23 on Friday. Matt 7:1-20 is read from Monday to Wednesday of the twelfth week.

2. J. Guillet, *Jésus devant sa vie et devant sa mort* (Paris: Aubier, 1971) 101.

3. See ''Lecture de l'Evangile selon saint Matthieu,'' *Cahiers Evangile* 9 (1974) 30, based on work of J. Dupont, *Les Béatitudes*.

4. In the Gospel of Matthew, each of Jesus' five great discourses is followed by the account of his acts that authenticate and illustrate his preaching.

Sixth Sunday—Pages 55-62

1. We all know how current this debate is, by reason of progress in psychology. Formerly, the discernment of responsibility was based on external circumstances, for example in the matter of an offense. Thus, the raped woman was presumed guilty if the deed took place in a town, since there would have been witnesses to her cries and to the manifestations of her resistance. She was presumed innocent if the aggression took place in the country since no one could have heard her calls for help (Deut 22:23-27).

2. "To hold the two ends of the chain" : "to act as if everything depended upon us, while knowing that everything depends on God." The mystery remains a mystery. But on the one hand, philosophical and theological reflection remains possible and legitimate as long as what must be absolutely safeguarded is intact. On the other hand, the road is wide open and free for the initiative, the freedom, and the responsibility of human beings who do not regard themselves as completely autonomous in relation to God.

3. The complementary affirmation that God intervenes in human life is found a little farther on (Sir 16:1-14).

4. Whatever the domain in which we must decide and choose, the assurance and the rapidity of the choice give the measure of our intelligence and freedom. The moral genius always chooses immediately and without hesitation what is good, true, just. We remain within the norm if the hesitations and errors are average. But it is quite another story when hesitations are endless and error is habitual.

5. This is what the sages do when reciting Psalm 119 (176 verses). It is called alphabetical because each of the twenty-two strophes of eight verses begins with a letter of the Hebrew alphabet. It is built around eight synonyms: law, statutes, commands, ordinances, decrees, precepts, words, and promise. Every verse contains one of these words, except v. 122.

See H. Duesberg, "Le miroir du fidèle. Le Ps 118 et ses usages liturgiques," *Bible et vie Chrétienne* 15 (1955) 125-42.

6. St. Gregory Nazianzen (329-389), *Discourse* 31, trans. P. Gallay and M. Jourjon (*Sources chrétiennes* 250), (Paris: Cerf, 1975) 329-31.

7. Needless to say, the term "Old Testament" is unknown to Matthew and, even more, to Jesus. The Greek translators used a word—*diatheke*, "testament"—to translate the Hebrew *berît*, "covenant." Hence, the expression "New Testament" to designate the new covenant established by Christ (1 Cor 11:25, Luke 22:20, 2 Cor 3:6-15). The Vulgate (Latin version of the Bible) gives the translation *vetus testamentum* ("Old Testament"). But the custom of calling the whole of the books of the old covenant and those of the new covenant, Old Testament and New Testament respectively, is more recent than Jerome.

We must add that "the teaching given by Jesus and recorded by the tradition is already somewhat 'ancient' for Matthew. It must be brought up to date on account of new needs in the Church of his time. The effort he made to do this is a model for the realization of pastoral tasks in any time: *Nova et Vetera.*" J. Dupont, "L'évangile de saint Matthieu," 40.

8. "I have come" introduces solemn affirmations on Jesus' mission: to call sinners, not the righteous (Matt 9:13); not to be served, but to serve and to give his life as a ransom (Matt 20:28); to seek and save what was lost (Luke 19:10).

9. One should not say, "After all, no matter the rank, provided one has a place in the kingdom."

10. The same condemnation is found in Mark 9:42 and Luke 17:2.

11. Chapters 18 and 23 say the same thing. In particular the reproach to those who "preach but . . . do not practice" (Matt 23:3), addressed again to scribes and Pharisees, is directed in Matthew to church leaders. See J. Dupont, "L'évangile de saint Matthieu," 24-25.

12. By saying, "I have come," Jesus identifies himself with the one the Scriptures announced: Matt 9:13, 11:2, 20:28, 21:9; Luke 19:10.

13. "It was said" is an impersonal formula used to avoid saying "God." It means "God has said."

14. J. Dupont, "L'évangile de saint Matthieu," 40 (n. 1).

15. The saying goes "Intention equals action." We must correctly understand this. There is a considerable distance to be covered in order to translate intention into action. We can indeed repel a bad intention, a murderous or adulterous thought, etc. The intention of doing good, for instance an act of charity, of sharing, is not enough. There is a vast difference

between having a good or a bad intention not followed through because we were prevented from doing so and because we have renounced our intention.

16. See J. Dupont, "Laisse là ton offrande devant l'autel . . . "*traditio et progressio. Studi liturgici in onore del Prof. Adrien Nocent* (*Studia anselmiana* 95, *Analecta liturgici*, 12), (Rome, 1988).

Jesus' demands agree with the prophets'. They too preached that it is necessary to act morally in order to render an acceptable worship to God (Isa 1:11-20, 29:13, 58:6-13; Jer 7:1-4; Amos 5:21-6; Mic 6:6-8; etc.).

17. This is clearly seen in the well-known narrative of chaste Susanna (Dan 13:1-62, Monday of the fifth week in Lent).

18. See Deut 14:1-4, Jer 3:1. In fact, the bill of divorce protected the woman by shielding her from her husband's fickleness. In case the husband changed his mind, the wife was under no obligation to resume conjugal life with her first husband in the case of a second marriage eventually dissolved through death or a second divorce. See A.-M. Dubarle, "Les textes évangéliques sur le mariage et le divorce," *La vie de la Parole. De l'Ancien au Nouveau Testament. Etudes d'exégèse et d'hermérméneutique bibliques offertes à Pierre Grelot* (Paris: Desclée, 1987) 334.

19. In that text too, this clear affirmation of the indissolubility of marriage is accompanied by the enigmatic parenthesis.

20. See "Lecture de l'Evangile selon saint Matthieu," 32, with this particularly interesting remark: "The problem of that time (both in civil law and among Christians) was not 'May I send away my adulterous wife?' but 'May I keep her?' for through her misconduct she has broken the sanctity of marriage. By continuing to live with her, the husband shared in her sin. Could he in this case remarry? No answer is known."

Hermas (second century) writes: "If the husband learns of his wife's sin and if she persists in it instead of repenting it, he would share her fault and participate in the adultery by continuing to live with her . . . Let him send her away and remain alone. But, having divorced her, he too commits adultery if he remarries." Hermas, *The Shepherd*, (*Sources chrétiennes* 53), (Paris: Cerf, 1958) 155.

21. A.-M. Dubarle, "Les textes évangéliques sur le mariage et le divorce, 335.

22. "If anyone thinks he is religious and does not bridle his tongue but deceives his heart, his religion is vain" (Jas 1:26). "If anyone does not fall short in speech, he is a perfect man, able to bridle his whole body also" (Jas 3:2).

23. "If one swears by the temple, it means nothing, but if one swears by the gold of the temple, one is obligated . . . If one swears by the altar, it means nothing, but if one swears by the gift on the altar, one is obligated" (Matt 23:16, 18).

24. See R. Guardini, *Le Seigneur: Méditations sur la personne et la vie de Jésus Christ* (Paris: Alsatia, 1945) 1:91.

25. We must not conclude that every oath-taking is forbidden and that Christians, by objection of conscience, must refuse to take an oath when it is required. In fact, the personal commitment so taken, should it be untrue, would incur the legal sanction for perjury. It is the reason why certain persons, particularly defendants, are not required to take an oath.

26. Commission Francophone Cistercienne, *Tropaires des dimanches*, 61.

Seventh Sunday—Pages 63-70

1. Only five texts in the Lectionary are taken from Leviticus, and two of them are almost identical: Lev 13:1-2, 44-46 (Sixth Sunday in Ordinary Time, B); Lev 19:1-2, 17-8 (Wednesday of the first week in Lent); Lev 19:1-2, 17-8 (Seventh Sunday in Ordinary Time, A); Lev

23:1, 4-11, 15-6, 27, 34b-37 (Friday of the seventeenth week in Ordinary Time, odd years); Lev 25:1, 8-17 (Saturday of the seventh week in Ordinary Time, odd years).

2. Lev 13:1-2, 44-6 is used again for the Sixth Sunday in Ordinary Time, B. The reason for this is that it enjoins on the lepers, when healed, to have the cure verified by a priest. And Jesus reminds the leper of this prescription (Mark 1:40-45—Gospel of this same Sunday).

3. These four parts are clearly distinguished by the subtitles in the *Bible de Jérusalem*. For a first introduction to Leviticus, refer to the *Traduction oecumémique de la Bible*.

4. "I am the Lord" recurs more that fifty times in Leviticus, and not only in the "Code of Legal Holiness." But there the expression means God's holiness more often than God's authority.

5. As already seen, this is a point Matthew particularly stresses. J. Dupont, "L'évangile de saint Matthieu," 21-25.

6. Under various forms, the apostolic writings—and in particular Paul's letters—speak of Christians as the body of Christ, temple of the Holy Spirit: 1 Cor 6:19; 2 Cor 5:1, 6:16; Eph 2:21, 3:17; Col 1:19, 2:9; 1 Pet 2:4-10; Heb 3:6, 11:1.

7. Origen (ca. 185–253), *Homélies sur Josué*, IX, 1-2, trans. A. Jaubert (*Sources chrétiennes* 71), (Paris: Cerf, 1960) 245–47.

8. This formulation is juridical in style. It alludes to the "Law of an eye for an eye": destruction for destruction (Exod 21:24, Lev 24:20, Deut 19:21), which is mentioned in the Gospel of this Sunday.

9. This applies to anyone exercising a responsibility in a community. Thus St. Benedict says that the abbot will have to give an account at God's tribunal of any loss found in the community. He will have to answer not only for his own soul, of course, but for the souls of the community members as well. St. Benedict, *The Rule of St. Benedict*, ed. Timothy Fry, O.S.B. (Collegeville, Minn.: The Liturgical Press, 1981), ch. 2, 171–77.

10. Balaï, Syrian bishop (fifth century), "Hymne pour la dédicace d'une nouvelle église," A. Hamman, *Prières des premiers chrétiens* (Paris: Club du livre religieux, 1951) 195.

11. Matt 5:17-37, Gospel of the Sixth Sunday.

12. "Talion" comes from the Latin *talio*, itself derived from *talis*, meaning "such."

13. In wartime, alas, such escalation reappears when for one person killed ten hostages are executed.

14. Thus in the current debate on the death penalty when, beyond all other elements of reflection, one resorts to the argument, "We must inflict on the murderer the same thing he inflicted on his victim."

15. See the notes in the *Bible de Jérusalem*, 1422, and the *Traduction oecuménique de la Bible*.

16. See Deut 7:1-6, 20:13-8, 25:19. However, we must recognize that such texts were—and still are—liable to be used to provide a justification for "holy wars," violent crusades, latent enmities. The danger also remains of regarding God's enemies as our own, or vice versa.

17. What must we think of the psalms of imprecation (Pss 17, 35, 54, 58, 69, 109, etc.) and especially of their use today in the Christian Liturgy of the Hours? Pope Paul VI advised the removal of the worst among them and the placement between parentheses of similar verses found throughout the Psalter. We have here cries of despair, even vengeance, inspired by the sufferings or the atrocious injustices inflicted upon an individual or group. Do not these cries of the unfortunate have their place in the prayer of the Church? Should they not resound in the praying community?

18. Martin Luther King, Jr., *La force d'aimer*, (Paris: Casterman, 1964) 51.

19. "They are Christians without knowing it, whatever they may say." Such reflections rightly anger those whom we presume to annex.

20. "Martinus, adhuc catechumenus, hac me veste contexit" (first antiphon of the first nocturn at Matins).

288 ORDINARY TIME A

21. See J. Dupont, "L'évangile de saint Matthieu," 30–32.

22. Commission Francophone Cistercienne, *Tropaires des dimanches,* 64.

Eighth Sunday—Pages 71–80

1. There are three parts in the Book of Isaiah. The first (Isa 1–39) is the work of the prophet of the eighth century before our era who gave his name to the whole collection of oracles. The second (Isa 40–55) was written by a disciple of Isaiah, who preached in Babylon between 558–550 B.C. Finally, the third (Isa 56–66) is the work of a third prophet who was contemporary with the rebuilding of the Temple about 520 B.C. See the introductions of the *Bible de Jérusalem,* 1077–79, and of the *Traduction oecuménique de la Bible.*

2. Isa 40–55 is rightly called the "Book of Consolation" not only because of its first words, "Comfort, give comfort to my people," but because comfort is its principal theme.

3. The "Book of Consolation" is thus interspersed with complaints and questions that express this discouragement and this disappointment.

4. The inmates of concentration camps knew this anguish. They knew their liberators to be near with their powerful forces, but not seeing them come, they thought, "They have forgotten us." It is the anguish of the sick when the promised help is slow in coming. It is the trial of the person who intently prays to God, who seems to stop his ears.

5. Solemnity of the Sacred Heart, Year B.

6. Hosea in particular develops this theme. God, a despised husband, has such a strong and faithful love for his people that not only is he ready to forgive but, besides, he entreats his wife to come back.

7. See for instance Matt 9:36, 15:32; Luke 1:78, 10:33, 15:20.

8. Excerpts from 1 Cor 1:1–4:20 are read from the Third Sunday to the present.

9. Matt 25:14-30; Mark 13:34-37, 12:35.

10. Spiritual masters speak in similar terms of the responsibility of every superior. St. Benedict, for instance, says to the abbot: "Let the abbot always remember that at the fearful judgment of God, not only his teaching but also his disciples' obedience will come under scrutiny. The abbot must, therefore, be aware that the shepherd will bear the blame wherever the father of the household finds that the sheep have yielded no profit . . . Let him realize that on judgment day he will surely have to submit a reckoning to the Lord for all their souls—and indeed for his own as well." St. Benedict, *Rule,* ch. 2, 173, 179.

11. This text is read on the Nineteenth Sunday of Year C. The parallel in Matthew (Matt 24:45-46) is read on Thursday of the twenty-first week.

12. St. Fulgentius, bishop of Ruspe in North Africa (ca. 467–533), "Homily on the servants of the Lord," 1:2-3, Common of Pastors, *Liturgy of the Hours* (New York: Catholic Book Publishing Co., 1975).

13. It is chapter 5 of the Gospel of Matthew: Matt 5:11-12—Fourth Sunday; Matt 5:13-16—Fifth Sunday; Matt 5:17-37—Sixth Sunday; Matt 5:38-48—Seventh Sunday.

14. The twenty-three verses not read on Sundays are read during the eleventh week: Matt 6:1-6 on Wednesday, Matt 6:7-15 on Thursday, Matt 6:19-23 on Friday. The three topics are almsgiving and prayer, the Our Father and mutual forgiveness, and the true treasure to gather in heaven with the conclusion, "For where your treasure is, there also will your heart be" and "The lamp of the body is the eye."

15. It is easy to see the advertisements that incite one to acquire more, to earn more. This race to the "more and more" is habitually disguised under high-minded, even disinterested motives like quality of life, dedication to others (parents, children). It rarely appears in the open as "I am interested in your money," or "How can I earn money without risks," etc.

16. Matt 5:3, 8:19-20, 16:24, 19:16-23.

17. Children instinctively exploit the situation when they find themselves between disagreeing parents or when they can play the strictures of the one against the leniency of the other.

18. The feast of the new moon or "neomenia," like the Sabbath, interrupted commercial transactions (Lev 23:24, Exod 20:8). This text from Amos is read on Friday of the thirteenth week.

19. See J. Dupont, "L'évangile de saint Matthieu," 12-13, 33-35.

20. M. Blondel, *L'action* (Paris: Presses universitaires de France, 1950) 355.

21. It is the conclusion of the parable of the seed (Fifteenth Sunday, A). It is also in Mark 4:19 (Wednesday of the third week) and Luke 8:14 (Saturday of the twenty-fifth week).

22. These two passages from the First Letter to the Corinthians are read on the Third and Fourth Sundays of Year B.

23. "Think of what is above, not of what is on earth. For you have died, and your life is hidden with Christ in God. When Christ your life appears, then you too will appear with him in glory" (Col 3:2-4). "For here we have no lasting city, but we seek the one that is to come" (Heb 13:14).

24. Saint Jean Eudes, French priest (1610-1680), *Le Royaume de Jésus*, 2nd part, 30, (*Oeuvres complètes* 1), (Paris: Lethielleux, 1922) 242-43.

25. As we see in St. Benedict, for instance, the spiritual tradition says the same thing. Benedict writes a Rule for those who devote their life to the exclusive search for God. "When they live by the labor of their hands, as our fathers and the apostles did, then they are really monks." St. Benedict, *Rule*, ch. 48, 249, 251.

26. "Of this day" or "daily" is the traditional and probable translation of a difficult word. See the note in the *Bible de Jérusalem*, 1422, and that, more developed, in the *Traduction oecuménique de la Bible*.

27. Eucharistic Liturgy, preparation of the bread.

28. Ibid.

29. Eucharistic Prayer II.

30. Commission Francophone Cistercienne, *Tropaires des dimanches*, 67.

Ninth Sunday—Pages 81-86

1. "Deuteronomy" means "Second Law." In the Hebrew Bible, it is simply called "Words" (of Moses). See the introduction to the Pentateuch in the *Bible de Jérusalem*, 23-30; the introduction to Deuteronomy in the *Traduction oecuménique de la bible*; J. Briend, "Une lecture du Pentateuque," *Cahiers Evangile* 15 (1976) 34-44; F. Garcia Lopez, "Le Deutéronome, une loi prêchée," *Cahiers Evangile* 68 (1988).

2. In particular, it is close to the famed Code of Hammurabi, king of Babylon (ca. 1955-1913 B.C.), who had it engraved on a stela discovered by M.-J. de Morgan, French archaeologist, during excavations at Suza (1901-1902) and kept in Paris in the Louvre Museum.

3. Taken literally, these prescriptions gave rise to the custom of wearing phylacteries ("tephillim" in Hebrew). They are small leather cases containing a parchment with the words of the Shema, "Hear, O Israel . . ." See Deut 6:4-9. At prayer time they are attached on the forehead and on the upper left arm at the level of the heart.

4. "Today" recurs more than seventy times in Deuteronomy, four times in the reading of this Sunday. This word expresses the concern for making the Law of Moses applicable to the present; hence, the title Deuteronomy, Second Law.

5. If we except the Gospels of Matthew, Mark, and Luke, there is not a single apostolic writing used as liberally and read with as much continuity in Sunday liturgies as the Letter to the Romans. However, it is not the longest of the apostolic writings. It comprises sixteen chapters divided into 433 verses, out of which seventy-two are read over sixteen Sundays. The Acts of the Apostles has 1,006 verses, the First Letter to the Corinthians has 437.

6. Paul often says, "my gospel." Rom 2:16, 16:25; 2 Cor 4:3; 1 Thess 1:5.

7. Paul had not yet visited Rome. He did not know the Christian community of that city. Besides, he had a rule not to meddle where others had preached the gospel (Rom 5:20). As a result, his letter does not deal with the concrete questions that might have faced the community.

8. The main topic of this letter is salvation through faith (Rom 1:16-11:36). A solemn declaration serves as a preamble to chapters one to eleven: the same salvation through faith is offered to all human beings, Jews or Pagans (Rom 1:16-17). The theme is then developed in four steps: 1. The whole of humankind, submerged in sin, is saved by the grace God grants in Jesus Christ (Rom 1:18–6:23). 2. Humankind is one in the death caused by Adam's sin; it is one also in the salvation that the risen Christ, who is the second Adam, gains for all. 3. Formerly slaves of the Law and unable to fulfill it, believers are freed by the gift of the Spirit, who makes of them children of God (Rom 7:1–8:39). 4. Since salvation through faith in Jesus extends to all human beings, Israel, now separated from the Lord, will be one day integrated into his risen body (Rom 9:1–11:32).

9. Exod 24:16, 40:34-35; Ezek 43:2-3; Isa 40:5, 60:1; Hag 3; John 1:14, 2:11; Rev 21. See the article "Gloire," *Vocabulaire de théologie biblique*, cols. 504-11.

10. The following chapters of the letter will show the significant parallelism between the gift of God's righteousness and the gift of the Spirit (second readings of the Fourteenth to the Seventeenth Sundays).

11. See J. Dupont, "L'évangile de saint Matthieu," 21-37.

12. Indeed the account of the Passion-Resurrection of the Lord follows immediately (Matt 26:1-28:20).

13. Matthew puts "Lord" eight times on the disciples' lips when they speak to Jesus (Matt 8:21, 25; 14:28, 30; 16:22; 17:4; 18:21; 26:22), eleven times on the lips of persons imploring a cure (Matt 8:2, 6, 8; 9:28; 15:22, 25, 27; 17:15; 20:30, 31, 33). When Jesus comes to act as a sovereign judge, he is also called "Lord" (Matt 7:21, 22; 25:11, 37, 44). See J. Dupont, "L'évangile de saint Matthieu," 11-13.

14. One often hears "orthopraxis," although this word does not appear with this meaning in dictionaries in current use.

15. This text is read on the Sixth Sunday.

16. See J. Dupont, "L'évangile de saint Matthieu," 13-17.

17. Matt 11:20-24; 13:54, 58; 14:2.

18. Paul makes this distinction in a rather obscure passage, "tongues are a sign not for those who believe but for unbelievers, whereas prophecy is not for unbelievers but for those who believe" (1 Cor 14:22).

19. Paul asserts this vigorously in the well-known passage, called the Hymn to Charity (1 Cor 13:1-3), "If I speak in . . . tongues . . . have the gift of prophecy . . . have all faith so as to move mountains, but do not have love, I am nothing." This text is read on the Fourth Sunday of Year C and on Wednesday of the twenty-fourth week, even years.

20. Literally "You who do evil," who are "lawless." *Anomia* is an important notion in Matthew's theology (Matt 7:23, 13:41, 24:12) since it is the antithesis of the *dikaiosune*, righteousness, that is conformity of life to the gospel. In apocalyptic literature, *anomia* designates sin par excellence, sin as violation of the divine law. Its intensification, foretold for the end of time, is due to false prophets and results in the cooling of fraternal charity (Matt 24:12).

21. The antithetical structure of this comparison connects it with the parables of the end times, built on the same plan. One thinks in particular of the parable of the ten virgins (Matt 25:1-13). After reminding the reader of the Law, the Old Testament often gives a warning. In the same way, Matthew likes to conclude a discourse with a parable that illustrates what Jesus has just been developing (Matt 18:23-35, Lev 26, 28; etc.).

22. Quoted by D. Marguerat, *Le jugement dans l'Evangile de Matthieu* (Genève: Labor et fides, 1981) 205.

23. Nersès IV Snorhali (the Gracious), Patriarch of Armenia (1102-1173), *Jésus Fils unique du Père*, trans. I. Kéchichian (*Sources chrétiennes* 203), (Paris: Cerf, 1973) 126.

24. Commission Francophone Cistercienne, *La nuit, le jour*, 114-115 (Fiche de chant P LH 168).

Tenth Sunday—Pages 88-93

1. Hos 4:1-14:1 constitutes a whole of 167 verses that the *Bible de Jérusalem* divides into thirty-one paragraphs or oracles, the *Traduction oecuménique de la Bible* into eighteen.

2. Not surprisingly, the liturgy often proceeds in this way. This legitimate method brings to mind the way one constructs a montage from slides. Among the many available photographs, one selects the proper one without altering it, leaving it stand as it was when among the others. What information these others would bring is not taken into account; in certain cases they could even confuse the meaning or disperse the attention. Who has taken this photograph? Where? When was the house, seen on the slide, built and by whom? In what circumstances? What do we see in the surroundings on other slides, etc.? To project the slides in the order in which they were taken corresponds to a different preoccupation, constitutes another approach.

3. Hos 2:10; 5:14; 6:3; 11:3; 13:4. See R. Martin-Achard, *Les prophètes et les livres prophétiques*, in *Petite bibliothèque des Sciences religieuses, Ancien Testament* (Paris: Desclée: 1985) 4:61.

4. Along with "knowledge," "love" is another key word in Hosea's vocabulary: Hos 2:21; 4:1; 6:4-6; 10:12; 12:17.

5. See Ch. Perrot, "L'Epître aux Romains," *Cahiers Evangile* 65 (1988).

6. The saying, "Outside the Church, there is no salvation," must be well understood. It does not mean, "All members of the Church are saved and all others are excluded." It does say that, since Christ is the only and unique Savior, the condition of salvation is to be a member of his Body, and the Church is this visible Body. But nothing is said about the individual salvation of baptized persons, nor about the fate of other people. See the scene of judgment at the end of the Gospel of Matthew (Matt 25:31-46).

7. This publican is called Levi by Mark (Mark 2:13) and Luke (Luke 5:27).

8. Charged with collecting taxes for the occupying power and with paying themselves out of the surplus of the sums they amassed, these functionaries were people who by the very nature of their position got rich at the taxpayers' expense. Their profession was a sort of lucrative and voluntary prostitution organized by foreigners. Therefore, the Gospels often lump them with prostitutes and sinners. See Matt 9:10-11; 11:9; 18:17; Luke 15:1.

9. Ch. Péguy, *Note conjointe* (Paris: Gallimard, 1935) 96, 100-101.

10. Commission Francophone Cistercienne, *Tropaires des dimanches*, 73.

Eleventh Sunday—Pages 94-99

1. Exod 13:17-18:27, five chapters out of Exodus' forty chapters. The first part of the book records how the Hebrews, oppressed in Egypt, were liberated under Moses' guidance (Exod 1:1-13:16).

2. Exod 19:1–40:38, more than half the book. This section borrows in part from the priestly tradition, so called because it is particularly concerned with the organization of the sanctuary, sacrifices, festivals, the person and functions of Aaron and his descendants. The exegetes think that the setting down of this tradition in the Pentateuch took place after the Babylonian Exile, that is, after 538 B.C.

3. The 176 verses of Psalm 119 celebrate this with thanksgiving. See, among others, verses 17, 32, 40, 50, 64, 68, 77, 80, 92, 93, 105, 116, 142, 144, 154, 156, 159, 166, and 174.

4. This applicability to the present was already underscored in the Old Testament. See n. 4 in the Ninth Sunday.

5. In the five prefaces of Easter.

6. See 1 Pet 2:5, 9; Rev 1:6; 5:10; 20:6.

7. It is no less heroic to die for an unknown person or in his or her stead, as Father Maximilian Kolbe did.

8. Matt 9:9-13, Gospel of the Tenth Sunday.

9. Matt 9:18-26. The parallel text for this miracle is read on the Tenth Sunday of Year B (Mark 5:21-43).

10. Matt 9:27-31, Friday of the first week in Advent.

11. Matt 9:32-34, Wednesday of the fourteenth week.

12. On God's tenderness see in particular Exod 34:6; Pss 103:8-13; 145:8; Jon 4:2; Hos 2:25; Jer 31:20; Isa 54:7.

13. See Isa 27:12; Joel 4:13. Prophets love word-plays: *quaïtz* (harvest) and *quetz* (end) have similar pronunciations.

14. Matt 20:1; Luke 17:7; Rom 15:16; 1 Cor 15:38; 2 Cor 5:4; Phil 1:12-13.

15. "I sent you to reap what you have not worked for; others have done the work, and you are sharing the fruits of their work" (John 4:38).

16. Obviously, tradition was more interested in the reality of apostleship and the definition of its task than in the names of the apostles themselves. The proof of this is that the lists found here and there do not exactly agree, except in regard to the main apostles. Peter, Andrew, James, and John, as well as Judas, are always named (see Mark 3:13-16; Acts 1:13). The title "apostle" became the rule only at the end of a long process. It is not at all necessary to think that Jesus used it for the twelve disciples whom he had first called.

17. Matt 9:1-34 (just before the text of this Sunday's Gospel; see nn. 9, 10, and 11); Matt 5:12-16 (cleansing of a leper).

18. See Matt 8:5-13 (the meeting with the Roman centurion whose son was sick, Monday of the first week in Advent) and Matt 15:21-28 (the meeting with the Canaanite woman and her daughter's cure, Twentieth Sunday).

19. Acts 13:5-14; 14:1; 17:2-10; 18:4; 19:8; 28:17.

20. The New Testament remained very suspicious on this point. Even when it occasionally happens to use the term "pastors" to designate ministers of the gospel (see Eph 4:11), it leaves no doubt that these never replace the Great Shepherd of the sheep, Jesus (1 Pet 2:25; Heb 13:20).

21. Commission Francophone Cistercienne, *Liturgie* 66 (1988) 210.

Twelfth to Fourteenth Sunday in Ordinary Time—Page 100

1. Matt 10:26-33 (Twelfth Sunday), Matt 10:37-42 (Thirteenth Sunday). The Apostolic Discourse or Discourse on the Mission includes the sending forth of the disciples (Matt 10:1-16, which was read in part, Matt 10:1-8, last Sunday) and includes the whole of chapter 10 (42 verses).

2. Matt 11:25-30 (Fourteenth Sunday).

3. "Le Mystère du Royaume des cieux" is the title the *Bible de Jérusalem* gives to the fourth "booklet" of Matthew's Gospel (11:1–13:51), which is neatly divided into a narrative section (Matt 11:1–12:50) followed by a parable discourse (Matt 13:1-51).

4. Jer 20:10-13 (Twelfth Sunday), 2 Kgs 4:8-11, 14-16 (Thirteenth Sunday).

5. Zach 9:9-10.

6. Rom 5:12-15 (Twelfth Sunday), Rom 8:3b-4, 8-11 (Thirteenth Sunday), Rom 8:9, 11-13 (Fourteenth Sunday).

Twelfth Sunday—Pages 101–106

1. These Confessions are found in five places of the Book of Jeremiah: Jer 11:18–12:6; 15:10-21; 17:12-18; 18:18-23; 20:7-18. See G. Behler, *Les Confessions de Jérémie* (Paris-Tournai: Casterman, 1959). On the Prophet Jeremiah see "Jeremiah, Prophet for a Time of Crisis and Conversion," *Days of the Lord, Lent*, vol. 2.

2. King Jehoiakim (609–597 B.C.).

3. Jer 20:7-18.

4. This text is read on the Twenty-second Sunday.

5. Jer 6:25; 20:3, 10; 46:5; 49:9.

6. Hos 9:7-8; Pss 38:12-22; 41:10.

7. See Jer 20:14, 18.

8. Isa 50:7-9; Pss 27:1-3; 144:1-2.

9. Jer 1:19; 15:20.

10. This call for vengeance, frequent in the psalms, can be explained. It expresses a need for justice against the powers of evil, always active in the world. For this reason, we still can read the psalms and make them our own. The Rule of St. Benedict uses a similar distinction when he asks the monks to "hate faults but love the brothers" (*Rule*, ch. 64).

11. Literally, the prophet "rolls" his cause, he unloads it on God like too heavy a burden that only the Lord can carry. We find the same image in the Vulgate translation of the Bible in Ps 38:5. See also Prov 16:3; 1 Pet 5:6-7.

12. See Zeph 2:3; 3:12-13; Jas 2:5.

13. Rom 5:1-11, Eleventh Sunday.

14. See the long notes in the *Bible de Jérusalem*, in the New Testament of the *Traduction oecuménique de la Bible*. See also, Gh. Lafont, "Il n'y a pas de commune mesure," *Assemblées du Seigneur*, 2nd series (Paris: Publications de Saint-André—Cerf, 1969) 43:13-28.

15. See the remarks of Gh. Lafont, "Il n'y a pas de commune mesure," 13–15.

16. The verb "to fear" is repeated three times in this passage.

17. Sick persons with run-down, ruinous bodies show that their "soul" keeps all its vigor. Men and women, tortured to death, prove that their tormentors remain powerless to subdue their fortitude in spite of all their efforts and fury.

18. See "Crainte de Dieu," *Vocabulaire de théologie biblique*, cols. 219-22.

19. P.-Y. Emery, "La crainte de Dieu: de la peur à l'amour," *La Vie spirituelle* 126 (1972) 749-50.

20. This text is read on the Eighteenth Sunday. It is also used at the celebration of the sacraments of matrimony and of the sick, as well as at Masses for the dead.

21. See 1 Tim 6:12; Matt 10:40; 18:20; 25:35.

22. Commission Francophone Cistercienne, *Tropaires des dimanches*, 79 (Fiche de chant A 209).

Thirteenth Sunday—Pages 107–113

1. See P. Gibert, "Les livres de Samuel et des rois," *Cahiers Evangile* 44 (1983). In Elisha's cycle (2 Kgs 2–9; 13:14-20) the main topic is the deeds of benevolence accomplished by the prophet and miracle-worker, until after his death. For, one day, people on their way to bury a dead person fled at the sight of a band of raiders. They threw the corpse into the prophet's grave. "But when the man came in contact with the bones of Elisha, he came back to life and rose to his feet" (2 Kgs 13:20-21). Elisha's miracles inspired various writers of edifying lives. Thus the second book of Dialogues, attributed to Pope Gregory the Great (540?–604), uses them to tell St. Benedict's story.

2. The story does not stop there. The woman gave birth to a son who grew up. But one day, going to see his father, who was with the reapers, he fell ill and died suddenly. Immediately, the mother went to find Elisha, who raised the child to life (2 Kgs 4:17-37). Later on, on the advice of Elisha, she left for the land of the Philistines so that she and her family might escape the famine that struck her country. Upon returning, seven years later, she found her house and land in other hands. She went to ask justice from the king. And, precisely then, Gehazi was telling the king about her son's resurrection. When she presented herself to the king, he ordered not only the restitution of her possessions, but also the payment of the income from her fields since the day on which she had left (2 Kgs 8:1-6).

3. Luke 8:1-3; 10:38-42; Acts 16:13-15.

4. St. Benedict, *Rule*, ch. 53.

5. It is the subject of the beginning of the Letter to the Romans (Rom 1:16–5:21): Salvation "depends on faith, so that it may be a gift" (Rom 4:16); ". . . we have been justified by faith" (Rom 5:1). The example of Abraham is the subject of chapter 4, a part of which is read on the Tenth Sunday (Rom 4:18-25), and most of it on the Friday and Saturday of the twenty-eighth week (Rom 4:1-8; 13:16-18) and on the Monday of the twenty-ninth week (Rom 4:20-25), odd years.

6. Has not Paul written, "where sin increased, grace overflowed all the more" (Rom 5:20)?

7. Two more answers will be developed later on: Rom 6:12-18; 6:19-23 (Wednesday and Thursday of the twenty-ninth week).

8. The Fathers of the Church had frequent recourse to this method; they took the sacrament and its celebration as the bases for their catechesis or even as the final argument in controversies. Today, we do rather the opposite; we invoke doctrine in order to explain the sacrament and its meaning. This second approach, a legitimate one, does not imply that we take less seriously the sacrament and its immediate meaning. It shows that the sacramental rite, as commonly regarded, has lost the expressive strength that so struck Paul and the Fathers.

9. Baptism given by pouring a little water on the head evokes more directly—although in a highly ritualized fashion—the sole purification. But this ritual formula is what comes to mind when we speak of baptism.

10. See Rom 7:6; Eph 2:10; 4:24; Col 3:9-10; 2 Cor 5:15; Gal 6:15; Rev 21:3-5.

11. Theodore of Mopsuestia (+ 428), *Commentaire sur saint Jean*, 1. II, in *Corpus scriptorum ecclesiasticum orientalium* 116, p. 55.

12. Certainly independent from one another in the beginning, these sentences were collected together thanks to what is called "hooking-words," which facilitate memorization. "Worthy of me" unites verses 37 and 38; "to take up one's cross" and "to lose one's life" unite verses 38 and 39. The phrase "to receive" occurs in verses 40 and 41; the word "reward," in verses 41 and 42.

13. "The love of Christ must come before all else" is a maxim of the Rule of St. Benedict in chapter 4, which lists "the tools of good works," that is, the tools of the "spiritual art."

These maxims make explicit in concrete terms the implications of the principle given at the beginning of the list: "First of all, love the Lord God with your whole heart, your whole soul and all your strength."

14. Luke 14:26-27 (Twenty-third Sunday, Year C) is closer to the Hebrew and says "to hate," which the Lectionary has translated by "to turn one's back."

15. History, even recent history, records such heroic acts and also cases in which certain persons have been unable to make the supreme sacrifice.

16. Besides, God does not behave like torturers, who odiously blackmail their victims by threatening to take revenge on father, mother, son, or daughter in case the parents or children refuse to yield to their will.

17. "Passion of St. Perpetua," quoted in A. G. Hamman, *Les premiers martyrs de l'Eglise*, in *Les Pères dans la foi* (Paris: Desclée de Brouwer, 1979) 75.

18. As Christians, we do not have to wish for death in order to express our desire to have a part in Jesus' passion. Such an interpretation can only be accepted insofar as the person wishing to die knows that Jesus went to life through the cross and that he calls out to be followed on that road.

19. The word on the necessity to carry one's cross is at the heart of the gospel. See Matt 16:24; Mark 8:28; Luke 9:23; 14:27.

20. When the Gospels speak of the cross, they speak of the disciples' cross. See X. Léon-Dufour, "Perdre sa vie selon l'Evangile," *Etudes* 351 (1972) 395–409.

21. Paul asked Philemon to welcome his fugitive slave as though he were Paul (Phlm 14, Twenty-third Sunday).

22. There is a similar conviction among rabbis for whom "they who are sent are as those who sent them." See J. Dupont, "Le nom d'Apôtre a-t-il été donné par Jésus?" *Etudes sur les évangiles synoptiques* 2 (Leuven, University Press-Peeters, 1985) 976–1010.

23. St. Benedict, *Rule*, ch. 53.

24. We must note that these narratives which hold the martyrs' heroic strength as an example demonstrate the humanity and the emotion of the writers. The way in which they relate the behavior of the heroes and what they say does not imply any lack of sensitivity to their readers' very human feelings. Besides, the executioners shameful cruelty is vigorously denounced. See the account of the seven brothers' martyrdom (2 Macc 7:1-42) and the stories presented by A. G. Hamman, *Les premiers martyrs de l'Eglise*.

25. Commission Francophone Cistercienne, *Tropaires des dimanches*, 82 (Fiche de Chant U LH 63).

Fourteenth Sunday—Pages 114–119

1. Another passage is used on the Twelfth Sunday of Year C (Zech 12:10-11, 13-1), and three passages during the week in odd years: Zech 2:5-9, 14-15a (Saturday of the twenty-fifth week); Zech 8:1-8 (Monday of the twenty-sixth week); Zech 8:20-23 (Tuesday of the twenty-sixth week). However, Zechariah is, second only to Isaiah, the most often quoted prophet in the gospels. especially in the context of the Passion: Matt 21:1-9; 26:31; 27:3-10; John 19:37.

2. The Book of Zechariah is no longer attributed to a single prophet. The first part (chs. 1–8) is the work of Zechariah himself, who was Haggai's contemporary, at the return from exile, between 520–518 b.c. We owe the second part (chs. 9–14) to a later author (third century b.c.?) See the introductions in the *Bible de Jérusalem*, 1089–90, and the *Traduction oecumé-*

nique de la Bible; S. Amsler, "Les prophètes de l'époque perse," *Les prophètes et les livres prophétiques,* in *Petite bibliothèque des sciences bibliques, Ancien Testament* 4 (Paris:Desclée) 284–89, 307–10.

3. See A. Gélin, *Les pauvres de Yahvé,* in *Témoins de Dieu* 14 (Paris: Cerf, 1953). This small book has lost none of its interest or relevance.

4. In the Bible, horses, a foreign import, are symbols of military force. The introduction of the war horse and of the horse-drawn chariot goes as far back as 1750–1580 B.C. The fortress of Megiddo in Israel demonstrates the evolution of military tactics that followed from this introduction. It is not surprising that the Bible kept an unfavorable memory of the horse, the invaders' war mount: Deut 17:16; Isa 31:1-3; Hos 1:7; 14:4; Ps 20:8. It prefers the ass, used by important persons before the establishment of the monarchy, or the mule that the king rode to his coronation: Judg 5:10; 10:4; 12:14; Mic 5:9; 1 Kgs 1:33.

5. Several oracles foretell this victory: Isa 9:3-4; Ezek 39:9; Mic 4:4; Ps 46:9-10.

6. See Isa 31:1-3; Hos 1:7.

7. On messianic peace see Isa 9:5; Ezek 34:25; Ps 72:3. On the extension of the kingdom see 1 Kgs 5:4; 1 Chr 22:9; Mic 5:3-4; Ps 72:7.

8. See J. Dupont, "L'évangile de saint Matthieu," 13–17.

9. Second reading of the Thirteenth Sunday.

10. The reading of this important chapter will continue until the Eighteenth Sunday. What portion is not read during that period is found in the weekly Lectionary, from the Saturday of the twenty-ninth week to the Thursday of the thirtieth.

11. Under a slightly different form, the same antithesis appears in the Second Letter to the Corinthians (2 Cor 3:4-18): on the one hand, the ministry of the Law, a ministry of death and condemnation; on the other hand, a ministry of the Spirit and the new economy inaugurated by Christ.

12. In other places of this same chapter, the word "spirit" takes on a different meaning. It is used to define the present condition of the reborn Christian.

13. See the article in the *Vocabulaire de théologie biblique,* cols. 146-52.

14. Gal 5:16-25 is read on Pentecost Sunday, Year B.

15. Matt 11:1-13:52.

16. Narrative section: Matt 11-12; Discourse in Parables: 13:1-52. These divisions are clearly indicated in the *Bible de Jérusalem.*

17. The beginning of chapter 11 (Matt 11:2-11) is read on the Third Sunday of Advent, Year A; the remainder, on Thursday and Friday of the second week of Advent (Matt 11:11-15; 11:16-20), on Tuesday, Wednesday, and Thursday of the fifteenth week (Matt 11:20-24; 11:25-27; 11:28-30).

18. In the Gospel of Luke (Luke 10:21-25), Jesus' prayer of thanksgiving is placed after the return of the seventy-two disciples sent on a mission.

19. See W. Marchel, *Dieu Père dans le Nouveau Testament,* in *Lire la Bible* 7 (Paris:Cerf, 1966).

20. These verses do not appear in the parallel text of Luke (Luke 10:21-22).

21. On these three verses, see J. Dupont, "L'évangile de saint Matthieu," 35–37.

22. Matthew insists on this point: Matt 22:36-39; 19:18-19.

23. "Learn from me, for I am meek and humble of heart" is often heard as an exhortation to imitate the meekness and the humility of Jesus.

24. This text is read on Saturday of the fifteenth week.

25. Evagrius Ponticus (lived from ca. 345 to shortly after Epiphany in 309), *Letters,* 36, quoted in *Revue d'ascétique et de mystique* (1934) 63–64.

26. St. Benedict, *Rule,* Prologue.

27. Commission Francophone Cistercienne, *Tropaires des dimanches,* 85 (Fiche de Chant U LH 62).

Fifteenth to Seventeenth Sunday in Ordinary Time—Page 120

1. "On that day" is a stereotyped formula that indicates a transition, but without chronological value. It is similar to the "once upon a time" in other narratives.

2. Matthew shows originality by placing six parables in the framework of a Discourse on the Kingdom of Heaven: The sower and its explanation, the weeds and its explanation, the mustard seed, the leaven, the treasure and the pearl, and the net, to which he adds two remarks on the reasons why Jesus uses this form of teaching. Mark records only three parables: the sower, the grain that grows on its own, and the mustard seed, all joined in a shorter and less clearly defined unit (Mark 4:1-34). Luke records the parable of the sower with its explanation, the barren fig tree, the mustard seed, and the leaven, but without gathering them together (Luke 8:4-15; 13:6-9, 18-19, 20-21). In contrast, he has joined into a unit (chapter 15) the three "parables of mercy." See *Days of the Lord, Ordinary Time Year C*, vol. 6.

Fifteenth Sunday—Pages 121-127

1. William Shakespeare, *Hamlet*, act 2, scene 2.
2. See "Parole de Dieu," *Vocabulaire de théologie biblique*, cols. 905-14; and "Parole humaine," *Vocabulaire de théologie biblique*, cols 915-16.
3. It is this situation that forms the background of the new exodus; we cannot doubt that this promise will be fulfilled because God does what he says. See Isa 55:12.
4. It is the refrain we find in the creation narrative (Gen 1:1-31). See Isa 48:13.
5. See Ps 148:5.
6. Rom 8:9-13 (Fourteenth Sunday).
7. The same opposition between the "momentary light affliction" and the "eternal weight of glory beyond all comparison" is stated in the Second Letter to the Corinthians (2 Cor 4:17—Tenth Sunday, Year B).
8. The Letter to the Philippians reminds its readers of the destiny common to Christ, suffering then glorified, and to the Christian (Phil 3:10-11). The same conviction is found in Peter's First Letter (1 Pet 4:13). We have here a constant of the early Christian tradition based on the oracles of the Suffering Servant (Isa 42:1-4—Baptism of the Lord, Year A; Isa 49:1-6—Passion Sunday; Isa 50:4-9—First Sunday, Year A; Isa 52:13–53:12—Good Friday).
9. Paul does not write, "We wait to be delivered from our bodies," but, "We wait for our bodies to be delivered."
10. D. Hameline, "Peuple où s'avance le Seigneur," strophe 4 (Fiche de chant K 82).
11. See "Comprenez les paraboles": 1. "Les paraboles des prophètes, des sages et des rabbins d'Israël," *Cahiers Evangile*, première série, 44 (1961); 2. "Les paraboles du Nouveau Testament, *Cahiers Evangile*, première série, 45 (1962); A. George, "La méthode des paraboles," *Assemblées du Seigneur*, première série, (Paris:Cerf-Publications de Saint-André, 1965) 15: 32–44; J. Dupont, *Pourquoi les paraboles? La méthode parabolique de Jésus*, in *Lire la Bible* 46 (Paris: Cerf, 1977); Association Catholique Française pour l'Etude de la Bible (ACFEB), *Les paraboles évangéliques. Perspectives nouvelles*, 12th Congress of ACFEB, Lyon (1987), ed. J. Delorme, in *Lectio divina* 135 (Paris: Cerf, 1989).

On the Discourse in Parables in Matthew's Gospel see J. Dupont, "Le point de vue de Matthieu dans le chapitre des paraboles," *L'évangile selon saint Matthieu. Rédaction et théologie*, Actes de la XXIe session des Journées bibliques de Louvain (1970), presented by M. Didier, in *Bibliotheca Ephemeridium Theologicarum Lovaniensium* 29 (Gembloux: Duculot, 1972)

221-60. See also "Parabole," *Vocabulaire de théologie biblique*, cols 891-94; and "Parabole," *Dictionnaire encyclopédique de la Bible*, 961-63.

12. J. Dupont, *Pourquoi les paraboles?* 102-03.

13. The parable and its explanation are found also in Mark (4:2-30) and Luke (8:5-15).

14. St. John Chrysostom (347-407), "Homélie sur saint Matthieu," 44:3, in M. Véricel, *L'évangile commenté par les Pères* (Paris: Editions ouvrières, 1965) 138.

15. Nersès Snorhali (1102-1173), *Jésus, Fils unique du Père*, in *Sources chrétiennes* 203 (Paris: Cerf, 1973), 133.

16. Commission Francophone Cistercienne, *Tropaires des dimanches*, 88 (Fiche de chant U LH 66).

Sixteenth Sunday—Pages 128-135

1. The author of the Book of Wisdom wonders when he considers the moderation shown by God towards Egypt (Wis 11:15-20) and Canaan (Wis 12:1-11).

2. The author of the Book of Wisdom restricts his reflection to the questions he poses. He does not address the serious problem of evil in general or of the suffering of the just in particular. This is the topic of the Book of Job. Moreover, not being catechetical in its intent, the Liturgy of the Word does not have to examine all the aspects, all the related developments of a question. Biblical texts are chosen within the framework of a montage for a liturgical celebration. We must not forget that the choice of the first reading for the Sundays in Ordinary Time is determined by the Gospel passage.

3. This is the second reading of the Fifteenth Sunday.

4. Origen (ca. 185-253), *La prière*, in *Les Pères dans la foi*, 21-22.

5. This sleep of everyone must not be understood as an allegoric feature—the explanation makes no use of it—but only as a manner of saying that the "enemy" has done his evil deed undetected.

6. See J. Dupont, "L'Evangile de saint Matthieu," 21-25.

7. Matt 13:1-23—Gospel of the Fifteenth Sunday.

8. We have the same lesson in the parable of the barren fig tree (Luke 13:6-9—Third Sunday in Lent, Year C).

9. The very money of the people was of no value, even to pay the taxes levied by the occupying forces who immediately used it to provide on the spot for their needs and their agents'.

10. See Dan 4:9, 18, where this symbolism is applied to the gathering of peoples in a great empire, and Ezek 17:23, where it is a question of the gathering into the kingdom at the end of time.

11. In our day, we are sensitive (attuned) to the biological development of everything: a plant, a tree for instance. People of biblical times wondered at the opposition between the smallness of the origin and what results from it. See J. Jeremias, *Les paraboles de Jésus*, trans. B. Hübsch (Le Puy, Lyon: X. Mappus) 151.

12. Likewise Mark 8:15 and Luke 12:1.

13. Gospel of the Fifteenth Sunday.

14. Gospel of the Eleventh Sunday, Year B. See "Nuit," *Vocabulaire de théologie biblique*, cols. 848-52.

15. See "Révélation," *Vocabulaire*, cols. 781-84.

16. To describe the behavior of "all evildoers," Matthew uses the word *anomia*, which means lawless conduct (Matt 7:23; 13:41; 24:12; 28:28). They have lived in impiety and debauchery.

17. "Live in fear of judgment day" is one of the "tools for good works" enumerated in the Rule of Benedict, chapter 4.

18. St. Augustine (354–430), *Lettres*, 153 (1:3–2:4), in Migne, ed., *Patrologie latine* 33, cols. 654-55.

19. Commission Francophone Cistercienne, *Tropaires des dimanches*, 91.

Seventeenth Sunday—Pages 136-141

1. This interview between the queen of Sheba and Solomon is recorded in 1 Kings 10:1-13 and 2 Chr 9:1-12. Solomon was thought to be the author of the Book of Wisdom (Wis 9:7-8, 12). The Greek Bible calls it "Wisdom of Solomon."

2. Chapters 3–11 of the First Book of Kings are entitled "Solomon in All His Glory" in the English version of *The Jerusalem Bible*. From the story of his reign, the Second Book of Chronicles has retained only what concerns the building of the Temple in Jerusalem.

3. This theme is found in a certain number of popular narratives, presenting for instance a fairy ready to fulfill the wish that will be made. This kind of story, which belongs to sapiential literature, is pedagogical in intent.

4. Ps 119:1, 24, 32, 45, 65, 104, 118.

5. Adam's sin was precisely to attempt such usurpation (Gen 2:9; 3:22). See. L. Ligier, *Péché d'Adam et péché du monde*, in *Théologie* 43, I (Paris: Aubier, 1960) 152–231.

6. See 1 Sam 16:11; 17:42; 2 Sam 3:39; 1 Chr 29:1; Prov 4:1-3; Sir 4:11-19; Wis 8:9; 1 Cor 1:27; 2 Cor 12:5, 9-10; 11:30. "I am a mere youth" has nothing to do with Solomon's age. The day when Jesus will take a child and place it among the disciples, he will present them their model. In New Testament language, the "little ones" are adults who have taken Jesus for their master. Cf. Matt 10:42; 11:25; Luke 10:21; Matt 18:6, 10; Mark 9:42; Luke 17:2. See S. Légasse, *Jésus et l'enfant. "Enfants," "petits" et "simples" dans la tradition synoptique*, in *Etudes bibliques* (Paris: Gabalda, 1969).

7. Rom 8:18-23, second reading of the Fifteenth Sunday.

8. Nicene Creed, recited at the Sunday Mass.

9. It is indeed conformity that is meant by image. This word implies that the life of faith really unites us to the earthly and heavenly destiny of the Son of God. See Rom 8:17; 1 Cor 15:44-49; 1 Thess 4:17.

10. See Rom 8:19, 23; 1 Cor 1:4; 15:49. Elsewhere, Paul expresses the same truth in terms of communion (1 Cor 1:9).

11. John Henry Newman, B.D., "A Particular Providence as Revealed in the Gospel," *Parochial and Plain Sermons* (London: Longmans, Green, and Co., 1916) 3:125-26.

12. Matt 13:1-23—Fifteenth Sunday.

13. Matt 13:24-43—Sixteenth Sunday.

14. J. Jeremias, *Les paraboles de Jésus* (Paris, Lyon: X. Mappus, 1962) 94, has established the complete listing of the double parables found in the Gospels.

15. It goes without saying that we must receive a parable at face value, concentrating on its lesson without discussing the elements of the narrative. For instance, we should not wonder whether the man had the right to rebury the treasure he had just discovered without saying anything to anyone, especially the field's owner; whether the value of the treasure or of the pearl was really worth the sale of all assets; whether the prices asked were high enough.

16. We find in both parables words and expressions such as "to separate," "the end of the age" "angels," "wicked and righteous," "wailing and grinding of teeth."

17. See Matt 11:2-6—Third Sunday of Advent.

18. Second Sunday of Advent.
19. Nersès Snorhali, Jésus, *Fils unique du Père*, 136, nos. 483-85.
20. Gospel of the Fifteenth Sunday.
21. See J. Dupont, "L'évangile de saint Matthieu," 40.
22. Commission Francophone Cistercienne, *Tropaires des dimanches*, 94.

Eighteenth Sunday—Pages 143–148

1. The second part of the Book of Isaiah is called the "Book of Consolation" because it begins with these words, "Comfort, give comfort to my people" (Isa 40:1) and because, in fact, comfort is its principal theme. These chapters included in the Book of Isaiah are attributed to an anonymous author living at the end of the Exile, called the Second Isaiah. See the introductions in the *Bible de Jérusalem* and the *Traduction oecuménique de la Bible*.

2. The people returning from exile face multiple difficulties, a severe famine to begin with (see Hag 1:6; Zech 8:18). They had dreamed that when they came back to their fatherland, everything would be wonderful: they were disillusioned. The Book of Consolation tries to give them courage and revive their hope.

3. This is not one of the least advantages of the liturgical use of prophetic oracles. There is no need to make laborious efforts of transposition in order to make relevant to the present oracles taken out of their original context that restricted their compass. In all literatures there are such texts that do not age; that do not acquire a wrinkle; that remain always timely by reason of the wisdom, the feelings they express. We must add that this characteristic is universal, inasmuch as this wisdom, these feelings, rest upon a concrete, a lived experience. Particular things can take on a universal value; the contrary is not true.

4. The thanksgivings and blessings at the beginning of the letters can be said to belong to the literary genre. Besides these, there are others: Rom 11:33-35 (hymn to God's merciful wisdom); Rom 16:25-27 (great doxology); 1 Cor 13:1-13 (hymn to charity); 1 Cor 15:54-57 (thanksgiving for Christ's victory over death); Phil 2:6-9 (hymn to Christ obedient unto death and, because of this, raised to glory); Col 1:15-20 (hymn to Christ's primacy); 1 Tim 3:16 and 6:13-16 (hymns to Christ).

5. In Paul's letters, "there are some things hard to understand that the ignorant and unstable distort to their own destruction, just as they do the other scriptures" (2 Pet 3:16).

6. Eph 4:14—Saturday of the twenty-fourth week, even years.
7. Eleventh Sunday.
8. Thirteenth Sunday.
9. Fourteenth Sunday.
10. Sixteenth and Fifteenth Sundays.
11. Seventeenth Sunday.
12. Literally, "the super-winners," "the super-champions," invincible.
13. Sören Kierkegaard, *La note de 1852* (Paris: Gallimard, 1941).
14. Tuesday of the thirteenth week, even years.
15. Two in Matthew (14:13-21; 15:32-38); two in Mark (6:31-44; 8:1-10); one in Luke (9:10-17); one in John (6:1-13). Perhaps Luke omits the second account because he includes in his Gospel the narrative of Jesus' appearance to the two disciples on their way to Emmaus, which culminates in the breaking of the bread (Luke 24:13-32). Small differences between accounts seem to attest that there were indeed two distinct miracles. See the notes in the *Bible de Jérusalem* and the *Traduction oecuménique de la Bible*.
16. Mark (6:30) and Luke (9:10) place this miracle in conjunction with the apostles' return to Jesus after their mission.

17. John Chrysostom (347–407), *Homélies sur saint Matthieu* 49:1-3, trans. M. Véricel, in *L'Evangile commenté par les Pères* (Paris: Editions ouvrières, 1966) 166.

18. See J. Dupont, "L'évangile de saint Matthieu," 13–17.

19. Liturgy of the Mass, preparation of the gifts.

20. Commission Francophone Cistercienne, *Tropaires des dimanches*, 49 (Fiche de chant D 237-1).

Nineteenth Sunday—Pages 149–155

1. Isaiah, Jeremiah, Ezekiel, and Daniel.

2. Hosea, Joel, Amos, Obadiah, Jonah, Micah, Nahum, Habakkuk, Zephaniah, Haggai, Zechariah, and Malachi. To these twelve, we must add Baruch, whose book is not found in the Hebrew Bible and which, for this reason, St. Jerome did not translate.

3. What is usually called "The Cycle of Elijah" comprises eight chapters in the Books of Kings (1 Kgs 17–2 Kgs 1). See *Vocabulaire de théologie biblique*, cols. 344-47.

4. The flour and oil multiplied in favor for the widow of Zarephath (1 Kgs 17:7-16—Tuesday of the twelfth week, even years); the raising of her son (1 Kgs 17:17-24—Tenth Sunday, Year C); the sacrifice on Mount Carmel when God sent the fire from heaven to consume the holocaust (1 Kgs 18:20-40—Wednesday of the tenth week, even years); the end of the drought (1 Kgs 18:41-46—Thursday of the tenth week, even years).

5. Matt 11:14; 16:14; 17:10-12; Mark 6:15; 8:26; 9:11-13; Luke 1:17; 4:25-26; 9:8; John 1:21-25; Rom 11:2; Jas 5:17. To these we must add Elijah's appearing, with Moses, at the Transfiguration (Matt 17:3-4; Mark 9:4-5; Luke 9:30-33).

6. Exod 19:1-23; Deut 4:10-15.

7. See the notes of the *Bible de Jérusalem* and the *Traduction oecuménique de la Bible*.

8. Moses' mystical experience is placed in this context. God says to him, "Lead my people out of Egypt." But God does not reveal his ways to him. "If you do not come yourself," says Moses, "If you do not lead us out of Egypt, how will people know that I found favor with you, I and my people?" The vision on Horeb is God's answer to this anguish of Moses, who wants to be faithful to his calling, but who knows a "night of faith."

9. The people are battling the temptation of false gods. The great gathering at Carmel has happened with splendor and has seemed to redress the situation (1 Kgs 18:20-40). But Queen Jezebel has not forgiven Elijah for what he has done, and he must flee for his life. Disheartened, he wishes to die: "This is enough, O Lord! Take my life, for I am no better than my fathers." Then the Lord sends him an angel to feed him and rouse him from his dejection, "Get up and eat, else the journey will be too long for you!" (1 Kgs 19:1-8).

10. Exod 3:2; 24:17; Deut 4:11-15, 24, 33-36; 5:4, 23-25; 9:15.

11. Great mystics have always attested to this fact, in particular, St. John of the Cross (1542–91), *La nuit obscure*, in *oeuvres complètes* (Paris: Cerf, 1980); also a good number of his poems. See J.-G. Hondet, *Les poèms mystiques de saint Jean de la Croix. Introduction, texte, traduction, commentaire spirituel* (Paris: Centurion, 1966).

12. Rom 8. We have read five excerpts from this chapter from the Fourteenth to the Eighteenth Sundays (8:9, 10-12; 8:18-23; 8:26-37; 8:28-30; 8:35, 37-39).

13. Rom 8:35, 37-39 (Eighteenth Sunday).

14. This reflection is the object of chapters 9–11. Two more excerpts will be read on the Twentieth and Twenty-first Sundays (Rom 11:13-15, 29-32; 11:33-36). It is little if we consider the complexity of the problem. But the liturgy is not the study of a theological question. The three passages it selects are sufficient to make Christians aware of the attitude they must have toward Israel, when they themselves celebrate the mystery of salvation

in which they share in the Spirit. Numerous studies have as a subject chapters 9–11 from the Letter to the Romans. See F. Refoulé, Bibliography, ''. . . *Et ainsi tout Israël sera sauvé''* (Rom 2:25-32), in *Lectio divina* 117 (Paris: Cerf, 1984) 282–87.

15. Fourteenth Sunday.

16. Seventeenth Sunday.

17. Eighteenth Sunday.

18. The history of relations between Jews and Christians has been stained with blood as far back as apostolic times. The anti-Semitism of Christendom did not always have only religious motives. These are explanations, not excuses.

19. Vatican II, "Declaration on the Relation of the Church to Non-Christian Religions," *Vatican Council II: The Conciliar and Post Conciliar Documents,* ed. Austin Flannery, O.P. (Collegeville, Minn.: The Liturgical Press, 1975) 740–41.

20. Mark 6:45-52; John 6:16-21. One sees immediately that Matthew's account is noticeably longer than Mark's or John's. This is because only Matthew records Peter's wavering walk on the water. On the other hand, all three mention that Jesus was not with his disciples because he had remained alone to pray.

21. See J. Gaide, "Jésus et Pierre sur les eaux," *Assemblées du Seigneur,* 2e série, no. 50 (Paris: Publications de Saint-André-Cerf, 1974) 28.

22. "For Matthew, the proper way to address Jesus is to call him 'Kyrie, Lord.' '' It is the title that befits disciples, and it expresses their true relation to Jesus; it is also the title that manifests the faith of those who are asking for a miracle.'' J. Dupont, "L'évangile de saint Matthieu," 12.

23. See Eighteenth Sunday: "Loaves Multiplied for the Multitude" and n 18.

24. See J. Dupont, "L'évangile de saint Matthieu," 9–13, 17–20.

25. Origen (ca. 185–253), *Commentaire sur l'évangile selon saint Matthieu I,* in *Sources chrétiennes* 162 (Paris:Cerf, 1970) 299.

26. A. Frossard, *Dieu existe, je l'ai recontré* (Paris: Fayard, 1969).

27. P. Claudel, *Contacts et circonstances* (Paris: Nouvelle Revue Française, Gallimard, 1940) 11–12.

28. A. Frossard, *Dieu existe, je l'ai recontré,* 12–13.

29. The catechesis of children baptized at birth and their education in faith have for their object to bring them to this personal acknowledgment.

30. P. Talec, *Un grand désir. Prières dans le secret, prières en commun* (Paris: Centurion-Cerf, 1971) 112.

Twentieth Sunday—Pages 156–161

1. See R. Martin-Achard, *Israël et les nations. La perspective missionnaire de l'Ancien Testament,* in *Cahiers théologiques* 42 (Neuchâtel-Paris: Delachaux et Niestlé, 1959).

2. His universalism will appear quite mitigated if we compare other texts that make explicit the spirit and the practice of this universalism. There we see that the stranger, although welcome, continues to be regarded as a servant belonging to a social condition normally inferior: Isa 49:22-23; 60:10; 61:5-6; Zech 8:20-23; Mal 1:11.

3. Acts 13:13-52; 14:1; 18:1-17; 19:8-10; 24:24-28; Rom 1:16; 2:10.

4. Pagans converted to the Jewish faith, but not circumcised, were called proselytes.

5. Acts 13:43; 18:8; etc.

6. Matt 10:5-6, Wednesday of the fourteenth week.

7. Matt 8:5-13, First Sunday of Advent.

8. Matt 8:16-17.

9. Matt 9:9-13—Tenth Sunday.

10. Matt 4:23—Third Sunday.

11. When he makes the twelve partners in this mission to proclaim on their way that the kingdom of heaven is at hand, he gives them this categorical instruction: "Do not go into pagan territory or a Samaritan town. Go rather to the lost sheep of the house of Israel" (Matt 10:5-7—Wednesday of the fourteenth week).

12. Matt 15:1-20—Fifteenth Sunday.

13. Today the region of South Lebanon.

14. The Bible calls the first inhabitants of Palestine Canaanites, the general term for pagans.

15. The *Traduction oecuménique de la Bible* translates the Greek verb by "send her away" (*dimitte eam* in the Vulgate). The Lectionary, like the *Bible de Jérusalem*, weakens its strength by saying "give her what she wants." We find the same word in the parable of the pitiless servant: "The master of that servant let him go and forgave him the loan" (Matt 27:17, 21, 26).

16. First Sunday, Year C. See *Days of the Lord, Ordinary Time, Year C*, vol. 6.

17. See Nineteenth Sunday with n. 22.

18. "Dog" is a polemical term to designate pagans. See Matt 7:6; Phil 3:2; 2 Pet 2:22; Rev 22:15. "Little dogs" somewhat softens the insult.

19. See J. Jeremias, *Jésus et les païens*, in *Cahiers théologiques* 39, (Neuchâtel-Paris: Delachaux et Niestlé, 1956).

20. Hesitations and perplexity on Peter's part when he had to baptize the first pagans (Acts 10:1-48); necessity to justify his action before the Jerusalem community (Acts 11:1-18); controversies about Paul's and Barnabas' preaching to pagans (Acts 13:44). The Council of Jerusalem settled the question (Acts 15:5-35) but did not eliminate all prejudices. Peter, at Antioch, again kept his distance from pagans, and Paul vehemently rebuked him for what he called Peter's "duplicity" (Gal 2:11-21).

21. "We are obliged to sing God's praises like little birds, without understanding anything" (private letter of a Christian Japanese monk).

22. Commission Francophone Cistercienne, *Sur la trace de Dieu* (Paris: Desclée, 1979) 43.

23. *La doctrine des douze Apôtres (Didachè)*, 9, 4, trans. W. Rordorf et A. Tuilier, in *Sources chrétiennes* 248 (Paris:Cerf, 1978) 177.

The Twenty-first and Twenty-second Sundays in Ordinary Time—Page 162

1. Matt 14:22-23—Nineteenth Sunday

Twenty-first Sunday—Pages 163–170

1. Threatened by Assyria, the kingdom of Judah tries to survive after a fashion, exhorted by Isaiah, who above all preaches faith in the Lord and distrusts unreliable alliances with human partners.

But in the court, intrigues abound. Shebna, a go-getter who has become master of the palace and whose arrogance and vanity have made him odious, is even more offensive, in Isaiah's view, by reason of his pro-Egyptian politics. The prophet has vehemently reproached him (Isa 22:15-18). Then Isaiah announces that this man will lose his position and will be exiled. One may suppose that the prophet used his influence to bring this disgrace about—only a partial disgrace—and to replace Shebna with a candidate more docile to God's politics, which are not those of humans. Eliakim, who will become first minister at the time of the Assyrian invasion (Isa 36:3–37:2), will distinguish himself by his astute resistance to Assyria and by his perfect interpretation of King Hezekiah's politics advised by Isaiah.

2. See *Days of the Lord: Advent, Christmas, Epiphany*, vol. 1.

3. An earlier hymn already accentuated his discourse on Christian life (Rom 8:31-39—Eighteenth Sunday). Paul several times inserts in his letters similar spiritual flights. 1 Cor 13:1-13; 15:54-57; Eph 1:3-14; 3:14-20; Phil 2:5-11; Col 1:15-20; 1 Tim 3:16; 6:14-16). To these one must add the great concluding doxology, (Rom 16:25-27).

4. In the biblical sense, knowledge is not the result of intellectual activity—although we make use of the intelligence in its various faculties—but a way of union with God. See the article ''Connaître'' in *Vocabulaire de théologie biblique*, cols. 199-204.

5. Although accepted and therefore taken in a particular and agreed-upon meaning, expressions like ''religion classes'' or ''catechism classes'' are in themselves inappropriate, or at least ambiguous. ''Class,'' indeed, does not have the meaning we use when we say ''history class, philosophy class, etc.'' In these cases, objectivity, understood as intellectual neutrality, is the rule. Whatever the teacher's deep convictions, the class must not turn into an argument in favor of an idea or into polemics.

6. As a first approach, one can read this text and compare it to other scriptural passages. For verse 33 (''Oh, the depth of the riches. . . .''): Job 41:7; Sir 24:28-29; Isa 40:28. For verse 34 (''Who has known. . . .''): Isa 40:13. For verse 35 (''Who has given him anything. . . .''): Job 41:3. See also Rom 11:25; 16:27; 1 Cor 2:7; Eph 3:10; 1 Cor 8:6; Col 1:16; Eph 4:6.

7. The word ''mystic'' must not frighten us. It is used here to mean the thrust, the flight toward God, that characterizes every Christian and not ''the mystical states'' experienced only by certain persons.

8. St. Louis-Marie Grignion de Monfort (1673–1716), *L'amour de la sagesse éternelle*, in *oeuvres complètes* (Paris: Seuil, 1966) 126, no. 65.

9. The same thing in Mark (8:27-30) and Luke (9:18-21). They, too, place this episode between the multiplication of the loaves and the Transfiguration.

10. The Constitution on the Sacred Liturgy, no. 2.

11. Penitential rite at the beginning of every Eucharistic celebration.

12. The expression ''flesh and blood'' is used in the Letter to the Galatians (1:16: literal translation in the *Bible de Jérusalem*; see the note in the *Traduction oecuménique de la Bible*). But nothing allows us to detect, in Matthew, Paul's influence. Rather, the expression is part of the rabbinic vocabulary. See J. Dupont, ''La révélation du Fils de Dieu en faveur de Pierre (Matt 16:17) et de Paul (Gal 1:16),'' in *Etudes sur les évangiles synoptiques* II (Leuven: University Press Peeters, 1985) 929–39.

13. See, for instance, in Matthew's Gospel, the theophany at the Jordan (3:17) and the prayer in which Christ blesses his Father (11:25-27—Fourteenth Sunday).

14. Perhaps we are insufficiently attentive to the fact that participation in the sacraments is, in the full force of the term, an ''act'' of faith accomplished not only personally but within a community, within the Church. Personal dispositions are certainly necessary. But instead of limiting our faith, they open it to the faith of the whole Church.

15. See also Matt 21:42; Acts 4:11; Rom 9:33; 1 Pet 2:6-8 with the quotation from Ps 118:22; Eph 2:20.

16. Certain persons deny the authenticity of this passage because the word'' church'' is used. Jesus would have here preached only the kingdom of the end of time and its closeness (imminence). Loisy's quip is well known, ''Jesus preached the kingdom and it is the Church that came.'' But how could we not recognize in the preaching in parables many texts that suppose a growth, a progressive development? Likewise, the calling of the twelve

supposes the constitution of a new community. By speaking of "my church," Jesus keeps its distance from other communities with messianic pretensions.

17. The *Bible de Jérusalem* translates "the gates of the underworld" (see its corresponding note).

18. The Gospel of Matthew hides nothing of those weaknesses and hesitations of Peter's faith: Matt 14:22-33—Twentieth Sunday; 16:21-24—Twenty-second Sunday; 26:69-75—Peter's denial.

19. Acts 10:47-48. Scribes who comment on the Law are said to be entrusted with the "keys of the kingdom of heaven" (Matt 23:13).

20. John 21:15-17.

21. In his preaching, Paul, from the very first, was going that far; he boldly announced a crucified Messiah, "a stumbling block to Jews and foolishness to Gentiles" (1 Cor 1:23; 2:2).

22. Humbert Clérissac, O.P., *Le mystère de l'Eglise* (Paris: ed. de La Vie spirituelle, 1925) 58.

23. Commission Francophone Cistercienne, *Tropaires des dimanches,* 104 (Fiche de chant W LH 159).

Twenty-second Sunday—Pages 171–176

1. On this image of fire compared to the divine word and to God himself: Isa 33:14; Exod 24:17; Jer 5:14; 23:29; Deut 4:24; Heb 12:29.

2. See Amos 3:3-8; Acts 4:20; 5:29-32; 1 Cor 9:16.

3. Rom 1:16–11:36.

4. Rom 12:1–15:13. Paul limits himself to two important domains: the Christians' relations between themselves and with other persons (Rom 12:3–13:14); the attitude toward weak fellow believers (Rom 14:1–15:13). From this section, we read Rom 12:1-2; 13:8-10; 14:7-9 from the Twenty-second to the Twenty-fourth Sundays. Four other excerpts are read from Tuesday to Friday of the thirty-first week, odd years: Rom 12:5-16a; 13:8-10; 14:7-12; 15:14-21.

5. 1 Sam 15:22; Isa 1:11-20; 29:13.

6. Jer 7:4-15, 21-22.

7. See 1 Cor 10:21; 11:18-19.

8. See 1 Cor 8:1.

9. St. John Chrysostom (ca. 350-407), *Homélie 20 sur la deuxième épître aux Corinthiens,* in *Patrologie grecque* 61, ed. Migne, col. 540.

10. Matt 16:13-20—Twenty-first Sunday.

11. This itinerary that leads to faith in the resurrection is admirably described in the episode of the disciples of Emmaus (Luke 24:13-35).

12. See *Days of the Lord: Ordinary Time, Year C,* vol. 6, Twenty-third Sunday.

13. Commission Francophone Cistercienne, *Tropaires des dimanches,* 106 (Fiche de chant U LH 64).

Twenty-third to Twenty-fifth Sunday in Ordinary Time— Page 177

1. Matt 18:1-5.

2. Matt 18:6-9.

3. Matt 18:10-14.

4. From the Twenty-fifth to the Twenty-eighth Sundays, we read four excerpts from the Letter to the Philippians: 1:20c-24, 27a; 2:1-11; 4:6-9; 4:12-14, 19-20.

5. Collect, Mass for Tuesday of Easter week (before the liturgical reforms mandated by Vatican II), quoted in The Constitution on the Sacred Liturgy, No. 10.

Twenty-third Sunday—Pages 178–185

1. A series of photographs may be presented in the order in which they were taken to show, for instance, the landscapes, the monuments, the people met in the course of a journey, the unfolding of a family festivity, etc. In this case, one indicates or recalls the dates, the names of places and persons. But it is possible also to pick out one photograph to place beside another one because this juxtaposition proves to be evocative and meaningful on account of similarities or contrasts. When were these pictures taken? in what circumstances? Where is this landscape? Who are the people in the photos? These questions and others of the same kind are of only secondary importance.

2. The exegete will point out that "in order to discern the crucial importance of these few lines at the place they occupy, one must take into consideration not only the whole book of Ezekiel but even more the prophetic vocation in Israel. We then realize that we are in a narrow location, at the vanguard of the Old Covenant, at the edge of the New." F. Smyth-Florentin, "Et toi, je t'ai établi comme sentinelle," *Assemblées du Seigneur*, 2e série, no. 54 (Paris: Cerf-Publications de Saint-André, 1972) 4.

3. In Ezekiel's time, the Babylonian army was preparing to invade all of the Near East. The Kingdom of Judah had taken precautions by placing sentinels on the borders, on the ramparts of fortified cities, in defiles and gorges strategically located along the invaders' route. To this day, all countries do the same thing, with more and more sophisticated means of surveillance.

4. Phil 1:1; 1 Tim 3:1-2; Titus 1:7.

5. The Rule of St. Benedict says that on Judgment Day, the abbot will have to render an account for every loss in the flock entrusted to him and for the monks' obedience (chs. 2, 3, 55, 63, 64, and 65).

6. Psalm 95 was for a long time the only one used as the "invitatory" at the beginning of the daily office.

7. Rom 12:1-2.

8. Between these two excerpts selected by the Sunday Lectionary, Paul preaches humility and charity, which must reign in the community (Rom 12:3-13) and be shown to all human beings, even enemies (Rom 12:14-21). Then he develops the demands of charity, especially toward the "weak" (Rom 14:1–15:13). Finally comes the closing section (Rom 15:14–16:27).

9. John 13:34-35; 15:12-13.

10. R. Voillaume, *Frères de tous* (Paris: Cerf, 1967) 14.

11. Isaac, Cistercian abbot of l'Etoile, Poitou, France (d. ca. 1168–1169), Sermon 31 (for the First Sunday in Lent), 20–21, in *Sources chrétiennes* 207 (Paris: Cerf, 1974) 203.

12. R. Swaeles, "La charité fraternelle accomplissement de la Loi," *Assemblées du Seigneur*, 2e série, no. 54 (Paris: Cerf-Publications de Saint-André, 1972) 15.

13. See Sixteenth Sunday.

14. This parable is read on the Third Sunday in Lent, Year C. See *Days of the Lord: Ordinary Time, Year C*, vol. 6.

15. Twentieth Sunday.

16. Tradition has understood and practiced Christian correction in this manner. The Rule of St. Benedict is a good example of it. A monk who commits a fault is first warned twice

in private; then if he does not amend, is rebuked in front of the whole community. If he remains recalcitrant and if he is capable of benefiting by it, he is submitted to monastic excommunication, which means he is excluded from the common table and from participation in the Liturgy of the Hours. If all this is of no avail, the whole community gives itself to prayer (chs. 23–28).

17. Charles Péguy, *Le mystère de la charité de Jeanne d'Arc* (Paris: Gallimard, 1943) 39.

18. Sixth Sunday.

19. Evening Vigil of Christmas. See *Days of the Lord: Advent, Christmas, Epiphany,* vol. 1.

20. Ascension, Year A, and Trinity Sunday, Year B.

21. The Code of Canon Law promulgated after Vatican II has been in force since the First Sunday of Advent, November 27, 1983. It replaced the previous one, in effect since Pentecost 1917.

22. The definition of the old catechisms suggested this conception: "The Church is the society of the faithful governed by the Pope and the bishops under the Pope's authority." Vatican II has not given a definition of the Church. It designates it as "sacrament of salvation," "People of God," "body of Christ," "Bride of Christ," "sheepfold," "flock," "field, building, household of God," "holy, spiritual temple," etc. For example, see Vatican II, Dogmatic Constitution on the Church, no. 6, *The Conciliar and Post Conciliar Documents,* ed. Austin Flannery, O.P. (Collegeville, Minn.: The Liturgical Press, 1975) 353–54.

23. I. Goma Civit, "Esprit et ordre dans la famille de Dieu," *Assemblées du Seigneur,* 2e série, no. 54 (Paris: Publications Saint-André—Cerf, 1972) 26.

24. Commission Francophone Cistercienne, *Tropaires des dimanches,* 109 (Fiche de chant U LH 68).

Twenty-fourth Sunday—Pages 186–192

1. To be convinced of this, it is enough to read what he writes on firmness and self-mastery (Sir 5:9–6:4), on friendship (6:5-17), on children (6:22-26), on parents (6:27-28), on tradition (8:6-9), on prudence (6:10-19), on humility (10:26-31), etc., and the many counsels he gives by way of proverbs.

2. Exod 34:6; Num 9:17; 14:18; Pss 86:15; 103:8; 145:8; Joel 2:13; Jonah 4:2; Nah 1:3; etc.

3. After the Letter to the Romans (433 verses) comes the Letter to the Hebrews (309 verses). The Acts of the Apostles contain 1006 verses and Revelation 404.

4. J. Vanier, *La communauté du pardon et de la fête* (Paris: Fleurus, 1979) 92–93.

5. The Rule of St. Benedict, for example, foresees that the dismissed brother can be received anew into the community up to three times (ch. 29).

6. The scribes obliged the husband to forgive his wife at least once and his brother five times. But four times was considered acceptable. The Church in the Middle Ages knew the "graduated penance" ("tariffed penance"). See the chapter "Lent and Sacramental Reconciliation," *Days of the Lord: Lent,* vol. 2.

7. Eighteenth Sunday. See *Days of the Lord: Ordinary Time, Year C,* vol. 6, 151-53.

8. Farther along in the narrative, a "master" will be mentioned, but an unusual one, since he is called "king."

9. "Ten thousand is the highest figure used and the talent is the highest gold standard known in the Near East." J. Jeremias, *Les paraboles de Jésus,* 200. L. Deiss, "Le pardon entre frères," *Assemblées du Seigneur,* 2e série, no. 55 (Paris: Cerf-Publications de Saint-André, 1974) 17, cites J. Jeremias, *Die Gleichnisse Jesu,* (Göttingen, 1956 [no publisher given]) 22—who quotes the Jewish historian Flavius Josephus (37—ca. 100), according to whom, in the year

4 B.C., Galilee and Perea paid about two hundred talents in taxes, hardly the fiftieth part of the sum mentioned in the Gospel.

10. See J. Dupont, "L'évangile de saint Matthieu," 10–11.

11. Seeing the crowds, Jesus "was moved with pity" (Matt 9:36). "When he disembarked and saw the vast crowd, his heart was moved with pity for them, and he cured their sick" (Matt 14:14).

12. When reading the parable, one could pay attention only to the numbers, ten thousand on one side, one hundred on the other. But the unit is not the same in both cases. The English language Jerusalem Bible notes that ten thousand talents are equivalent to sixty million dollars. Then the right proportion between the two debts clearly appears.

13. This is a characteristic of this teaching method. The parable leads the hearers to take sides when they see the situation described and the behavior of the persons introduced. The lesson either endorses this spontaneous reaction or, on the contrary, shows that the point has not been understood. Thus, for instance, Jesus shows those who approve the elder son's conduct to be in the wrong; they should have sided with the father and rejoice with him over his younger son's return (Luke 15:11-32—Fourth Sunday of Lent, Year A). Jesus teaches those who regard as unjust the landowner's actions that one must not murmur on account of his goodness (Matt 20:1-16—Twenty-fifth Sunday). See J. Dupont, *Pourquoi des paraboles.*

14. Isa 29:13, quoted in Matt 15:8-9.

15. John Cassian, *Conférences* IX, 22, in *Sources chrétiennes* 54 (Paris: Cerf, 1958) 60.

16. Commission Francophone Cistercienne, *Tropaires des dimanches,* 112.

Twenty-fifth Sunday—Pages 193–201

1. It is part of the "Captivity Epistles," along with the Letters to the Ephesians, the Colossians, and Philemon. These were more probably written during Paul's imprisonment in Rome. It is likely that the Letter to the Philippians was not sent out from such a distance, but perhaps from Ephesus. See the introductions in the *Bible de Jérusalem* and the *Traduction oecuménique de la Bible.*

2. Of all Paul's letters, the one to the Philippians least resembles a treatise. It is an outpouring of the heart, a testimony of affection and gratitude addressed by Paul to a community that has welcomed him. He began the evangelization of Philippi with the small Jewish colony of this cosmopolitan city; he preached to Jews near a river used by them for their ritual ablutions (Acts 16:13). He was so well received that he even accepted, contrary to his custom, the hospitality of one of his new converts. Later on, he again will accept— another exception to the rule he had made for himself—the financial aid of this Church, so faithful to his preaching. He will come back to it at least twice (Acts 20:6), which indicates particularly close ties.

3. Sulpicius Severus (ca. 360-420), *Vie de saint Martin. Lettre à Basulo* (Paris: Payot, 1927) 133–34.

4. Ch. de Foucauld (1858-1916), "Méditation 194 sur les évangiles," *Oeuvres spirituelles* (Paris: Seuil, 1958) 212–15.

5. Thus St. Gregory (Pope, 590-604) sees in the different hours the periods going from Adam to Noah, from Noah to Abraham, from Abraham to Moses, from Moses to Christ, from Christ to the end of the world (*Homélie 19 sur l'Evangile,* no. 1, read at Matins in the Liturgy of the Hours for Septuagesima Sunday prior to the reforms of Vatican II). This kind of allegorical interpretation of all the details of a parable holds, in the last analysis, little interest for most people. Besides, it probably does not correspond to the gospel mode of

teaching, which precisely aims at being direct, readily understandable, without recourse to subtleties. Here, it was necessary that the hiring take place at different hours—and singularly at dawn and in the evening—to make possible the principal lesson.

6. In current parlance, when we speak of "a worker of the last hour," we think more of "la mouche du coche" (a busybody), from La Fontaine's fable "Le Coche et la Mouche," than of the Gospel parable.

7. See the article "Vigne" in *Vocabulaire de théologie biblique*, cols. 1355-57.

8. This parable is read on Tuesday of the nineteenth week and, in the parallel passage from Luke's Gospel (15:4-7), on the solemnity of the Sacred Heart of Jesus, Year C.

9. The narrative speaks only of these two groups to make the master's behavior even clearer. And, of course, it is necessary to start with the last group so that the first group, seeing the salary of their companions, can express their reaction.

10. Ch. Péguy, "La Pléiade 69," *Oeuvres poétiques complètes* (Paris: Gallimard, 1957) 617.

11. In Matthew's text, this sentence comes at this place, at the end of the parable. But is it its conclusion? Exegetes point out that if one takes the parable of the workers in the vineyard out of context, this sentence can be omitted. Indeed, in the composition of Matthew's Gospel, this sentence "justifies" Jesus' answer to Peter's question: "We have given up everything and followed you. What will there be for us?" Jesus declares, "In the new age . . . everyone who has given up houses or brothers or sisters or father or mother or children or lands for the sake of my name will receive a hundred times more and will inherit eternal life." And he concludes, "But many who are first will be last, and the last will be first" (Matt 19:27-30—Wednesday of the twentieth week). Therefore, it is the same formula we find here, but reversed since it mentions the last first. See J. Dupont, "Les ouviers de la onzième heure," in *Assemblées du Seigneur*, 2e série, No. 56 (Paris: Cerf-Publications de Saint-André, 1974) 17-19.

12. See St. Gregory's interpretation (n. 5 above).

13. Twenty-seventh Sunday, Year C. See *Days of the Lord: Ordinary Time, Year C*, vol. 6.

14. Commission Francophone Cistercienne, *Tropaires des dimanches*, 115 (Fiche de chant U LH 69).

Twenty-sixth to Twenty-eighth Sunday in Ordinary Time—Page 202

1. Constitution on the Liturgy, no. 7.
2. Ibid., no. 11.
3. See J. Dupont, "L'évangile de saint Matthieu," 37-39.
4. Constitution on the Liturgy, no. 10.

Twenty-sixth Sunday—Pages 203-208

1. Dogmatic Constitution on the Church, no. 4.
2. One could translate "one heart and mind" as in Acts 4:32 ("The community of believers was of one heart and mind.")
3. It is not surprising that all religious lawgivers have so insisted on the necessity of humility. Thus St. Benedict, who devoted the longest chapter of his *Rule* to this virtue (ch. 7).
4. See Mass of Passion Sunday in *Days of the Lord: Lent*, vol. 2.

5. To be a publican was to be a sort of prostitute. These tax collectors sold themselves to the Roman occupying forces. Not only did they benefit from their profession, but they freely wrung money out of the people.

6. Second Sunday of Advent. See *Days of the Lord: Advent, Christmas, Epiphany*, vol. 1.

7. See Matt 9:10-11; 10:1.

8. One must not forget that at the time Matthew was writing his Gospel, John the Baptist's preaching and Jesus' ministries already belonged to the past.

9. Y. de Montcheuil, *Le Royaume et ses exigences* (Paris: Epi, 1959) 65.

Twenty-seventh Sunday—Pages 209–213

1. Hos 10:1; Isa 3:14; 27:2-5; Jer 2:21; 5:10; 6:9; 12:10; Ezek 15:1-8; 17:3-10; 19:10-14; Ps 80:9-17; John 15:1-2. In the Old Testament, the vine is also the symbol of love: Cant 1:6-14; 2:15; 8:12. See the article "Vigne" in *Vocabulaire de théologie biblique*, cols. 1355-57, and "raisin, vigne, vin" in *Dictionnaire encyclopédique de la Bible*, pp. 1091–92.

2. Vinegrowers do not forget those sad years without a crop, because hail, for example, has destroyed everything. Hail may even have harmed the vine–stock, thus compromising the hope of a normal harvest the next year.

3. Preface of Holy Men and Women 1.

4. Others, perhaps, would see here a convenient justification of the absolute right of big landowners to suppress any revolt by those they have paid to work the land and who resort to violence.

5. In the Synoptic Gospels, there is a marked dramatic progression in the narration: entry of the Messiah into Jerusalem, cleansing of the Temple, symbolic cursing of the barren fig tree. To these, Matthew (21:23-27) adds the episode of the questioning of Jesus' authority.

6. The Bible willingly calls God's prophets "servants." It also tells of their martyrdom: 1 Kgs 18:13; 22:27; 2 Chr 24:21; 36:15; Neh 9:26; Matt 23:37; Luke 4:24-29; 13:34; Heb 11:37. According to tradition, Jeremiah was stoned and Isaiah was sawed in two in the tree trunk where he had hidden. Furthermore, Matthew frequently associates in his Gospel the two categories of "prophets" and the "just"; this could explain the two deputations sent by the Master (Matt 10:41; 13:17; 23:29, 44).

7. *Lettre à Diognète* (anon. from 2nd century), VII, 2, in *Sources chrétiennes* 33, trans. H.-I. Marrou (Paris: Cerf, 1951) 67-69.

8. See Vatican Council II, Declaration on the Relation of the Church to Non-Christian Religions, no. 4, *The Conciliar and Post Conciliar Documents*, ed. Austin Flannery, O.P. (Collegeville, Minn.: The Liturgical Press, 1977).

9. Commission Francophone Cistercienne, *Tropaires des dimanches*, 121.

Twenty-eighth Sunday—Pages 214–221

1. It is difficult to imagine this slow composition of such diverse writings, their preservation, their transmission, for at least two reasons. First, today this ensemble forms one single book. Second, we are accustomed to the intensive production of books that, though important, have an ephemeral duration. They are kept in libraries the world over. They are catalogued. They are consulted. But none of these constitutes "The Book," transmitted from generation to generation, copied and published over and over again, preciously

owned by so many men and women—Jews and Christians—who unceasingly read and reread it because it is, for them, God's revelation. This slow elaboration of the Old Testament, founded on oral tradition, assimilated, enriched in the course of centuries, faithfully transmitted, helps us to realize that faith is first of all a "memorial," a living "memory" of what God has said through his prophets—in the broad sense of the term—and of what he has done. The role of the writers-prophets and hagiographers has been considerable, not only because they have put down in writing the former traditions but also because they have reread them and because their writings have stimulated the progress of reflection, of memory. However, nothing would have happened and nothing would have reached us without the innumerable crowd of the others, those who have written nothing, the entire people whose collective memory the writings nourished.

2. Chapters 24–27 constitute what is customarily called the "Apocalypse of Isaiah" because they deal with events concerning the last judgment. These events are evoked in poetry; their description is interspersed with prayers, entreaties (psalms), and hymns of thanksgiving. The apocalyptic literature will be developed in the chapters 9–14 of the Book of Zechariah (beginning of 4th century B.C.) and the Book of Daniel (end of 2nd century B.C.)

3. Judg 4:10; 1 Kgs 3:15; 1 Sam 25:36; 11:15; 1 Kgs 1:9-25; Esth 1:3.

4. Hos 4:11; 8:13; 9:1; Amos 2:8; Isa 28:7.

5. Lev 4:35; 1 Sam 2:15; Prov 9:1; Isa 55:1; 65:13.

6. For the author of this text from the Book of Isaiah, things were less clear. The exegetes think that the oracle expressed the hope of a national restoration seen as a resurrection (see Isa 29:19; Ezek 37), which marked a new progress of revelation (see Isa 65:20-22). The idea of resurrection properly so-called will need still more time to clearly assert itself. This will come in the aftermath of the persecutions undergone during the revolt against hellenistic domination at the time of the Maccabees, under Antiochus Epiphanes (175–164 B.C.): 2 Macc 7:9-22; 14:46; Dan 12:2-3. But in the liturgy, the Church reads the Old Testament in the light of her faith today, a faith which has developed in continuity with yesterday's faith. This going-beyond is a fulfillment.

7. See above, p. 210 ("Last Advice from an Apostle in Prison") for a discussion of why we can speak here of a "note."

8. Taking care to remain brief, the liturgists have omitted verses 10-11 and 15-18. But the integral reading of this note, written by Paul as a prisoner, is well worthwhile. This is what we shall do here.

9. See Phil 2:6-11; 3:4-11; 1 Cor 9:16-23. These texts shed light on Paul's state of mind.

10. See Acts 18:5; 2 Cor 8:1-3; 11:8-9; Phil 4:16; 2:25-26.

11. Commission Francophone Cistercienne, Guetteur de l'aube (Paris: Desclée, 1976) 137 (Fiche de chant D LH 117).

12. The Lectionary offers a "short form" that stops before the episode of the wedding garment. The result is a text that is easier to understand but truncates the reach of the teaching. It goes without saying that here we read the integral text.

13. We also have a king in the parable of the insolvent debtors: Matt 18:23-35—Twenty-fourth Sunday.

14. See Matt 8:11; 9:15; 25:1-13.

15. Matt 3:7; 4:17.

16. He has even recorded it in a version peculiar to him, as can be seen by a simple comparison with Luke (14:15-24).

17. The burning of "their" city could be an allegorical trait alluding to the ruin of Jerusalem in A.D. 70 (see Matt 24:1-3).

18. The parable of the sower and the seed is read on the Fifteenth Sunday.

19. Ninth Sunday.

20. See Matt 5:12; 10:17, 18, 41; 13:17; 23:29-36.

21. One might find the manner in which the narrative is built strange: the meal is ready and yet the king takes the time to organize a punitive expedition against those first called and against their city. But a parable is not an ordinary narrative. The mention of the chastisement at this point is a way of having done with the first group preparing their exit from the story. From then on, our attention is focused on those invited in the second place.

22. Matthew shows great care to reflect on the present conditions of the life of the Church, starting from Jesus' teaching. He does not hesitate to transpose into the present what Luke, for instance, speaks of in the future tense. Thus, concerning "narrow gate," Luke writes, "Many . . . will attempt to enter but will not be strong enough" (Luke 13:24). Matthew, for his part, says that we must find it and enter it right now (Matt 7:13-14). See also Matt 3:8-10; 7:19; 13:24-30, 36-43, 47- 50; 20:1-16; 21:28-32; 25:1-13, 31-46.

23. Gospel of Christ the King.

24. Rom 13:14; Gal 3:27; Eph 4:24.

25. Luke (13:23-24) explicitly says that the parable of the narrow gate was the answer of Jesus to someone who was querying him concerning the elect's number.

26. Constitution on the Sacred Liturgy, no. 2: "For it is the liturgy through which, especially in the divine sacrifice of the Eucharist, 'the work of our redemption is accomplished,' and it is through the liturgy, especially, that the faithful are enabled to express in their lives and manifest to others the mystery of Christ and the real nature of the true Church."

27. Ibid., no. 10.

28. Commission Francophone "Cistercienne, *Tropaires des dimanches,* 125.

Twenty-ninth Sunday—Pages 223–228

1. "Messiah" is the literal meaning that the Lectionary translates by "anointed."

2. To endow any power with a sacred character tends to encourage—even to engender—justification of absolutism and its worst abuses. What is the cause, what is the origin of such a process if not the will of those who benefit by power and seek to give it a legitimacy that would be sacrilegious to deny? To limit ourselves to the history of the Church and to a remote past, let us think of the ambiguities of Constantinian Christendom. The Christian world does not have a monopoly on endowing something with a sacred character. In our own times, we saw it practiced in Nazi Germany on the basis of a frankly pagan ideology.

3. On these various events see Ezra 1:1-6, 7-11; 5:14-15; 6:2-5. The edict of reconstruction would be in full effect under Darius, Cyrus' second successor (522–486 B.C.).

4. Curiously, this is what still often happens in a world however strongly secularized, if not atheistic. That certain people exploit this tendency is understandable; they are political schemers. But the genuine believers owe it to themselves to denounce such shameful exploitation of God and religious sentiment.

5. Paul founded this community during his second missionary journey (end of 49—end of 51). According to his custom, he first addressed himself to the Jewish community on three consecutive Sabbaths. Some were convinced and joined Paul and Silas (called Silvanus in the Letter to the Thessalonians) along with a vast number of Greeks who were worshipers and many women of high rank. But there was such a violent reaction among certain Jews that Paul and Silas-Silvanus were forced to leave during the night. They went to Beroea, then to Athens. Silas-Silvanus returned to Thessalonica (Acts 17:1-15). From Athens, Paul went to Corinth, being joined there by Timothy and Silvanus, bringing good news from the community in Thessalonica, about which Paul was concerned because of his sudden departure.

6. It has been generally used to designate the diverse Christian communities founded by Christ's disciples in the pagan world: Acts 13:1; 14:23; 15:41; 16:5.

7. The Greek word *ecclesia* signifies "assembly," "congregation."

8. 1 Thess 1:3–2:16.

9. 1 Thess 2:17–4:12.

10. 1 Thess 4:13–5:11.

11. Paul's stay in Thessalonica was probably not as short as one could construe from what the Book of Acts says (Acts 17:2). It must have lasted at least for the whole summer of 50 (see 1 Thess 2:9; Phil 4:16). Still it was relatively short.

12. Ephesus is the place where Paul stayed the longest during his third journey. Acts speaks of two years and three months (19:8-10) and three years (20:31). See *Cahiers Evangile* 21 (1977), p.6.

13. Y. de Montcheuil, *Aspects de l'Eglise*, in *Livre de vie* 23 (Paris: Cerf, 1949) 176.

14. Mark (12:13-17) and Luke (20:20-26) also have this episode. This indicates its importance in the gospel tradition.

15. The etymology of "Pharisee" shows a link between this word and a root meaning "to separate" or "to explain." "Pharisees owed their name to their assiduous practice of the commentary on the Law or to the rigor of their moral discipline, which separated them from the rest of the population. . . . It is usually agreed that the Pharisees were recruited from the lower classes of society. Furthermore, certain doctors held manual work in honor. . . . As a general rule, the strictness of their life gave them a large following among the lowly folk." (*Dictionnaire encyclopédique de la Bible*, 1013. See also *Vocabulaire de théologie biblique*, cols. 992-93.) We must guard against caricatures and the tendency to attribute to Pharisees as a whole what belongs to pharisaism. Before his conversion, Paul was a Pharisee (Acts 23:6; Phil 3:5). The Pharisees' hostility to Jesus was caused by his teaching on the practice of the Law, which excluded a punctilious and, so to speak, material observance with its attendant casuistry and emphasis on appearances. Pharisees could not fail to feel attacked. Moreover, Jesus' attitude toward sinners and tax collectors was diametrically opposed to the Pharisees'. In sum, their religious universe, their conception of the Law, their ideals were destabilized, if not overturned. By the same token, their credit with the people was undermined.

16. Known especially through the Jewish historian Flavius Josephus (ca. 37-100), the Zealots, fierce adversaries of the occupying forces, went so far as to engage in terrorist actions against the Romans and even against their fellow Jews when the latter were judged to lack conviction or to be collaborators. It would be an exaggeration to label them the armed faction of the Pharisaic movement. But most of them came from the ranks of the Pharisees, and their active determination manifested their position.

17. In order to pay the tax, people needed money minted by the Romans. Thus the latter recovered for their treasury money sold to the inhabitants at a prescribed rate. With this money, the Romans defrayed the expenses incurred by the occupation: soldiers' pay, local functionaries' salaries. The system was flawless: it came down to having the inhabitants of the occupied country support the cost of their own subjection. In the transaction, the money sold and immediately recovered acquired a greater value. It is needless to mention how humiliating these demands were for the population.

18. Negotiation was often ratified by the signing of concordats. Elsewhere, it was a *modus vivendi* which came to be established, sometimes, as in France for instance, after a time of battle between secularism and clericalism.

19. St. Augustine (354–430), "24th Sermon," 8, in Raulx, *Sermons inédits*, vol. 2, 468, quoted in *Assemblées du Seigneur*, 2e série, no. 60 (Paris: Publications de St. André-Cerf, 1975), 26.

Thirtieth Sunday—Pages 229–235

1. The formation of the Book of Exodus, in the framework of that of the Pentateuch (Genesis, Exodus, Leviticus, Numbers, and Deuteronomy) is the result of a complex and very long history. See the introductions in the *Bible de Jérusalem* and the *Traduction oecuménique de la Bible*, as well as Cl. Wiener, "Le Livre de l'Exode," *Cahiers Evangile* 54 (1985).

2. Exod 20:22–23:33.

3. Exod 20:1-20.

4. In the Bible, the alien, the widow, and the orphan are the poor par excellence, deprived of all human help. This is why God is their recourse, to whom they can always appeal with the certainty of being heard.

5. More recent legislations will not fail to repeat this instant admonition to love the strangers who live in the country. Deut 10:18-19; 24:18-22; 26:12; Lev 19:10, 33-35; 35:35; Jer 7:6; 22:3; Ezek 22:7; Zech 7:10; Mal 3:5; Ps 146:9.

6. Deut 10:18; 14:29; 16:11, 14; 24:17-21; 26:12-13; 27:19; Isa 1:1.

7. Deut 23:20; Lev 25:37; Prov 28:8; Neh 5:1-13; Ps 15:5; Ezek 18:8, 13, 17; 22:12.

8. See "Aumône," *Vocabulaire de théologie biblique*, cols. 95-98.

9. We cannot conclude from this text that every form of lending at interest is condemned by the Bible. Evidently it could not have legislated for an economic system it did not know.

10. 1 Thess 1:2-5b, Twenty-ninth Sunday.

11. Because of the success of their preaching, Paul and his companions have been the objects of violent reactions on the part of certain members of the Jewish community. Jason, who gave hospitality to the preachers, and some other brothers were dragged before the authorities and let out on bail. Paul and Silvanus were obliged to hide, then flee during the night (Acts 17:5-10). This departure did not put an end to persecutions (1 Thess 2:14).

12. See Twenty-ninth Sunday, n. 11.

13. "Worshipers of God" is the expression that designates those who sympathize with Judaism without going so far as integrating themselves with the Jewish people by circumcision.

14. P. de La Tour du Pin, "Essai d'hymne de marche," in *Une somme de poésie* (Paris: Gallimard, 1983) 3:256 (Fiche de chant T 9).

15. The episode is also recorded by Mark (12:28-34) and Luke (10:25-28). Each one of the Synoptic narratives is found several times in the Lectionary: Matthew's twice (Thirtieth Sunday and Friday of the Twentieth Week), Mark's three times (Thirty-first Sunday, Year B, Friday of the Third Week in Lent, and Thursday of the Ninth Week), Luke's twice (Fifteenth Sunday, Year C, and Monday of the Twenty-seventh Week).

16. In a Bible class, it would be interesting and fruitful to compare in detail the three Synoptic accounts, particularly Matthew's and Mark's, which are approximately the same length. Luke's is shorter and introduces the parable of the Samaritan. See *Days of the Lord: Ordinary Time, Year C*, vol. 6.

17. Twenty-ninth Sunday.

18. Discussing this question, the lawyers had deduced 613 precepts and 365 prohibitions, arranged according to their gravity. In an effort to reduce things to the essentials, some were seeking, out of that mass of prescriptions one precept that would include all the rest, for instance, the observance of the Sabbath or the rejection of idols. Shortly before Christ, Rabbi Hillel (20 B.C.) said, "Do not do to your neighbor what you would not want done to you. This is the whole Law. The rest is explanations."

19. Sometimes this intention is conscious. But it often happens that we do not fathom the profound meaning of such a question.

20. Human experience proves this. We may have nothing to reproach a relative with because he or she is dutiful and "does everything that must be done," even with generosity; and yet we cannot say that this person loves us.

21. Thirty-fourth Sunday, Feast of Christ the King.

22. St. Augustine (354–430), *Homélie sur l'Evangile de Jean*, 17:7-9, quoted in the *Liturgy of the Hours*, vol. 1, 511-13.

Thirty-first Sunday—Pages 236–242

1. From the fifty-five verses of this book, the Lectionary has retained only four passages: 1:14b–2:1, 2b, 8-10 (this Sunday); 3:1-4, 23-24 (December 23); 3:13-20a (Thursday of the Twenty-seventh Week, odd years); 3:19-20a (Thirty-third Sunday, Year C)—a total of eighteen verses.

The oracles of this book clearly point to a period following the rebuilding of the Temple and the resumption of services, therefore well after 515 B.C. but preceding the reforms of Nehemiah and Ezra (ca. 440 B.C.). This prophet was a vigorous reformer of the religious and moral life in Israel; hence, the harshness of many of his oracles.

The Book of Malachi struck its readers because of its messianic content. It still occupies an important place in Judaism.

2. Vatican II, Constitution on the Sacred Liturgy, no. 7.

3. Ibid., no. 9.

4. Ibid., no. 10.

5. Ibid., no. 11.

6. Ibid., no. 11.

7. What does the excuse "I don't have time" mean if not precisely this?

8. Vatican II, Constitution on the Sacred Liturgy, no. 2.

9. The last verse of the liturgical reading belongs to a new development in the Book of Malachi. It is a warning against marriages with pagans on account of the danger of religious contamination. An example of this is Solomon, whose heart turned to other gods under the sway of his foreign wives (1 Kgs 11:1-13). By attaching this verse to what precedes it, the reading emphasizes the fact that unfaithfulness toward God is unfaithfulness toward brothers and sisters.

10. See 2 Thess 3:8; 2 Cor 11:9.

11. On scribes and Pharisees, see *Vocabulaire de théologie biblique*, 1013, 1178-79.

12. See "Good Grain and Weeds in the Same Field," Sixteenth Sunday, and "The Net Filled with Good and Bad Fish," Seventeenth Sunday for a discussion of "good and bad."

13. One could say this is the case of every society and every group. However, there are important differences.

14. St. Benedict has explicitly incorporated this doctrine into his Rule: "Furthermore, anyone who receives the name of abbot is to lead the disciples by a twofold teaching: he must point out to them all that is good and holy more by example than by words, proposing the commandments of the Lord to receptive disciples with words, but demonstrating God's instructions to the stubborn and the dull by a living example. Again, if he teaches his disciples that something is not to be done, then neither must he do it, *lest after preaching to others, he himself be found reprobate*" (ch. 2); "Obey the orders of the abbot unreservedly, even if his own conduct—which God forbid—be at odds with what he says. Remember the teaching of the Lord: *Do what they say, not what they do*" (ch. 4).

15. Second reading, Thirtieth Sunday.

16. Phylacteries: small cases containing the essential words of the Law (Exod 13:1-10; 13:14-16; Deut 6:49; 11:13-21) attached to the left arm and the forehead. Tassels: fringes fixed to the corners of the cloak; Jesus, like all pious Jews, wore these (Matt 9:20).

17. Rabbi means "my master."

18. Y. Congar, *Pour une Eglise servante et pauvre* (Paris: Cerf, 1963), describes the invasion of honors and privileges in the Church, especially from the Middle Ages on.

19. Second reading, Third Sunday, Year C. See *Days of the Lord: Ordinary Time, Year C*, vol. 6.

20. "The abbot must always remember what he is and remember what he is called" (St. Benedict, *Rule*, ch. 2).

21. Some forget, for instance, that when the functions are easy to recognize, the members of an assembly are not in danger of feeling manipulated by just anybody.

22. Commission Francophone Cistercienne, *Tropaires des dimanches*, 133 (Fiche de chant U LH 80).

Thirty-second Sunday—Pages 244-249

1. It was written in Greek in Alexandria, around the years 50-30 B.C., by a Jewish author who was perfectly conversant with Greek thought. He seeks to express the Jewish faith in the framework of the culture that he has made his own. In particular, he exalts the role of Wisdom by personalizing it and adorning it with traits that, in the Bible, belong to the Word and the Spirit. There are three large parts: human destiny according to God (Wis 1-5), the praise of Wisdom (Wis 6:1- 11:3), and Wisdom at work in history (Wis 11:5-19:21).

2. If they study the book in this perspective, the readers are led to see in Wisdom much more than a personified attribute of God: God himself and, in the Christian tradition, Christ, true light, perfect image of the Father. See Matt 12:42; 1 Cor 11:7; 2 Cor 3:18; 4:4; Col 1:15; 3:10.

3. It is distressing to see that some persons, reassured by this hope, exploit nature, compromising the future without a thought for those who will follow them. Such conduct, powered by the sole research of immediate maximum profit, is unworthy of a believer.

4. It is fortunate because there is nothing more erroneous and dangerous than the mixture of computations and supposed human revelations on the destruction of the world, along with the fears they generate, and the Christian faith concerning the end of time and the return of the Lord, object and basis of our hope.

5. Did Paul share his correspondents' conviction of the imminent manifestation of the Lord? Nothing allows us to answer this question, not even the expression "we who are alive," which may simply be a way of speaking. But it does not matter; in any event, Paul's teaching remains the same.

6. How would it be possible to evoke these realities without images?

7. Paul limits himself to answering the question of his correspondents. But he does not exhaust the subject. For instance, he does not even allude to the problem of those who die in unfaithfulness. He acts as a good teacher who says everything that those who put question to him must know, here and now.

8. It is safer to avoid speaking of eternity in terms belonging to the category of time, for instance, "a time that lasts forever." Eternity has nothing in common with a duration that would be divisible without end.

9. Matt 24:36; Mark 13:32; Luke 17:26-27, 34-35; 12:39-40.

10. Matt 24:1-3, 15-24; Mark 13:1-4, 14-23; Luke 21:5-7, 20-24.

11. Jerusalem and the Temple had been destroyed and sacked before. But this time, it was worse. After four months of siege causing famine and atrocious suffering, Titus's troops made the final assault on the Temple on August 6, 70; it was totally destroyed and would not be rebuilt. The Jews were not deported together as had happened before, but they were sold as slaves. The city was in ruins. Renamed AElia Capitolina, a pagan name and thus an abomination to the Jews, and rebuilt by Hadrian, emperor from 117 to 138, it would become a pagan city.

12. Matthew's Gospel must have been written in its present form around 80-90, perhaps even a little earlier, but without a doubt after the tragic events of 70.

13. The other one—the parable of the faithful servant (Matt 24:45-51) is read on Thursday of the Twenty-first Week.

14. A certain delay was in good taste. But until the middle of the night . . .

15. The account of the wedding at Cana implicitly shows that the festive hall was largely open to all comers. If the wine failed, was it not by reason of an unforeseen number of guests? Jesus and his disciples? Others with them?

16. "The Eschatological Discourse" insists several times on this sudden character: Matt 24:36-42, 50.

17. Certain homilists, especially in patristic times, have interpreted all the details of this parable in the allegorical sense: the bridesmaids' sleep, the lamps, the oil. They drew useful lessons, often very much to the point. But we should be wary of the tendency to give an allegorical sense, supposedly willed by Jesus, to all the details of a parable. The risk is to distract the readers from the principal lesson which was certainly meant and which all can immediately understand.

18. St. Augustine (354-430), *Sermons*, 223 D, in G. Morin, *Miscellanea agostiniana* (Rome, 1930) 685.

19. Commission Francophone Cistercienne, *La nuit, le jour*, 28 (Fiche de chant P LH 107, 109).

Thirty-third Sunday—Pages 250-255

1. It contains 915 maxims or verses. This literary genre and the fact that proverbs usually follow one another without logical order explains why, not surprisingly, the Lectionary uses it but little: 8:22-31 (Trinity Sunday, Year C); 9:1-6 (Twentieth Sunday, Year B); 31:10-13, 19-20, 30-31 (Thirty-third Sunday, Year A); 3:27-34; 21:1-6, 10-13; 30:5-9 (Monday, Tuesday, and Wednesday of the Twenty-fifth Week, even years).

2. Two remarks: First, this commendation is in alphabetic form: the first word of each sentence—each verse—begins with one of the twenty-two Hebrew letters (aleph, beth, gimel, etc.). Such a constraint restricts inspiration. Second, the liturgy utilizes only a few verses which reflect the tone of the whole piece but which find their meaning only in verse 30.

3. Psalms praise those who fear God: Pss 1:7; 111:5; 112:1; 128:1. Likewise, the New Testament: Luke 1:50 (Magnificat); Acts 10:34-35; Rev 11:8. See "Crainte de Dieu," *Vocabulaire de théologie biblique*, cols. 219-22.

4. Eight more passages from this letter are read from Monday of the Twenty-first Week to Tuesday of the Twenty-second Week, odd years.

5. Matt 24:36; Mark 13:32, 35; 12:39-40; Luke 17:26-27.

6. Joel 3:4-5; 4:16-21; Zech 14; Mal 3:2-5, 19-21. See "Jour du Seigneur," *Vocabulaire de théologie biblique*, cols. 618-25, and "Jour du Yahvé," *Dictionnaire encyclopédique de la Bible*, 688-90.

7. This does not mean that the Lord will act like a thief, but that he will come unannounced.

8. Centre National de Pastorale Liturgique (Fiche de chant A LH 188).

9. The *Traduction oecuménique de la Bible* says that the talent was worth about six thousand gold francs. The *Dictionnaire encyclopédique de la Bible*, 1237, goes into more detail: the talent, ancient weight of sixty minas, that is, six thousand drachmas, corresponded to 34.2 kilograms of gold or silver. The *Bible de Jérusalem*, 1892, ("Table des monnaies," table of monetary units) gives even more precise information: the drachma (a Greek coin) was equivalent to the Roman denarium. Therefore, one talent represented the salary for some six thousand workdays. Whatever the value of these calculations, the master entrusts a considerable sum of capital to his servants, even to the one who receives only one.

10. Nersès Snorhali, *Jésus, Fils unique du Père*, nos. 694-700, pp. 174-75.

Thirty-fourth Sunday—Pages 256–269

1. Pius XI, Encyclical *Quas primas*, December 11, 1925.

2. Pius XI, Encyclical *Ubi arcano Dei*, December 23, 1922.

3. The quotations from *Quas primas* are translated from the French translation of L. Picard, *La royauté du Christ* (Louvain: Ed. de la Jeunesse catholique, 1926) with reference to Joseph Husslein, S.J., *The Reign of Christ* (New York: P. J. Kenedy & Sons, 1928).

4. The works cited in n. 3 are symptomatic of this combative spirit. For further information see H. Brun, *La Cité chrétienne d'après les enseignements pontificaux* (Paris: Bonne Press, n.d.).

5. And the verses—"You are truly King by . . ." (your birth, etc.)—that enumerate the various titles of Christ to kingship were quite aggressive toward his opponents: "Those who defy your power, Jesus, are the work of your hands."

6. This is the second version. At the time of the battles over the papal states, people sang, "Save Rome and France." In many churches, there was the tricolor with the Heart of Jesus superimposed on the central panel.

7. Sometimes there was what we must call a rather unexpected political exploitation of these religious manifestations. Thus, at the Eucharistic Congress at Carthage in 1930, the secular French government financed the participation of seminarians from France in this celebration taking place in its protectorate of Tunisia.

8. We are the more surprised to see that the interventions in ethical matters—although these are eminently the province of spiritual ministry—encounter the greatest number of objections and disputations, even on the part of the faithful.

9. John XXIII, *Pacem in terris*, in *Seven Great Encyclicals* (Glen Rock, N.J.: Paulist Press, 1963) nos. 151-52.

10. Vatican II, Pastoral Constitution on the Church in the Modern World, no. 2.

11. Ibid., no. 3.

12. The addition of "of the universe" removes all ambiguities.

13. See "Pasteur et troupeau," *Vocabulaire de théologie biblique*, cols. 917-21.

14. This oracle dates from the Exile. Ezekiel wants to restore the hope of the people while at the same time exhorting them to avoid falling again into past errors. The liturgical reading for the feast of Christ the King omits verses 13 and 14, which speak of the people's return from exile to their own land: "I will lead them out from among the peoples and gather them from the foreign lands; I will bring them back to their own country and pasture them upon the mountains of Israel [in the land's ravines and all its inhabited places].

In good pastures will I pasture them, and on the mountain heights of Israel shall be their grazing ground, and in rich pastures shall they be pastured on the mountains of Israel.''

15. Gospel of the Ninth Sunday.

16. ''For it is love that I desire, not sacrifice'' (Hos 6:6 quoted in Matt 9:13 and 12:7). See also Matt 5:21-26; 6:14-15; 7:12; 18:23-35; 22:40; 24:12.

17. St. Augustine (354-430), *Sermons*, 58:9-10, quoted by M. Véricel, *Les évangile des dimanches. Commentaires des Pères de l'Eglise. Année A* (Paris: Les Editions Ouvrières, 1983) 246-47.

18. Commission Francophone Cistercienne, *Sur la trace de Dieu* (Paris: Desclée, 1979) 94 (Fiche de chant M 53).

Postscript—Pages 270-271

1. Constitution on the Sacred Liturgy, no. 10.